REAL FAITH

Knowing the Will of God
Believing for the Impossible

To: Gary Cobb,
My brother in
Jesus – may this
be a blessing to you.
Yours in Him,
Shad

"Thus speaketh the Lord God of Israel, saying,
Write thee all the words that I have spoken unto thee in a book."
Jeremiah 30:2

REAL FAITH

Knowing the Will of God
Believing for the Impossible

"The author who benefits you is not the one
who tells you something you did not know before,
but the one who gives expression to the truth
that has been struggling for utterance in you."
Oswald Chambers

Shad Williams

SWEA
2009

Cover Design

The cover of this book was designed by our daughter, Rachel Busse, but it is not just another one of her creative and clever designs. It actually comes from an experience I had with God early one morning in the summer of 1976. One year earlier, God had unmistakably spoken to Sheila and me about going into international evangelism. A year later, however, I was still wrestling with just how to go about it.

During that summer , the Lord began waking me up every morning at 4:30. Every day I would throw on some jeans and a tee shirt, grab my Bible, and go down to a park near our house to walk and pray. This went on for weeks, and one morning as I was praying out loud I uttered these words, "Lord, I guess there is just no other way for us to do this; I guess it has to be by faith." As soon as the word "faith" came out of my mouth the heel of my shoe caught on something in the grass. When I looked down, I saw a large piece of concrete and in it was written the word *FAITH*. I could not believe my eyes. I knelt down and ran my hand across the word to make sure I was seeing what I thought I was. Right then and there, while I was kneeling, I said, "Lord, we don't need to discuss this any longer. My question is answered for good. We are going to do this and we are going to do it by faith." As I stood to my feet, I knew in my heart that I had embarked upon a new journey, the journey of faith. I also sensed that I was about to take some higher-level classes in the school of faith. I was right. I have never graduated from Faith University and never will, but I have taken many challenging and interesting courses. Much of what I have learned so far is contained in the pages of this book.

Ten years later my friend, Dr. Philip Eyster, was supervising the production of a video for our ten-year ministry anniversary. As part of the video I shared with him the story of what happened in the park that day. He went to the park to see if the concrete was still there and sure enough it was. He outlined the letters in white and took a picture of it. He used that picture in the video and gave me a framed print of it, which has hung on my office wall ever since. When it came time to design a cover for this book, there was no question as to what it should look like. It had to be THAT picture that Phil took in the park long ago. The word "real" was fabricated by my talented daughter, but the word "faith" appears exactly as it is in that photo taken long ago. As we walk through life, stumbling is usually not considered to be a good thing. But as I discovered that day in the park, when we stumble across real faith it can be the greatest moment in our life. May it be so for you, my dear brother or sister in Christ, may it be so for you.

This book is dedicated to:

My pastor – Rev. Don J. Milam
(1910 – 1995)

Brother Don was the man God used to introduce Sheila and me
to Jesus and to help us through the difficult beginning stages
of our Christian life. He was our constant source of
encouragement and spiritual guidance until his death.
He correctly viewed our life and ministry as an extension
of his own. Because of Brother Don's relentless pursuit
and determination to see us saved, Sheila and I are in the
Kingdom of God, and because of his example to us
of what it truly means to live for Christ, we are now
being used of God to help expand it.

My friend – Rev. Dr. W. Wayne Allen
(1939 – 2005)

Brother Wayne was the man God used to help propel us along
in the life of faith. He was one of the most outstanding examples
in my life of what it means to believe God for the impossible.
He was the living embodiment of the verse of Scripture he
so often quoted, Matthew 19:26, "With men this is impossible;
but with God all things are possible." Brother Wayne believed
in our ministry as much as any person we have ever known
and enthusiastically encouraged us to push forward by faith.

My Father – Leland S. Williams
(1920 – 2002)

My Dad was the man God used to provide me with a picture
of what it means to be a father. From my earliest memory
he was always the man who could do anything and get anything,
and he was always ready to do it for me. In my childhood
he represented total security and unconditional approval.
He not only provided but did so in excess. Because of my Dad
the word *father* produces an image in my mind of total love,
provision, and acceptance. It is that image transferred into
my Christian life that makes it so easy for me to believe
that my Heavenly Father can be trusted to do anything and
provide everything – and He will do it for ME.

Contents

Preface

This book is written to provide the Christian church and the world-wide Christian mission force with a practical guide as to how to truly live by faith and thus overcome the powers of darkness, enhance their Christian life, and expand the Kingdom of God. The majority of Christians throughout the world live far below their privilege and potential because they are deceived by the lies of the devil and enslaved by the limitations of the visible. So many enter the Christian life by faith and then attempt to live it by sight. The vast majority of the church is unknowingly wandering in the wilderness of unbelief, in search of freedom and power that they will never possess without discovering a life of real Bible faith. This book is intended to help God's children, new Believers and seasoned warriors alike, escape the status quo and the deceptions of satan and enter into the promised land of real, overcoming, life-altering faith.

It is my intent and goal to help my brothers and sisters in Jesus discover the liberating truth that it is absolutely possible to clearly know the will of God and boldly believe Him for the impossible. The content contained in these pages has been arranged in such a way so as to lead the reader from start to finish through the process of actually knowing the will of God and accessing the power and resources of God in relation to specific needs and circumstances in his or her life.

There is a great deal of error and misunderstanding regarding the subject of faith in the modern church. On the one hand are those who attempt to trust God by faith without an adequate understanding of what is required to make that possible. On the other hand are those who reject any idea of believing God for the impossible as an impossibility in itself. The corresponding result is confusion, disillusionment, disappointment, discouragement, and defeat. An extended purpose of this book is to help protect the church, the body of Christ, from misguided and erroneous ideas and to help them find the true, balanced, scriptural life of faith that is available for all Believers.

My wife and I were saved in the summer of 1968 and sensed the call of God upon our life immediately. It did not take long for us to realize that God was not only calling us to the ministry of evangelism but also to a life of faith. As young new Believers we were perfectly willing to cast ourselves upon the Lord and trust Him by faith. We were even enthusiastic about it. All we had, however, was enthusiasm. We were excited about trusting God, but we did not have a clue as to how to go about it. We needed an instruction book and there wasn't one. We read the great exploits of faith in the Bible and believed all of them. We read every biography we could get our hands on – Hudson Taylor, George Muller, C.T. Studd – and marveled at their faith. But the question remained, how do we make this work in our lives?

When God called us into this ministry that we have been in now for the past thirty-two years, we embarked upon it by faith, which we were happy to do. But, again, we did not have a clear grasp as to how to go about it, how to live it out practically in our daily life. And I will be the first to admit that in those early years I made a lot of mistakes, mistakes that cost my family unnecessarily, mistakes that slowed the development of the ministry, and mistakes I would not have made if I had had a practical, definitive guide as to how to go about knowing the clear will of God and trusting Him by real, legitimate faith. It would have saved me a lot of time just to have a clear and accurate understanding of what faith really is. My goal in this book is to provide for my brothers and sisters in Jesus the guide and the help that I so desperately needed and did not have.

Someone asked me one day during a seminar on field evangelism in Malawi, Africa, "Brother Shad, where did this material come from that you are teaching us in this seminar?" I told him, "Brother, I spent twenty years making mistakes and eliminating everything that does not work in field evangelism, and what you are getting in this seminar is everything that is left." I could say the same thing about this book. I have discovered over the past forty years of living by faith, many things that may sound good and look good but are not true and don't work. They are not in this book, but the things that are true and that do work are. They are the component parts of the life of real Bible faith. It is my prayer and desire that this book provide you with a guide that will take you to the summit of "faith mountain" and allow you to look across the landscape of the victorious Christian life that you have suspected to be possible but have not yet fully enjoyed.

NOTE: Even though it is gramatically correct to capitalize all proper names, I have, as a matter of personal conviction, deliberately not capitalized the name "satan" throughout this book unless it appears at the beginning of a sentence.

Acknowledgement

If it were not for the help and encouragement of my wife, Sheila, this book would not exist.

Because of her expertise in so many areas applied to this work, and because of her stubborn refusal to allow me to give up on it, it has reached its completion. I did not realize just what a spiritual battle it would be to put in writing the things God has taught us over the years about living by faith. But it certainly has been, and Sheila has stood by me and with me in the warfare for more than four years of work on this project.

It is her strength that has sustained me in the most difficult hours. It is her unwavering belief in me that has on so many occasions enabled me to write the next page, the next chapter. It is her vast knowledge of Scripture, her grasp of theology, and her deep understanding of living by faith that has helped me maintain dead-on accuracy from beginning to end. It is her walking with me through more than forty years of life and faith experiences that has provided me a dependable, reliable sounding board. It is her believing prayers with me and for me that have provided me with the supernatural strength and understanding needed to write this book.

To all of this must be added Sheila's great literary skill, her command of the English language, her expert editing ability, and her computer proficiency. This book reads the way it reads because my wife took what I wrote and made it readable. It looks the way it looks because she worked tirelessly to make it attractive, interesting, and appealing. It settles upon your heart as "right" because Sheila made sure that it is.

My wife is the most amazing woman I have ever known, and nothing in my life would be complete without her, including this book. I thank God that because of her, you hold *"Real Faith"* in your hand.

14)

Introduction
to the Second Edition

Dear friend, I rejoice that God has led you to read this book. I pray it will be a blessing and an encouragement to you as you walk with God day by day. I pray it will enhance, deepen, and expand your Christian life and enable you to better minister to others. I assure you the devil does not want you to read it because there are many empowering, liberating, and life-changing truths contained in these pages he does not want you to know. There are two things you can expect from the enemy. To begin with, he will attempt to prevent you from getting started in the first place. Then once you do begin, he will try to stop you before you finish. Therefore, I have a couple of suggestions for you. First, do not put off starting this study. Don't wait until you "have time" or "have no distractions" or "go on vacation." DO IT NOW. Then once you have begun, do not stop and start over, as many have told me they have done. Do not begin by "studying" the book. Just read it – all the way through from beginning to end. Don't worry about what you are retaining or what you are missing. Just read it. This will provide you with a panoramic overview of the life of faith. Then once you have read the book in its entirety, go back to the beginning and study it chapter by chapter. Underline, outline, highlight, make notes, and whatever else helps you to retain and apply what you study. Also, do not skip around from place to place. The chapters are arranged in a certain sequence because one builds upon the other.

Chapters 1-12 deal with the fact that living by faith is God's PLAN for every Christian. Then in chapters 13-25 we find that real Bible faith exercised in the life of the believer is the PROCESS by which God transfers His will from heaven to earth. Finally in chapters 26-31 we discover that real faith is God's PROGRAM for the victorious Christian life.

Now let me say one more thing before you begin reading. When I wrote this book, I did so assuming that everyone who reads it would be a born-again child of God. Since publishing it, however, I have discovered that is not always the case. Therefore, if you have any doubt or question whatsoever regarding your relationship to Jesus Christ, I suggest you begin by looking at the appendix in the back of this book entitled "How to Have a Clean Heart." There you will find very simple instructions on how to be sure you are saved. Once that is settled, begin your study in faith and may God bless you as you do.

Chapter 1

Getting Started

A New Approach to the Christian Life

*"The Christian experience, from start to finish, is a journey of faith.
Through it we come into possession of a new life and through it
we walk by this new life. Faith is the life principle of a Christian."*
Watchman Nee (1)

In order for our Christian life to be pleasing to God it must be lived by faith – REAL faith. For most Christians the concept of living in total dependence upon God for everything at all times is a very radical and totally new idea. It is a whole new approach to the Christian life. I have entitled this chapter "Getting Started" in faith, but the truth is, if you are a child of God you have already begun. You took your first step in real faith the moment you invited the Lord Jesus to come into your heart. The impossible became reality by your act of believing upon Jesus Christ to do for you what you could not do for yourself, to transfer you from the domain of hell into the Kingdom of God. You started in faith by making a simple choice to believe in what you could not see or touch. Now you must live in faith by continuing to make that same choice. *"As ye have therefore received Christ Jesus the Lord, so walk ye in Him"* (Colossians 2:6). How did you receive Him? By faith. How do you continue in Him? By faith. In order to live the life that God intends for you to live, the life that you were born by God's Spirit to live, you must discover how to live by faith. There are many reasons why, but the most important one is that *"Without faith it is impossible to please him…"* (Hebrews 11:6). As children of God, we are endowed by our Heavenly Father with the capacity for faith for the purpose of bringing honor and glory to Him.

Now - let me ask you a question; when you hear the word "faith", what do you think of? Is it Moses standing at the Red Sea and the waters parting? Is it Joshua marching around the walls of Jericho? Or is it blind Bartimaeus stumbling through the crowd to get to Jesus to be healed? Maybe it is Peter stepping out of the boat and walking to Jesus on the water. Those are certainly remarkable examples of the exercise of faith as related to special faith events in Bible history. But, as we will learn, God never intended that the demonstration and living out of faith should be confined to the events that took place in the Bible. Faith is a way of life, and we are going to discover that living by faith is the privilege and the responsibility of every person who knows Jesus Christ as Savior and Lord.

We will develop a full definition of faith later on, but to get started, let's make four brief beginning observations.

1. First, faith is the **plan** of God for every Believer. *"...as it is written, The just shall live by faith"* (Romans 1:17).
2. Second, the capacity of faith is **provided** by God and is given to every child of God as a **personal possession**. *"...according as God hath dealt to every man the measure of faith"* (Romans 12:3).
3. Third, faith is the **power** of the Christian life. *"...and this is the victory that overcometh the world, even our faith"* (I John 5:4).
4. Fourth, God's word makes it very clear that the exercise of faith is required to **please** God. *"But without faith it is impossible to please him..."* (Hebrews 11:6).

Learning a New Language

So we see from the start that faith is essential to the Christian life. You could accurately say that faith IS the Christian life. We are going to learn that the subject of faith is vast and takes time to grasp. I know you want to learn as much as you can as fast as you can. That is why you are reading this book. It is best, however, to not get in too much of a hurry. Learning to live by faith takes time, so let it. It is like learning a new language. It may be a struggle at first, but in time an amazing thing happens; you just wake up one day and you are speaking the language. That thing you have struggled so hard to grasp has now grasped you. You will find the same to be true with learning to live by faith. Faith is the language of the Spirit of God, the language that enables us to fully and freely communicate with Him.

I remember my first day in New Testament Greek class. I looked at the first page of that Greek grammar book and thought, "You have to be kidding! There is no way I can ever learn this stuff!" I was right; I couldn't learn it. I had to discover it; I had to absorb it. It had to become part of me. Then one day an amazing thing happened, I opened up the Greek New Testament and could actually read it! It was a miracle! Dear friend, my advice to you is to approach this study in faith the same way. Discover it, absorb it, and allow it to become part of you.

Scaling New Heights

Embarking upon the study of faith is also somewhat like climbing a mountain. The only way to do it is to start at the bottom and slowly work your way up. Experienced climbers know that it is necessary to stop at base camps along the way in order to get acclimated to the thinning oxygen supply. Well, the one who is making the climb of faith will discover the same thing. God will take you along for a certain distance and then you will need to stop and get acclimated in your experience. Then you can move on to the next level. The mountain climber must learn as he goes along to rely on less oxygen than he has been accustomed to. Likewise the faith climber must learn to rely on less of his own resources, his own abilities, his old way of life, and his old way of thinking. Again let me suggest that you not expect to absorb it all by just reading one or two isolated chapters of this book. It won't happen that way. But as you read and absorb, chapter by chapter, the light will begin to dawn and you will begin to see clearly the way of faith. For most it is a new way and requires making adjustments. As reflected in the subtitle of this chapter, we are talking about,what may be for many an entirely new approach to the Christian life. Again, just give it time, and as you pray each chapter back to God you will assuredly begin to "acclimate."

Have you ever wondered why some climbers make it to the top and some don't? At the beginning of the climb everyone has the same goal, the same distance to climb, the same equipment, the same clothing, the same instructions, and the same guide leading them. So what makes the difference in who makes it and who doesn't? Well, of course, sheer strength and stamina play a part, but quite often the key factors are desire, determination, and just plain old refusal to quit. Friends, the faith climb is very much like that. It is not a question of how much faith a person has. Faith is not a force; it is a capacity. Every Believer is endowed by God with the exact same capacity to trust, to believe, and to walk by faith. No Christian has any greater capacity for faith than anyone else; again quoting Romans 12:3 *"...according as God hath dealt to every man the measure of faith."* It is not a question of having, but of using. It is not faith possessed that conquers, but faith exercised. As we go through this study you will very likely need some of that "plain old refusal to quit." The devil does not want you to discover how to live by faith, because if you do you will become a serious threat to the powers of darkness. Satan is going to try to prevent you from ever beginning the climb, and if you do start, then he will try to knock you off the mountain with discouragement and confusion. Don't you listen to him. Just follow the instructions of your Guide and keep focused on the peak. I talked to a doctor one day who was going to Tanzania to climb Mount Kilimanjaro. I asked him why he was going to do that. He replied very simply, "I want to." There it was; there was the defining ingredient. Dear Christian, if you master the life of faith it will be for one reason, not because you have to but because you want to.

It is my prayer that this study will ignite in you a desire to learn the language and ascend the heights of faith. Don't get discouraged when you have to rest and review, when you have to stop occasionally at a base camp and catch your breath. Everybody does. As we have said, base camps (resting places) are part of the process. That is why opportunities for rest, reflection and review are provided for you at the close of each chapter. Remember, and I can't say it often enough, learning to live by faith is a process.

Clearing the Way for Real Faith

Speaking of processes, let me share one with you. Our home in Tennessee, which my wife Sheila named "Pilgrim's Rest," was built on a beautiful piece of property that came to us as a tremendous blessing from God. But, there were a few obstacles to overcome before building could begin. First the deed had to be settled, which was made challenging by the fact that the surveyors incorrectly shot the south boundary three hundred feet too far north, putting it right through our kitchen. It was quite an ordeal, but it was all eventually settled, the deed was filed at the courthouse, and we could finally say with confidence that we really owned the property. But then there was another problem; there was no access to the property from the road. We discovered, however, that the property between our land and the road was

Faith is unutterable trust in God which never dreams that He will not stand by us.

Oswald Chambers (2)

owned by a wonderful Christian man who was willing to sell us enough of it for a driveway . So now we had a deed to the land and a way to get to it, but there were still two more hurdles to clear. There was not a flat spot on the property large enough to adequately contain the footprint of the house, and the property was completely covered with trees. Sheila always said that she would like to move out of the city and find a place in the country with lots of trees. Well, we had trees all right - nothing but trees.

It became apparent from the very beginning that every aspect of this building project was going to be an issue of faith and it would be a while before these pilgrims could rest at Pilgrim's Rest. But, the process did

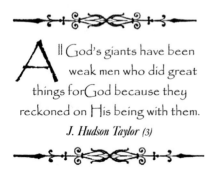

A ll God's giants have been weak men who did great things for God because they reckoned on His being with them.

J. Hudson Taylor (3)

begin. First, the footing was dug and the concrete poured. Then the blocks were laid and the floor joists were set. Next came the sub-floor and then the walls were framed. Then came the roof rafters, shingles, bricklaying, and so on until the structure was complete and we had moved in. After it was finished I realized that it was a perfect picture of the development of the faith life. Let me show you.

Before the faith life can be built into a person, God must first secure the deed to the "property." He did that in you and me by paying the highest price possible with the shed blood of His Son. But ownership is not enough, evidenced by the fact that many of God's children are not yet living by faith. In addition to ownership, God, through the Holy Spirit, must be given free access to our life. As we will discuss later on, many people receive Christ as Savior but then go no further. They escape the slavery of Egypt but then become trapped in the "wilderness." They seem to never develop a real, working, productive fellowship with God.

So how does God gain full access to a Christian's life? He does it by means of two things: *de*struction and *con*struction. II Corinthians 5:17 says that in the life of every Believer, *"...old things are passed away; behold, all things are become new."* Before we began preparing our property for the construction of Pilgrim's Rest, some destruction had to take place. The first time we saw the property was in the fall and it was absolutely beautiful. The issue, however, was not appearance but suitability for building. That required making some changes on the land. The bulldozers, backhoes, and gravel trucks came in and attacked that place with a vengeance. Trees were cleared to create a driveway and more trees came down to make room for the house. Then deep utility ditches were dug along each side of the drive and huge mounds of dirt were formed on the property along with gigantic piles of logs and brush. Within a couple of days the place looked like a disaster area. In time, however, the ultimate goal was realized. On that land there now sits the envisioned house. It is surrounded by beautiful landscaping, railed fences, and ornamental trees which take the place of some of the ones cleared away. Now the property is not only more beautiful than it was before, but it is also *occupied.* It all happened because Sheila and I made a decision. We allowed the contractor to do the <u>de</u>struction so that he could then do what we really hired him to do - the <u>con</u>struction of the desired building. You see, it is not enough for your Christian life to just look good. In order for it to be useful to God, it must be completely occupied by the Holy Spirit. In order for that to happen some changes are going to have to be made. You must be willing for the Contractor of Heaven to remove some things from your life and replace them with Himself, with His plan and purpose, with the one thing that brings glory to Him - the life of real faith. Are you ready to do that?

I suspect that as you consider the task of learning this new language of faith, as you gaze upwards to the highest peak of "Faith Mountain", and as you consider turning the page to the next chapter of this book, there may very possibly be some questions, doubts, or objections arising in your mind and heart. I would be surprised if that did NOT happen. The very last thing that satan wants for any child of God to discover is that it is possible to live beyond the limitations of the visible. The devil does not want you to know that you have been given the capacity and privilege of believing God for the miraculous and impossible. When Sheila and I first stood down in the woods on our property, it was very hard for us to envision a house standing there. Why? Because we were totally surrounded by trees. All we could see were the hindrances. As you make the effort to embark upon the climb of faith, you may very well encounter some hindrances, some "trees" growing on the property of your Christian life, that need to be cleared away so that God can begin building in you the life of faith.

There is an old expression that says, "You can't see the forest for the trees." Very often there is a forest growing on the property of our life that we cannot see through and therefore cannot escape. It is deep and dark and hinders the formation of the life of faith. I call it the "Devil's Forest." But how does it get there? The same way all those red oak trees got on our property at Pilgrim's Rest, they grew from seeds. As we have said already, the moment you were saved, the deed to your life was registered in Heaven and belongs to God. Satan cannot get the property back, but he can scatter seeds on it that quickly grow into trees, hindrances that prohibit the building of the life that God intends for every Believer to experience and enjoy. In the next chapter we are going to look at some of these trees. Each one bears its own poisonous fruit and conveys its own deceptive lie. It only takes one to prevent us from ever taking the first step toward a life of faith.

Now before we examine these possible hindrances to faith in your life, let me just tell you that before the first tree came down on our property and before the first yard of dirt was moved, Sheila was already at the paint and wallpaper store picking out colors and patterns. She even had little pieces of furniture-shaped paper cut out to scale and was placing them on the floor plan. Unlike me, she was not really into all that heavy equipment stuff. She had already jumped way ahead to what she called the "fun part."

Of course, I thought all that stuff involving bulldozers, backhoes, and concrete trucks was the fun part. I guess, however, that's a "guy thing." The point is, however, that not one piece of wallpaper could go up and not one roller of paint could be applied until the process had developed far enough along to make that possible. So it is in learning to walk by faith. I promise you that we will get to the fun part in this process, the part where we are actually seeing God do the impossible. We will speak this faith language. We will stand on top of Faith Mountain and look out across the expanse of God's spiritual world. But first, we must make sure that all the trees are cleared, and we must begin to lay the foundation.

> Our God specializes in working through normal people who believe in a supernatural God who will do His work through them.
>
> Dr. Bruce Wilkinson (4)

As I said before, you began in faith the moment you asked Jesus into your heart, but that was only the beginning. That simple initial act of receiving Christ was like standing on the beach and putting your toe in the ocean. There is a vast ocean of experience awaiting you as you move on beyond receiving Jesus to walking in partnership with Him, trusting the Father for the impossible. There is a world awaiting you that is overflowing with wonder and excitement. It is filled with the blessings of God. Listen to the words of Paul in I Corinthians 2:9, *"But as it is written* [Isaiah 64:4], *Eye hath not seen, nor ear heard, neither have entered into the heart of man, the things which God hath prepared for them that love him."*

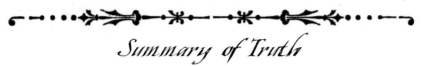

Summary of Truth

- ❖ Our first step in real God-faith is believing on Jesus Christ for salvation.
- ❖ Without faith it is impossible to please God.
- ❖ Learning to live by faith is the privilege and responsibility of every child of God.
- ❖ Faith is the language of God and must be learned in order to communicate with Him.
- ❖ Becoming acclimated to the faith life is a process that takes time.
- ❖ Every Christian is endowed by God with the exact same capacity for faith, for the purpose of bringing glory to Him.
- ❖ The faith life IS the Christian life.
- ❖ If we learn to live by faith it will be because we <u>want</u> to, not because we <u>have</u> to.
- ❖ It is not enough for our life to <u>belong</u> to God; it must also be <u>occupied</u> by Him.
- ❖ In order for faith to develop in our life, changes must be made. We must trust God to do <u>de</u>struction in order for Him to do <u>con</u>struction.
- ❖ As we embark upon the climb of faith we will surely encounter opposition from satan.
- ❖ It is God's will for us to live by faith.

NOW LET'S TAKE A MOMENT AND PRAY TOGETHER:

DEAR FATHER, I HAVE UNDERTAKEN THIS STUDY BECAUSE I DESIRE TO KNOW MORE ABOUT LIVING BY REAL FAITH. I BELIEVE YOU HAVE LED ME INTO IT AND I ASK YOU TO HELP ME CONTINUE IN IT. I ADMIT TO YOU THAT THE LANGUAGE OF FAITH IS NOT FAMILIAR TO ME, BUT I AM WILLING TO LEARN. LORD, MORE THAN ANYTHING, I WANT TO LIVE A LIFE THAT IS PLEASING TO YOU, THAT HONORS YOU AND THAT BRINGS GLORY TO YOU. LORD I ASK YOU TO DO WHATEVER DESTRUCTION IS NECESSARY IN MY LIFE IN ORDER TO MAKE WAY FOR YOUR CONSTRUCTION. MAKE MY LIFE A SUITABLE GROUND FOR THE BUILDING OF A LIFE OF REAL FAITH THAT HONORS YOU. THANK YOU, LORD JESUS, FOR SAVING ME AND INDWELLING ME BY YOUR SPIRIT. TEACH ME TO LIVE BY FAITH. I THANK YOU, AND I LOVE YOU, LORD JESUS. IN YOUR NAME I PRAY. AMEN.

Chapter 2

Hindrances

Resisting the Lies of the Enemy

*"Faith is the heroic effort of your life, you fling yourself in reckless
confidence on God. The real meaning of eternal life is
a life that can face anything it has to face without wavering.
If we take this view, life becomes one great romance,
a glorious opportunity for seeing marvelous things all the time."*
Oswald Chambers (1)

Satan's aim for every Christian is a life lived apart from the supernatural intervention of God. Previously we made the observation from Scripture that without faith it is impossible to please God and that living by faith is not only the privilege but also the responsibility of every child of God. When God's Word says, *"...The just [saved] shall live by faith"* (Romans 1:17, Hebrews 10:38, Habakkuk 2:4), He means every Christian, not just a select few. Having that settled, we also concluded that if we do learn how to live by faith it will ultimately be for one reason, because we *want* to. Knowing that we *can* and that we *should* will never be enough; there must be a desire that produces a choice. Now we could reasonably ask this question; if a Christian knows that it is not possible to please God without living by faith, and he has the God-given capacity to do so, and there is a wonderful new world of experience waiting for him if he does, then why would he not have the desire and make the choice? There are several possible reasons which can all be grouped under one heading, satan's deception. Remember, his ultimate goal for every Christian is a life that is lived out apart from the intervention of God. Why? Because a life lived without the intervention of God produces no glory to God.

Later on we will discuss some things that we will label "enemies of faith." These are things that oppose real faith once it has actually begun in a Christian's life. But here we are going to deal with some hindrances that satan uses to prevent Believers from ever getting started in the faith life to begin with. They are like trees growing on the property of our life, property that God owns and wants to fully occupy for His own purpose and glory. These trees form the "devil's forest" that I mentioned previously. I know that deep within your heart there is a desire to trust God and a longing to see Him work supernaturally through your life. If that were not so you would not be reading this book. So why have you not started before now? Perhaps you have fallen victim to satan's deception. Are you being hindered by things of which you are not even aware? If you discover that you are, then take heart. All you have to do to remove the hindrances to faith in your life is to know they exist, claim your freedom in Christ, and declare that you are going on with God. Now, let's look at some possible "trees" that may be hindering your beginning in faith.

1. IGNORANCE of the truth of faith.

Satan's lie: "You are saved, but there is no need to go any further."
Result – Form of godliness with no power.

There are multitudes in the modern church who do not live by faith simply because they do not <u>know</u> about it. They do not know that the possibility of the faith life even exists, and they have gone no further because their eyes have been blinded to the fact that there is any further to go. It is easy to be satisfied with where you are if you don't know that there is anything better. That is the case with many Christians, because the principles of faith and the truths of the faith life are not taught or preached in their churches. Also, they have never heard testimonies of God's miraculous intervention or His supernatural provision, and they have never had an opportunity to read the biographies of the ordinary men and women in Christian history who lived extraordinary lives of faith. There have been many great books written over the years chronicling the wonderful exploits of faith in the lives of those who have dared to believe God, but satan has kept them virtually hidden from the Christian mainstream. He does not want God's church at large to know just how practical and productive it is to trust in the Living God. If that news ever gets out, the kingdom of darkness is in trouble. Dear Christian, one of satan's most effective ways of hindering you from beginning in faith is to just keep its truths hidden from you.

2. INCORRECTNESS regarding the truth of faith.

Satan's lie: "Faith is praying until you receive what you desire."
Result – False concept of the faith life.

We are not going to spend much time on this topic because it will be covered in detail later. Suffice it to say that there are many misconceptions about faith, and there is a lot of incorrect teaching. If satan cannot keep the truth of the faith life hidden from you, then he will try to distort it. A very effective ploy of the devil in robbing the church of a dynamic legitimate faith walk is to place an out of balance emphasis on my hopes and desires in connection with trusting God. Real faith is based upon the will of God, not my will. It is for the expansion of HIS Kingdom, not mine. Many times well meaning Christians try to live by what they believe to be faith, but their faith is misplaced or misdirected. Therefore, it produces nothing and ends in disappointment and defeat. Well, dear reader, as you continue in this study you will discover real faith, and I promise you will not be disappointed.

3. INVOLVEMENT without the truth of faith.
Satan's lie: "The important thing is to be busy working for God."
Result – Fleshly activity that does not glorify God.

The very first instruction that most new Christians receive is that they need to hurry up and get involved and get busy for the Lord. So, before long, we are all just like little "Energizer Bunnies"; we are going and going, attending and attending, doing and doing, serving and serving. We are beating our little drums and making a lot of noise, but in actuality we are accomplishing little for the glory of God. Why? Because, so much of what we are doing is being accomplished out of our own energy and resources. We are led by our own intellect and feeling rather than by the Spirit of God. Before we realize what has happened, we have gotten caught up in doing rather than being. We are not told that we are to be anything; we are just supposed to show up and do things. Our Christian life has become based entirely upon behavior rather than believing. Sadly, many churches measure success by the same measuring stick that the world uses; attendance, income, programs, and buildings. Unfortunately, these things often testify to man's achievement rather than God's faithfulness. Millions of Christians across the world are never taught that the most important thing in their life is their personal relationship with God and learning to trust Him by faith.

So is it not a good thing to be involved in work for God? Yes, of course it is, and we should be, but only if our involvement and our activity is initiated by God and carried out by faith in accordance with His will through the guidance and power of the Holy Spirit. That is the only way it brings glory to God. Anything else is just fleshly religious activity. The only Christian work done <u>for</u> God that brings glory <u>to</u> God is that which is done <u>by</u> God <u>through</u> the Believer.

We must learn that the secret to the Christian life is not our working <u>for</u> God, but it is God working <u>through</u> us. *"For it is God which worketh in you both to will and to do of his good pleasure"* (Philippians 2:13). Are you so busy in "service" to the Lord that you do not have time to wait upon Him, to know His will, and then act according to what He tells you? If so, then it is very likely you are being hindered from faith. Ask yourself, "Why am I doing all that I am doing? Is it a result of God telling me in my spirit to do it? Or, am I just responding to the requests and expectations of men, the needs I see before me, and my own desire to do something for God?" In I Corinthians 3:12, Paul warns us that there are two kinds of work for God. He calls one *"gold, silver, precious stones"* (work that will last), and the other he calls *"wood, hay, stubble"* (that which will not last). In verse 13 we are told *"Every man's work shall be made manifest; for the day shall declare it, because it shall be revealed by fire; and the fire shall try every man's work of what sort it is."* Only the life of faith produces work that lasts. Ask yourself this question, "Am I living a life of trusting God to execute HIS will through me, or am I just busy?" Involvement is good as long as it is according to God's will and does not hinder you from a life of real faith.

4. INDOCTRINATION *against the truth of faith.*

Satan's lie: "God does not speak to you in your heart."

Result – <u>Failure</u> to recognize the ministry of the indwelling Holy Spirit.

Many children of God have been indoctrinated against the truth of faith by listening to misguided teaching that is set forth in an effort to counteract extremes and false doctrine concerning faith. Some would have us believe that God, by His Spirit, does not make His specific will known to individual Believers. If that were true then real faith would be impossible because faith is simply acting upon the received will of God. It is persuasion of fact (God's will) followed by corresponding action (believing). Some Christians have been led to believe that they cannot hear from God personally and directly. In other words, the Holy Spirit speaking the will of God in our hearts (the inner man, Ephesians 3:16) is unnecessary, in fact impossible, and the written Word of God is all there is. They have been taught that we are supposed to just read the Bible and apply it as best we can to our situation, without the inner guidance of the Holy Spirit, and then do what we think is right. Not only does this leave the Christian on his own to determine the course of his life, it places him exactly where satan wants him to be. This narrow view of God's interaction in our life has been adopted by many in reaction to another equally erroneous position. The opposite extreme is that whatever I think God has said to me or that I feel good and positive about is OK, even if it contradicts God's written word. This view places the Christian in extreme danger of hearing a lie from the devil and believing it because it sounds good. So you see, one erroneous extreme fosters overreaction by another causing division, discord, and polarization in the Body of Christ. In the end, the only one who wins is satan because he has deceived both sides. The truth is that both are wrong and do not live by real faith, because real faith requires knowing the will of God first and acting upon it. The Holy Spirit will reveal the will of God to your inner man, and it will **never** contradict the written Word of God. This is the balanced life of faith. Have you been hindered from real faith by one wrong teaching or another? The truth lies between the two points, and you are going to discover it as you continue this study.

5. *INTELLECTUALISM instead of the truth of faith.*
Satan's lie: "We must always do what makes the most sense."
Result – Focus upon logic and reason rather than trusting God.

Intellectualism is the enthronement of reason over the truth of faith. How many times have you heard some well-meaning church leader stand up and say, "Yes we need to pray, but we must also use good business-sense?" Or you may have heard some one say "We really don't have to pray about that, it's a no-brainer. It just makes sense." Or what about this one, "Yes we do need to trust God, but we also need to be practical and use good common-sense. God did give us a brain, you know." Yes, God did give us a brain, but He also gave us a spirit. And, as we will observe in depth later on, it is the spirit of man that He communicates with and reveals His will to, not the mind or emotions. If you are living your Christian life within the confines of merely what you can reason, think or figure out, then you are stopping short of where God wants you to go and are living a very limited life.

Some Christians tend to value great learning over child-like faith in a loving Heavenly Father. They sometimes look upon those who choose to trust God by simple faith as immature, inferior, or lacking in intelligence. If you have been guilty of harboring that kind of attitude, or if you have fallen victim to it, I would encourage you to read the biographies of the men and women who have made the greatest impact on the world for Jesus Christ. You will find that many of them did not hold high degrees and most of them did not always abide by "good common-sense." In fact many, at first, were called foolish by their learned peers, who later had to recant in the face of all God did through their lives. In I Corinthians 1:20 Paul asked a probing question, *"Where is the wise? where is the scribe? where is the disputer* [learned one] *of this world? hath not God made foolish the wisdom of this world?"* Then in verse 27 he tells us, *"But God hath chosen the foolish things of the world to confound the wise; and God hath chosen the weak things of the world to confound the things which are mighty."* Dear child of God, do not be afraid to be numbered among those who would be called foolish for believing that God still works miracles and performs the impossible. According to the Apostle Paul, it is not a bad group to be in. In fact, that is just the very group God is looking for. It is this group that ultimately makes it to the top of Faith Mountain.

When Hudson Taylor, founder of the China Inland Mission, was about to depart for his first trip to China at age twenty-one, he shared with an elderly minister what he was about to do. When the elder brother asked how he intended to support himself, Hudson Taylor told him that he was going by faith, trusting God to supply all his needs. The man said, "Some day you will be older and wiser and you will see that that won't work." After forty years of trusting God by faith, never asking any man for anything, and being used of God to place hundreds of missionaries in China, Mr. Taylor remembered what the man had said. Then he said, "He was partly right, I <u>have</u> grown older, but I am no wiser because I still believe that I can trust God by simple faith to meet all my needs."

So are we saying that we should not use our intellect? Are we saying we should not study and learn and use our brain? No, not at all. What we ARE saying, however, is that reason and intellectualism should not be allowed to take the place of simply trusting God with child-like faith. Our intellect is not at odds with faith. God gave us our mind to use for serving Him and for relating to the physical world we live in. It is not our intellect that opposes faith; it is intellectualism - the use of intellect to the exclusion of trusting God. In referring to His followers, Jesus repeatedly used the word "children." In I John the author used the expression "little children" nine times in referring to followers of Christ. Then in Ephesians 5:1 we find Paul instructing the church to *"Be ye therefore followers of God, as dear children."* The message from Scripture is clear. God wants us to trust Him as a child trusts his father – by faith, not by "figuring." If you are willing to humble yourself, become like a child, and learn to trust God by simple faith, this study is going to show you how.

6. INTIMIDATION by the truth of faith.

Satan's lie: "Faith will work for others, but not for you."

Result – Fear of becoming a disappointment to yourself and to God.

Most people are afraid of three basic things – the unknown, rejection, and failure. Some Christians are afraid of living by faith because they don't know anything about it. It is simply unknown territory to them. Others, such as those in the indoctrinated group or the common-sense crowd, may be afraid of being thought of as strange or foolish. But then there are some Christians who experience another type of fear – the fear of failure. They may be part of a Christian fellowship that actually embraces the truth of the faith life and would readily support their efforts to live by faith, but they are still afraid to try it for themselves. They have seen it "work" for others and have heard and read encouraging testimonies regarding the validity of simply trusting God, but there is a hesitancy in making the attempt themselves. Why? Because the devil has convinced them that it won't "work" for them and they are going to end up looking foolish. Satan tells them that it is all just too hard and they will never get it right. Of course that is a lie. God has called and enabled every child of His to live by faith, but there are those who don't because they are afraid they will fail and God will be disappointed in them. I promise you that you cannot fail at faith, because God, by His indwelling Spirit, has equipped you for it. You have absolutely nothing to lose in trusting God by faith. He will respond to you with nothing but love and encouragement for making even the feeblest attempt at faith. Look again at that crowd gathered in Hebrews eleven. They were just as ordinary as you and me, and they did not all succeed the first time out. But they did eventually, and they all ended up in the "Hall of Faith." If satan has stopped you with fear, then right now stand up and resist that fear on the ground of the cross of Jesus. Say out loud, "I will trust God by faith!" As you continue in this study you will discover just how to make that statement come true.

7. INDIFFERENCE *towards the truth of faith.*
Satan's lie: "We should be content to just accept whatever God sends."
Result − <u>Fatalistic</u> view of God's will and plan for our life.

To say, "I'll just take whatever God sends" may sound good, but in reality it is not good, because it is not faith. Real faith is knowing the will of God and then trusting Him to perform it. Statements like the one above are only made by complacent Christians. They live clean, moral, doctrinally correct lives and are well thought of in their churches. On one end of the spectrum are those whose good Christian lives form a neat and attractive package, and many are well supplied with all they want and need. These Christians (and often their churches) have all the money, talent, and resources to do whatever they desire to do. So why change anything? As comfortable as the status quo is, it <u>must</u> be right. At the other end of the spectrum are those who think it is holy and righteous to barely get by. They believe that God is somehow pleased by their willingness to do without and their acceptance of whatever happens as "from the Lord." At both ends of this spectrum, though, God receives <u>no</u> glory. Your Heavenly Father does not want you to live a passive life of "just taking what comes." He wants to reveal His will, His plan, and His purpose to you and work through you in His eternal enterprises. He wants to draw you into the aggressive, conquering, dynamic life of faith. He wants to use you in the building of His kingdom. If you have gone through your Christian life thus far with a "take it or leave it" attitude concerning faith, then ask God to forgive you and to help you embrace the life He so wants to give you. God does not want you to live a self-satisfied or self-sacrificed life; He wants you to live a <u>sanctified</u> life, which means a life that continues in the faith that led you to Jesus in the first place.

8. INDECISION *about the truth of faith.*
Satan's lie: "Yes you should enter the life of faith, but do it later."
Result − <u>Forfeited</u> life of faith.

The sooner you make the choice to live the life of faith, the sooner you begin living a life that brings glory and honor to God. Every day you postpone your decision is another day of opportunity lost in establishing a fresh and present testimony to the faithfulness of God. Why wait another hour in making your decision to enter the only life that is truly pleasing to God, a life that makes room for His supernatural intervention? Why wait any longer to enter a life that will bring you more joy than you have ever imagined? Make the choice, do it <u>now</u>! Do not forfeit the extraordinary life that you were born to possess. Do not be deterred from a life that depends on God alone and operates by His supernatural intervention. From the very beginning, satan's goal was to create in man a spirit of independence from God, an attitude of self-reliance and an absence of faith. Oswald Chambers reminds us, "Every element of self-reliance must be slain by the power of God. Complete weakness and dependence will always be the occasion for the Spirit of God to manifest His power" (2).

Timberrrrr!!!

Now, I ask you to go back and review satan's most often used lies and allow the Holy Spirit to show you if you have fallen victim to any of them.

If you have, then take a stand against the lies of the devil. Go to your knees in prayer and ask God to clear those lies away in order to make room for faith. As you do, you will hear the trees crashing in the devil's forest. Yes, the trees are coming down. As you continue in this study you are going to learn who you <u>are</u> in Christ. You are going to discover what you <u>have</u> in Christ. You are going to learn to <u>walk</u> in Christ. And you are going to learn to live by the <u>faith</u> of Christ. You are going to discover how to fight the "good fight of faith."

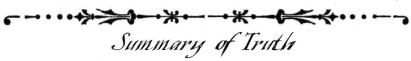

Summary of Truth

❖ Satan puts hindrances in the lives of Christians to prevent them from discovering the joy and freedom of trusting God for the miraculous and the impossible. The hindrances are:

• IGNORANCE of the truth of faith
• INCORRECTNESS regarding the truth of faith
• INVOLVEMENT without the truth of faith
• INDOCTRINATION against the truth of faith
• INTELLECTUALISM instead of the truth of faith
• INTIMIDATION by the truth of faith
• INDIFFERENCE towards the truth of faith
• INDECISION about the truth of faith

❖ The result of believing satan's lies is a powerless, fruitless life that brings no honor and no glory to God.

❖ The hindrances can be removed by making the simple choice to believe that God has given every Christian the power and privilege of living by faith.

❖ I have made that choice, and through this study I am going to discover how to know the will of God and trust Him for the impossible.

Now Let's Take a Moment and Pray Together:

Dear Father, I thank You again for saving me and I ask You to create a burning desire in me to live by simple faith in You. Reveal to me by Your Spirit all that has been hidden from me by believing satan's lies. Deliver me from all fleshly activity. Teach me the difference between my working <u>for</u> You and Your working <u>through</u> me. Help me to understand the ministry of the Holy Spirit in my life, and protect me from false teachings concerning faith. Lord, teach me how to make the choice of faith rather than relying solely on reason and common sense. Deliver me from the fear of failure. Give me the courage to step out and trust You with child-like faith. Help me to never again just take things as they come but to boldly believe You for the miraculous and impossible. And Lord, help me to start right now. I renounce and refuse all lies from the devil, and I choose to receive from You everything You want to reveal to me through this study in faith. Lord, I love You and I thank You for the privilege of trusting You. In Your powerful Name I pray. Amen.

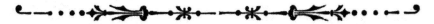

Chapter 3
Explainable Only in Terms of God

*"Our calling in Christ Jesus is to live supernatural lives,
to be more than conquerors day by day."*
Mrs. James Hudson Taylor (1)

*I*f I asked you to give one word that would define or explain or summarize your life at this very moment, what would it be? Think about it carefully; it is an important question. In Nairobi, Kenya, where I have preached hundreds of times, the main mode of public transportation is a mid-sized bus called a "matatu." Want to test your faith? Ride one of those! They are always painted in bright colors and they are always overloaded. They also have names. Across the back window of each vehicle there is always one word painted in big bright letters. It may be a word like "joy" or "danger" or "light" or maybe the name of a famous rap music star or sports figure. One day as we were entering Machakos bus terminal to preach, we followed a matatu in that had the word "HOPELESS" written on it. Of course I used it in my message and asked the crowd if their life had a word written across it, what would it be? Would it be "hopeless", "desperate", "lonely", or what? I also asked them if they would want to change it. Now let me ask you, what one word would you give at this very moment that would explain your life to this point? Would you want to change it? I told those people they could change from "hopeless" to "saved", "redeemed", and "Christian" by simply placing their faith in Jesus. Thank God hundreds of them did. As a Believer, your life should be summarized and explained by one name only, the Name of JESUS. If it isn't, it can be by making the choice to go on with God into a life of real faith.

When we read the list of names in Hebrews eleven, the great "by faith" roster in the Hall of Faith, we have to ask ourselves what it was about the lives of those people that qualified them to be there. The answer is simple; every one of them made the choice of faith that resulted in a life that was explainable only in terms of God Himself. When we read the biographies of George Whitefield, Hudson Taylor, George Muller, Amy Carmichael,

Corrie ten Boom, C.T. Studd, Adoniram Judson, Billy Graham, and Charles Spurgeon, we find ourselves asking the same question; what is it that makes these people such giants in Christian history? All of them were plain, ordinary people and most were raised up from obscurity. So what was it that set them apart? Again the answer is simple; their lives are explainable only in terms of God. In his book, *The Prayer of Jabez*, Bruce Wilkinson observes, "How encouraging it is to find very few supersaints listed among those God has placed on His honor roll. They are mostly ordinary easy-to-overlook people who had faith in an extraordinary God and stepped out to act on that faith" (2). Oswald Chambers adds, "In the history of God's work you will nearly always find that it has started from the obscure, the unknown, the ignored, but the steadfastly true to Jesus Christ"(3).

During one of our campaigns in Malawi, Africa in 1985 I met a remarkable woman in the city of Blantyre. She was an elderly missionary lady from Scotland and was operating a Christian bookstore near the bus station where we were preaching. You might call her one of those easy-to-overlook folks. She shared with me that at age nineteen she was a student at a Bible college in Scotland. One morning during a chapel service she heard a man speak on missions. At that instant God spoke to her and told her to leave Scotland and go to Africa. She quit school in 1939, boarded a ship for Central Africa and settled in Blantyre where she opened the bookstore right away. She had no support, no backing, nothing to stand upon other than the promises of God and the certainty of His will. She told me that since the day she arrived she had spent every morning from 5:00 to 7:00 sharing the Gospel with people passing through the bus station. She said she had led people to Christ from all over the world at that place. She also said she had never missed a day - not one single day in 46 years. I asked her did she ever get sick or tired. She said, "Yes, my brother, I do, but God gives me strength and enables me to go on. He has enabled me to be here every morning for the past 46 years." When I left her that day I had three thoughts. First, if there was an awards ceremony in heaven she would be at the front of the line. Second, compared to her I was doing nothing. And third, there is only one possible explanation for that woman's life - GOD Himself.

Coming up Empty

I was talking one day with a very dedicated, elderly Christian man about our recently completed India campaign. Being a businessman, as well as being familiar with our non-solicitation policy, he was especially interested in how the project was funded. I certainly did not mind sharing the information with him since it was such a testimony to God's faithfulness. So, I told him the story. On the morning of our departure day, we did not have one penny to cover expenses for the campaign or for home either. We needed a total of no less than $22,000. He asked, "Well, what did you do?" I told him we did the only thing we could do. Knowing it was God's will for us to go, we just kept moving in that direction, believing that God would provide in His own way and time. We put our bags in the car and went to the post office to check the box. There was nothing in it. We then went to our ministry office to finish up last minute details before leaving for the airport. Then at about 9:30 we received a FedEx delivery from a man in Texas. There was a check in it for $12,000. Then at about 10:00 a man called and told me that he had wired $7,000 into our account that morning. I was stunned. God had provided $19,000 by 10:00! But,

There should be only one explanation for our lives. God is the only explanation for what we are and what we are doing. If we can explain it on any other level, we are a failure.

Manley Beasley (4)

what about the remaining $3,000? After the phone call, I sat at my desk thanking God on one hand for His amazing supply, but on the other, wondering how we were going to get along without the $3,000 balance. Then, all of a sudden, Sheila called out in an "excited" tone, "Shad, come here!" I couldn't imagine what was wrong. I jumped up from my desk and ran into her office. She said that she had made a mistake in the checkbook. My first reaction was, "Oh no! How bad is it?" But then she explained; she had made a deposit in the bank a few days earlier and had forgotten to enter it. It was for $3,000, exactly what we needed! That was the only time in the history of the ministry that she had ever forgotten to enter a deposit. God had supplied the entire amount, $22,000, four hours before our departure.

My friend was thrilled to hear the story, and I was pleased to speak of the Lord's faithfulness. At the same time, however, he seemed a little disturbed, and said to me, "You know, I have never had anything like that happen to me." Then I told him it did not happen to us every day either. In fact, we have gotten on the plane several times over the years without the money, trusting God to provide as we went. And, of course, sometimes the funds are available ahead of time. I said to my friend, "I'm sure, brother, that you have seen God do many things for you over the years." As he looked at me, saying nothing, the silence told me that he was coming up empty. He could not remember one single time in over sixty years of being a Christian where God did something for him that was personal and so obviously of God that only God could get the credit. All of a sudden I felt bad about telling him the story at all, because it seemed to bring sadness into his heart. That was certainly not my intention. Of course, it wasn't the story that made him feel sad, but the realization that he had missed opportunities in his life to trust God. He came face to face with the reality that, thus far, his life was explainable in terms of his own best efforts, not in terms of the God he knows and loves. It was apparent that this realization brought disappointment and regret. Over the course of his life, my friend has been a successful businessman, a faithful church member, and has led a good Christian life. But as we talked that day, I felt as if I was speaking to a man who had inherited a great fortune, had somehow failed to use it, and had lived on welfare all his life.

That's All Folks - Or Is It

So what causes a Christian, like my friend, to stop short of a life that can be explained only in terms of God? It is believing the subtle lie of the devil. Satan cannot prevent a person from being saved, from leaving the slavery of Egypt. But just after crossing the spiritual border out of hell into heaven, there stands satan, holding up a sign that reads "YOU HAVE AR-RIVED." He attempts to convince the newborn child of God that salvation is the end of the story rather than the beginning, that he has arrived and there is no need to go any further. If the new Christian can be persuaded of that lie, then he can be diverted away from the spiritual promised land of Canaan, that place of faith and rest available for every Believer. If he can be convinced to live his life in the barren religious wilderness of "churchianity" and wander in circles producing nothing, then satan has won. Why is it that so much of the church, the body of Christ, throughout the world seems to be so powerless in storming the gates of hell, so anemic in spiritual growth, and so ineffective in expanding the Kingdom of God? Could it be because so many believers have settled for so much less than God wants them to have? The Bible tells us in Colossians 2:6, *"As ye have therefore received Christ Jesus the Lord, so walk ye in him."* We received

Him by faith and we are now to *"...walk by faith, not by sight"* (II Corinthians 5:7). We are to *"...look not at the things which are seen, but at the things which are not seen..."* (II Corinthians 4:18). We are to trust God Who *"...calleth those things which be not as though they were"* (Romans 4:17). We are born into the family of God to live a supernatural life, but many believers settle for far less, often because they are in churches that are led by pastors who have settled for far less. Sad to say, many do not even realize it because their life and situation seems so normal in the Christian world and environment they are a part of. Dear friend, satan does not mind if you attend church and get involved with "Christian activity." In fact he will even encourage it, if it will pacify you and keep you from sensing the need of going on with God into the life of real faith. What satan does <u>not</u> want you to do is to learn to reach into the invisible and trust God for the impossible. Brother Manley Beasley expressed it this way, "You can be saved from hell and yet not go on with God, and be destroyed. Not your soul, but your life can be shortened, shipwrecked and ruined. There is no neutral ground. There is no turning back" (5).

The New Testament Church pictured in Acts chapter two was unified, bold, power-packed, aggressive, reproducing, and a witness to the supernatural acts of God. Why? Because, it was Spirit-filled and led by men who could, by faith, see into the invisible and trust God for the miraculous and the impossible. There was no explanation for it other than God. The glory of the early church was Jesus Christ, not buildings, programs, or personalities. The gates of hell cannot stand against a faith-filled church or a faith-filled Christian. That is why satan tries so hard to keep us satisfied in the weekly religious grind, the status quo of the wilderness. The last thing satan wants is for us to discover the liberating power of living by faith. He does not want our life to be explainable only in terms of God. Satisfied, wilderness-Christians are no threat to the kingdom of darkness. Dear Christian, is your life a threat to satan and the powers of darkness? It should be, and it will be when you begin to walk by real faith.

Getting beyond the First Step

A picture that is almost as sad as that of an unsaved man who is separated from the person of God by sin, is that of the Christian who is separated from the power and provision of God through unbelief. He has a <u>relationship</u> with God but he does not have meaningful <u>fellowship</u> because he has not made the transition into a life of real God-faith. He has not entered into the new life he has been given. There are so many who have taken the first step of salvation, but have not gone on with God. Again they are like the children of Israel who had been delivered from the bondage of slavery in Egypt and yet wandered in the wilderness. They were surviving day by day but not going on into the promised land of Canaan, that land of victory and blessing God had prepared for them. What a tragedy and what a disappointment that must have been to the heart of God to see those people wandering around in circles, experiencing and possessing so much less than He intended for them. It was all because of unbelief. They just simply would not believe. In spite of all they had seen God do, they just would not make the transition into God-faith. In fact their unbelief was so intense that it even made them look at times back into Egypt, into the old life, and wish they had never been delivered in the first place.

How easy it would have been for that missionary lady to ignore the prompting of God and just stay in Bible College in Scotland. She could have gotten her degree and spent the rest of her life in Christian work and no one but her would have ever known the difference. She would probably have been admired by her friends and family and would have surely been loved dearly by the husband and children she never had. She could have lived out her life in the comfort and security of her homeland "serving God," and no one would have known that she had missed the will of God. No one would have suspected she was actually wandering in the wilderness - no one but her and God.

I have never met anyone who said they wished they had never been saved, but I have met thousands of Christians who are, from all appearances, wandering in the wilderness. They have been made alive in Christ but are experiencing no life at all, or at best, a limited life that does not look much different than what they had prior to salvation. Oh, they have given up their old habits, their language is better, they attend church, and they even read their Bible and pray. Below the surface veneer, however, they still live pretty much within the boundaries of the old life. For so many millions of Christians it cannot be said that their life is explainable only in terms of God. Why is that? It is because so many have not made the transition into God-faith. They believe in it intellectually, they believe it is possible, and they may even desire it emotionally, having seen stirring examples of it in the Bible or perhaps even in the lives of other Christians. They themselves, however, have not crossed over and have never seen God do anything supernatural. They are, therefore, deprived of the intimate, personal fellowship that God wants to share with them – a fellowship made possible only by God-faith.

Where Do We Live?

As an analogy, there are three types of life possible for a human being: Egypt Life, Wilderness Life and Canaan Life. Correspondingly, there are three categories of faith. The first two are in the realm of natural faith and the third is in the realm of spiritual faith. "**Egypt Faith**" is simply natural human faith being exercised by the unsaved man. It is man doing something for man using his own abilities and resources to accomplish it. It produces no honor, glory, or gratitude to God. Then there is **"Wilderness Faith",** which is still just natural human faith, but exercised by a saved person in a futile attempt to serve God. It is man doing something for God, but still attempting to accomplish it out of his own abilities and resources rather than by trusting God. Again, God receives no glory. Finally we come to the only life that pleases God - the life lived by real spiritual God-faith or **"Canaan Faith."** In this category, man trusts God to work through him and provide for him, using His supernatural power and resources to accomplish the task. When it is finished, there is no doubt as to who receives the glory because it is explainable only in terms of God.

An example of Egypt faith, or human faith (man doing for man), would be someone using everything he had to build a good business for the benefit of himself, his family, his employees, and his customers. It is a noble, wonderful achievement but brings no glory to God. As we have said, unsaved people can accomplish many great things for themselves and for humanity, but the end result does not accomplish the ultimate goal that all human activity should accomplish and that is to bring glory to God.

An example of Wilderness faith (man doing for God) would be a group of church members who decide that it is time to add on to the church building without taking the time to know the will of God first. Or, they may take the time to pray and determine the will of God, but when it comes down to the planning process, that is where "good business sense" takes over rather than real God-faith. They look at how much money is being received in the weekly offering and decide whether or not it is enough. If they conclude that it isn't, they postpone their plans. Or they may hire a professional fund-raiser to devise a scheme to extract more money from the congregation. After that is done, they add up how much they have and then plan to build within the limits of what they can see in the visible. Or they may decide to take out a loan to make up the difference. Of course some churches and some individuals are in that dangerous position of having so much man-power and so much money-power of their own that they do not see the necessity to consult God about anything. They just decide what they want and then do it. The bottom line, however, in either case is that the project does not involve trusting God by faith. So often when it is finished we say, "Oh, look how God has blessed us." But the truth is, we just decided what we wanted, rather than knowing the will of God, or waiting on God to do it in His time and in His way. We just used our own scheme to get it done. Oh, we may attach God to it, because as Christians we understand that the rules say He is supposed to get the glory. In reality, however, He had nothing to do with it and will not take credit for it. <u>God is a God of integrity and will not take credit for things He does not do</u>. So, without God's direct supernatural intervention, we end up with just another monument to man's achievement. <u>There is nothing more futile or phony than Christian activity performed in the Name of the Son, that is not initiated by the Father, and therefore not carried out by the power and guidance of the Holy Spirit</u>. It is explainable by something other than God's intervention.

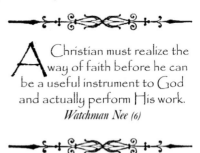

A Christian must realize the way of faith before he can be a useful instrument to God and actually perform His work.
Watchman Nee (6)

Finally, Canaan faith (God doing through and for man) would be that same group of church members going before God together in prayer and waiting until He speaks in their hearts in unity, revealing His will. He might tell them to do nothing just yet. Or He might lead them to build a specific structure, which may or may not fit into what their resources and "feasibility study" say they can do. Then they step out in the will of God, by faith, and trust Him to provide for them supernaturally - miraculously, if need be. When it is finished, it is obvious that God gets the glory and gratitude, because it could not have been done without Him. Canaan faith is trusting God to take you out beyond where your abilities, resources, circumstances and good business sense say you can go. It is reaching out into the invisible and trusting God for the impossible. Real faith will always cause you to reach beyond your grasp. Egypt faith can enable a lost man to build a good business. Wilderness faith can enable a group of Christians to add a wing onto their church building. But, only Canaan faith will result in adding to the Kingdom of God and bringing glory to His name.

The Caterpillar and the Butterfly

Romans 12:2 tells us that we are to be "transformed." Into what? Into a new creature. The word "transform" comes from the Greek word *metamorphoo*, which means to change from one thing to another. An outstanding example from nature is the caterpillar becoming a butterfly. The caterpillar spins a cocoon around itself, dies, and then emerges as a new living creature - a butterfly. Now let's use this picture as an analogy of the Christian life. First we are born into the world as a caterpillar, crawling through the dirt of sin, not able to see above the grass and living a limited life. But one day we hear that a new life can be had if we are willing to die to the old one - a life that has wings! At first we may be afraid to give up that old caterpillar life. It may not be much, but it is all we know and it is all we have. Finally, though, we come to the place where we are tired of crawling and eating dirt, and we place our faith in Jesus, the beautiful "Heavenly Butterfly" Who spread His arms on the cross for us.

We emerge on the other side of the cross as new creatures, alive in Christ (II Corinthians 5:17). Now we can spread our wings of faith and fly above the earth, above the circumstances, above the old life of the visible to which we were once enslaved. We find it to be a glorious existence. Then we notice that not all the butterflies are flying. In fact most are just sitting around or just walking, hardly using their wings at all. Their lives are still explainable in terms of themselves. They all meet together and talk about flying and sing about it and even hear sermons about it, but they don't fly. Furthermore they ask you, "Why do you fly so much? Why don't you settle down and join the rest of us?" So, you heed that suggestion, and in order to fit in you too stop using your wings. Oh you move them occasionally and fly every once in a while, but for the most part, you are living pretty much as you did before. Christians whose lives are explained by self effort do not want a Spirit-controlled, faith-filled Believer in their midst because light exposes darkness.

Strange as it may seem, it is much easier for a carnal "folded wings" Christian to live among Spirit-filled Believers than for a Spirit-filled child of God to live among those who are not. The reason is that the Believer who is not living by faith will be encouraged and lifted up by those who are. They desire to see him enjoy what they have. On the other hand, if you place a Spirit-led, faith-filled Christian in the midst of a group that is living with folded wings and satisfied with the status quo, they will discourage him and make every effort to pull him down to where they are. Why? Because most "folded wings" Christians do not want to be reminded that there is some other explanation for their life other than God. That knowledge makes status quo Christians feel uncomfortable and guilty, unless they are willing to change.

I told you about sharing with my friend how God supplied for our campaign in India and how it seemed to bring sadness to his heart. I believe it was because he realized his wings had been folded for a long time, and he had missed out on opportunities to see God work in his life. He realized his life was explainable in terms of himself rather than in terms of God. Now, where are you in your walk with God? Are you flying in the freedom of faith, or have you folded your wings? Perhaps you have never begun to use them in the first place. Well, it is not too late to start. You may have been living a powerless Christian life up to this point - a life that, for the most part, has brought little glory to God because there is little about it that requires His supernatural intervention. But that can change, because you can change. You can spread your spiritual wings and fly. You were born to fly.

All you need to do is to choose to begin living out what God has put in you. The devil will probably tell you, "You have missed your opportunities to trust God. You are stuck in the wilderness and there is nothing you can do about it. You can never be a truly spiritual Christian. You may as well put this book down and forget it. It's too late for you." That is a lie from the pit of hell. Don't you listen to a word of it. Remember that climbing Faith Mountain can be challenging and it is a process. Part of the process is finding out where you are and then charting a course to go on from there.

Now let me go back to the original question; what one word would you use to explain or summarize your life at this very moment? Maybe before beginning to read this book or this chapter it was "satisfied", "comfortable", or "safe." Maybe it was "normal", "practical", "successful", or "ambitious." Or could it have been "searching?" Would you like to change it? You can by simply making the deliberate decision to go on with God into a life of real faith. Your name can become "victorious", "spiritual", and "pleasing to God", all of which are incorporated into the one matchless Name of Jesus. Earlier I asked another question; what placed all those ordinary people on God's honor roll in the Bible and in Christian history? It's simple – at some point in their walk with God their life had a name change; from "self" to "Jesus", from "natural" to "spiritual", from "reason" to "faith", from "mine" to "His." Are you ready for a name change? Are you ready to spread your wings? Are you ready to enter Canaan? Are you ready to live a life explainable only in terms of God?

Footprints That Last

On the "Cover Design" page at the beginning of this book, I referred to the time in my life (1976-77) when God was dealing with me about going into the ministry we are in today. It involved many early morning discussions with God while walking in a public park near our house. On one of those mornings God brought me to a point of making the same kind of decision I am talking about in this chapter, a decision to unfold my wings and fly in the freedom of real faith.

While walking in the park one morning I passed by the baseball diamond, and as I did I noticed hundreds of footprints in the dust that had been put there during a game the night before. I thought about all the activity it took to produce them, and as I was think about it, a man came over the diamond on a tractor equipped with a blade. He made a few turns around the diamond and wiped out every single print. When he finished, the ground was completely smooth and there was no trace left of the activity from the night before. There was no evidence that anything had happened there at all.

Then I walked over to the other side of the park where there was a concrete sidewalk. In it was one single footprint and beside it was written the date, 1957. It was made 20 years earlier and was still there. At that moment God spoke to me and said, "Shad, you can spend the rest of your life in useless activity making footprints in the dust that time, satan, and circumstances can easily wipe away. Or, you can plant your feet in the concrete of My will and make footprints that bring glory to My Name and last forever."

That morning, long ago, I made my choice and, my beloved brother or sister in Christ, so can you. Determine in your heart right now, at this very moment in time, to allow God to write across your life, "BY FAITH." Decide right now to unfold your wings and fly.

Summary of Truth

- ❖ God wants our lives to be explainable only in terms of Himself.
- ❖ Salvation is only the first step. God wants us to move on to a life of faith.
- ❖ Many Christians miss opportunities to see the glory of God because they do not trust Him by faith.
- ❖ There are three types of people - natural, carnal and spiritual.
- ❖ The Spirit-filled life of faith is available to every Believer.
- ❖ Any Christian can choose to be transformed, to know God's will and live by faith.

NOW LET'S TAKE A MOMENT AND PRAY TOGETHER:

DEAR FATHER, I THANK YOU AGAIN THAT I AM YOUR CHILD AND YOU ARE MY FATHER. BUT LORD I WANT TO BE MORE THAT JUST YOUR CHILD. I WANT TO BE A CHILD THAT HAS MANY OPPORTUNITIES TO BRAG ON HIS FATHER. I WANT TO BRING GLORY TO YOU. LORD FILL ME WITH YOUR HOLY SPIRIT AND MAKE ME A SPIRITUAL CHRISTIAN. HELP ME TO GO ALL THE WAY INTO CANAAN. HELP ME TO LEARN TO TRUST YOU BY FAITH. BRING ME TO THE PLACE WHERE MY LIFE IS EXPLAINABLE ONLY IN TERMS OF GOD. LORD, HELP ME TO UNFOLD MY WINGS AND FLY. HELP ME TO FACE, HEAD ON, WHERE I AM AND THEN MOVE ON TO THE HEIGHTS OF FAITH. I PURPOSE IN MY HEART TO DO IT. RIGHT NOW I PLACE YOU ON THE THRONE OF MY LIFE AND GIVE YOU TOTAL CONTROL OF EVERYTHING. I LOVE YOU, LORD JESUS. IN YOUR NAME I PRAY. AMEN.

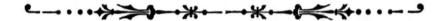

Chapter 4

Living in Two Worlds

Part One:
The Way It Was Supposed to Be

"One of the most important truths in the Christian life is the reality of a world beyond which our senses can perceive and our reason can understand. When we are born again we are given a new set of faculties capable of seeing and hearing into this spiritual world."
Manley Beasley (1)

THE RESULT OF CREATION - A PERFECTLY BALANCED LIFE

CREATED MAN
(PERFECT MAN)

PERFECTLY BALANCED
ALIVE IN BOTH WORLDS

EARTHLY ◄———————► HEAVENLY

COMMUNICATION
INTACT WITH
BOTH WORLDS

The fundamental basis for living the Christian life, as well as a life of real faith, is an understanding of how we were created and what we were created for. There is a crucial foundational Biblical truth that we must comprehend in order to fully grasp the meaning and operation of real faith, a truth that is largely neglected these days in the Christian mainstream. That truth is that we are created by God as three-part beings for the purpose of living in two worlds at the same time. He made us this way so that we can be one with Him continually, execute His will, and bring glory to Him. Man was created with a body, a spirit, and a soul, which equipped him to live in the natural world and the spirit world simultaneously. As human beings we were uniquely designed by God to be the connection between the two. **Living by faith means living the complete, balanced, unlimited life that God intended for a human being to live in the first place.**

In 1975 Sheila and I made our first trip overseas – to east Africa via Amsterdam, Athens and Cairo. It was the first time that either of us had traveled outside the USA. We were so excited we could hardly stand it, because we were entering a New World. We had heard about it and read about it, but we had never seen it or experienced it personally. We did not realize it at the time, but when we stepped on to that plane, we were taking a step that would change our lives forever. From that day forward we would never be the same, because our lives were being expanded beyond the borders of all we had known before, of all we had grown up with, of all we were accustomed to. We were not just crossing geographical boundaries, but our vision was being expanded as well. God was opening our eyes to see that there was a much bigger world of experience and opportunity for ministry out there than we had ever suspected. I remember how excited we were just looking out the airplane window as we crossed the coastline of Ireland en route to the Netherlands. At that moment we had no idea what was in store for us, just how little we were getting excited about, or just how vast this New World would prove to be. We were not aware at first that we were entering a discovery process that would continue for the rest of our lives. We also did not realize that in a very real sense we were taking on a dual citizenship. No longer would we, or could we, be satisfied to just live and minister within the borders of the Old World. We could do both, but we could no longer be limited to just one.

Now let me ask you, have you ever thought about why getting saved is so wonderful, so overwhelming? Of course there is the grateful realization that you have been transferred out of hell into heaven, but it is even more than that, isn't it? Our old friend, Manley Beasley, summed it up when he wrote, "The greatest thing that happens to you when you are saved, is not that you are going to miss hell and go to heaven, but that you take on a capacity to know God and live in the spirit world

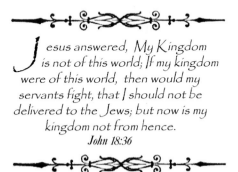

Jesus answered, My Kingdom is not of this world; If my kingdom were of this world, then would my servants fight, that I should not be delivered to the Jews; but now is my kingdom not from hence.
John 18:36

while you are still here physically"(2). You get excited about being saved for the same reason Sheila and I got so excited about going on that first trip – you have entered a vast New World, the spiritual and supernatural realm of God. It is new, different, somewhat mysterious, and even a little intimidating, but as a new child of God you just can't wait to get at it. You can't describe it to those who are not yet in it, but you know that YOU are in it and you can't learn about it fast enough. That is why you have a hunger to read the Bible, your New World map. That is also why you want to go to church and be around other Believers, New World citizens. You quickly realize that you now possess a new kind of **communication ability** you did not possess before you were saved – the ability to communicate with God. From within your new-born spirit you now pick up "signals" from another realm, the spirit realm. It is almost as if you now have a sixth sense. You do; it is a spiritual sense. Now you can see and hear with the eyes and ears of your spirit. You also possess a new kind of **convicting awareness,** the awareness of sin. It becomes apparent to you very quickly that you are now playing by a new set of rules, the rules of the New World. In short, everything has changed.

Before Sheila and I left to go to Africa, we were each issued a document by the US Government - a passport. That little book gave us permission to do something we could not do before we received it; we could now pass back and forth from one country to the other at will. Upon receipt of that official document we suddenly had access to a world beyond all that we had known before. Dear Christian, let me tell you something that is fantastic. When you received Christ into your heart you received a spiritual passport, purchased by the blood of Jesus and issued by the God of the universe. As a Believer, the indwelling Holy Spirit gives you the ability and the authority to live and operate in two worlds, natural and spiritual, at the same time. You now have a channel (your born-again human spirit connected to the Holy Spirit) through which to communicate with God, and God has a channel (His Holy Spirit indwelling your human spirit) through which He can flow His will into the physical realm. That is the operation of faith.

Over the years an interesting thing has happened to Sheila and me; a process has taken place that we would have never expected. As we have traveled from one country to another over the past 30 years, we have become as comfortable and as functional in the world outside the borders of the US as we are within them. We find now that we can be just as much at home in Nairobi, Kenya or Chennai, India as we are in Tennessee. Well, maybe not <u>quite</u> as comfortable as at home, but you get the point. I did say it is a process. Adjusting to and becoming comfortable in the New World of the spiritual realm is a process also. Today I realize that it will never end, and in a very real sense I have only just begun. After I was saved I began to study my spiritual world map, the Word of God. I began to learn His ways, and the Holy Spirit began revealing things to me about this New World I was now living in. Again, the discovery process had begun and continues to this day, and it will go on until I see Him face to face. I can honestly say though, and in time so will you, that in many ways I actually feel more at home now in the spiritual realm than I do in the natural. And I certainly feel more secure.

Let me say it again; learning to live by faith is simply learning to live in two worlds at the same time. Living by faith means becoming a channel through which God can flow His will and His provision from the spirit realm into the natural, from the invisible to the visible. Before the fall, Adam and Eve did not have to learn how to live by faith; they did it naturally, or you might say "automatically." All of that changed with the fall, of course, thus making it necessary for man to now learn to live by faith. That process begins when we are saved, and it continues as we grow in Christ. In this chapter and in the two that follow, we are going to examine three crucial questions that will help lay a foundation for us to build on in our study of faith.

1. How was life supposed to be - what was God's original plan for all human beings?
2. What went wrong – how was the plan interrupted?
3. How do we get back – how is the plan restored?

Created to Be Citizens of Two Worlds

Human beings were specially designed and equipped by God at creation to live in two worlds at the same time; the natural and the spiritual, the visible and the invisible, the earthly and the heavenly. In their original state, Adam and Eve enjoyed dual citizenship. They were as comfortable and as functional in the spiritual realm as they were in the natural. God, operating from the spiritual world, created man in and from the natural world. His plan was that through man He would give definition to the natural, physical world and populate it with human beings that would love and worship Him forever. In order to accomplish this, God made man in a certain way. When His creative process was complete, a being emerged unlike any other in the universe – a human being. This being was created in the image of God with three component parts: a body, a spirit, and a soul. It is clear from Scripture that man is a three part being and it is essential for our understanding of the operation of faith to get this truth embedded in our hearts.

> *"And the very God of peace sanctify you wholly; and I pray God your whole spirit and soul and body be preserved blameless unto the coming of our Lord Jesus Christ."* I Thessalonians 5:23

> *"For the word of God is quick, and powerful, and sharper than any twoedged sword, piercing even to the dividing asunder of soul and spirit, and of the joints and marrow, and is a discerner of the thoughts and intents of the heart."* Hebrews 4:12

By means of his body man could relate to, and function in, physical reality. Through his spirit he could relate to, and function in, spiritual reality. His soul (made up of intellect, emotions, and will) would act as a middle man or bridge connecting the two. By God's perfect design, man could exper-ience three levels of life simultaneously. The lowest was his physical, body life since he was created of and from the earth. It connected him to the earthly realm. The highest was his spiritual life since his spirit was breathed into him by God. It connected him to the heavenly realm. The soul stood between the two and was the connection between the earthly and the heavenly.

Genesis 1:26-27 tells us WHY God created man the way he did, *"And God said, Let us make man in our image, after our likeness…So, God created man in his own image, in the image of God created he him; male and female created he them."* Then Genesis 2:7 tells us HOW, *"And the Lord God formed man of the dust of the ground, and breathed into his nostrils the breath of life; and man became a living soul."* So God created man to live in two worlds (natural and spiritual) at the same time, to be as much at home in one as the other. In fact, before the fall Adam and Eve did not distinguish between the two. The sense of separation between natural and spiritual, visible and invisible, that exists in us today did not exist in the beginning. In order for man to interact with both realms, he had to have faculties (instruments of communication) that would be perfectly suited to both. Therefore, God created the body for the earthly realm, the spirit for the spirit realm, and the soul to provide expression for both. Now before going on, let's summarize the three component parts of a human being and their functions. (Please refer to the diagram at the beginning of this chapter.)

Our BODY, with its five senses, connects us to the physical world of earth. God has a divine order and a divine purpose in everything He does, and so it was in the creation of man. He first made his body, *"And the Lord God formed man of the dust of the ground..."* (Genesis 2:7). God created a material, physical realm, and He made man material and physical so that he could inhabit it, affect it, and rule over it. Man's physical body was perfectly suited to the environment that God created it from and placed it in. God does everything perfectly. Therefore, He made man in such a way that his interaction with the world around him was perfect and complete by means of his five senses. He was equipped to see, hear, taste, touch and smell. No area was left out. But, physical life alone was not enough. It did not make him a person, or personality, and it did not put him in contact with God. It did not make him complete and balanced. Without spirit and soul, man would be no more than an animal. His existence would be limited to only one dimension - earthly, and God never intended for man to be one-dimensional. He must be connected to and have communication and interaction with God. It was not God's design for our lives to be limited to the physical and the visible.

Our SPIRIT connects us to the spiritual world of heaven. God created within man a faculty, his spirit, which would place man in contact with Himself and with the spiritual dimension in which He lives. The Bible tells us that God *"...breathed into his nostrils the breath of life."* "Breath" is derived from the Hebrew word "neshamah", which is translated in Proverbs 20:27 as "spirit," *"The spirit* [neshamah] *of man is the candle of the Lord, searching all the inward parts..."* Additionally we read in Zechariah 12:1, *"... the Lord, which stretcheth forth the heavens, and layeth the foundation of the earth, and formeth the spirit of man within him."* This formation took place when God breathed into Adam the breath, or spirit, of

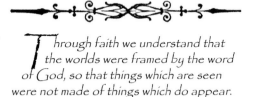

Through faith we understand that the worlds were framed by the word of God, so that things which are seen were not made of things which do appear.
Hebrews 11:3

life. At that instant, his human spirit came into existence. The formation of the spirit provided him with the ability to worship God, to fellowship with God, and to receive the will of God. He was now living in complete, unhindered communion and communication with God. His body made him perfectly suited for the tangible physical world, and his spirit made him equally suited for the intangible spiritual world. Now it was possible for him to have perfect interaction with the world around him as well as unbroken communication and interaction with God Who created him.

Our SOUL connects the two worlds. Man was alive physically and spiritually, but there had to be a connection between physical life and spiritual life, something to provide expression for both. There had to be a way of interaction between the two realms. So, at the same moment the spirit came to life in the body, the soul was formed, *"...and man became a living soul."* Man's soul made his existence complete. Now he was able to think, feel, and choose - that is, to express himself. The soul is a channel connecting the visible with the invisible, the material with the immaterial, the earthly with the heavenly. It is the soul that makes us an individual, a distinct being, and gives us personality.

So, through the body and its five senses we relate to physical reality. Through the soul we relate to the higher reality of thought, emotion, and choice. We can reason, feel, imagine, calculate, approve and disapprove, and make decisions. And then, with our spirit we relate to the highest form of reality, the Reality of God. By means of our body we have world-consciousness, by means of the soul we have self-consciousness, and by means of our spirit we have God-consciousness. It was contact with the third reality, God-consciousness, which was lost in the fall and is regained only by grace through faith in Jesus Christ.

God's Unique Creation Makes the Faith Process Possible

We will see later in our examination of the mechanics or process of faith, that our ability to reason, approve and decide, not only makes us a complete person but also makes us usable in the hands of God for the carrying out of His will and purposes. It makes us a suitable container for the capacity of faith. We receive the will (or thought) of God in our spirit, referred to as the *"inner man"* in Ephesians 3:16, the *"inward man"* in Romans 7:22 and II Corinthians 4:16, and the *"hidden man of the heart"* in 1 Peter 3:4. Then the thought (the directive, the guidance) received from God is processed through the intellect, emotions, and will. It is then carried out by means of our physical being, thus forming a perfect channel linking the invisible world with the visible world and the spiritual realm with the physical, material realm. That is the **process of faith,** our interacting with God in such a way so that God's will is transferred through us to earth. Before the fall of the human race, this process was effortless.

Faith was operational in that it resided in the spirit of man and functioned automatically. The thought of not cooperating with God did not occur to Adam until the temptation. Therefore, faith was un-conscious. **It was only after the fall that faith became a matter of conscious choice.**

Complete and Balanced

So then, God's complete and perfectly balanced man and woman were three-part beings living in two worlds, possessing three forms of life, and relating to three levels of reality - all at the same time and all without effort or conflict. They could think, feel, and choose in relation to the invisible world as easily as the visible. They were alive physically, spiritually, emotionally, intellectually, and volitionally. They were simultaneously conscious of, and equally comfortable with, operating by the physical laws of the visible (the natural laws of thought, emotion, and choice) and the spiritual laws of God. They worshipped God continually and had constant, unbroken fellowship with Him. They were in the position of continuously receiving from God. With the mind, emotions, and will, they joyfully carried out the thoughts of God perceived in their spirit. Their physical being responded to the perfect directives of God's will without fear or hesitation. Their component parts worked in perfect harmony, and they, in their entirety, were perfectly related to their Creator. They were complete, perfectly balanced, totally unlimited, and free. Man was unlimited in his access to God and God was unlimited in His access to man. Regards for the restraints of space and time were not necessary, and the invisible was considered to be no less real than the visible. There were no boundaries to cross in relating to one world or the other. That was the way it was supposed to be and, as we will see, the way it can be again by means of faith. Life restored to this description is the real Christian life, the Spirit-filled life, the life of real faith.

Obviously boundaries, restraints, limitations, and conflicts are clearly part of human experience now, even for most Christians. So, what went wrong? How was the connection lost? How did man go from being perfectly balanced and unlimited to completely out of balance and totally limited to what he can see, touch, think, and feel? How did we become so enslaved to the visible? What was it that changed faith from an automatic response to God into a necessary conscious choice, thus making it all seem so difficult? It was a thing called The Fall. We are going to take a brief look in the next chapter at just what went wrong and how it happened. Thank God, however, we do not have to stop there and we are not going to. Because of God's wonderful plan of redemption, because of the precious blood of Jesus, we can quickly move on and get back to the way it was supposed to be - and we do it by faith.

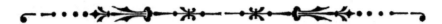

Summary of Truth

- ❖ We were created to live in two worlds at the same time.
- ❖ We were created in a unique way with a body, soul, and spirit.
- ❖ Because of the way we were designed, we are perfectly suited to the faith process.
- ❖ By faith we can live a perfectly balanced life.

Now Let's Take a Moment and Pray Together:

DEAR FATHER, I WAS CREATED BY YOU TO LIVE IN THE NATURAL WORLD AND THE SPIRITUAL WORLD AT THE SAME TIME. THANK YOU FOR CREATING ME IN SUCH A UNIQUE AND WONDERFUL WAY. THANK YOU FOR MAKING IT POSSIBLE FOR ME TO HAVE A PERFECTLY BALANCED LIFE. LORD, AS I CONTINUE IN THIS STUDY HELP ME TO UNDERSTAND HOW I CAN EXPERIENCE THAT PERFECTLY BALANCED LIFE BY EXERCISING THE CAPACITY OF FAITH THAT YOU PLACED IN ME. IN YOUR NAME I PRAY. AMEN.

Chapter 5

Living in Two Worlds

Part Two:
What Went Wrong

*"Wherefore, as by one man sin entered into the world, and death by sin;
and so death passed upon all men, for that all have sinned."*
Romans 5:12

THE RESULT OF THE FALL - LIFE OUT OF BALANCE

FALLEN MAN
(NATURAL)

OUT OF BALANCE
ALIVE IN PHYSICAL WORLD ONLY

EARTHLY ← → HEAVENLY

COMMUNICATION
WITH GOD
WAS LOST

Through the fall, the human race lost its relationship with God and therefore its ability to trust God by faith. God's purpose in the creation of man was that, through Him, the earth would be inhabited by a race of unique beings that would fellowship with Him and worship Him continuously. Through the creation of the spirit, God endowed man with the ability to know Him and worship Him. Through the creation of the soul, God endowed man with the ability to express Him and experience Him. Through the creation of the body, God enabled man to maintain his existence and carry out the will of God on earth. God had instructed Adam and Eve in Genesis 1:28 to *"...Be fruitful, and multiply, and replenish the earth, and subdue it: and have dominion over... every living thing that moveth upon the earth."* But, before the first child could be born, before that dominion could be realized, satan tempted them, they yielded, and they lost everything. The plan of God was seemingly interrupted.

One Deadly Question

The fall of the human race, the beginning of man's limitations, the establishment of boundaries, his loss of freedom, and his enslavement to the visible, all began with one question. Satan, disguised as a serpent, approached Eve and uttered the words, which he has so often repeated down through the ages, *"Yea, hath God said?"* (Genesis 3:1). He took an issue from the physical world, the need for food, and made it the focal point of a doubt-producing question presented to the mind. It did not matter, though, what the question was in reference to, because the implication would have been the same; God was withholding something from them, He was not going to meet their needs, and He could not be trusted. It is the same pitch that satan has been making to the human race since it began. It is the same accusation that he attempts to level against God in the mind of every Believer today. He never changes his approach. He doesn't have to because the old one continues to work so well.

Look at the disciples in the storm in Mark 4:35- 41. Jesus said, *"...Let us pass over unto the other side."* There it was, the clear will of God made known by the spoken word. Then the storm came and what did the disciples say? They repeated the accusation that satan whispered in their ears, *"...Master, carest thou not that we perish?"* They believed the lie from the devil rather than the spoken Word of God. What about us today? What do we do when the storms and trials come, when the sudden emergency arises, when we have a problem that will require a miracle from God to solve? Do we listen to the voice of God telling us that "He will never leave us nor forsake us," or do we listen to satan and try to answer his accusing questions? How many times have we heard him ask, "What are you going to do about this?" That question is always designed to make us doubt and react to the external in fear, rather than wait on God's guidance from within. To do so is always a mistake. It was a mistake for the disciples, it was a mistake for Eve, and it is a mistake for you and me.

Eve's first step in the wrong direction was attempting to answer the devil's question. She should never have entered into that conversation in the first place, and neither should we. But she did, and in doing so, she allowed satan an entrance. His first line of attack, his first step in his efforts to capture and control the will, is always through the **mind**, and so it was with Eve. He appealed to her reason and in effect said to her, "Think about this, has God REALLY said…? Are you sure?" He began the process of contaminating man's soul by injecting the mind with doubt. When Eve attempted to answer the question, she opened the door to the devil, giving him access, and then he took the next step. He moved from the mind to the **emotions**. In Genesis 3:4-5 satan said, *"...Ye shall not surely die; For God* *doth know that in the day ye eat thereof, then your eyes shall be opened, and ye shall be as gods, knowing good and evil.* " This lie incited Eve's emotions and caused her to believe that God was withholding something good from her.

The final stage in the corruption of the soul took place in the **will**. Adam and Eve made the deadly choice to partake of the tree of knowledge (Genesis 3:6). At that moment sin entered the human race and death by sin, *"Wherefore, as by one man sin entered into the world, and death by sin; and so death passed upon all men, for that all have sinned"* (Romans 5:12). Through one fatal act of disobedience, sin entered the human race and contaminated the entire physical world. Now man's soul was darkened; his intellect was dulled, his emotions were deluded, and his will was diverted. His body, which was created pure, was contaminated and changed by the foreign element of indwelling sin and was therefore condemned to die. But the ultimate consequence, the greatest tragedy of all, was that man's spirit died within him and his communion and communication with God was severed. The unconscious automatic response of faith to the will and directives of God was lost.

Sequence of Influence

In looking at how the tragedy of the fall took place, we must see that there is a satanic sequence of influence and a Godly sequence of influence. First, let's look at how God deals with man. When God speaks He always moves from the inside to the outside. He first reveals his will to our spirit. Then God's will, received in the spirit, is interpreted by the intellect, approved of and embraced by the emotions, and obeyed by the will. Finally, it is carried out by means of his physical being. God's will begins in the spirit, moves through the soul, and culminates in the physical. God always calls upon man to act in response to guidance received in the inner man, not to react to the external stimuli of need and/or circumstances or to the pressure of fear, reason, logic, common-sense, public opinion, or "practical" suggestion. God deals with man by giving instruction and guidance to the spirit not by presenting questions to the mind or by making appeals to the emotions.

Satan, on the other hand, operates in just the opposite manner. He always approaches man from the external, usually with some sort of threat or enticement, just as he attempted to do with Jesus in the wilderness. His tactics have not changed from the beginning until now. But then, he has no choice because he does not have access to man's spirit. We will see later on that the spirit is the equivalent to the most holy place in the tabernacle, which could only be occupied by God. It was there that God's directives were given for the nation of Israel, and it is in the spirit that His guidance is given to the Christian. Satan's objective is always to gain control of the will thus causing man to choose contrary to the will of God.

The Struggle for Balance

Our physical being was designed for the sole purpose of carrying out the will of God in the physical realm. Without the ability to receive God's direction in the spirit, however, man is left to the limitations of his own abilities and resources and can never be completely satisfied. Likewise, our soul was created for the singular purpose of representing and expressing God. That function was lost in the fall. Without the spirit, the body and soul are left to serve and express nothing but self.

There is, however, a residual need resident in the soul - the need to worship and express God. Tragically, from that need is born a monster that speaks of God and yet does not know Him. It is called "Religion." It was religion that rejected Jesus and crucified Him. It will not, and cannot, provide balance, because it cannot provide connection to God. Religion is simply man doing his best, and it will not satisfy. He must have a relationship with the living God.

Because of sin indwelling the human race, the spirit does not come alive at physical birth. Physical cannot give birth to spiritual. John 3:6-7 says, *"That which is born of the flesh is flesh; and that which is born of the Spirit is spirit. Marvel not that I said unto thee, Ye must be born again."* The only way a man's spirit can come to life is by the same means it did in creation; life must be breathed into him by the Spirit of God. Man's human spirit comes to life when it is touched by the Holy Spirit, and that happens the instant that man turns in faith to Jesus. Then, and only then, is a relationship established between man and God. The natural man, having not had his spirit brought to life, cannot communicate with God. Therefore, the realization of a balanced, faith filled, God-honoring life is not possible for the unsaved. Jesus said in John 3:3, *"... Verily, verily, I say unto thee, Except a man be born again, he cannot see the kingdom of God."* Jesus told Nicodemus that without coming alive spiritually he would never be able to see the Kingdom of God; he would never have contact with the spiritual realm and would forever remain disconnected from God. He would be doomed to live a life out of balance, limited to the visible, and imprisoned by sin.

A Sad Picture

The Bible tells us that because of the fall the natural man is an enemy of God (Romans 5:10), is far from God (Ephesians 2:17), is guilty (Romans 3:19), is condemned (John 3:18), and is under God's wrath (John 3:36). He is alienated from the life of God (Ephesians 4:18), is without God in his life (Ephesians 2:12), and furthermore, is without God in the life to come (II Thessalonians 1:9).

Man without God lives totally unto himself. Everything about him is completely dominated by self - his thoughts, affections, words, will, and behavior. He is under the dominion and control of satan and is hopelessly and helplessly enslaved to sin. Tragically, he cannot comprehend the seriousness of his condition or the consequences of continuing in it. II Corinthians 4:4 reveals that, *"...the god of this world* [age], *hath blinded the minds of them which believe not, lest the light of the glorious gospel of Christ, who is the image of God, should shine unto them."* Unsaved man has no power to know God (Galatians 4:8), to love Him (I John 4:10), to receive Him (I Corinthians 2:14), or even seek Him (Romans 3:11). Furthermore, he is incapable of gratitude toward God (Romans 1:21), can have no faith in God (John 3:18), and no fear of God (Romans 3:18). He cannot worship God (Romans 1:21, 25), he resists the truth of God (II Timothy 3:8), disobeys the Gospel (II Thessalonians 1:8), and therefore continues in condemnation (John 3:18). It is a sad picture, but thanks be to God, it is a picture that can be changed. There is a way back - through faith in Jesus Christ.

The whole human race was created to glorify God and enjoy Him forever. Sin has switched the human race on to another track, but it has not altered God's purpose in the tiniest degree.

Oswald Chambers (1)

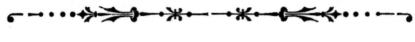

Summary of Truth

- ❖ God's plan was to inhabit the earth with a race of beings that would love and worship Him forever.
- ❖ The plan was interrupted by the fall, through which man lost his relationship with God.
- ❖ Satan always approaches man from the external. God works from the inside only.
- ❖ The human race is in a desperate struggle for balance, which can only be obtained through redemption.
- ❖ The only way back to the way it was intended to be is by faith.

NOW LET'S TAKE A MOMENT AND PRAY TOGETHER:

DEAR LORD JESUS, I KNOW THAT I WAS BORN IN SIN AS A RESULT OF THE FALL, BUT I THANK YOU THAT I DO NOT HAVE TO LIVE MY LIFE UNDER THE LIMITATIONS IMPOSED BY IT. THANK YOU THAT YOU HAVE PROVIDED A WAY TO FREEDOM FROM THE POWER OF SIN THROUGH FAITH. THANK YOU LORD THAT I DO NOT HAVE TO LIVE MY ENTIRE LIFE IN A STRUGGLE FOR BALANCE. IT IS MINE THROUGH FAITH IN YOU. THANK YOU FOR LOVING ME ENOUGH TO DIE FOR ME. IN YOUR NAME I PRAY. AMEN.

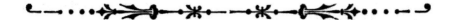

Chapter 6

Living in Two Worlds

Part Three :
How Do We Get Back

*"Therefore, being justified by faith, we have peace with God
through our Lord Jesus Christ, By whom also we have access by faith
into this grace wherein we stand, and rejoice in hope of the glory of God."*
Romans 5:1-2

THE RESULT OF REDEMPTION - BALANCE RESTORED

REDEEMED MAN
SPIRITUAL
(CONTROLLED BY SPIRIT)

BALANCE RESTORED
AND MAINTAINED BY FAITH - ALIVE AGAIN IN BOTH WORLDS

EARTHLY ←——— [BODY SOUL SPIRIT †] ———→ HEAVENLY

COMMUNICATION
WITH GOD
RESTORED

As you already know, there is a way back to life as it is supposed to be. That way back is through Jesus alone. If you are a born-again person, you took your first step in the direction of a fully restored life when you received Jesus into your heart. Now you must continue. Through Jesus Christ man regains his position of dual citizenship and his ability to walk before God by faith.

Every unsaved person is faced with a choice - to remain as he is, separated from God, or to be reunited with God by believing on Jesus Christ and receiving Him as Lord and Savior. He must make the radical choice of faith. He must reach out into the invisible and take hold of what he cannot see, thus receiving from God the impossible – that is, the miracle of salvation. Likewise, every saved person is also faced with a similar choice - to live a mediocre Christian life or to live the dynamic God-pleasing life of faith. How? By doing the same thing – by reaching out beyond the limits of the visible and taking hold of the will and promises of God.

Walking in the Grace of God

In fallen human nature, there is an innate resistance to trusting God, first in relation to salvation and then in relation to living beyond the visible as a child of God. Man, in his pride, wants to think his way to God, or feel his way, or work his way. But God says there is only one way - he must "faith his way," that is, he must believe on Christ. *"For by grace are ye saved through faith; and that not of yourselves: it is the gift of God: Not of works, lest any man should boast"* (Ephesians 2:8-9). There is no room for boasting in salvation or in the Christian life. Many unbelievers are hindered from being saved because they want to do it in such a way that they feel they have a part in it. They want to take credit for it in some way rather than simply coming to Jesus in child-like faith. Many Christians, however, are just as guilty but in another sense. They come to Jesus by faith for salvation, but then they try to continue in their own strength rather than by simple faith. There is only one way to be saved and there is only one way to live the real Christian life - by the act of reaching out and receiving from God. The Christian life is not entered into by works, or as a result of what we deserve; it is entered into by faith. The grace of God is initially received in our life by the Holy Spirit drawing us into faith for salvation. We are not saved by thinking, feeling, or manipulating; we are saved by reaching out into the invisible and receiving from God by faith. The same choice that is required for salvation is required for a life that is pleasing to God - the choice to walk in the grace of God by faith in Christ alone.

The Way Back

The pathway that initially leads us out of darkness into light, back to where God intended for us to be, is called "grace." The Door that provides access to that pathway is the Lord Jesus. *"I am the door: by me if any man enter in, he shall be saved... "* (John 10:9). The key that unlocks the door to salvation is faith. It is also the key that continues to unlock the door to the unseen resources of God. *"By whom also we have access by faith into this grace wherein we stand, and rejoice in hope of the glory of God"* (Romans 5:2). What is grace? It is God's free and unmerited provision for need – spiritual or otherwise. By an act of faith, by choosing to believe upon the Son of God, we become recipients of salvation and participants in that wonderful plan of God called redemption. God's word tells us that we are *"...justified freely by his grace through the redemption that is in Christ Jesus: Whom God hath set forth to be a propitiation through faith in his blood...*"(Romans 3:24-25). We read in Colossians 1:13-14, that God *"...hath delivered us from the power of darkness, and hath translated us into the kingdom of his dear Son: in whom we have redemption through his blood, even the forgiveness of sins."* <u>The way back to where God wants us to be is through the Lord Jesus,</u> *"I am the way, the truth and the life: no man cometh unto the Father but by me"* (John 14:6). We get there by redemption, which is made possible by grace, through faith in the blood of Jesus shed for us on the cross.

Real Faith Made Possible through the Gateway of the Cross

Embarking upon the faith life is made easier by understanding exactly what happens when we are saved, and to do so we must return to the truth that man is made up of spirit, soul, and body. Through Adam, sin and death were dispensed to every area of man's being. His spirit  died, causing him to lose contact with God. His intellect was darkened, his emotions were deluded, and his will was diverted from God to sin, satan, and self. This caused him to think contrary to God, to love that which is not godly, and to make decisions based solely upon fallen human judgment, all of which is opposite to faith. In addition, his body became corrupted and began to die. But by salvation through Jesus Christ, the capacity to function according to God's original design is restored to every part of man's being through the operation of faith from the spirit. II Corinthians 5:17-18 tells us that *"...if any man be in Christ, he is a new creature: old things* [self-life] *are passed away; behold, all things* [faith-life] *are become new; And all things are of God, who hath reconciled us to himself by Jesus Christ..."* In short, redemption "fixed" everything in man that was "broken" in the fall, replacing death with life, separation with fellowship, and fear with faith.

It was "fixed" the only place it could be, at the cross of Jesus. The cross of Jesus Christ is the centerpiece of time and eternity. It is the pivotal point of human history. It is the place where sinful man and Holy God merge, and the explosive force of the love of God issues forth through the power of forgiveness, which results in that marvelous and mysterious outcome called redemption. The cross of Christ stands in defiance against all human logic and exceeds the limits of human understanding. It is the monument to faith. The cross is foolishness to those who perish in unbelief, but to those of us who believe upon Him Who died there, it is cherished and precious. It is no wonder that the Apostle Paul wrote to the church at Corinth, *"For I determined not to know any thing among you, save Jesus Christ, and him crucified"* (I Corinthians 2:2). Through the cross it is possible for God to see us as sons and for us to see Him as Father. Through the cross the operation of God-faith is possible for every human being. Through the cross the world of the visible and the world of the invisible are joined. It is because of the cross of Jesus that it is now possible for us to live in two worlds at the same time. The cross is the gateway from one to the other.

The cross serves as the dividing marker in history between dead religion and a living relationship with God. Every religion has devised some scheme to try to deal with the problem of sins. But the problem that needs solving is sin (the cause), not sins (the effect). The problem is heredity, not behavior. Through self-effort, any man can change his behavior to some extent. But no amount of struggle or determination will change his heredity, what he is from birth. *"That which is born of the flesh is flesh; and that which is born of the Spirit is spirit"* (John 3:6). Sin is not just the things we do that break the laws of God; it is a condition of the heart. If the condition is dealt with, then the symptoms will diminish. It is not wrong <u>doing</u> that needs to be corrected in man; it is wrong <u>being</u>. That is what Jesus did on the cross - He solved the problem of the heredity of sin. Redemption means that through His death on the cross, Jesus can put within any man His own heredity of holiness, His own disposition, thereby making it possible for the man to live up to the standards He imposes. Jesus took our heredity of sin and gave us His heredity of righteousness, *"For he hath made him to be sin for us, who knew no sin; that we might be made the righteousness of God in him"* (II Corinthians 5:21). We are born into this world under the heredity of fear and failure, but through the cross of Jesus we are placed into the heredity of faith.

The transaction, the exchange of sin for righteousness, takes place in our spirit, *"Not by works of righteousness which we have done, but according to his mercy he saved us, by the washing of regeneration, and renewing of the Holy Ghost"* (Titus 3:5). The first step in God's marvelous salvation is the regeneration of the spirit. When we first turn to Jesus by faith in repentance, His redeeming blood is applied to cleanse our conscience and our deadened spirit is made alive. The Holy Spirit takes up residence in our human spirit, and our communication, fellowship, and worship are restored. The Bible tells us, *"But ye are not in the flesh, but in the Spirit, if so be that the Spirit of God dwell in you. Now if any man have not the Spirit of Christ, he is none of his. And if Christ be in you, the body is dead because of sin; but the Spirit is life because of righteousness. But if the Spirit of him that raised up Jesus from the dead dwell in you, he that raised up Christ from the dead shall also quicken your mortal bodies by his Spirit that dwelleth in you"* (Romans 8:9-11). In Romans 8:15-16 we read, *"For ye have not received the spirit of bondage again to fear; but ye have received the Spirit of adoption, whereby we cry. Abba, Father. The Spirit itself beareth witness with our spirit, that we are the children of God."* Our spirit, then, is made alive by the entrance of the Holy Spirit. We were born physically and soulishly into the physical world, and we are born again spiritually into the spiritual world.

The Way It Is Supposd to Be

The moment you said "yes" to Jesus, the Holy Spirit of God entered your spirit, made it alive again, and you entered the pathway of life - the faith life. You took your first step back into the way God intended for life to be. Now you are alive in two worlds. Now you can communicate not only with the world around you but also with the God Who created you. You have been restored to a place of perfect balance. You have a new relationship with God. Love of self no longer reigns supreme. It has been exchanged for a love for God, which surpasses all other affections. You are no longer bound to slavery to the kingdom of this world and the kingdom of darkness. Now you are free to be loyal to the Kingdom of God - the kingdom of light. Now, you can be used by Him as an instrument for its expansion. You are no longer part of this world system, alienated from God. You are now a citizen of heaven, an ambassador for Christ to the world. You are no longer <u>of</u> the world but you are left <u>in</u> the world as a representative of Jesus. You

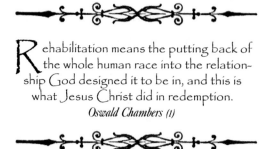

Rehabilitation means the putting back of the whole human race into the relationship God designed it to be in, and this is what Jesus Christ did in redemption.
Oswald Chambers (1)

once walked the earth alone, disconnected from God and connected to other human beings only by physical birth. Now you are a child of God, connected to His Church by His indwelling Spirit. You are a container for God and a channel through which He can work. You are now a suitable instrument for the operation of faith.

We said earlier that before the fall, Adam and Eve occupied a unique position as the connection between the spiritual world and the physical world. They were never conscious of need, because they lived in the continuous, uninterrupted stream of God's supply. They were in a state of continuously receiving from Him. The concept or possibility of need was never thought of until it was introduced by satan. It is crucial to our study of faith for us to understand that when we came alive in Christ, two things happened. First, we again became a connection between the two worlds, a channel through which God can flow His will into the earth. Second, we were once again placed in the stream of God's continual supply, to which we have constant access to by faith. Again, the faith life is simply a receiving life. It is receiving from God in the invisible that which is needed to carry out His will in the visible.

Balance has been restored to our life in every sense. But balance in the Christian life is not automatic like it was in Adam and Eve before the fall. Balance in the Christian life is potential and only becomes practical by the continuous choice of faith to obey the will of God. Balance in the Christian life must be maintained and can be interrupted by yielding to sin and self. We either walk by faith or by the flesh. In Christ, we have become everything mentioned above, but satan will do everything in his power to prevent us from living out who we are in Jesus. He will attempt to draw our focus away from the spiritual to the physical and soulish, to act out of our intellect and emotions rather than the spirit. He will try to delude us into believing the need rather than God's supply. He will try to interrupt our communication with God through the cares of the world. He will make every effort to distract us into "doing good things" rather than receiving the will of God in our spirit, fulfilling His will, and trusting Him to work through us. So, how do we guard against being led astray? How do we maintain our walk of faith?

Maintaining spiritual balance is made easier by remembering that God created us for three purposes: to love Him, to worship Him, and to cooperate with Him in populating the earth with a race of beings that do the same. That was God's design for the human race, but through the fall the plan was interrupted. What failed to happen through Adam by physical propagation, however, can now happen through Jesus Christ by spiritual propagation. The battle that was lost by Adam in the Garden of Eden was won by Jesus in the Garden of Gethsemane. Because of the blood of Jesus shed on Calvary, the earth can now be populated with a race of beings who love and worship God and who can be inhabited by Him, thus providing a channel through which He can flow His will. After being born again, our purpose while we remain on the earth is to participate in the agenda of God so that we might bring glory to Him. Our participation in that agenda is made possible by our spiritual ability to make the choice of faith, our spiritual capacity to believe, our spiritual ears to hear the voice of God, and our spiritual eyes to see into the invisible. Spiritual balance is maintained by remembering that we are alive in two worlds at the same time - two worlds connected by the operation of faith.

Salvation Is Only the Beginning

It is imperative that we understand that getting back to where God intended us to be is more than just being saved. Let me strongly stress the point that salvation is not the end, but the beginning. *"As ye have therefore received Christ Jesus the Lord* [by faith]*, so walk ye in him"* (Colossians 2:6). We received Christ by faith and we are to live out the Christian life by faith. We are saved to *"walk in newness of life"* (Romans 6:4*)*, with the goal in view *"...to be conformed to the image of his Son..."* (Romans 8:29), not to just sit down and occupy space. We are not trophies or ornaments; we are ambassadors and warriors for Christ. We are channels through which God wants to pour His will into this world. The Christian life is an active, dynamic believing life, not a passive one. It is a life of real faith.

Many Believers act as if they think that entering the Christian life is the same as entering a waiting room where they just bide their time, doing the best they can, until that day comes when they die, go to heaven, and finally become what God intended for them to be. Canaan is not "over there" and it is not later on in "the sweet by and by." It is right here and right now. We are *"translated... into the kingdom..."* NOW (Colossians 1:13). We *"...sit together in heavenly places in Christ Jesus"* NOW (Ephesians 2:6). We are *"...no more strangers and foreigners, but fellowcitizens with the saints, and of the household of God"* NOW (Ephesians 2:19). We *"...which have believed do enter into rest..."* NOW (Hebrews 4:3). Through the cross of Jesus we are joined to the Eternal God Who lives in the Eternal NOW. "Getting there" is a two-step process, salvation and sanctification. It is birth and growth. By faith we are born into His family (salvation), and by faith we grow up and continue to function in His family (sanctification). The choice to believe upon Christ as Savior creates the <u>potential</u> for living by faith. The choice to follow Him, to walk in Him, and to obey Him as Lord, creates the <u>practice</u> of living by faith.

Real Faith Is Always Opposed

Now, let me just tell you, satan does not want the potential for real faith to become practical in your life. If it does, you will become a serious threat to the kingdom of darkness. He will do all in his limited power to keep you unaware of the fact that **you are alive in two worlds and you have God's Kingdom authority in both**. Dear Christian friend, your involvement in the plan of God, in the building of His Kingdom, will not go unchallenged. Satan will make every attempt to divert you away from the plan of God by diverting you away from the walk of faith. Before you were saved, your intellect argued that salvation through simple faith in Jesus was illogical or too easy, and your emotions were afraid of giving up cherished evil affections. Opposition from the enemy is fierce, and against such, it was a battle for your will to yield to the drawing of the Holy Spirit. Finally, however, God broke through the wall of separation, and you emerged on the other side as a child of God. But the war is not over. The battle of the will still rages after you are saved. Even after you are born again, you still face tremendous opposition to the leading of the Holy Spirit. You are still opposed by the world, by satan, and by self (your own emotions and intellect). Let's look at a revealing truth that explains why.

Only One Part Is Saved

Essential to understanding the battle you are in, and to your grasp of the meaning of the faith life, is realizing that only one part of you is saved. When you came to Jesus for **salvation**, you were saved forever from the <u>penalty</u> of sin. But, the only part of your three-part being that was saved completely was your spirit. The rest of you was saved <u>positionally</u> (all of you is "in Christ") but not yet <u>practically</u> (you still sin and your body is still dying). But, doesn't your thinking change after you are saved? Yes, but it has to be transformed (Romans 12:1,2). Do you not have a love for God and a hatred of sin that you did not have before? Yes, but your emotions are still capable of setting their affections on things that are not of God. Colossians 3:2 says, *"Set your affection on things above, not on things on the earth."* Why does God say that? Because it is still possible for a Believer to "feel" contrary to the will of God. It is also obvious that your intellect has not been redeemed because it still has the capacity to oppose God's will. Paul refers to the "carnal mind" in Romans 8:7 and says it *"...is enmity* *against God: for it is not subject to the law of God, neither indeed can be."* Doesn't your outward behavior change? Yes, because we now have power in Christ to choose not to sin (Romans 6:11-13), but it is a choice - it is not automatic. There is a powerful influence imposed upon your soul and body now that did not exist before salvation. That influence is the Holy Spirit indwelling your spirit. But, the influence of the Holy Spirit does not eradicate the influence of sin, self, and satan. In Romans 7:14-25, Paul describes a terrible conflict in himself, a battle between the "law of sin" and the "law of God." Then, in Romans 8:1-2, he finds relief that, *"There is therefore now no condemnation to them which are in Christ Jesus, who walk not after the flesh, but after the Spirit. For the law of the Spirit of life in Christ Jesus hath made me free from the law of sin and death."* It is, however, a freedom that must be recognized, claimed, and exercised. This is the ongoing process of **sanctification** where you are being saved daily from the <u>power</u> of sin. The choice to obey the law of the Spirit rather than the law of sin will always be a choice of faith.

Your physical body will be redeemed someday (Romans 8:23, Ephesians 1:14, 4:30) and that is the final process - **glorification**. On that day you will be saved from the <u>presence</u> of sin. I Corinthians 15:52 says, *"...the dead shall be raised incorruptible, and we shall be changed."* But until that happens, you and I will continue to live in the same dying bodies we were living in before we were saved. Our bodies are undeniably benefited now that they are now temples of the Holy Spirit (I Corinthians 3:16), but they are still dying just the same.

The point is this - the day will come, thank God, when you will be redeemed entirely and your positional redemption will become practical. But for now, there is a part of you that has been redeemed (the spirit), a part that is being redeemed (the soul), and a part that will be redeemed (the body). Faith (believing God) will always be the automatic response of the spirit. But trusting God and venturing out where you cannot see with the eyes of reason, logic, and common sense will always pose a struggle for the flesh. Going out beyond where you feel emotionally comfortable will always be a difficult decision and a battle. But take heart and be encouraged, because it does become easier with time and with experience in watching God do the impossible. I promise you that the outcome is worth the battle. You may ask, "But am I up to the battle?" Yes, you are very much up for it. In fact, you were born for it. You were born to live in two worlds at the same time. You were born to live by faith.

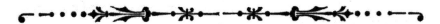

Summary of Truth

❖ The way back to the way it was supposed to be is through faith in Jesus Christ alone.

❖ The cross "fixed" everything that was "broken" in the fall.

❖ Through the cross of Jesus Christ, balance is restored to the human race and to our life personally.

❖ Salvation is only the beginning. We are citizens of heaven NOW.

❖ Faith will always be opposed by satan and self, but we are victorious in Jesus.

NOW LET'S TAKE A MOMENT AND PRAY TOGETHER:

DEAR LORD JESUS, THANK YOU FOR COMING INTO THIS SINFUL WORLD AND DYING FOR ME. THANK YOU FOR GIVING ME A WAY BACK TO YOU AND TO THE LIFE YOU INTENDED FOR ME TO HAVE. I KNOW, HOWEVER, THAT SALVATION IS ONLY THE BEGINNING, AND I PRAY THAT YOU HELP ME TO GO ON BY FAITH, WALKING WITH YOU AND BEING USED BY YOU FOR YOUR GLORY. LORD, I KNOW THAT MY LIVING FOR YOU AND MY WALK OF FAITH WILL BE OPPOSED BY SATAN, BUT I THANK YOU THAT YOU HAVE ALREADY GIVEN ME THE VICTORY. I AM IN A BATTLE, BUT IN YOU I AM UP FOR IT BECAUSE THROUGH YOU I WAS BORN FOR IT. THANK YOU FOR MAKING IT POSSIBLE FOR ME TO LIVE IN TWO WORLDS AT THE SAME TIME. THANK YOU FOR MAKING IT POSSIBLE THROUGH THE CROSS FOR ME TO LIVE BY FAITH. IN YOUR NAME I PRAY. AMEN.

Chapter 7

An
Operational Definition

*"Now faith is the substance of things hoped for,
the evidence of things not seen."*
Hebrews 11:1

*"Faith is choosing to act upon the revealed will of God,
using power and resources that only He has access to."*
Shad Williams

*D*oes the term "real faith" suggest that there is a faith that is not real? It most certainly does. For everything in the Christian life, satan has a counterfeit or substitute and real faith is no exception. Satan knows that real faith is the one and only thing that connects lost people to God for salvation, and it is the only thing that connects saved people to God's will and purpose. Faith is the means by which earth is moved to heaven and heaven is moved to earth. From the very first pages of Genesis we see a contrast between real and counterfeit faith, a contrast that is illustrated repeatedly throughout the entire Bible. Hebrews 11:4 sums up what took place in Genesis chapter four, *"By **faith** Abel offered unto God a more excellent sacrifice than Cain, by which he obtained witness that he was righteous..."*. Abel offered a sacrifice of faith and Cain offered a substitute.

In Genesis 12 we see the contrast again between Abraham and Lot. Verse 4 tells us that *"Abram departed **as the Lord had spoken** unto him."* And then it says *"and **Lot went with him.**"* What was the difference? Abraham was stepping out on the promise of God, obeying the express will of God, and trusting God to bring about an outcome that could only be produced out of the power and unseen resources of God. He went through the process of real faith (revealed will – choice – action). Lot, on the other hand, just had a good idea. Abraham was following and trusting God and Lot was following and trusting Abraham. See the difference? They both went, but only one should have. Real faith operates by God's revealed will, not good ideas, good intentions or good common sense. Both Abraham and

Lot believed in God (II Peter 2:7) and they both went to heaven, but oh what different routes their lives took on the way. Every born-again Believer is going to heaven, but only those who live lives of real faith will bring pleasure, honor and glory to God in this life.

The real core bedrock issue being dealt with throughout the entire Bible is the issue of believing God, the issue of faith. The central thing that God wanted the Israelites to do was to trust Him, to believe Him, and thereby be a blessing to the nations. The one thing that Jesus wanted His Disciples to do was to believe Him. He repeatedly asked them, "Where is your faith?" He never asked where is your love, your enthusiasm, your commitment, or your loyalty. All He asked was that they believe. The one issue that Paul stressed over and over in his letters to the churches was the issue of faith. Why? Because he knew that it was only by real faith that they would survive and grow. Satan's target in the life of every human being is real, life-altering and life-sustaining, faith in God, and he uses two approaches. One is to persuade the believer to avoid trusting God altogether by reverting back to the old way of self-effort and self-reliance. If that doesn't work, then the devil will offer a counterfeit of the real thing, such as positive thinking, hoping and wishing, mysticism, or self-determination.

Satan's first attempt at counterfeit faith is in relation to salvation. Millions who carry the name "Christian" are deceived, believing that they are saved by means of church membership, religious activity, baptism, good behavior, denominational affiliation, or adherence to certain creeds. They believe in Jesus with their heads, but they have never believed in Him with their hearts. Therefore there has never been a change in their life that is produced by the indwelling Holy Spirit of God. All they have is an empty, substitute religion built on counterfeit faith.

In John 2:23-25, we find an interesting situation involving a great multitude of people who believed in Jesus and yet were not saved. The Bible tells us *"...many believed in his name when they saw the miracles which he did."* Now that sounds good except for the fact that it goes on to say *"But Jesus did not commit* [entrust] *himself unto them, because he knew all men."* He knew what was going on in their hearts and that all they were believing was what they saw with their physical eyes. When the show was over, they all went home and that was the end of it. There was one man, however, who did not go home. His name was Nicodemus. His heart had been stirred by what he had seen during the afternoon, and now at nightfall, after the crowd disbursed, he came to Jesus in search of the truth. At that point Jesus explained to him that there was another world beyond what he could see – a world beyond the miracles that he and the others had witnessed earlier – the world of the Spirit of God. Jesus told Nicodemus that his faith, which was based on keeping the law, was not suffiicient before God. It was not enough to simply believe Jesus was a good man or a prophet. Nicodemus had to be born of the Spirit by believing in Jesus as Savior.

Real faith is not mere mental assent. James 2:19 says, *"...The devils also believe, and tremble."* Real faith goes beyond mental assent to actually receiving from God. The folks on the hillside that day gave mental assent to the miracles they saw. But, they went home empty because they were only emotionally intrigued; they did not believe in their hearts. It appears from Scripture (John 19:39) that Nicodemus went away from Jesus as a changed man - someone who had made the choice of real faith. Anyone who desires to "see the kingdom of God" must make the choice of real faith in Jesus.

But what about those who have truly been born again? Can they be deceived also? The answer is yes. As mentioned already, Paul's main concern in writing to the churches was the condition of their faith. He covered different concerns with different churches, but he dealt with the issue of faith with all of them. His concern for every new Believer in every church could be summed up in what he wrote to the church in Corinth in I Corinthians 2:5, *"That your faith should not stand in the wisdom of men, but in the power of God."* His concern was that their faith be real, that they not settle for a counterfeit.

> Faith is the substance of things hoped for, and not mere shadow. It is not less than sight, but more. Sight only shows the outward form of things; faith gives the substance.
>
> *James Hudson Taylor (1)*

Let's look at Colossians 2:6-7 again, *"As you have, therefore, received Christ Jesus the Lord, so walk ye in him, Rooted and built up in him and stablished in the faith, as ye have been taught, abounding therein with thanksgiving."* We were saved by choosing, in real faith, to believe upon Jesus for salvation. Now we are to live by continuing to choose to believe upon Jesus for everything else. That is what satan does not want us to do.

The Bible tells us in verse 8, *"Beware lest any man spoil you through philosophy and vain deceit, after the tradition of men, after the rudiments* [principles] *of the world, and not after Christ."* In other words, after you are saved do not revert back to the ways of the world and the old life. Rather, live by real faith. We were saved by reaching out into the invisible and receiving God's provision of eternal life. Now we must continue as children of God by reaching out into the invisible and receiving God's provision for everything else. Real faith is the act of receiving and using.

In Hebrews 11 we find a list of people we refer to numerous times throughout this study. It is called the "Great Hall of Faith." It is not, however, made up of great people but of simple, ordinary folks, just like you and me, who made the choice to trust in a Great God to do extraordinary things. As a result, God poured His supernatural power through them and performed the miraculous and the impossible. He did it because they made the choice of real faith. The faith of each person in the list was proven to be real by the five actions that each one took. These actions are listed in verse 13. They *"received the promises"* of God, they *"saw them afar off"*, they *"were persuaded of them"*, they *"embraced them"* and they *"confessed them."*

Jesus asked an interesting question in Luke 18:8b, *"Nevertheless when the Son of man cometh, shall he find faith on the earth?"* If Jesus returned today would He find a church (local or universal) that is living by real faith, a church that is fulfilling the revealed will of God? Would He find one that is honoring God by actively trusting Him for the miraculous and the impossible, thereby continually establishing a fresh testimony to the goodness and faithfulness of God? The devil knows that it is only by real faith, exercised by God's children, that the church can storm the gates of hell. Only by real faith can the ministry of the ascended Christ continue upon earth. It is only by real faith that the Kingdom of God can be built, that the impossible can become possible, and that God can be glorified. And the devil knows that it is only by real faith that a local church, or an individual Believer, can see things happen that are explainable only in terms of God. Therefore, he will make every attempt to get every Believer and every church to settle for less than real faith – faith that is based upon the express will of God and bids circumstances to bend in conformity to that will.

So how do we know if we have real faith? My dear friend, that is what this book is all about - how to recognize, embrace, and live by real faith.

There is a rational, balanced, scriptural, doctrinally correct life of real faith available to every child of God. It is not strange or mystical but is, in fact, the normal Christian life. Real faith is living in cooperation with, and reliance upon, God. We are going to begin by looking at some observations that a few others have made. You will recognize some of them because they are outstanding examples of people who lived by faith. Then we are going to look at some characteristics of faith; what faith is, and what it is not. These lists will not exactly define faith, but they will help us to at least begin to get an idea of what we are talking about.

Manley Beasley

"Faith is reason at rest with God" (2).

"Faith is treating the future as present and the invisible as visible" (3).

"Faith is being as much at home in the realm of the impossible as in the possible" (4).

"Faith is an act that bids eternal truth to become present fact" (5).

"Faith is not believing God can or wanting God to, but acting upon God's Word as if it is being done now" (6).

"Faith is an active principle of trust in Jesus Christ which is ready to venture on every word He speaks" (7).

Oswald Chambers

"Faith is unutterable trust in God that never dreams He will not stand by us" (8).

"Faith is looking unto Jesus for salvation from everything" (9).

"Faith is endurance combined with absolute certainty that what we are looking for is going to transpire" (10).

"Faith is the heroic effort of your life. You fling yourself in reckless confidence on God"(11).

"Faith is making the thing inevitable, finding out what God says and acting upon it" (12).

"Faith is being so confident in God that in a crisis we are the reliable ones" (13).

James Hudson Taylor

"Faith is reckoning upon God's faithfulness" (14).

"Faith is entering into the finished work" (15).

Andrew Murray

"Faith is the ear which has heard God say what He will do, and the eye which has seen Him do it" (16).

George Muller

"The province of faith begins where probabilities cease and sight and sense fail" (17).

Ruth Paxson

"Faith is the cable that connects and transmits the life of the ascended Lord in heaven to the Believer on earth" (18).

The observations listed above along with the many others quoted throughout this book reveal many aspects of real faith and the real faith life. But when you put them all together there is one very clear collective message that comes through; **real faith is not man made, it originates with God**. It cannot be manufactured or "worked up." One mistaken idea that is prevalent among the church today is that a Christian can choose at will to trust God for this or that. That is not true, and attempting to do so only leads to false or counterfeit faith. **Real faith begins by first knowing the will of God and then acting in accordance with it**. You cannot believe God for anything unless He first bids you to do so. **Real faith begins with God, continues with God, and ends with God**.

Below we are going to list a few characteristics of real faith. We will see some of them again later, but I believe that taking a quick look at them here will help us to begin developing an overall idea of what we are talking about when we say "real faith." First, lets look at what real faith is NOT and then at what it IS.

Real Faith Is Not:

1. **Self-confidence or self-reliance** - it has nothing to do with temperament or personality.
2. **Positive thinking** - it has nothing to do with thinking at all, positive or negative.
3. **Emotional** - it is not "having a good feeling" about something and therefore thinking it will come to pass.
4. **Hoping or wishing** - that will not move God to do anything.
5. **Reactionary** - real faith does not react to pressure produced by need, logic, circumstances, emotional appeal, "deadlines", or human opinion.
6. **Determination and will power** - these will enable a person to use his natural resources and abilities to the fullest, but they will not move God.

7. **Intellectual conclusion** - faith not only has nothing to do with logical conclusions drawn in the mind, but it more often stands in opposition to them.
8. **Passive** - faith is not something that happens TO me. It happens THROUGH me as I make a deliberate choice to believe.
9. **Mystical** - faith is only "strange" or "other-worldly" in the sense that it is not what the natural man is accustomed to, and it puts the Believer in contact with the spirit realm.
10. **Based upon circumstances** - real faith is usually opposed by circumstances at the outset. It more often requires that the circumstances bend into conformity to God's will.
11. **Limited to what I see, know, think, touch and have** - real faith is based upon the Will and unseen resources of God.
12. **Vague or abstract** - faith is based upon the fact of the will of God and focuses upon a definite definable object.
13. **Based upon "common sense", reason, or logic.**
14. **Thinking God can or wanting Him to** - it is believing that He IS - right now.
15. **Making a plan and then expecting God to bless it** - it is knowing His plan and cooperating with Him in it.
16. **Manipulating circumstances** to fit a desired outcome.
17. **Helping God out** with our good ideas, man-made schemes, or human resources.

Real Faith Is:

1. **Confidence in God** plus nothing else and no one else.
2. **Belief that results in God releasing His creative power** to produce substance from nothing.
3. **Based solely upon the promises of God from His Word and upon His guidance** by His Spirit from within our inner man.
4. **Based upon the fact** of His revealed will in our spirit.
5. **Acting** in accordance with the express will of God. It is acting upon the truth of God in such a way that circumstances are changed and situations are altered to conform to God's will.
6. **Based upon hearing** the voice of God in our spirit.
7. **Results in speaking** to the world what God has spoken in our heart.
8. **Assurance** of the object or outcome based upon the fact of God's will.
9. **Seeing** in the invisible with the eyes of the spirit.

10. **Specific** - real faith has a specific, well-defined object or outcome.
11. **Substance.**
12. **Based upon absolutes** - the Person, purpose, plan, and provision of God.
13. **Based upon God's will** - whether it makes "sense" or not.
14. **Always requires a definite choice.**
15. **Receiving** from God, taking, possessing, using.
16. **Childlike obedience** to the will and plan of God.
17. **Based upon the past** - real faith is entering into the finished work of Christ. It is believing upon what God has already done, not what He is going to do. It is operating according to the truth that God has no future, from His perspective it is all finished.
18. **Waiting** until the last minute - standing still and seeing the salvation of God.
19. **Letting go** of everything and clinging to God alone.
20. **More practical** than anything that stands against it.

A Revealing Word Study

Now we are going to add to our lists of observations and characteristics another list made up of three Greek words, which I believe will help define faith in a more precise way. These three words combined provide us with a clear panoramic picture of the operation of real faith. They are PEITHO, PISTIS, and PISTEUO. Yes I know they sound strange, but after all, they are Greek.

The first word is a verb, PEITHO. It is translated into English as "to be confident" (Galatians 5:10), "to persuade" or "to be persuaded" (Acts 26:28), "to trust" (II Corinthians 1:9), "to obey" (Hebrews 13:17), and "to believe" (Acts 28:24). This word is never translated as "faith", since it is a verb, but it is important because it is the word from which PISTIS (faith) is derived. It contains the idea of obedience or action, based upon trust, persuasion of truth, and inward certainty. It conveys the idea of faith even though it is not translated "faith." Paul uses the word "peitho" in Romans 8:38-39 where he names a list of things and says he is "persuaded" that none of them will separate him from the love of God. In other words, he is saying that he has faith (persuasion of fact) that he will not be separated from the love of God.

Now, from the word "peitho" comes the second word, PISTIS, which is a noun. It is used 244 times in the New Testament, being translated "faith" 239 times. Every time the word "faith" appears in the New Testament, it is the word "pistis" (with one exception in Hebrews 10:23). The word means "a firm persuasion, a conviction based upon hearing." *"So then faith cometh by hearing and hearing by the word of God"* (Romans 10:17). So, the word "faith" actually means to "consider as fact" or "to be assured of reality." It is an assurance that is so strong that it cannot help but to result in action. That brings us to our third word in the list.

Interestingly, the first two words, "peitho" and "pistis" are used in Matthew, Mark and Luke, but never in the Gospel of John. Rather, in John's Gospel, the Holy Spirit uses the verb PISTEUO and uses it ninety-nine times. "Pisteuo" means "believe", in the sense of reliance upon something or some one to do for us what we cannot do for ourselves. It means to "make a commitment", to "take action."

So then, we have three words, which help us understand the concept of faith and formulate a definition. Putting them all together helps us see that faith involves three things; an inward <u>certainty</u> (peitho), a <u>choice</u> that results from persuasion of fact based upon hearing (pistis), and finally an overt <u>action</u> (pisteuo). Let's say it this way, faith is **persuasion** (peitho) followed by **choice** (pistis) followed by **action** (pisteuo). From the intertwining of these words we see that faith is like a three-legged stool, and all three legs

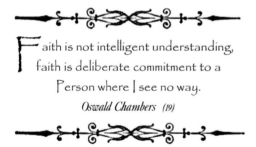

Faith is not intelligent understanding, faith is deliberate commitment to a Person where I see no way.

Oswald Chambers (19)

must be secure in order for it to stand. There must first be a certainty of God's will, then a choice must be made to venture out on His will, and finally, a definite action must be taken in accordance with His will.

This same sequence is also seen repeatedly in the Old Testament. The word "faith" appears only twice in the Old Testament, in Deuteronomy 32:20 and in Habakkuk 2:4. The examples, however, of applied faith are numerous. A partial, yet convincing list is provided in Hebrews, chapter eleven. In every instance of faith, in the Old Testament or New, the people involved are required to go where they cannot see or to take action using power and resources they themselves do not possess. They are required to act upon the truth of God's promise, upon the fact of God's unseen provision, and upon the reliability of God's command; all of which cannot be seen in, or by, the world around them.

Real Faith - An Operational Definition

As you can see from looking at the various observations about faith, from our list of what faith is and is not, and from our word study, arriving at a concise working definition of faith is still not easy. That is because faith is not just a word, it is a concept, it is an experience, it is a process, it is a powerful creative force, and it is a way of life. It is a living principle. In fact every life that has been lived out by faith in the Bible or in Christian history has given its own definition to the word. Each life offers a fresh explanation and demonstration of how faith works. It paints another unique picture which illustrates that faith is God working originally, intimately, directly, and supernaturally in and through the life of His child in order to fulfill His will on earth and bring glory to Himself.

Faith is not tangible, but it makes tangible the intangible. It cannot be touched, but when exercised, it brings into existence those things that can be. It is not visible, but it makes real the invisible. Life content may change from one child of God to another, but the characteristics of faith-living, the sequence of operation, and the process of faith remain constant. **Faith begins with knowing the will of God in the inner man, then making a choice to act upon His will, and finally, trusting Him to do the impossible in order for faith's object to become real.** Therefore, the definition for faith that I have settled upon in my life and experience, and that we are going to often refer to in this study, reads as follows:

"REAL FAITH IS CHOOSING TO ACT UPON THE REVEALED WILL OF GOD, USING POWER AND RESOURCES THAT ONLY HE HAS ACCESS TO."

Watch What It Does

Sometimes in trying to define a thing, a clearer definition comes from watching what it does and being a participant in the doing of it. Let's take an illustration from the natural world – an airplane. If you were called upon to define the word "airplane" to some one who had never seen or heard of one before, what would you say? I have found myself in that very predicament. Sheila and I have traveled for many years in parts of the world where there are still people who have never seen an airplane. So where do you start? "It is a big machine that has wings with motors attached, and you sit in it, and it rolls along getting faster and faster until it rises above the ground and, and..." See what I mean? Okay then, let's turn to the expert on definitions. Webster says it is "a powered heavier-than-air aircraft that has fixed wings from which it derives most of its lift" (20). Well, that just clears it right up doesn't it! No, I think I like my attempt better. But, I will tell you what will clear it up – going to the airport and watching one take off, fly around, and then land. And even better still, get in it and experience it for yourself.

I remember one time when one of our overseas brothers flew with us for the first time across his native land. He was so excited. We went to the airport where he saw a plane close up for the first time in his life. Then we actually got in it and sat down, and soon it taxied down the runway and took off. He couldn't look at everything fast enough. He looked out the window on one side and then the other.

It was really fun watching him enjoy himself so much. Then after about an hour we landed in another city, and he couldn't wait to tell everyone about his experience. Now, after that flight, what do you think he would have said if someone had asked him to define an airplane? He could not have put it into words, but there would be no doubt in his mind from that day forward that he knew exactly what an airplane was. He didn't need words to define "airplane" because he had now experienced "airplane" for himself.

The same is true with faith. Watch how it operates in the lives of people in the Bible as well as others in Christian history. Then, better still, you yourself begin to practice the principles of faith in your own life. Then you will know what faith is. If you cannot define it verbally, it will not matter because you will have the experience. When you get involved in faith "up close and personal" you won't need a definition, all you will need or want is more opportunity.

The day my friend and I boarded that plane, something happened in our lives. We took a step – a step of faith. It was an elementary step in the natural realm, but a step nonetheless. We completed a process – the process of faith. It was **revealed** to us that the plane was going where we wanted to go and was available to take us. Then, being **persuaded** of its reliability (peitho), we **made a choice** (pistis) to get in it. Then we **took the actual step** of placing ourselves inside (pisteuo). At that point, there was nothing left to do but rest (the ultimate result of real faith). We trusted that machine to do for us what we could not do for ourselves. We took action and ascended above the earth, using power and resources, which we ourselves did not possess prior to taking that step of faith. The law of gravity was over-ruled by the law of aerodynamics, and the impossible became possible.

God Only Responds to Real Faith

Now let's say it again, **real faith is a trustworthy knowledge of God's will followed by solid persuasion of fact followed by decisive action which relates to a definite object or outcome**. But remember it MUST begin with God. Real faith is "choosing to act upon the revealed will of God, using power and resources that only He has access to." Dear child of God, earlier we asked the question, how do you know if you have real faith? Well, are there any situations or occasions in your life where you are acting upon the revealed will of God in such a way that it will require God's supernatural intervention to bring it to pass? Again quoting Brother Manley Beasley, "Faith is so acting upon the revealed word of God that God has to perform a miracle to keep it" (21). Are you doing that? Have you ever done that? You may ask, "Can I EVER do that?" Yes, you most certainly can! If you couldn't, God would have never placed the capacity for faith in you to begin with. But He did, and you can, and you will. You are going to learn to live by faith because it is your birthright, your privilege, and your responsibility. And remember, you were born to fly!

Summary of Truth

* ✢ Faith is choosing to act upon the revealed will of God, using power and resources that only He has access to.
* ✢ Faith is a way of life, a personal living principle.
* ✢ Each life lived by faith offers a fresh definition of what it is.
* ✢ The sequence of faith is Persuasion, Choice and Action.
* ✢ Jesus Christ alone is our Source for everything, including faith.
* ✢ The best way to understand what something is, is to watch what it does and to participate in it personally. This applies to understanding faith.
* ✢ It is the birthright, privilege, and responsibility of every Believer to live by faith.

Now Let's Take a Moment and Pray Together:

Heavenly Father, I not only want to understand what faith is, but I also desire that it become a living principle in My life. I pray that my own life will offer a fresh definition of what faith is. Help me to learn how to know Your will and to make the choice to obey. Lord Jesus, You are my Source for everything. Help me to live up to my birthright, to exercise my privilege, and to assume my responsibility to live by faith. Lord Jesus, I love you. Thank You for being my Savior. In Your Name I pray. Amen.

Chapter 8

Two Realms :
Natural and Spiritual

"We need a faith that rests upon a great God, and expects Him
to keep His own word and to do just as He promised."
James Hudson Taylor (1)

*T*o understand fully the meaning and operation of faith and how to utilize faith as a Christian, we need to realize that in a sense, we have been exercising faith since we were born. When we use the term "real faith" what we are talking about is not something new, a new concept or capacity, but something expanded into a new realm. Real faith, i.e. God faith, is simply faith that has been extended to its highest level. It has moved beyond the realm of the visible into the invisible. From the time we are born until we accept Christ, the use of our capacity of faith is limited to the natural realm because we are functioning only as a two-part being: body and soul. After we are born again, however, our capacity of faith becomes operational in the spiritual realm as well.

All human beings, lost and saved, experience and exercise faith. It is necessary for the sustaining of life. The exercise of the faculty of faith is unavoidable in human experience because no person possesses all knowledge. Therefore all perceived truth can only be verified as factual and reliable by acting upon it. That's what faith is in its basic form: **persuasion of fact followed by corresponding action**. The question is what *kind* of faith does he exercise? What kind *should* he exercise? For a person who has been made complete in Christ, the answer should be *both*. Human faith operates up to the limits of humanity - that is, up to the limits of what man can produce from his body, mind, emotions, and will. God faith operates beyond these limits into the realm of the invisible, the supernatural and the "impossible."

Most of us tend to think of faith as only a spiritual thing, as something that is related only to God or church or religion. That is because, as a result of the fall, there is a separation in our thinking between the natural and the spiritual. In the purely natural realm, that is within the sphere of human existence apart from God, there seems to be the operation of something that looks like faith, but we hesitate to call it that. Well, we should call it that, because that is exactly what it is. Faith is not a "religious" thing, it is a human thing; it is a gift from God to all men. It is the capacity to believe. The thing that makes the operation of faith natural or spiritual is its object and its source.

Natural faith originates with man and has as its object that which is in the visible. Spiritual faith originates with God and has as its object that which is in the invisible. Natural faith is based on my will and spiritual faith is based on God's will. Again, simply put, faith is the persuasion that something is true, factual, and reliable followed by corresponding action. This applies to the natural realm as well as the spiritual. Faith is a capacity that was given to man in creation and it is not confined to the realm of the spiritual. In fact, after the fall it was just the opposite; it was confined to the natural. Faith can be classified as "natural" or "spiritual" if we are talking about which realm it is operating in at the moment, but in reality, in function, it is the same thing. It takes place in both realms, on both sides of the cross, before salvation and after. The difference is that before salvation the operation of faith is limited and after salvation it is unlimited.

So, categorically speaking, aside from its sphere of operation, what is the difference between natural faith and spiritual faith? Two things: source and object. Natural faith could also be called "soulish faith" in that it operates out of our intellect and emotion. It is based in and upon what we want (our will), what we have, and what we can do using our own intellectual and physical abilities and our resources. Spiritual faith could also be called "God faith" in that it operates out of our spirit by the knowledge of God's will and guidance from the Holy Spirit. It is based in and upon what God wants (His will), what God has, and what He can do using power and resources that only He has access to. Natural faith operates in the visible, and spiritual faith operates in the invisible. Natural faith holds on to what it can see, what it possesses right now in the visible, and to what it hopes to see and possess eventually. Spiritual faith holds on to what it cannot see, what it possesses in the invisible, and what it knows will appear eventually in the visible. Natural faith operates according to what it views as yet to come, and spiritual faith operates according to what it views as already finished.

Now, natural faith is SO natural that we tend to not think of it as faith at all. We think that way because the objects and projected outcomes of natural faith are usually easy to believe in. They are easy because they can be seen in the visible by means of physical sight, or they can be imagined as real, as "doable," based upon my own calculations and human efforts. Therefore it does not feel like faith at all because it is not seen as difficult. Somehow we have the mistaken idea that in order for faith to be faith it has to be a struggle. But by observing how faith works in the natural realm we come to see that it does not have to be a struggle at all. In fact, it was never intended to be, in the natural realm or the spiritual.

Now, let's look at a couple of examples of natural faith. A very simple one is something I am doing right now – sitting in a chair. I became persuaded of the fact that the chair is reliable, that it would hold me up, and then I acted upon that persuasion by actually sitting in it. The action of placing all my weight on the chair verifies that the perceived truth can accurately be accepted as actual fact. Another example is the act of eating. You look at the food, consider it trustworthy, then take it and eat it. Faith is taking and using in one realm or another. This morning I wrote an email to send to our prayer team. After reading over it I clicked "send" because I was persuaded that my internet server is reliable and the message would be delivered. Then there is the example we used in a previous chapter – getting on an airplane – you just see it, judge it reliable, and get on. It doesn't feel like faith because it is not hard to do. But, as pointed out already, the entire faith process is completed by the simple act of getting on that plane. Forty years ago, Sheila and I completed the faith process in a way that goes beyond the physical, yet is still in the natural realm. We exchanged wedding rings at the marriage altar. We were persuaded of our love for each other and we acted upon that persuasion by saying "I do." Now, sitting, eating, sending an email, getting on a plane and meeting your fiancée at the altar doesn't feel much like faith because all these things are easy to do. But they are, in fact, all acts of faith – **persuasion of fact followed by corresponding action**.

You see there is no rule that says that faith has to be hard in order to be faith, regardless of which realm it is in. In fact God never intended that trusting Him would be hard at all. So then why do we usually view natural faith as easy and spiritual faith as hard? It has to do partly with the object. Natural faith has its object in the realm of the visible, the possible, and the known. Spiritual faith has its object in the realm of the invisible, the impossible, and the unknown.

There is also the issue of control. I have had many Christians say to me over the years, "There is no way I could live the way you and Sheila do." What they are saying is they could not live without a stated "guaranteed" income from somewhere, a predictable visible anchor in the natural realm. When I ask why, they always reply, "It's just too hard." One brother told me that he would have a nervous breakdown living the way we do. Well, let's look at that. In the natural realm (going back to our illustration) I look at a chair, evaluate it, judge it reliable, and sit in it. There you go - an act of faith. He does the same thing – no nervous breakdown. We go to a restaurant, order the same thing, look at it, judge it reliable, and eat it - another act of faith. Nothing hard about that. Then we get into the same car and drive home. No panic, no nervous breakdown, no fear. So far, so good. Now we move into the realm of the spiritual. Why should it be any more difficult to look at the record of God's performance in His Word and in Christian history, judge Him reliable, and just trust Him to provide all we need? It has to do with control. In the natural realm I may not actually be in control, but I <u>feel</u> like I am. Therefore I feel secure. In the spiritual realm I <u>know</u> I am not in control, and that makes me feel vulnerable. When faced with problems we can't solve, we often say, "Well, God is in control." Friend, God being in control is not the issue. Of course He is in control – He is GOD! The real issue, the real question, is: is it "okay" with me for God to be in control? Many times, in our heart, the truthful answer is no.

Let's ask ourselves something, though. If we can sit in a chair that was made by a man, entrust our lives to a machine that was made by men, and eat food prepared by a cook we have never seen, then why can we not trust in the Living God? My friends, it is so important for us to see that faith is faith, regardless of the realm in which it operates. All God is calling upon us to do is just simply trust Him by means of the same faculty of faith we have been using all along. All He wants us to do is to continue doing what we did when we came to Jesus in the first place. Placing our trust in Him as Savior was our very first act of faith in the spiritual realm. Now, let me ask you - how did that turn out? Are you saved? Yes. For how long? Forever. Now here is another question – was it really THAT hard? Once you became persuaded of your need for Christ and the legitimacy of His death, burial, resurrection, and ascension, was it "hard" to receive Christ Whom you cannot see or touch? No, it was not. All you did was reach out into the invisible and receive the unseen supply that God had prepared to meet your need.

Real faith is the capacity to see, receive, use and apply, regardless of which realm it operates in. The capacity, however, is of no use unless there is material provided for it to use or act upon. For example, our lungs would serve no purpose if there were no air to breathe. Our stomach would have no function if there were no food to eat. Now notice, before man had any need or use for anything in the visible realm, God had already provided it. **The supply existed before the need**. The same is true in the spiritual realm. Before the fall ever occurred, God had already provided redemption through His Son. Faith is appropriation of supply and God has provided everything that any of us could ever make use of in both realms – visible and invisible alike.II Peter 1:3 tells us, *"According as his divine power hath given unto us all things that pertain unto life and godliness, through the knowledge of him that hath called us to glory and virtue."* Dear Christian, it is the intention of our Heavenly Father that spiritual faith becomes as "easy" to us, as "natural" to us, as the natural itself. God wants us to live and function easily in two worlds at the same time. All He is asking us to do is to believe that His supply, His provision, is available and then trust Him to give it to us.

Real Faith Is Completed Faith

Real faith is a completed faith. It is not natural or spiritual; it is natural plus spiritual. In another chapter we talked about counterfeit or substitute faith in the life of a Christian. By this we mean a faith that stops short of the spiritual. Real faith is unlimited, except for the boundaries of the will of God. An unsaved person can only exercise limited human faith, and he does so out of the natural abilities and resources he was born with. Only a born-again child of God can exercise real spiritual faith. Jesus revealed this truth when He told Nicodemus in John 3:6, *"That which is born of the flesh is flesh* [natural]; *and that which is born of the Spirit is spirit* [spiritual]. *"* The flesh will never be capable of exercising faith in God, because it is incapable of knowing God. In order to know God and trust God, man's spirit, which was deadened in the fall, must be brought to life, and that takes place only when he makes the choice to believe upon the Lord Jesus Christ as his personal Savior. Therefore, Jesus told Nicodemus, *"...Ye must be born again."*

The unsaved person, the natural man, may possess many innate talents and abilities. And by exercising natural faith in them, he can accomplish many great things for himself and for mankind. Through the creativity of his intellect, the passion of his emotions, the decision-making ability of his will, and the force of his physical being, he can produce phenomenal human achievement. In so doing, he exercises a certain kind of faith, natural faith, whereby he believes in, and acts upon, his own abilities and resources to bring his ideas, thoughts, and plans into visible reality. Before a person is saved, he uses the God-given capacity for faith for his own ends. He uses the abilities and resources provided by God through creation. The tragedy is that unsaved man does not realize or appreciate the fact that his capacity for faith comes from God, because he has not been made alive to God in his spirit. Therefore, created man receives all the glory, praise, honor, and gratitude, rather than Creator God.

One of the greatest examples I ever saw of a man operating to the fullest by natural faith was my Dad. He did not become a Christian until later in life and lived as far away from God as a man can. But while my brother and I were growing up in the Mississippi Delta, we heard him say many times, "Boys, you have to have faith." Now, he did not mean faith in God but in ourselves. And, he did have faith in himself. As far back as I can remember, Dad was always adding a room on to the house. He never had the money to do the project on the front end, but that did not

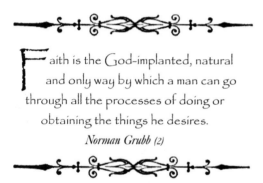

Faith is the God-implanted, natural and only way by which a man can go through all the processes of doing or obtaining the things he desires.

Norman Grubb (2)

deter him. He would tear the back wall off the house, not having a clue as to how he was going to buy the materials to begin building. In his mind, however, he could visualize the room complete, and in his emotions he could feel the joy and satisfaction of his accomplishment. In addition, he had tremendous drive and will power and he used it all to the fullest. Dad did not make much money managing a dry goods store in a small town. But when he got paid he would go and buy a hundred two-by-fours, at thirty-five cents each, and build as much as he could with that. Then he would wait, and when more money was available, he would continue, until the addition was completed. He poured every ounce of his personal abilities and resources into the project and would not quit until it was finished. When it was finished, he took great pride in what he had done. Now, is that a bad thing? No, not for an unsaved man. What else is a lost person going to do? He is just living like the natural man he is, serving himself and bringing glory to himself. Now you may ask is it wrong for some one to believe in himself? No it is not wrong. In fact we encourage our children to believe in themselves, to have confidence in themselves, so they will develop a good self-image. The problem is not in believing in ourselves, but in believing ONLY in ourselves to the exclusion of God.

In later life, Dad did receive Christ and his life was radically changed. In fact, God gave me the privilege of leading him to Jesus eight months after I was saved. About that time, he took a job with a life insurance company. He knew absolutely nothing about selling insurance. But, as always, he believed he could do it. Now, however, to faith in himself, he added a new faith - faith in God. He began reading the Bible daily and praying over his business. He constantly asked me to pray for him. He would say things like, "I am trusting God to help me reach this goal." Dad still believed in himself, but now he was trusting God to enable him to do more than he knew he could do in his own strength. He became very successful in the insurance business and was soon the top salesman in his district. He was even rewarded for his success with a trip for him and Mom to the Caribbean. While there, he was presented a trophy at an awards banquet and asked to make a speech. When he stood up he said, "I just want to give all the credit for this to the Lord. Without Him I could not have done it, and I praise God for making it possible." What happened to Dad? It is very simple - he was making the transition from natural, human faith into spiritual, God faith. He was now operating with a completed faith – real faith. Now instead of bringing glory to himself, he was bringing glory to God.

In and of himself, the natural man can only operate within the parameters of the visible and the possible. That is as far as natural human faith will take him. Without Christ, he is forever locked into a limited existence, surrounded by boundaries from which there is no escape. But, man possesses an innate knowledge of God, and therefore senses and suspects it might somehow be possible to reach out beyond what he knows and where he can see, into a reality that cannot be grasped with mere mind and emotion. Man's innate knowledge of God, coupled with his God-given capacity of faith, makes it possible for the Holy Spirit to draw him to Jesus. And when he comes, that glorious thing called redemption takes place; his spirit comes to life, and there is born within him the ability to trust in the Living God in the realm of the invisible. In other words, he now possesses a faith that is complete, a faith that is operative in the natural and spiritual realm at the same time. He now possesses a faith that is real. Now, before we pray lets look at a brief comparison between mere limited, natural faith and unlimited, completed, spiritual God-faith.

NATURAL HUMAN FAITH	SPIRITUAL GOD-FAITH
Rests upon me, what I have, and what I can do	Rests upon God's power and resources
Looks to the visible	Looks to the invisible
Sees with the eyes of the flesh	Sees with the eyes of the spirit
Initiated by my will	Initiated by the will of God
Limited to the possible	Reaches into the impossible
Operates by reason, feeling, and circumstances	Operates by guidance from the Holy Spirit
Brings glory and praise to self	Brings glory and praise to God
Possible for every man	Possible only for the saved man
Operates within the limits of natural laws	Operates beyond the limits of natural laws

There is so much more in store for us as a child of God than we can even comprehend. God has a vast storehouse of experience and blessing and joy prepared for those who love Him. And it will all be revealed to us, by His Spirit, if we will trust Him by real faith. Listen to the inspired words of Paul in 1 Corinthians 2:9 - 10, *"But as it is written, Eye hath not seen, nor ear heard, neither have entered into the heart of man, the things which God hath prepared for them that love him. But God hath revealed them unto us by His Spirit: for the Spirit searcheth all things, yea, the deep things of God."* The key to having our eyes and ears opened and to receive all that He has prepared for us is to trust God by real faith.

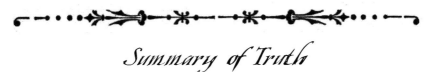

Summary of Truth

❖ Every human being possesses the capacity of faith.

❖ Faith has been operational in our lives since we were born.

❖ Real faith is not a new faith, but an expanded, completed faith.

❖ Faith is not a religious thing; it is a human thing, a faculty, a capacity, a gift from God.

❖ Faith is persuasion that something is true or reliable, followed by corresponding action.

❖ The thing that makes faith natural or spiritual is its object.

❖ Faith does not have to be difficult in order to be faith. It does not have to be a struggle.

❖ Real faith is not natural <u>or</u> spiritual; it is natural <u>plus</u> spiritual.

❖ Our first act of spiritual faith was receiving Christ as Savior.

NOW LET'S TAKE A MOMENT AND PRAY TOGETHER:

HEAVENLY FATHER, THANK YOU FOR PLACING WITHIN ME THE CA-PACITY OF FAITH, ENABLING ME TO TRUST YOU FOR EVERYTHING INCLUDING SALVATION THROUGH JESUS. LORD, HELP ME TO UNDER-STAND FULLY HOW FAITH OPERATES AND HOW TO APPLY IT TO EVERY AREA OF MY LIFE, ESPECIALLY MY WALK WITH YOU. HELP ME TO GET BEYOND SEEING FAITH AS A STRUGGLE. HELP ME TO REACH THE PLACE IN MY LIFE WHERE TRUSTING YOU IN THE SPIRITUAL REALM IS AS EASY AND AS NATURAL FOR ME AS SITTING IN A CHAIR. LORD, I DESIRE THAT MY LIFE CONTINUOUSLY BRING HONOR AND GLORY TO YOUR NAME. I THEREFORE PRAY THAT YOU TEACH ME BY YOUR SPIRIT TO LIVE BY REAL FAITH. IN YOUR NAME I PRAY. AMEN.

Chapter 9

Real Faith: The Real Issue with Jesus

"...I say unto you, If you have faith as a grain of mustard seed, ye shall say unto this mountain, Remove hence to yonder place; and it shall remove; and nothing shall be impossible unto you."
Matthew 17:20

How can you tell what is really important to someone? There are two ways - listen to what they talk about and observe what makes them happy and excited. Watch what makes them "light up." That being true, what would you say is more important to Jesus than anything else? Well, when you read through the Gospels, what do you find Him talking about more than anything else? What was it that so evidently pleased or displeased Him in His relationship with His disciples? It was clearly their choice to believe Him or not to believe Him. It was indisputably the issue of faith. The same is true for you and me. More than sentiment, service, or sacrifice Jesus is interested in one thing from us – real, simple, childlike faith. The disciples asked Him in John 6:28, *"What shall we do, that we might work the works of God?"* In verse 29 Jesus answered very clearly, *"...This is the work of God that ye believe on him whom he hath sent."* In John 7:38 Jesus said, *"He that believeth on me...out of his belly shall flow rivers of living water."* It is believing that creates the flow. Then in John 14:12 He said, *"Verily, verily, I say unto you, he that believeth on me, the works that I do shall he do also; and greater works than these shall he do; because I go unto my Father."* It is believing that creates the works. Everything about our Christian life hinges upon one thing and one thing only - choosing to believe upon Jesus by faith, not just for salvation but for everything.

Throughout the Gospels we repeatedly hear Jesus speaking phrases such as *"seeing their faith," "your faith has made you whole," "according to your faith," "if you have faith," "your faith has saved you," "as you have believed,"* *"do you believe I am able,"* and *"if you can believe".* The constant, predominate theme of His teachings is faith, and in His dealings with people it was the one issue that most often elicited from Him expressions of joy or disappointment. Let's look at some examples.

A Roman Centurion with Great (Vast) Faith

The first time the words "faith" and "believe" are used in the New Testament in a positive sense is in the story of the Roman Centurion (Matthew 8:5-13, Luke 7:1-10). As Jesus entered Capernaum He was approached by a group of Jewish elders representing the soldier. He had sent them to ask Jesus to come and heal his beloved servant who was sick. The elders gave a good report to Jesus, telling Him how worthy the soldier was to be helped in that he loved the nation of Israel and had even built a synagogue for them. Jesus responded by going with them, but before He arrived at the man's house, He was met by another group of the soldier's friends. They told Jesus that the Centurion did not consider himself worthy to approach Jesus or to even have Him under his roof. He said that if Jesus would just speak the word, the servant would be healed. He explained his thinking by saying, *"...I am a man under authority, having soldiers under me: and I say to this man, Go, and he goeth; and to another, Come, and he cometh; and to my servant, Do this, and he doeth it."* Then Jesus responded by saying, *"...I say unto you, I have not found so great faith, no, not in Israel."* He told the Centurion, *"Go thy way: and as thou hast believed, so be it done unto thee..."* The word Jesus used to describe the faith of this man is the Greek word "totos" (total), which is only used once in the Bible. It means "vast." What Jesus was saying, and what pleased Him so much, was that this man had a faith that was real.

Now let's look at two things that you might think would have some degree of influence on the situation. First there is the merit of the Centurion. He was a good man, he loved his servant, he was generous, and he was interested in the things of God. He was highly spoken of by the Jews, he was humble, he even understood the power of the spoken word, and he recognized the authority and the Lordship of Jesus. Second there was the desperation of the servant. He was sick, helpless, hopeless, and was probably going to die. Now notice, though, the one thing that impressed Jesus; that made Him "light up," pleased Him to the point of verbal response, and moved Him into action. It was not the merit of the soldier or the malady of the servant. It was faith – the Centurion's total, unflinching faith in Jesus. His love for his servant, his deep desire, resulted in his critical choice to believe, the choice that Jesus seeks to elicit from everyone who follows Him – the choice of real faith.

A Desperate Mother with "Mega" Faith

In Matthew 15:21-28, Jesus was confronted by a desperate mother whom He appeared at first to ignore. In reality, however, He was not ignoring her at all; He was provoking her to real faith. She cried out to Jesus asking for mercy for herself and for her demon possessed daughter. The disciples wanted to send her away, and Jesus Himself told her that He was sent only *"...unto the lost sheep of the house of Israel."* But she would not be deterred and fell to the ground and worshipped Him and begged for His help. Continuing to draw her to a place of faith He said, *"It is not meet to take the children's bread and cast it to dogs."* Then she spoke the words that opened the door, *"Truth, Lord: yet the dogs eat of the crumbs which fall from the master's table."* Then Jesus said to her, *"O Woman, great is thy faith: be it unto thee even as thou wilt* [choose]... *"* The word that Jesus used to describe faith in this instance is another Greek word "megas" (mega), which means "very large." Again, it is the only time in the Bible this word is used.

What was it that caused Jesus to help this woman? Was it her desperate need, her relentless persistence, her loud cries for help, her falling on the ground to worship Him? Apparently not, because He saw all that and kept on walking. But there was something that stopped Him in His tracks - faith. Jesus was only moved to action by the thing that her need drove her to, the thing that her persistence brought her to, the thing that her cries voiced from deep within her. He was moved to action by her faith.

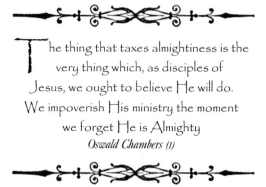

The thing that taxes almightiness is the very thing which, as disciples of Jesus, we ought to believe He will do. We impoverish His ministry the moment we forget He is Almighty

Oswald Chambers (1)

Once more we observe that the only thing that draws a response from Jesus is faith, not need, or crying, or desperation. That is why He deliberately provoked that woman to move beyond begging to believing, beyond crying to choosing, beyond desperation to a decisive faith that was equal to her situation. The thing that altered this situation and changed these circumstances was real faith. Jesus will very often allow a Christian to come to his wit's end before doing anything, because it is there that the capacity for faith is engaged.

In reading this account, you might wonder if Jesus really cared about this woman at all. You might ask how could the Good Shepherd appear to be so unconcerned about someone who was in such desperate need? Did He not love her? Did He not have compassion on her? Yes, He did care. He cared enough and loved enough and had a level of compassion for her that caused Him to draw her to a level of faith that would meet her needs. He drew her beyond little faith to "mega faith." That woman had reached a point in her experience and in her circumstances where she was convinced that Jesus was her only hope, her only possible solution. But that was not enough - not for her or for us. She had to move beyond the point of intellectually thinking that Jesus could help her and beyond the point of emotionally wanting Him to. She had to reach the place of believing that He was doing it right now. That was the place Jesus was drawing her to - the place of active faith. Need and desperation will draw us to Jesus but only real faith will draw a response from Jesus.

When we, as human beings, want to elicit a response from another person, or convince someone to do something, we very often use the methods of intellectual reasoning or emotional appeal. We do that because it works. So, when we have a need in our life, many times we try to approach God on the same level using persuasion, logic, manipulation, and bargaining. We tell God how desperate our situation is and how reasonable it is for us to expect Him to help us. We often make promises we can't keep in pleading with Him to fix our problem or meet our need. Of course, we are only telling God what He already knows. We will even weep before the Lord about it. But we discover that the problem remains unchanged because God is trying to get us to a place where we will trust Him by faith. It is not that God does not have compassion on us, or that He does not want to meet our needs. But trying to appeal to God on an intellectual or emotional basis simply does not work. If God responded to us every time we told Him how pitiful we are, we would never learn to trust Him. All we would learn is how to sound more pitiful. We would play the "emotion card" on God every time, because it is easier than trusting Him. God wants us to trust Him by faith, to find out what His will is and trust Him to perform it. God does not allow adverse circumstances in our life to destroy us, but to provoke us, to draw us into faith. The storm that overwhelmed the disciples in Mark 4:37-41 did not take Jesus by surprise. He *brought* the storm. He *caused* the storm. Why? So that His disciples could have an opportunity to trust and bring glory to God.

A Begging Blind Man with Enough Faith

Now, let's look at one more situation. In Mark 10:46-52, we find the account of Bartimaeus, the blind beggar who sat by the roadside, desperate and hopeless – until he heard Jesus coming. He began crying out, *"...Jesus, thou Son of David, have mercy on me."* People told him to be quiet, but he cried out even more, and Jesus gave instruction to call him. Bartimaeus jumped up in his darkness, cast off his coat and stumbled to Jesus. Now, after tripping over things and bumping into people in order to get to Jesus, Bartimaeus found himself standing in front of the Son of God. Then he heard Jesus ask a very strange question, *"...What wilt thou that I should do unto thee?"* Didn't He know? Wasn't it obvious? Yes He did and yes it was, but again, the Lord was provoking the man to real faith. He was drawing him out beyond thinking and wanting to receiving. The word "wilt" is the same word Jesus used with the mother of the demon possessed daughter and it means "to choose." Jesus was asking him, was giving him opportunity, to make a choice – the choice of real faith. The beggar replied, *"...Lord, that I might receive my sight."* He did not hesitate, but verbally expressed a specific request. Real faith always verbalizes and is always specific. Then Jesus said to him, *"...Go thy way, thy faith* [choice] *hath made thee whole."* Jesus intended to heal Bartimaeus all along. He knew he would be sitting there, just as He knew He would encounter the Centurion as He entered Capernaum and the desperate mother on the road. In each instance **the supply was provided before the need was presented**. All that was necessary was for the person involved to come to a place where their will was joined to Jesus' will in the choice of real faith.

Jesus did not apply a quantifying word to faith in this instance. The faith of Bartimaeus was not called vast or large. It was just faith, a simple deliberate choice to believe – and it was enough. It was enough because it was real. Even in the case of the Centurion and of the desperate mother, it was not the quantity of faith that mattered to Jesus, it was the choice of faith. It is not an amount of faith that moves God to action; it is simply the choice to believe.

Twice in the Gospels Jesus made the point that the issue in faith is not quantity, but quality. In Matthew 17:20, the disciples were perplexed over not being able to cast out a demon and Jesus told them that the problem was unbelief, a failure to exercise faith. They were attempting to do a spiritual work without real spiritual faith. Jesus told them that with the faith of a grain of mustard seed they could tell a mountain to be removed and it would be. Then in Luke 17:5-6, the disciples asked Jesus to increase their faith, and again Jesus responded by telling them that if they had faith as a grain of mustard seed they could tell a tree to be uprooted and it would be. Now Jesus did not

And Jesus answering saith unto them, Have faith in God.

Mark 11:22

actually intend for them to go around uprooting trees and casting mountains into the sea, but He was making a point - a strong one. He was telling them that any shred of faith that is real will yield results. In the face of real faith, God responds, satan flees and circumstances are altered.

Dear fellow Christian, right now in your time of need, in your crisis, your trial, how are you approaching Jesus? Have you yet moved beyond the point of knowing He <u>can</u> solve your problem or grant your desire? Have you gone further than just <u>wanting</u> Him to? You must! In order to get a response from Jesus, in order to receive from Him, you must choose to believe - believe that He is doing it now. The desperate mother came to Jesus for help. With her intellect she <u>knew</u> He could. That was a good and necessary first step, but it was not far enough. She cried out to Him expressing her specific request. With her emotions she <u>wanted</u> Him to. That was a good and necessary second step, but it was still not far enough. Then finally with her will she chose to believe. That third step was the key. Her will was joined to God's will in faith. In all three cases - the Centurion, the mother and Bartimaeus - it was the will of God to heal. It had already been decided before Jesus met them. All He needed was for some one to believe. Dear Child of God, is Jesus waiting for you to believe? You may say, "But I don't understand <u>how</u> to believe." You will; just keep reading.

Disciples with Little Faith

In Matthew 6:24-34 and Luke 12:22-32, Jesus spoke to the Disciples about their worry and anxiety over the daily necessities of life. He told them (and us), *"Take no thought for your life..."* If God feeds the birds and clothes the grass of the field, will He not much more take care of you – *"...O ye of little faith?"* Jesus used the expression "little faith" in both Matthew and Luke. Little faith is the English translation of the Greek word "oligopistos" and it means "small, short, limited, and temporary." Jesus wanted the disciples, as well as all believers, to walk in faith that takes for granted that He is going to meet every need. He tells us in Matthew 6:33, *"Seek ye first the kingdom of God, and his righteousness; and all these things shall be added unto you"*. That was His plan and His desire for His disciples, both the ones He was immediately speaking to and those who would follow throughout generations to come. Our primary concern and focus in the Christian life should be our relationship to God and the expansion of His Kingdom.

Jesus also used that word, "oligopistos" (little faith), in three other familiar accounts. After calming the wind and the waves in the storm in Matthew 8:23-27, Jesus asked the disciples, *"...Why are ye fearful, O ye of little faith?"* Of course, He asked the question and answered it all in the same breath. Their fear was so big because their faith was so weak. In Mark 4:40, He asks, *"How is it that ye have no faith?"* or "Why do you not yet have faith?" And in Luke 8:25 He just asks, *"...Where is your faith?"* The phrasing is a little different from one account to the other, but the message is the same in all three – what Jesus was looking for out of His disciples was the exercise of faith. He wanted them to make the choice of faith, to believe His words, "Let's go to the other side" rather than the visible circumstances, which caused them to say, "We perish."

In Matthew 14:30-31, we find Peter making the same mistake. After stepping out of the boat and walking briefly on the water, after a heroic beginning, he became fearful, focusing on the wind and the waves rather than Jesus, and he began to sink. Jesus, of course, rescued him and while doing so asked him, *"...O thou of little faith, wherefore didst thou doubt?"* The answer is obvious. Peter had not yet learned that faith in the word, in the power of Jesus, could override the natural laws by which he, like us, was so accustomed to being governed. Did Peter not have faith? Yes, he did. If he had not, he would have never walked on the water to begin with. The problem was that his faith was temporary, limited, and shortened by looking at and believing in the reality of the visible more than the greater reality of the word of Jesus.

In Matthew 16:6-12, Jesus warned the disciples about the treachery of the Pharisees and Sadducees. *"...Take heed and beware of the leaven of the Pharisees and of the Sadducees."* They misunderstood what He was saying and thought that He was concerned about the fact that they had brought no bread. He said to them, *"O ye of little faith, why reason ye among yourselves, because ye have brought no bread?"* He asked did they not remember the five loaves and the five thousand, or the seven loaves and the four thousand, and how many baskets of food they had left over? You can almost hear Him saying, "How much are you guys going to have to see me do, and how often am I going to have to do it, before you understand the simplicity and importance of just trusting Me by faith?" In each one of these cases we see that the big issue with Jesus was faith. He did not ask, where is your love, or your loyalty, or your obedience. His question was, "Where is your faith?" In instance after instance you can just hear Jesus asking, "How long am I going to be with you, how long is it going to take for you to get this right?" He knew they had to "get it right;" they had to become strong in faith, because they would be the foundation of the Church. To them, and to us, would be given the responsibility to spread the Gospel throughout the world.

In Luke 22:31-32, Jesus said to Peter, *"...Simon, Simon, behold, satan hath desired to have you, that he may sift you as wheat; But I have prayed for thee, that thy faith fail not: and when thou art converted, strengthen thy brethren."* What was Jesus' concern for Peter? It was for his faith. What would enable Peter to strengthen his brothers? It was his faith. Jesus did not say I have prayed for your love to be increased, your commitment to be deepened, or your loyalty to be more evident. He said, "I have prayed for your faith." And in Acts 3:1-7, after the coming of the Holy Spirit, we see that Peter "got it right." When asked by the lame man for money, Peter said to him, *"...Silver and gold have I none; but such as I have give I thee."* What did Peter have? He had what Jesus prayed he would have, the most important thing he could have - Holy Spirit energized faith. Peter could not give the man money because he had none. It would not have helped even if he could have given money to him, because money could not make the man walk. But Peter could activate the man's capacity for faith - the one thing that would result in his healing. There is a limit to what money, or material resources, or human skill can do, regardless of the quality or quantity. But real faith has no boundaries and no limits except the will of God.

God revealed something to me many years ago in relation to ministry team members. It is imperative that they learn to trust in God alone, and they cannot do that by trying to live on my faith. It has always been my desire and my tendency to meet every need in every life connected to our ministry, but God has never allowed me to completely do that and I know why. Because if I did, they would never learn to trust God and therefore would never be able to stand on their own. Their growth as a Christian and their development as a servant of God would be hindered for lack of opportunity to look to God alone. I will never have enough money to meet the never-ending needs of their life and ministry, but there will always be enough of God's supernatural supply as well as enough capacity of faith within them to access it. The very worst thing that I could ever do for another Christian, especially a called servant of God, is to rob him of the privilege, responsibility, and joy of trusting God personally. God can use me as a channel through which He can send His supply to others, but I dare not become the source. We are to have only one Source and only one object of faith and that is the Lord Jesus Himself. Real discipleship, as demonstrated by Jesus, is helping Believers grow in their relationship with God to the point that they can trust God alone by real faith at all times for everything.

The Ministry of Jesus Continues with Our Faith

Now we come to the heart of the issue of faith – the continuation of the ministry of Jesus. Before entering the Garden of Gethsemane, Jesus spoke to the Father concerning the disciples, *"As Thou hast sent me into the world, even so I have also sent them into the world"* (John 17:18). Real faith in the disciples and real faith in you and me is so vitally important to Jesus because it is essential to the continuation of His ministry on this earth. Jesus was going to leave this world, but His ministry of redemption was not going to end. It had just begun. He was going to continue saving souls, delivering from bondage, and meeting needs, just as He had been doing all along in the sight of the disciples and the multitudes. Now, however, He was going to perform His ministry through them, through the church that would be born at Pentecost, and ultimately through those of us who believe on Him today.

How did Jesus perform His ministry? Through simple obedience to, and trust in, the Father. He performed His ministry by faith. Jesus lived in continuous cooperation with the will of the Father. His was a life of real faith. He said, *"I can of mine own self do nothing: as I hear, I judge: and my judgment is just; because I seek not mine own will, but the will of the Father which hath sent me"* (John 5:30). Then He said, *"For I came down from heaven, not to do mine own will, but the will of him that sent me"* (John 6:38). Jesus received the will of the Father, cooperated with Him by speaking the word of faith, thus releasing the Holy Spirit to do the work. We will look at this se-

Faith and nothing but faith avails for us to receive the gifts and graces of our ascended Lord

Ruth Paxson (2)

quence more closely later, but for now suffice it to say that Jesus was the channel through which the Father flowed His will (and so are we to be) by the operation of faith. Again we read, *"He that believeth on me, as the scripture hath said, out of his belly shall flow rivers of living water"* (John 7:38).

Everything that Jesus said and did during His public ministry illustrated how His ministry was to continue through the disciples and through the coming church. Through every person healed, every demon cast out, every person raised from the dead, every storm calmed, every need met, every soul salvaged, the collective message came through – it is all by faith, and without real faith it is not possible. It was said of Jesus in His own hometown, *"He did not many mighty works there because of their unbelief"* (Matthew 13:58). Jesus *"did not many mighty works there"* not because He could not but because He <u>would not</u>. **God requires real faith on our part before He will do His part**.

Jesus took the disciples through three years in the school of faith and used every possible opportunity to teach them, because He knew where He was leading them – into hand-to-hand combat with the powers of darkness. In order for Jesus to fulfill His continuing ministry through them, through us, they had to learn to live and operate by real faith. So do we. There is no other way. Why is our faith so important to Jesus? <u>It is important to Him because the continuation of His ministry and the building of His Kingdom depend upon it.</u>

Summary of Truth

- ❖ The one thing we can do that is certain to bring joy to Jesus is to trust Him by faith.
- ❖ Jesus will "delay" His answer in order to provoke us to believe.
- ❖ The key issue is our choice to believe, not quantity of faith.
- ❖ The crucial concern with Jesus in relation to the disciples was their faith.
- ❖ The ministry of Jesus on earth continues through us as we trust Him by faith.

NOW LET'S TAKE A MOMENT AND PRAY TOGETHER:

LORD JESUS, I NOW KNOW THAT THE MOST IMPORTANT THING IN MY RELATIONSHIP WITH YOU IS FAITH. LORD, HELP ME TO CHOOSE TO TRUST YOU IN EVERYTHING, IN EVERY CIRCUMSTANCE. HELP ME TO SETTLE FOR NOTHING LESS THAN REAL FAITH. LORD USE ME AS A CHANNEL THROUGH WHICH YOU CAN CONTINUE YOUR MINISTRY ON EARTH. MAY THE GREATER WORKS BE ACCOMPLISHED THROUGH ME. IN YOUR NAME I PRAY. AMEN.

Chapter 10

Real Faith:
Beyond the Gospels

"Faith in the Bible is faith in God against everything that contradicts Him."
Oswald Chambers (1)

Throughout the Gospels we see Jesus continually leading the disciples into one situation after another in which they would be called upon to act in faith and in which they would likely fail. He did it because they were learning, and they had to. They were in the school of faith. Jesus knew that if they learned nothing else they must learn to live by faith. The reason, as already stated, was that in order for Jesus to continue His ministry on earth, He would have to do it through them and the coming Church. That could only be possible if they learned to apply the same faith process He used to the situations they would face.

Now notice how Jesus dealt with His disciples. He was firm and persistent in His teaching regarding their faith but He was gentle and never condemning. He dealt with them as a teacher with students, not as a taskmaster with servants. There are two words in the New Testament for "unbelief." One is the Greek word "apeithia" which is a very hard, harsh, and condemning word. It means to be obstinately opposed to the will of God or to God Himself. Jesus never used that word in dealing with the disciples because it did not apply. They were not opposed to trusting God, they just didn't know how. Accordingly Jesus chose the softer word "apistia", which means a weakness or smallness of faith. They <u>wanted</u> to believe and they were <u>willing</u> to believe, but they did not possess the <u>power</u> to believe beyond a certain point. There were boundaries around their faith, the boundaries of the visible. That is why Jesus told Peter in Matthew 14:31 that he had "little faith," or "limited" faith. It was faith that would extend only up to the limits of what he could see in the visible. His "small" faith could get him out of the boat and hold him up on the water for a while, but it could not sustain him once he was confronted with the opposing circumstances of wind and waves. It wasn't a <u>refusal</u> to believe, but an <u>inability</u> to believe.

Jesus knew, however, that once the Holy Spirit came, then everything they had learned theoretically, would become theirs experientially. The things that they did not yet understand would eventually become crystal clear, and their willingness to believe would be accompanied by the energizing power of the Holy Spirit. Jesus said, *"These things have I spoken unto you, being yet present with you. But the Comforter, which is the Holy Ghost, whom the Father will send in my name, he shall teach you all things, and **bring all things to your remembrance**, whatsoever I have said unto you"* (John 14:25-26).

Now this transitions us beyond the Gospels into the book of Acts. Here everything changes with the coming of the Holy Spirit and the formation of the Church, the body of Christ. As recorded in chapter two, the Holy Spirit did come just as Jesus had promised, and with Him came the empowering of Believers to enter into a supernatural relationship with God. In the Gospels the Disciples were often discouraged and defeated in their attempts to utilize their God-given capacity of faith. They could not make the transition from visible to invisible, from natural to supernatural. They could not move beyond the limitation of the five loaves they could see in their possession to the thousands of loaves they could not see in Jesus' possession (Matthew 14:17). They were experimenting with faith, trying to believe upon the Lord Jesus Who was walking with them, but more often than not they were failing in their attempts. In chapter 22 of Luke's Gospel, he tells how Peter was powerless to live up to his promise to follow Jesus to prison and to death, to stay awake and to pray, or to walk with Jesus when He was led away. He told how Peter even denied Jesus three times, claiming that he did not even know him.

Then in Acts 3:1-9, Luke tells an entirely different story about the same exact man. At the temple gate Peter and John encountered a man who had been lame from birth. He asked for money, and Peter told him that he had none, *"...but such as I have give I thee: In the name of Jesus Christ of Nazareth rise up and walk."* What did Peter have that he did not have before? He now had real faith that could move beyond the boundaries of the visible, the possible, and the sensible. He had the power of God to believe for the miraculous. What had happened to Peter? Very simply, he had become empowered by the Holy Spirit. He had become a citizen of a world that exists beyond mere thought, feeling, sight, sound and touch and he had learned how to draw upon it. Now instead of trying to believe in Jesus Who was walking with him, he was enabled to actively believe in

Jesus Who was living <u>in</u> him. The foundation and energy of real faith is *"...Christ in you, the hope of glory"* (Colossians 1:27). To the unbelieving onlookers who marveled at the healing of the lame man, Peter explained how it happened in Acts 3:16, *"And his name through faith in his name hath made this man strong, whom ye see and know: yea, the faith which is by him* [Jesus] *hath given him this perfect soundness in the presence of you all."* Before, he could not "see" himself walking on the water, but now by Spirit-energized faith he could "see" this man walking on his feet. He could see with the eyes of faith, made possible by Jesus living in him.

Dear Christian, before going on, I want to pause here and inject an important point that is easy to pass over. While we view this scene in Acts as remarkable, we also tend to relegate it, and others, to Bible history. We feel detached from it and tend to put it in the "that was then and this is now" category. But the truth is, God can and will do things just as remarkable through any born-again believer who chooses to trust Him, regardless of the age he lives in. All God needs in order to perform the miraculous is a human channel through which to flow, some one who will join his will to the will of God and believe. Now you might say, "Yes, but those men in the Bible were different from me; they had power that I don't have." No, my

Faith is the one thing that pleases God. In all worship and work that is acceptable to God in Christ Jesus, it is faith that receives the testimony that we are well pleasing to Him.

Andrew Murray (2)

Christian friend, they were not different from you. They were plain ordinary folks made of flesh and blood just like you and me. They were indwelt by the same Holy Spirit as you are. They were ordinary people who made the choice to believe in an extraordinary God. They did not even have the New Testament. What they had is what you and I have, the God-given capacity to believe.

It was Jesus' plan that after His ascension His followers, then and now, would occupy the same position He did when He was on earth, the position of mediator between heaven and earth. Jesus was the channel through which the will of the Father flowed and so are we to be. The Holy Spirit was sent at Pentecost for the express purpose of continuing the ministry of Jesus on earth by the formation of the Church, by the indwelling and empowering of those who believe upon Him and follow Him. It was the coming of the Holy Spirit to indwell our human spirit that made it possible for us to hear the in-spoken voice of God, to be empowered to confess the will of God in a creating spoken word of faith, and then to act upon it with the activity of faith.

With empowering, however, comes responsibility. The indwelling of the Holy Spirit in our spirit makes us responsible before God to live by faith. Because of His indwelling, we are without excuse. The Holy Spirit gives us the ability to receive instructions from the Father and the supernatural power to obey, a power that the disciples did not have before Pentecost. As we read through the book of Acts, we see that with the indwelling Holy Spirit, comes the greatest gift of all, the supernatural ability to believe God for the impossible. In Acts 6:8 we are told that Stephen *"did great wonders and miracles among the people."* How? It was because he was *"full of faith and power."* Then in Acts 11:24 it is said of Barnabas that *"he was a good man, and full of the Holy Ghost and of faith: and much people was added unto the Lord."* Throughout the book we see that by faith thousands were saved and added to the church, people were healed, and demons were cast out. By faith, missionary journeys were made and churches were founded. By faith, prison chains fell off and prison doors were opened. By faith, Paul and those with him were enabled to survive stoning, snake bite, and ship wreck. God used Peter's faith to bring physical healing, Stephen's faith to enable him to die for Christ, and Barnabas' faith to bring people into the Kingdom. But in each case, the key was real faith energized by the power of the Holy Spirit.

In Acts 7:57-60, we see Stephen, the man full of faith and the Holy Ghost, being martyred for Jesus. But his faith held right to the very end. Watching the whole thing and consenting to it was a young man named Saul. To this man, that harsh word "apeithia" (unbelief) could have appropriately been applied because he was certainly standing in obstinate opposition to God. The Bible tells us that he was *"...breathing out threatenings and slaughter against the disciples of the Lord"* (Acts 9:1). Then came the life-changing event on the Damascus Road - his encounter with the Lord Jesus. The faith he had witnessed in Stephen entered his own heart. Now the obstinate opposition of "Saul" was replaced by total devotion to Jesus by "Paul." Now he was possessed by a compelling to proclaim to the world the message of faith in Christ. The drastic contrast between the old totally faithless life of Saul and the new all-consuming life of faith of Paul may explain to some degree why, under the inspiration of the Holy Spirit, he placed such great emphasis on faith in all of his letters to the churches. He stressed that it is by faith we are saved, we live, we walk, we are liberated from the law, and we have access to God.

From Paul to the Churches

Faith in the disciples was the key issue to Jesus, and faith in the churches was one of the key issues to Paul, probably second only to the Lordship of Christ. In his letters to the churches, Paul dealt with a wide range of issues, which varied from church to church, but he expressed the importance of real faith, and his concern regarding the steadfastness and quality of faith, with all of them. We are not going to deal with every reference to faith in the Bible, we would have to write another book to do that, but we will take an abbreviated look at a few.

Paul begins his letter to the church at Rome (1:8) by telling them that above all else it is their faith that is spoken of throughout the whole world. In verse 17, he sets the tone for the rest of the letter by stating that *"the just shall live by faith"*. Throughout chapter 3, Paul stresses that righteousness is established and salvation is obtained only by faith. In Chapter 4, he further illustrates this truth with the account of the faith of Abraham. Throughout the entire book of Romans, Paul emphasizes that faith is the foundation of the Christian life and the facilitator of the grace of God.

Then to the Corinthians he stressed that real faith *"should not stand in the wisdom of men, but in the power of God"* (I Corinthians 2:5) and that it must rest in the reality of the resurrection of Jesus (I Corinthians 15:14). He emphasized that it is by faith the Christian stands for God (II Corinthians 1:24) and conducts his Christian life (II Corinthians 5:7). In writing to the Galatians, Paul dealt with the issue of the law and stressed that it is not by the law that we are justified but by faith (Galatians 2:16). It is by faith that we live (2:20), we receive the Spirit (3:2), we are grafted into the spiritual family of Abraham (3:7), and we have access to the blessing of Abraham (3:9). Again, it is by faith that we live (3:11) and are liberated (3:25).

In the first chapter of Ephesians, Paul began by saying that he did not cease to give thanks for them in his prayers because **"...I heard of your faith** in the Lord Jesus, and love unto all the saints" (1:15). He stressed again that salvation is by faith (2:8) and it is by faith that we have boldness and access to God (3:12). Then Paul nears the conclusion of the letter by telling the church that above all else they should take the **"shield**

of faith" (6:16) so they would be able to withstand the onslaught of the devil. In chapter one of Philippians, Paul told the church that there was one reason why he wanted to remain with them - to increase their faith. *"...I know that I shall abide and continue with you all **for your furtherance and joy of faith**"* (v. 25). To the Colossians he expressed his reason for finding joy in them, *"For though I be absent in the flesh, yet am I with you in the spirit, joying and beholding your order, and the **stedfastness of your faith** in Christ"* (2:5).

In writing to the church at Thessalonica, Paul told them that he remembered without ceasing their **"...work of faith**, *and labor of love, and patience of hope in our Lord Jesus Christ"* (I Thessalonians 1:3). In chapter three, he told them that he had sent Timothy to them for one express purpose - to know the condition of their faith. *"For this cause, when I could no longer forbear, **I sent to know your faith**, lest by some means the tempter have tempted you, and our labour be in vain"* (v.5). In verse 7, Paul said that he was comforted in his afflictions by their faith, and in verse ten he expressed a desire to help perfect (mature) their faith. Why? Because Paul knew it was faith, and faith alone, that would enable the infant church to withstand the attacks of satan. In chapter 5, verse 8, he again stressed the importance of the overall covering of faith, *"But let us, who are of the day, be sober, putting on the **breastplate of faith** and love; and for an helmet, the hope of salvation."* Then in his second letter Paul told them that he was able to rejoice in them because their *"**faith groweth exceedingly**"* (II Thessalonians 1:3).

Toward the end of his life Paul wrote two letters to Timothy, whom he called his own son in the faith. In those letters Paul expressed deep concern over the issue of faith in Timothy's life and ministry. By this time in his own life, he had been serving the Lord for many years, and as he reflected back over his years of experience, he clearly saw that faith was the most critical issue in his life and he knew it would be in Timothy's also.

In the first letter (1:18-19), Paul warned *"This charge I commit unto thee, son Timothy, according to the prophesies which went before on thee, that thou by them mightest war a good warfare; **Holding faith** and a good conscience; which some having put away concerning **faith** have made shipwreck."* In 4:12, he instructed Timothy to be an example to other Believers in six areas: *"...in word, in conversation, in charity* [love], *in spirit, in **faith**, in purity."* In 6:11, Paul told him to follow after six things: *"...righteousness, godliness, **faith**, love, patience, meekness."* Then in the next verse Paul gave Timothy the strong exhortation to *"Fight the good fight of faith"* The words used in this verse clearly reveal what Paul was trying to get across to Timothy. The first word "fight" is the Greek verb "agonizomai", which means to struggle, to strive, to labor fervently, or to agonize. The second word "fight" is the noun "agon", which means an assembly place of conflict, an arena, a battle, or a contest. A modern day equivalent would be a boxing ring. So what was Paul telling Timothy? He was telling him that if there was any fight or conflict that he *must* win, if there was any arena in life that he could not afford to lose in, it was the arena of **faith**. Whatever amount of effort, agony, or struggle it took, he *must* succeed at faith. There are many words that Paul could have used to sum up his own life, but in his second letter to Timothy he said this, *"I have fought a good fight, I have finished my course, I have kept the faith"* (II Timothy 4:7).

The Great Hall of Faith

Now we turn to the book of Hebrews, which was written to Jews who had become professing Christians but who seemed to be wavering in their commitment to Christ. The writer reminds them in chapter 4, verse 2 that the Gospel must be *"mixed with faith"* or it is of no profit, and that once the foundation of repentance and *"faith toward God" (6:1)* are laid, it is not necessary to do it again. In verse 22 of chapter 10 they are told to *"draw near with a true heart in full assurance of faith."* And in verse 38 they are reminded again that, *"The just shall live by faith."*

Then in chapter 11, to further press the point and the importance of faith by means of example, the author leads the reader into the GREAT HALL OF FAITH. Upon entering we read these words, *"Now faith is the substance of things hoped for, the evidence of things not seen"* (11:1). Then a little further in we read *"Through faith we understand that the worlds were framed by the Word of God, so that things which are seen were not made of things which do appear"* (11:3). *"But without faith it is impossible to please him: for he that cometh to God must believe that he is, and that he is a rewarder of them that diligently seek him"* (11:6). Real faith believes that God *is* and that God *does.*

Once inside we encounter an amazing gallery of portraits of plain ordinary people who "pleased God" and whose lives vividly illustrate the faithfulness of God and the wisdom of trusting Him by faith. First we see Abel (v.4) who *"By faith...offered unto God a more excellent sacrifice than Cain, by which he obtained witness that he was righteous."* Then there is Enoch (v.5) who by faith *"was translated that he should not see death."* It was said of him that *"he pleased God."* Next is Noah (v.7) who demonstrated that a man can obey God and stand upon a faith that sees into the invisible. In verses 8 and 9, we encounter one of the greatest examples of faith-living in the Bible, Abraham. He *"went out, not knowing"* and *"By faith he sojourned in the land of promise..."* He demonstrated that faith enables us to go where we cannot see and to enjoy that which we do not yet have in our hand. The faith of Abraham provides one of the first glimpses in the Bible of the truth that we do not have to live within the boundaries of the visible. In verse 13, we observe the entire process of faith. The saints of God SAW the promises afar off, became PERSUADED of their reality, RECEIVED them in their heart, EMBRACED them as real, and CONFESSED them with their mouth – even though they had not yet received them in the natural realm. In verse 17, Abraham demonstrated his belief in the promise of God by offering up his only son in obedience to God, by faith, believing they would come down from the mountain together.

The next portrait is that of Isaac, who shows us that real faith can boldly speak with assurance of those things that are yet to come. *"By faith Isaac blessed Jacob and Esau concerning things to come"* (11:20). On and on the list goes with Jacob, Joseph, Moses, Joshua, Rahab, Gideon, Barak, Samson, Jephthae, David, and Samuel. Their lives demonstrated that **by faith**, the domination of the world can be refused, the walls can come down, the sea can be crossed, and those who trust in God can be protected. **By faith** kingdoms can be subdued, promises can be obtained, the mouths of lions can be stopped, fire can be quenched, the sword can be escaped, armies can be set to flight, and the dead can be raised. The portraits hanging in the Great Hall of Faith prove beyond doubt that **by faith**, God's children, you and I, can fulfill God's purpose for our lives, whether it ends in living another day to testify to His goodness or in dying with praise on our lips for His unwavering faithfulness.

As we exit the Great Hall we are confronted with another compelling message which reads, *"Wherefore seeing we also are compassed about with so great a cloud of witnesses, let us lay aside every weight, and the sin which doth so easily beset us, and let us run with patience the race that is set before us, **Looking unto Jesus the author and finisher of our faith**"* (12:1-2). With all this evidence in front of us as to the faithfulness of God, how can we <u>not</u> make the choice to trust Him? With Jesus as the Author, the Initiator, and the Completer of our faith, how can we not believe Him for the impossible? How do we dare to imprison ourselves within the boundaries of what we can see and feel when it is obviously so unnecessary? Who was it that initiated the faith of Abel, of Moses, of Noah, of Daniel, of Abraham? It was Jesus. It was Jesus who brought each situation to a conclusion that glorified God. Who was the fourth man in the fiery furnace with Shadrach, Meshach and Abednego? It was Jesus, and He will enable each one of us to trust Him by faith if we will choose His will. What are the "weights" we must lay aside? They are the things in the visible that tell us we cannot trust God. What is *"the sin which doth so easily beset us?"* It is unbelief, that awful thing that hinders so many from entering into the promised rest of God. The writer warns, *"Take heed, brethren, lest there be in any of you an **evil heart of unbelief** [weakness of faith], in departing from the living God"* (3:12).

Coming to the end of the New Testament we find James, Peter, John and Jude continuing to stress the urgency of faith. James emphasizes the importance of faith, especially in the sense of balance. He presents the Christian life, in a practical way, as a two-sided page, with faith in God on one side and our actions on the other. He is quick to say that one is never operational to the exclusion of the other. He points out that our faith must be tried, unwavering, without respect of persons, and *active*. James points out that real faith is always accompanied by works. The Greek word he uses for "work" is "ergon", which means "an act, deed, or doing." James is simply saying that real faith results in corresponding action.

Peter points out that real faith is also accompanied by trials and conflict. He writes in I Peter 1:7, *"That the trial of your faith, being much more precious than of gold that perisheth, though it be tried with fire, might be found unto praise and honor and glory at the appearing of Jesus Christ"*. The thing that is more precious to the Lord Jesus, more valuable to Him than anything else, is our faith. The one thing that will bring praise, honor, and glory to Him at His appearing is our faith. John underscores the importance of real faith by telling us that the only way to experience victory over the world is by faith. *"For whatsoever is born of God overcometh the world: and this is the victory that overcometh the world, **even our faith**"* (I John 5:4). Then Jude instructs us in verse 21 to *"Keep yourselves in the love of God, looking for the mercy of our Lord Jesus Christ unto eternal life."* In verse 20 he tells us how, by ***"…building up yourselves on***

your most holy faith*, praying in the Holy Ghost."*

So we see that the Word of God, in its entirety, presents the unshakable truth that faith is the most crucial issue in our Christian life. Whether the message comes through Jesus speaking in the Gospels, or through the New Testament writers, or through the many examples from the Old Testament, it is the same; in order to please God, in order to live a victorious life, Christians *must* live by faith. Below our closing prayer is a compelling list of things that would not, and can not, exist apart from real faith. I encourage you to take a look at it before going on, and allow it to impress upon your heart the urgency of faith in your Christian life. There are 68 items on the list. May I suggest that as part of your daily Bible study and devotion time you read and study two items per day. Allow these Scripture passages to soak into your heart, and ask the Holy Spirit to make them part of your life and experience.

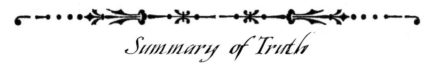

Summary of Truth

❖ The Holy Spirit was sent for the continuation of the ministry of Jesus on earth.

❖ His coming makes all Believers responsible before God to live by faith.

❖ God will perform remarkable, supernatural acts through and for any Christian who will trust Him by faith.

❖ Jesus Christ is the initiation and the completion of every act of faith.

❖ Faith was a key issue in Paul's letters to the churches.

❖ He considered it of the utmost importance in his own life and ministry.

❖ The portraits in the Great Hall of Faith illustrate that we do not have to live within the boundaries of the visible and possible.

❖ The Word of God, in its entirety, stresses the importance of faith.

❖ There is no victory in the Christian life apart from faith.

NOW LET'S TAKE A MOMENT AND PRAY TOGETHER:

DEAR LORD JESUS, AGAIN I OFFER MYSELF TO YOU AS A CHANNEL THROUGH WHICH YOU CAN CONTINUE YOUR MINISTRY. BY THE IN-DWELLING OF YOUR SPIRIT I AM RESPONSIBLE TO LIVE BY FAITH, AND I ACCEPT THAT RESPONSIBILITY. LORD I ASK YOU TO BE THE CONSTANT INITIATION AND COMPLETION OF FAITH IN ME. I ASK YOU, LORD, TO MAKE MY LIFE ONE OF THOSE THAT WILL SOMEDAY HANG IN THE GREAT HALL OF FAITH. I LOVE YOU, LORD JESUS. IN YOUR NAME I PRAY AND THANK YOU. AMEN.

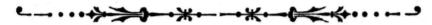

DAY BY DAY – BY FAITH

DAY 1 - I HAVE ALL I NEED

Anxiety and worry are overcome - Matt. 6:25-34

Healing is secured - Matt. 8:10, 9:2, 22, 29, Mk. 5:34, 10:52, Lk. 17:19, Acts 3:16

DAY 2 - I HAVE THE IMPOSSIBLE

We have power - Matt. 18:19

The impossible is made possible - Matt. 17:20, 21:21, Lk. 17:6

DAY 3 - I HAVE ANSWERED PRAYER

Prayer is answered - Matt. 21:22; Mk. 11:24

The work of God is performed - Jn. 6:29

DAY 4 - I AM A CHANNEL OF LIVING WATER

We are rivers of living water - Jn. 7:38

Wonders and miracles are performed - Acts 6:8

DAY 5 - I AM PURIFIED

People are added to the church - Acts 11:24

Our hearts are purified - Acts 15:9

DAY 6 - I AM FORGIVEN

Churches are established - Acts 16:5

We are forgiven of sin and sanctified - Acts 26:16-18

DAY 7 - I AM COMFORTED

Christian testimony is established - Rom. 1:8; Eph. 1:15; Col. 1:4

We are comforted - Rom. 1:12

DAY 8 - I AM RIGHTEOUS

The just shall live - Rom. 1:17; Gal. 3:11; Heb. 10:38

Righteousness is obtained - Rom. 3:22, 4:5, 9, 11, 30, 10:6; Phil. 3:9

DAY 9 - I AM JUSTIFIED

Boasting is excluded - Rom. 3:27

All are justified - Mk. 16:16; Rom. 3:30, 5:2, Gal. 2:16, 3:8, 24, Eph. 2:8

DAY 10 - I HAVE AN INHERITANCE

The law is established - Rom. 3:31

We have the inheritance - Rom. 4:13

DAY 11 - I HAVE THE PROMISE OF GOD

Grace is made effective to all who believe upon Jesus - Rom. 4:16

God is glorified - Rom. 4:20

DAY 12 - I OVERCOME

Impossible circumstances are overcome - Rom. 4:16-19; Heb. 11:33

We are enabled to stand upon the promises of God - Rom. 4:20

DAY 13 - I HAVE PEACE WITH GOD

We have peace with God - Rom. 5:1

We have access into the grace of God - Rom. 5:2

DAY 14 - I REJOICE

We are made to rejoice in hope of the glory of God - Rom. 5:2

The Gospel is preached - Rom. 10:8, 12:6

DAY 15 - I THINK CLEARLY AND STAND FIRM

We think soberly - Rom. 12:3

The Christian stands - II Cor. 1:24

DAY 16 - I SPEAK WITH CONFIDENCE
We speak authoritatively - II Cor. 4:13
The Christian is to walk - II Cor. 5:7

DAY 17 - MY MINISTRY IS ENLARGED
Our ministry is enlarged through others - II Cor. 10:15
We are to live - Gal. 2:20

DAY 18 - I HAVE RECEIVED THE HOLY SPIRIT
We receive the Holy Spirit - Gal. 3:2
We are grafted into the family of Abraham - Gal. 3:7

DAY 19 - I AM LIBERATED
We partake of the blessings of Abraham - Gal. 3:9, 14
We are liberated from the law - Gal. 3:25

DAY 20 - I AM IN THE FAMILY OF GOD
We are the children of God - Gal. 3:26
We wait for the hope of righteousness - Gal. 5:5

DAY 21 - I HAVE BOLDNESS
We have boldness and access with confidence - Eph. 3:12
Christ dwells in our hearts, we are rooted and grounded in love -
Eph. 3:17

DAY 22 - I KNOW THE LOVE OF JESUS
We comprehend the breadth, length, depth and height of God's love -
Eph. 3:18
We know the love of Christ which passes knowledge - Eph. 3:19

DAY 23 - I AM RISEN WITH CHRIST
We are filled with all the fullness of God - Eph. 3:19
We are risen with Christ - Col. 2:12

DAY 24 - I AM PROTECTED
We have protection from satan - Eph. 6:16; I Thess. 5:8
The shipwrecked life is prevented - I Tim. 1:19

DAY 25 - I AM A GOOD EXAMPLE TO OTHERS
We become a good example to other believers - I Tim. 4:12
We become wise in the scriptures - II Tim. 3:15

DAY 26 - I AM NEAR TO GOD
We inherit the promises of God - Heb. 6:12
We draw near to God - Heb. 10:22

DAY 27 - I AM PLEASING TO GOD
We understand that the worlds were framed by the word of God - Heb. 11:3
We please God - Heb. 11:6

DAY 28 - I GO WITHOUT KNOWING

We act in accordance with things not seen as yet - Heb. 11:7

We go out without knowing - Heb. 11:8

DAY 29 - I CONFESS THE PROMISES

We judge God faithful - Heb. 11: 11

We see, believe, embrace, and confess the promises - Heb. 11: 13

DAY 30 - I WORSHIP GOD

We may speak things to come - Heb. 11: 20

We worship God - Heb. 11: 21

DAY 31 - I FORSAKE THE WORLD

We can forsake the world - Heb. 11:27

The invisible is made visible - Heb. 11:27

DAY 32 - I ENDURE ALL THINGS

We are able to endure trial, suffering and death - Heb. 11:35-38

Our actions are made meaningful and effective - Js. 2:14-26

DAY 33 - I AM KEPT BY THE POWER OF GOD

We are kept by the power of God - I Pet. 1:5

Satan is resisted - I Pet. 5:9

DAY 34 - I HAVE VICTORY

We have victory that overcomes the world - I Jn. 5:4

We continue to be built up - Jude 3

Chapter 11

Real Love :
The Driving Force
of Real Faith

"Whoso loves, believes the impossible."
Elizabeth Barret Browning

*L*ove and faith are the two driving forces in the universe, in the Word of God, and in our life. To fully comprehend the dynamic of real faith we must see clearly the relationship between the two because they are counterparts of each other. Stating it simply, faith is the <u>facilitator</u> for love and love is the stimulus or <u>motivation</u> for faith. When a person comes to the point of trusting God, it is because he is motivated by love. Natural love motivates to natural faith and love for God motivates to spiritual God-faith. All human beings love and therefore exercise their God-given capacity for faith towards something. The question is what?

I John 4:7-8 tells us that *"...love is of God"* and *"God is love..."* In Mark 12:30, we are given what Jesus called, the *"first and great commandment"*, which is to *"...love the Lord thy God with all thy heart, and with all thy soul, and with all thy mind, and with all thy strength...."* It is the God-given capacity of faith that makes possible the fulfillment of that commandment as well as the second, *"...Thou shalt love thy neighbor as thyself..."* (Mark 12:31). We are told in Hebrews 11:6, *"...without faith it is impossible to please him..."* That is because, without faith it is impossible to keep His commandments. Our life is like a sailing ship that is propelled by the wind. Without sails there is nothing to catch the wind, and the ship will not move. But without wind, the sails are useless. Either way, the ship is motionless, dead in the water. In our life, love is the wind, and faith is the sail. One is useless without the other, but the two operating together create the power that is needed to propel the life. It is these two forces, love and faith, working together that create motion. As we said, all human beings are moving toward something - either the satisfaction of self and the flesh or toward the fulfillment of the will of God.

We see the forces of love and faith connected repeatedly in God's Word, as if making up two sides of the page of our Christian life. In numerous places throughout the New Testament, we find the forces of love and faith connected. Let's look at a few.

"For in Jesus Christ neither circumcision availeth any thing, nor uncircumcision; but faith which worketh by love" (Galatians 5:6).

"Peace be to the brethren, and love with faith, from God the Father and the Lord Jesus Christ" (Ephesians 6:23).

"But let us, who are of the day, be sober, putting on the breastplate of faith and love; and for an helmet, the hope of salvation" (I Thessalonians 5:8).

"Now the end of the commandment is charity [love] *out of a pure heart, and of a good conscience, and of faith unfeigned"* (I Timothy 1:5).

"And the grace of our Lord was exceeding abundant with faith and love which is in Christ Jesus" (I Timothy 1:14).

"Hold fast the form of sound words, which thou hast heard of me, in faith and love which is in Christ Jesus" (II Timothy 1:13).

"Hearing of thy love and faith, which thou hast toward the Lord Jesus, and toward all saints" (Philemon 5).

Which Is More Important – Love or Faith?

Now let's ask this question, which is more important in the Christian life, love or faith? We are instructed in Ephesians 5:2 to *"walk in love"* but, in II Corinthians 5:7 we are also told to *"walk by faith."* So which is it? Well, that question cannot be answered in an either-or fashion. Love and faith are two sides of the same coin. One cannot function without the other. It is not possible to spend one side of the coin and not the other. That is why God endowed man with the capacity for both. Before we were saved, our faith was limited to the things of the world and to our own resources, because our love was limited to the world and to self. But after we were born of the Spirit of God, our faith was expanded to God, because our love was transferred from the world and self to Him.

In his book, *The Law of Faith,* Norman Grubb explains, "[Man] loves long before he is redeemed. He loves from the time he becomes a living soul. But what does he love? Love is the driving force. Desire (love pure or perverted) controls, contrives, creates all that ever comes to pass. Emotion, not reason, is at humanity's helm. Love motivates, but faith acts. Faith is action. By faith alone can a man act. Faith carries out the urges of love. Faith works by love" (1).

The issue is not <u>does</u> man love, but <u>what</u> does he love? I have heard some Christians say that before they were saved they did not have the ability to love. That is not true. What they did not have was the ability to love God. Likewise, the issue is not does man have faith, but what is the object of his faith? Every person, lost or saved, loves something supremely and exercises faith in that direction. The question is, what? Man can love darkness or he can love light

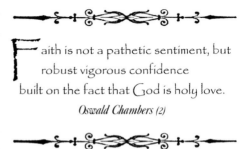

Faith is not a pathetic sentiment, but robust vigorous confidence built on the fact that God is holy love.

Oswald Chambers (2)

(John 3:19). He can love pleasure or he can love God (II Timothy 3:4). He can love the world (I John 2:15), or money (I Timothy 6:10) or the praise of men (John 12:43), or his own self (II Timothy 3:2), or he can love Jesus. Whatever is the object of his supreme love, that will be the direction of his faith also.

So we see that love is the motivation for faith, and faith is the activation of love. Love provides the desire to act, and faith makes the decision to act. Faith provides expression for love. Without love, faith would lie dormant because there would be nothing to rouse it to action. But without faith, love would be powerless, because there would be no means of expression. Love provides the "why" and faith provides the "how." Love says, "I want to", and faith says, "I am going to." Love "says", and faith "does."

Focus of the Light

There are times in our walk with God when it appears that the issue of our love for Him comes to the forefront. Then there are times when it seems that our focus is drawn more to the issue of faith, of trusting Him.

That is because the workings of God in our heart, and the formation of His will in our life, take place in two stages. He begins to speak to us in our spirit concerning His will, His direction, and we respond to His leading, initially, out of our love for Him and out of our desire to please Him. That is the love side operating. But once we become convinced of His will, once His guidance becomes clear, then the faith side awakens to do it. The light of the Holy Spirit shines <u>inward,</u> upon our hearts, revealing His will, and we respond in love by saying, "I want to obey You, Lord." Then the light shines <u>outward</u> through us, into the world, as we say, "I will obey You, Lord." The motivation of love becomes the action of faith.

Sheila and I went into a rug store one day looking for a rug to go in the living room. We looked at many, in the price range we thought we could afford, but nothing really excited us. Then we noticed a rug against a far wall that caught the attention of both of us at the same time. It was absolutely beautiful. We walked toward it, and so did the salesman. We stood right in front of it, dreaming of how it would look in our house. The salesman said, "No, don't stand right in front of it, stand to the side." So we moved to the left side of the rug. Gorgeous! Then he told us to move to the right side. Amazingly, as we did, it changed colors. It was still gorgeous - and way out of our league. He explained that this exquisite rug was woven in such a way that the color was determined by the angle of the light shining upon it. It was the focus of the light that made the difference. The Bible tells us that Jesus is the Light that shines upon our life. God has woven the fabric of our walk with God in such a way, that at one moment it seems that the issue before us is love and at another moment the issue is faith. But in reality, it is always both. It just depends on the angle of the Light at any given moment.

Balance Is the Key

The key word in the Christian life is *balance.* Paul writes in Ephesians 5:15, *"See then that ye walk circumspectly, not as fools, but as wise."* The word *circumspectly* is the Greek word *akribos,* meaning perfect or "most straightest." From it we get the English word, acrobat. Picture a tightrope walker. He walks on a thin wire, high above the ground in the circus tent, maintaining his balance by holding a balancing pole, which helps him to walk perfectly or "most straight." He accomplishes the daring feat by using the pole for balance and by fixing his eyes upon the platform at the end of the rope. If he drops the pole or loses his focus, he will lose his footing and fall.

Dear Believer, it is possible to live a perfectly balanced Christian life if the two dynamic forces which God placed within us, love and faith, are equally and fully operational. It is the combination of the two, the tension between the two in our life, that produces power and poise. Understandably, it was the two driving forces of love and faith that satan attacked in the garden. Through question and suggestion, satan cast doubt in the mind and resentment in the heart. He implied to Adam and Eve that God could not be trusted to meet their needs, that He did not love them, and that they should not love Him. The devil's aim was to cause separation between God and man, thus making it impossible for God to fulfill His plan through them. Many people enter the circus tent to see the tightrope walker for one reason - to watch him fall. And on rare occasions he does. But underneath him there is a net to break the fall, to save him. Satan entered the garden for the same reason, to draw man's attention away from God and to watch him fall. And fall he did. But beneath him there was something that satan did not count on - a net provided by God. It is called redemption. And by redemption through the blood of Jesus, God imparts to man a new life, which has within it the purified forces of love and faith. At the moment of salvation, God, by His Spirit, places within us His capacity of love, *"...the love of God is shed abroad in our hearts by the Holy Ghost which is given unto us"* (Romans 5:5). At the same time, He extends our capacity for faith beyond the natural into the spiritual, *"...according as God hath dealt to every man the measure of faith"* (Romans 12:3). "But," you ask, "what about those who are not saved, who die without Christ? Why did the net of redemption not save them?" The anser is, the net only saves if it is used. Some acrobats choose not to use one, and when they fall, they die.

Love Complete

God tells us in I John 4:18 that *"...perfect love casteth out fear..."*, indicating that we are to have a certain kind of love, a perfected love, that is, a love that is complete. We are also to have a perfected faith. In 1 Thessalonians 3:10 Paul expressed a desire to the church to *"...perfect that which is lacking in your faith."* Again, the word perfect means complete. Paul desired that they have a complete faith. How is love made complete? By faith. How is faith made complete? By love. Love provides motivation for faith and faith provides activation for love. On one end of our balancing pole is love and on the other end is faith. And at the end of our tightrope is Jesus, our Focal Point, *"Looking unto Jesus, the author and finisher of our faith... "* (Hebrews 12:2).

On several occasions we find Jesus rebuking His disciples over one issue – their faith, or rather, their weakness of faith. In Luke 8:25, Jesus asked the disciples in the storm, *"...where is your faith?"* He did not ask where is your loyalty or commitment or enthusiasm. No, He was looking for that thing that love activates. He questioned their faith. He did so because he knew their faith could only be operational by the motivating power of love. Jesus told the Pharisees in John 5:39-42 that they did not believe Him because the love of God was not in them. No love – no faith. He asked Peter three times in John 21:15-17 if he loved Him. Why? Because Jesus knew that love was the only motivating factor that would move Peter into action. Jesus was stirring up his capacity for love in order to stimulate his capacity for faith. A faithless life often indicates a loveless life or a love that has not yet learned to express itself through faith. Jesus told the disciples in John 14:15, *"If ye love me, keep my commandments."* In other words, if the motivation of love is present in you, then act by faith in obedience to Me. *"And why call ye me Lord, Lord, and do not the things which I say"* (Luke 6:46)?

Head over Heels in Love

Living the faith life, the only life that really pleases God, is made possible by two things: falling in love with Jesus, and then learning to express that love through obedience to His will. Do you have faith to believe God for the supernatural, for the impossible? Of course you do. Every child of God does - potentially. You have the <u>capacity</u> for faith because every Christian has been given that as a gift from God. But perhaps what you are lacking is the <u>reality</u> of trusting God and seeing Him move supernaturally on your behalf. If so, it is either because you have never really fallen in love with Jesus, or you have not yet learned how to express that love through faith.

Most attempts to illustrate spiritual truth from the natural world fall short of the mark, and this one may also. But I am going to try anyway. We have said that love motivates to action, to believing. I remember when I met my wife, Sheila, in the fall of 1966. She was eighteen and I was twenty. We will save the details for another book. But suffice it to say, when I saw her for the first time I was almost in shock. She had long blonde hair (still does) and was absolutely beautiful (still is). At the very instant I laid eyes on her, something happened to me that I thought had happened before. It was love - full blown, the real thing. I thought it had happened before, until the genuine article came along. The first time we went out I told myself that I was going to marry her. I wanted to spend every minute of every day with her, talking to her, and learning all I could about her. I wanted to give her everything, whether I could afford it or not. I wanted everyone to know that she was my girl (and still do). My overwhelming love for Sheila issued forth in a word of faith, which became an action of faith, which culminated in our marriage. Along with that love came trust – we had faith in each other. Of course it was faith in the natural realm, but it was faith nonetheless.

The same thing happened when I met Jesus in 1968. I fell in love with the Son of God. All of a sudden I wanted to spend all my time with Him, to give to Him, to talk to Him, to learn all I could about Him. I wanted everyone to know He is my Lord (and I still do). I vowed from the very first moment He came into my heart that I would serve Him for the rest of my life. And when I fell in love with Jesus, that dimension of trust came into being, but in the spiritual realm. I believed in Him. I had faith in Him.

Now let me ask you, have you ever fallen in love with Jesus? I am not asking if you are saved, but have you fallen head over heels in love with the One Who saved you? Some people are married for a lifetime, "going through the motions", but they never know the excitement and joy that comes from real love. They make a home, have kids, and live their life, but never enjoy the meaning of a real love relationship. Likewise, some people come into the Kingdom of God, but never fall ridiculously in love with Jesus. They just spend their Christian life going through the motions. They go to church, tithe, sing the hymns, refrain from overt sins, and live a "good Christian life." But there is no joy, no excitement, no thrill in just being alive in Christ. Therefore, there is no activity of faith, no supernatural intervention of God, because the motivation of real love is not there. Their Christian life is explainable in terms of self, not in terms of God.

Now let me ask you, where are you in your walk with Jesus? Have you fallen in love with Him? How do you know? If you have, your love will issue forth in faith, in obedience to His will. Love is more than feeling, more than affection. Love involves emotion and affection, but it moves beyond that into the will, into action. *"For God so loved the world that He* gave..." (John 3:16). He *did* something. Love creates because love is of God. *"If ye love me, keep my commandments"* (John 14:15). *"Love your enemies...bless...do good"* (Matthew 5:44). *"...lovest thou me?...Feed my sheep"* (John 21:17). *"...by love, serve one another"* (Galatians 5:13). *"My little children, let us not love in word, neither in tongue; but in deed and in truth"* (I John 3:18). II Corinthians 5:14 tells us, *"For the love of Christ constraineth us..."* Love is activated by faith and faith is motivated by love.

Love That Launches Out

In Luke 5:4-6, Jesus told Peter to launch out into the deep water and let down his net for a catch. Peter's response was, *"...Master, we have toiled all the night, and have taken nothing: nevertheless at thy word I will let down the net."* Do you have the kind of love for Jesus that motivates you to launch out into the deep of the unknown, the unfamiliar, and the impractical in obedience to His word, to forsake all, and follow Him? Will your love obey His "come" and step out of the boat to join Him on the water? Does your love for Jesus cause you to want to spend time with Him, to serve Him, and to make Him known to others? Do you delight in talking about Him? Are you listening for His voice, anxiously awaiting His next command so that you may quickly move into action in obedience to Him? Is your love for Him sufficient to take you out beyond your comfort zone? Will your

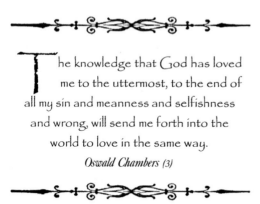

The knowledge that God has loved me to the uttermost, to the end of all my sin and meanness and selfishness and wrong, will send me forth into the world to love in the same way.

Oswald Chambers (3)

love risk all for Him? Is your love the kind that produces faith? Yes, dear child of God, it is! "But," you say, "can any ordinary person have that kind of love?" Again the answer is yes. The disciples were just plain ordinary men, and yet they launched out, stepped out, went out, and reached out, standing on nothing but the word of Jesus. And you can too. They were not yet indwelt by the Holy Spirit, but you are. Again quoting Romans 5:5 we see *"...the love of God is shed abroad in our hearts by the Holy Ghost which is given unto us."* When we were saved, the love of God was placed within us (in our spirit) by the Holy Spirit.

You may ask, "Well then, if I have that God-given, faith-producing love resident within me, why have I never launched out by faith to trust God for the miraculous? Why do I not see the supernatural intervention of God in my life? Why is my love not motivating to faith? Why is there a hesitation, a fear within me, of following Jesus into the unknown? Why do I spend my Christian life playing it safe?" The most likely answer to these questions is this - your love has been distracted and diverted away from its true and intended object, the Lord Jesus Himself. Your vision of Jesus has become clouded by other things. "Well, then is it possible" you ask, "to fall in love with Him all over again?" Yes, it certainly is. Jesus told the church at Ephesus in Revelation 2:4 that they had left their first love, not lost it. All you need is a new fresh look at Him with the eyes of your heart.

Do you want to live a life that is pleasing to God (the faith life)? Do you want to receive everything that is yours by inheritance as a child of God? Do you want to see God do the miraculous in your life? Do you want to lift the sails of your faith in the wind of God's love? Do you want to fall in love with Jesus all over again? Then let me suggest that you do some things. Right now go to the Bible and take a fresh look at the Savior. Read again Psalm 22 - 24 and Isaiah 53. Read the Gospels and walk with Him through the days of His ministry. Spend the hours in the garden with Him. Stand at the foot of the cross and watch Him die for you. Then go to the grave and see the stone rolled away. Ask God to open the eyes of your heart to see Him as He really is. Spend some time in prayer with Him. Confess to Him that your love has grown cold and ask Him to rekindle your love for Him in your heart. Think back on the time you were saved and how your life was before you knew Jesus. Then share your testimony with a friend. The very act of sharing with some one else what Jesus has done for you will ignite your love for Him. There have been some excellent films made over the past few years about the life of Jesus. Rent them or buy them and watch them again and again. You may be surprised as to how much you will be stimulated by them. If you have a shred of love in your heart for the Lord Jesus, then just watching a reenactment of His death will stir you in your heart and soul. You have the capacity for faith, just like every other child of God, but it must be stimulated and energized by love. As our love for Jesus grows, so will our faith.

There are two equally dynamic forces at work in the universe, in the plan of God: love and faith. Now allow them to explode in you. As you do, your life will become an exciting love affair with Jesus and an adventure in faith. It will be explainable only in terms of God and will thereby glorify Him. If you ever live by faith, it will be because you <u>want</u> to, not because you <u>have</u> to. That "want to" is produced by one thing only - falling in love with Jesus. When you do, you will discover that your desire to pray to Him, to give to Him, to worship Him, to talk about Him, to serve Him and to believe Him for the impossible will be inexhaustible. You just can't do enough or be enough for someone you truly love.

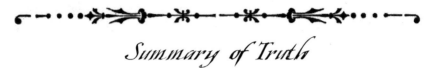

Summary of Truth

- ❖ The two driving forces in the universe are love and faith.
- ❖ Love is the motivation for faith and faith is the facilitator for love.
- ❖ The object of our love will determine the direction of our faith.
- ❖ The key to the Christian life is balance, and balance is maintained by love and faith being equally operational in our life.
- ❖ Learning to live by faith is made possible by two things - falling in love with Jesus and expressing that love by trusting Him for everything.

Now Let's Take a Moment and Pray Together:

Dear Lord Jesus, I do love You, but I want to fall in love with You all over again right now. I want the kind of love that makes me want to trust You by faith for the impossible. Lord, do whatever it takes in my life to cause that to happen. Teach me how to express my love for You through faith. I am willing to learn. Make my life glorifying to You. Thank You, Lord Jesus. Amen.

Chapter 12

Misconceptions

"He who lives by faith is as unchanging as God; he expresses
the same kind of life through darkness or through light."
Watchman Nee (1)

*I*n chapter two we talked about a number of hindrances to beginning in faith. One we mentioned briefly was <u>incorrectness regarding the truth of faith</u>. In this chapter we are going to expand on that by discussing some commonly held misconceptions about what real faith actually is. Just a few wrong ideas about what spiritual faith is, and how it operates, is all it takes to prevent even the most sincere Believer from getting started. Of course, these incorrect and often innocently held views are fostered by the devil in an attempt to create enough confusion to prevent real faith from ever taking root in the Christian's life. Distortion of spiritual truth comes from looking at the things of God from a natural, human point of view, and that is always satan's temptation. The key to understanding real God-faith, and all other spiritual truths and concepts, is to simply get on God's side of the page. To help us do just that, let's look again at our operational definition of real Bible faith, **"Choosing to act upon the revealed will of God, using power and resources that only He has access to."** Internalizing that definition will help dispel some of the wrong ideas we may have about faith. Now let's look at some of them .

Misconception #1 – Faith Is Only for a Select Group of People

The first wrong idea is that living by faith is only for a special few – not for everyone. Most Christians believe that living by faith is for some one else. It is only for missionaries, or evangelists, or some other type of Christian worker who does not have an underwritten income. Or it is for people who are going through some sort of trial or crisis. This wrong view has greatly weakened the church throughout the world, especially the Western world. The church is dangerously anemic because it works so diligently and successfully at modeling itself after the secular, corporate world system. It works hard at insulating itself from actually having to trust God for anything. The problem, though, is that a faithless life is a spiritually powerless life. And a faithless church is a spiritually powerless church, no matter how large, prestigious, or prosperous it may be. Power against the rulers of darkness is not determined by how much money is in the bank, how large the building is, or by how many members are in the pews. Spiritual power is determined by one thing only, our ability and our choice to believe God for His will.

I was recently talking with a lady about the subject of faith and she asked a question that reflected just what we are talking about. She said, "Well some Christians don't have to live by faith, do they?" I asked what she meant by that question and she said, "Well some Christians don't have any problems or needs or trials and therefore don't have any reason to live by faith." I said to her, "Okay, let me get this straight; what you are saying is that the Christian who is financially secure, has a good family, a good marriage, no kids on drugs, no health problems, no trials, is involved in church and is living a 'good Christian life' has no need of faith." She said, "Yes, that is exactly what I mean. I know a lot of people like that and they seem to have no reason to live by faith." Her question, though sincere, revealed that she had bought into the same wrong view of faith that is held by so many Believers. The reason we are to live by faith is not just to provide a safety net for us in times of crisis but to bring glory to God and expand His Kingdom.

I agree with the lady in that there are certainly a lot of people who fit the description she outlined. Their life is very secure (at least for the moment), very well ordered, and comfortable. It forms a very neat and attractive package. But the question is, does the package bring glory to God? It can, if it is a product of faith and believing God. More often, however, that is not the case. Rather it is often a product of self and self-effort. The truth is that most Christians work very hard at arranging things so they do not have to trust God at all - for anything - ever! Why is that? It is because most Christians view and use faith as a "last resort" when nothing else works, rather than a first choice. They often equate faith with a life of trouble, poverty, risk, foolishness, uncertainty and despair, rather than what it really is; a life of power, adventure, abundance, assurance, peace and supernatural cooperation with God in His eternal enterprises.

Now to further address the question of whether or not faith is for every Christian, let's look at the Word of God. First of all, when Jesus exhorted His followers to believe Him by faith, was He talking to just a few of them or to all of them? The answer is obvious. Once again, in Romans 1:17,

Galatians 3:11, and Hebrews 10:38, we are told, *"The just* [saved] *shall live by faith."* Is that talking about just some saved people or all of us? Again the answer is obvious. Romans 3:27-28 tells us that we are saved by the "law of faith." Does the law of gravity apply to just a select group of people or do all people who jump off of a rooftop fall to the ground? The reason something is called a law is because it applies to everyone, and faith is no exception. All human beings live and exist by the natural laws of the physical world, and likewise all Believers are to live by the spiritual law of faith. The Bible tells us that it is by faith that the grace of God is accessed (Romans 4:16), that we are to walk (II Corinthians 5:7), that we are protected (Ephesians 6:16), that we please God (Hebrews 11:6), that we endure trials (I Peter 1:7), and that we have victory (I John 5:4). Do these truths apply to just some Christians or to all? Obviously, they apply to all. The key issue in every Believer's relationship with Jesus is faith. Every child of God is to live by faith, without exception or exemption. Again, Hebrews 11:6 tells us *"But without **faith** it is **impossible** to please him..."* Very often the individual or church that has no *perceivable* need has the *greatest* need of all, because the thing that is needed most is an opportunity to see the reality of God. Dear friend, the Bible is clear, the faith life is for every Christian - including YOU.

Misconception #2 - Faith Is Only for Occasional, Critical Situations

Many Christians, even those who believe that faith is for them personally, still hold the erroneous view that it is only to be used sporadically from time to time when a crisis arises, or when we find ourselves in more trouble than we can get ourselves out of. Faith is looked upon as just another tool in the spiritual toolbox to be taken out, dusted off, and used in special situations of extreme need and trial. Sadly, most Christians treat trusting God as something they do only when they are forced to as a last alternative. It's like finally giving up and going to the doctor when you are sick and you realize you are not going to get over it without a shot or a prescription. The problem with this kind of thinking is that God never *forces* His child to do anything, including trusting Him. Additionally, faith should never be our last choice, but our first. Faith is for ALL times, good or bad, favorable or adverse. Just as the whole of our human existence is a walk of faith in the natural realm, the whole of our Christian life is to be a walk of faith in the spiritual realm. Remember that **God-faith is acting (at all times) upon the revealed will of God (in every situation) using power and**

resources that only <u>God</u> has access to. That applies to every moment we live as a child of God, not just times of trouble. The truth of the matter is that there should be no activity or decision in our Christian life that is not the product of faith exercised toward God in obedience to His leading. Another problem with "faith as a last resort" thinking is that if we are not accustomed to exercising faith on a continual basis, it will be very difficult to do so in a time of crisis. A crisis moment is the wrong time to try to learn faith. It cannot be done as a "crash course." The time to learn CPR is **before** you have occasion to use it. You certainly wouldn't want to have to read and learn the instructions while trying to administer it. <u>Faith is action not reaction</u>. It is positive not negative. The Christian who is living by faith will be prepared for the crisis long before it arises. Adverse circumstances may awaken us to the need for the <u>activation</u> of faith but they will not teach us faith. Trials are not designed to teach us faith, but if we are trusting God they will always <u>demonstrate</u> faith. Trials give us opportunity to live out what we have ALREADY learned. Oswald Chambers puts it this way, "The big crisis will only reveal the stuff we are made of, it will not put anything into us" (2).

Misconception # 3 - Faith Is a Blind Leap in the Dark, into the Unknown

God faith is NOT blind. It is not a leap in the dark. Rather, it is crystal clear vision and a step into the light. Let's look again at the first part of our definition of faith, "Faith is **acting** upon the **revealed will** of God…" It is intelligent, deliberate acting upon the guarantee of God. Faith is persuasion of *fact* followed by corresponding *action*. An example of faith from the natural realm is sitting in a chair. You see it, judge it reliable, and sit in it. You would never ask a guest to sit in a chair that isn't there. In the same way, God will never ask His child to believe Him for something that does not exist or for something He is not going to do. <u>Faith is hearing God tell us what He is going to do and then acting and speaking in accordance with what He says</u>. There is nothing blind, vague, abstract, or uncertain about that. I have heard people say something like, "Well, I don't know what else to do so I guess I'll just have to step out on faith." What they are saying is that their ideas and schemes in the visible realm haven't worked, so as a last ditch effort they are going to attempt to "step out on faith." Sadly, most Christians don't have a clue as to what that means. The phrase itself implies two wrong beliefs. The first is that it is stepping **out**. Many times I have heard people say, "I guess I'm just going to have to go out on a limb with God." You don't step **out** on faith, you step **in**. Trusting God does not take you out on a limb, to a place of danger, uncertainty, and risk. It brings you back to the Trunk, the Lord Jesus, the place of safety, certainty, and security. The second wrong belief concerns the meaning of the words "on faith." In the minds of most people that phrase implies "on nothing," at least on nothing tangible or solid. We do not have faith in faith. We have faith (or trust) in GOD Himself and in His will. "Stepping out on faith" guarantees nothing, but venturing all on <u>God</u> guarantees everything. What we need is to step <u>in</u> to the will of God, trusting <u>Him</u> to bring it to pass. <u>That</u> is faith.

The only sense in which real faith is blind is that it is blind (and deaf) to opposition from the world, the flesh, and the devil. The world system will always tell us how foolish and impractical it is to trust God and what fools we are for attempting to live the life of faith. Even some Christians will advise us to "just be normal" like everyone else. Then the flesh (our emotions and intellect) will always tell us that it doesn't make good common sense to trust in what we "can't see." And of course satan is always on hand to threaten us by telling us that God is not only going to take us out on an unreliable limb, but He is also going to saw it off behind us. It is the same lie He told Eve in the Garden of Eden, that God cannot be trusted. But, dear Believer, there is nothing more sensible or practical than total trust and absolute reliance upon the all-knowing, all-powerful, and all-present God of the universe. Real God-faith is not foolish and it is not a blind leap into the dark. It is a practical, sure-footed step into the light of God's will settled in eternity. It is entering into the "finished work."

Misconception # 4 – Faith Is Based in the Future

As strange as it may sound, real faith is NOT based in the future; it is based in the PAST! It is not believing in what we <u>want</u> to have or what we <u>might</u> have; it is believing in what we <u>already</u> have. Real faith is not trusting for what <u>will</u> happen, but in what has <u>already</u> happened. We will cover this more fully later on, but for the moment we need to drive this truth home in our thinking. It is **foundational** to our understanding of the operation of faith. As we said earlier, you would not attempt to sit in a chair that does not exist. You cannot eat food that is not there and you cannot spend cash that you do not have in your pocket. Natural faith is taking and using what your senses and intellect tell you that you already have in the natural realm. By the same token, spiritual faith is taking and using what God tells you that you already have in the spiritual realm, whether it is an object or an outcome. As we stated before, real faith is entering into the finished work of God. Hebrews 4:3 says, "...the works [of God] were finished from the foundation of the world." Then in chapter 11, verse 1 we also read, "Now faith is the substance [the assurance, the title deed] of things hoped for, the evidence [proof] of things not seen." Now let's look at one more verse, Mark 11:24, "Therefore I say unto you, what things soever ye desire [in the will of God], when ye pray, believe that ye [have already] receive[d] them [past tense], and ye shall have them." As I said, we will deal with this more later, but for the moment let's just observe that the reason that trusting God by faith is so practical is that it is simply acting in agreement with what He has already provided and with what He has already accomplished. Granted, from the human perspective it looks like future, but from God's point of view it is all in the past. God does not have a "future." From His viewpoint it is all completed. Again, it is a matter of looking at things from God's side of the page. When we do, we see much more clearly.

Misconception # 5 - Faith Begins with Me

There are seven stages in the faith process (which we will discuss in Chapter 22). The first is the establishment of an atmosphere for faith in our life and the second is the *activation* (or initiation) of the actual process. Now the question is who does the activating? The answer is God. Real Bible faith **always** begins and ends with God. "*Looking unto Jesus, the author and finisher of our faith...*" (Heb. 12:2). In spiritual faith, whether in relation to salvation or to Christian living, God always takes the initiative in providing opportunity for His child to believe Him for the impossible. Looking into the lives and experiences of the disciples, you will see that trusting Jesus for something that took them beyond their own abilities and resources was never their idea. The same was true in the lives of the heroes of faith in Hebrews eleven. It was not Moses' idea to go to the Red Sea. It was not Abraham's idea to go to the mountain to sacrifice Isaac, and it was not Elijah's preconceived idea to end up at Mount Carmel after leaving Gilead. In I Kings 17:4 we find the Lord telling Elijah, "*And it shall be, that thou shalt drink of the brook; and I have commanded the ravens to feed thee there.*" Then in verse nine we read, "*Arise, get thee to Zarephath, which belongeth to Zidon, and dwell there; behold, I have commanded a widow woman there to sustain thee.*" The key word in these verses is there. Each step of obedience brought Elijah closer to the ultimate "there," Mount Carmel, where God would be glorified. In the life of every saint it was God Who took the initiative and arranged for the individual to come to a place where the choice of faith had to be made. The same is true for you and me. God is always working to bring each of us to our own individual "there" where we can choose to believe for the impossible and see the glory of God. The question we must all answer is, are we willing for God to do that?

There are basically five means by which God draws us into the exercise of faith. They are <u>need</u>, <u>desire</u>, His <u>Word</u>, <u>prompting</u> from the Holy Spirit and <u>calling</u>. The only sense in which we activate the faith process is by placing ourselves in a position to hear God speak, receiving the knowledge of His will in our spirit, and then making the choice to believe (act in accordance with) what He says. But even the desire to "get in position" comes from God. Dear friend, is that desire rising up in your heart as you read this book? I suspect it is, and the reason is that God is putting it there. Your part is to simply yield to the drawing of the Holy Spirit in your life and let Him take you "there."

Misconception # 6 – Some Christians Have More Faith Than Others

How often have you heard some one say, "Well, I guess I just need more faith," or "I just don't have enough faith to get through this." Or how about this one, "I guess God is testing me to see if I have enough faith." Do those statements sound right to you? They shouldn't, because they are terribly wrong. They come from a serious misconception about faith – that one person has more than another. **Faith is not a <u>quantity</u> possessed; it is a <u>capacity</u> exercised**. The capacity for faith does not differ from one Christian to another. Jesus did not discriminate from one disciple to another in His repeated commands to exercise faith. He did not tell Peter, "Oh that's okay Peter, you don't have to believe as much as John, because after all, you don't have as much faith as he does." No, His demands were equal for all the disciples, because they were all equipped with the same capacity to believe.

In Matthew 17:14–21, we find the disciples trying to cast a demon out of a young boy, and they could not do it. So they brought the boy to Jesus and He did it. Afterwards they asked Jesus why they could not do it and He answered in verse 20, *"Because of your unbelief..."* We said earlier that there are two Greek words translated "unbelief." The first, "apeithia", means to obstinately oppose the will of God. It is a refusal to believe. It means no faith. The second, "apistia", means weakness in faith, not the absence of it. It is the second word Jesus used here with the disciples. What He was telling them is that the amount of faith is not the issue; it is the exercise of it that matters – or in this case, the failure to exercise. He made that point by telling them that even the smallest amount of faith, even *"as a grain of mustard seed"* would be enough to move mountains and produce the impossible. Again in Luke 17:5 we find the disciples asking Jesus to *"increase our faith."* The word they used was the word "prostithemi", which also means to strengthen. What they needed was not "more faith," but to exercise or strengthen what they already had. Again Jesus makes the same point with the mustard seed example. What they needed was not more capacity to believe, but to make the choice to believe.

The capacity for faith does not differ from one Believer to another, but what does differ from one to another is the <u>sphere or area of faith</u>, the area or parameters in which it operates. Those parameters are set by the will of God. In Romans 12:3 Paul wrote, *"For I say through the grace given unto me, to every man that is among you, not to think of himself more highly than he ought to think; but to think soberly, according as God hath dealt to every man the measure of faith."* Why should one man not think more highly of himself than another? Because, they were all equal. The key to understanding Paul's message in this verse is to understand the meaning of the words "dealt" and "measure." It would appear at first glance that he is talking about a quantity such as water in a bucket or grain in a bag, but that is not the case. Rather he is talking about a sphere or area. In his *Expository Dictionary of New Testament Words,* W.E. Vine gives this definition of the word "dealt" (Gr. merizo), "to divide into parts, a portion, to distribute, to divide out"(3). Then he gives two definitions for the word "measure" (Gr. metron). The first is "a container or measuring stick, a measuring device." The second is "that which is measured, a determined extent, a portion measured off, Romans 12:3, II Corinthians 10:13, Ephesians 4:7" (4).

In II Corinthians 10:13-16, Paul is talking about the scope of his ministry, and in doing so he gives a very clear picture of the meaning of the word "measure" (metron) as it is used in this verse and in Romans 12:3. Let's look at it, *"But we will not boast of things without our measure* [area], *but according to the measure* [area] *of the rule* [field of ministry] *which God hath distributed to us, a measure* [area] *to reach even unto you."* In verse 14 he says, *"For we stretch not ourselves beyond our measure* [area of ministry]... *"* Then in verse 16, Paul says, *"To preach the gospel in the regions beyond you, and not to boast in another man's line* [area of ministry] *of things made ready to our hand."* The idea set forth here is that of territory and authority. **God establishes, within the circumference of His will, in each one of our lives, a territory for our faith to operate in**. He gives us authority to believe (that is, carry out the activity of faith) up to the limits of that territory.

God has not given you an "amount" of faith, or even an "ability" of faith, that differs from any other Believer. What He has given you that differs from others is a sphere of faith, an area of faith, a commission of faith, or a field of faith. You could also say it is a jurisdiction of faith. Our state, Tennessee, is divided (like every state) into counties, and each county has within it law enforcement officers. Now, the sheriff of our county, McNairy, has jurisdiction or authority all over the county, but not across the county line. Once you cross over into the neighboring county, the authority moves to another sheriff. Both men have the same exact kind of authority and the same exact amount, but they exercise it in different areas. Think of God's will as if it was a state divided into counties or as a large country divided into states. You see, the capacity of faith, or the jurisdiction of faith, that God has given me does not encompass his entire will, but it does encompass some of it. My responsibility as a child of God is to know His will for ME, to know what my field of faith is and to trust God for that. I am not responsible for what happens in the next county or state – that is someone else's concern, and it is between them and the Father. The question we should ask ourselves is not how much faith do I have, but what is my field of faith and am I trusting God for everything that lies within that area.

God called my wife and me to oversee an international ministry and to do it without soliciting funds, and for the past thirty years we have focused our capacity of faith in that direction. As a result, we have seen God perform one miracle after another. We have exercised our God-given authority to act in faith within our God-given sphere or territory. Now, you might say, "There is absolutely no way I could live like that." You are probably right. But why? Why can we do it and you can't? Is it because we have more faith than you? Absolutely not. What we do have is a commission from God that you do not have. The reason we can trust God by faith for the operation of our ministry, and you cannot, is because it is God's will for our lives and not yours. But, by the same token, there are many things you can believe God for and we can't, because they are in your sphere of faith, your commission, your area or field, and not ours. George Muller of Bristol, England fed and housed over 2,000 orphans every day and never asked for a penny. How could he do that when others couldn't? He could do it because God gave him the authority to believe within a certain commission that included the care of those orphans. You can see that it is crucially important for every Christian to know God's will in relation to the various areas of his life, because it is God's will that sets the boundaries for faith, defines faith, makes opportunity for faith, and provides for the fulfillment of faith.

You can also see that as born-again Believers, we may not excuse or exempt ourselves from living by faith by saying, "Well, I would live a life of trusting God, but I just don't have the faith that some people do." Dear friend, you have exactly the faith that every other Christian has, and you have the authority and responsibility within your commission from God to exercise it. Within the parameters of your province of faith God will reveal His will to you and will provide many opportunities for the operation, or the activity, of faith. When those opportunities come, don't ever say, "I guess God is just testing me to see if I have faith." He doesn't have to test you; He *knows* you have faith because He put the capacity for faith, the ability to believe, in you when you were born again. The big question we must all answer is not do I have faith, but am I willing for God to draw me into situations in which I am required to exercise the faith I have.

God has given a commission of faith, the scope of His will, to every child of His. It is like a vast land laid out before them just waiting to be discovered. The sad thing is that so many Christians never make the discovery. They are like some one who lands in a new world, but after coming ashore won't go any further than the beach they landed on. Can you imagine how much territory of faith has never been explored, discovered, and claimed by the children of God simply because so many have been deceived into believing they do not have the ability to make the discovery? How much blessing to the saint, and benefit to the Kingdom of God, has been forfeited because so many Christians have bought into the lie that they do not have enough faith. If the joy of seeing God perform the impossible through you is missing in your life, it is not because you do not have faith, or "enough faith." It is because you have not made the choice to begin exercising what you have. You will never have any more faith than you have right now, but as you exercise it you will have more and more opportunity.

Misconception # 7 – Faith Insulates Us from Trials and Suffering

There is a false and dangerous teaching being spread throughout the worldwide church today which says that if a Christian has enough faith he will not have trials, poverty, sickness, or suffering in his life. Dear friend that is a lie from hell and cannot be substantiated anywhere in Scripture. The implication is that if a Believer has trials and suffering in his life it is his own fault because he does not have enough faith. That is such a damning accusation that only satan could be the source of it. Trials, poverty, sickness and suffering are part of the common human experience as a result of the fall and the presence of sin in the human race. They are unavoidable, and they occur in every person's life, even Christians who are legitimately trusting God with real Spirit-energized, God-honoring faith.

In Hebrews 11, we find a wonderful list of ordinary people whom God used to accomplish extraordinary feats because they chose to believe God. Noah built the Ark, Abraham became the Father of Israel, Sarah miraculously gave birth, Moses forsook Egypt and led Israel through the Red Sea, and on and on the list goes. Wonderful! Fantastic! Amazing! Yes, there is a marvelous list of people in the Great Hall of Faith who did great exploits of faith and lived to tell the story. But then there is another list. In verses 35-39 we are told that many of those who were trusting God by faith were tortured, sawn asunder, stoned, slain with the sword, wandered about in sheepskins and goatskins, were destitute, afflicted and tormented. What was wrong with those people? Why did they not stay healthy, get rich, and avoid trials and suffering? Did they not have faith? Yes, dear Christian, they had faith, real God-honoring faith. Verse 39 says, *"And these all, having obtained a good report* [God's approval] *through faith..."* As we will talk about later, it is not just the outcome of faith that honors God, but it is also the process.

The men and women throughout Christian history who have made the greatest impact for the Kingdom of God are those who lived by faith and at the same time suffered greatly. I Peter 4:19 clearly indicates that there are times when the will of God involves suffering, *"Wherefore let them that suffer according to the will of God commit the keeping of their souls to him in well-doing, as unto a faithful Creator."* There are times when faith will deliver you from the storm, the trial, the suffering, but there are other times when it takes you <u>through</u> it. There are times when faith <u>overcomes</u> hardship and poverty, but there are also many times when it <u>sustains you in it</u>. For the first seven years of our ministry my wife and I did not know more than twenty-four hours at a time, humanly speaking, where our next meal was coming from, but we were sustained by real faith. There have been many times when we have seen God provide miraculously with great abundance, but there have also been many times when we have had to hang on day by day waiting upon God. Does that mean we had faith one time and not another? No, it simply means that God does it both ways and He receives glory in each case. Sometimes the miracle of faith is in the abundant supply and sometimes it is in the supernatural ability to wait upon God in the midst of extreme trial and suffering. If trials, suffering, poverty, and hardship indicate a lack of faith, then the apostle Paul, the Lord's disciples, and even Jesus Himself were all failures in faith. Dear friend, a faith-filled life may not be free of trials and suffering, but it will be filled with victory. Real faith does not always produce what the world calls "success," but it always brings glory to God. Real success for the Christian is doing the will of God, and sometimes that involves trials and sufferings. When you go through a trial, that does not mean you are a substandard Christian; it means God is trusting you with an opportunity to trust Him by faith and bring glory to His Name.

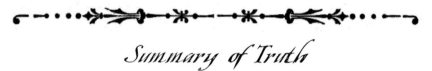

Summary of Truth

- Spiritual power is determined by our ability and choice to believe God.
- Most Christians work harder at not trusting God than they do at believing.
- It is the will of God for every Christian to live by faith.
- Living by faith is not just for special occasions but for every moment of life.
- Living by faith is not a blind leap into the dark; it is a step into the light of God's will.
- Real faith is based upon the finished work of the will of God.
- The process of real faith always begins by God's initiation, not mine.
- Every Christian has the same capacity of faith; it is only the application that changes from one life to another.
- Faith does not prevent trials and suffering, rather it provides a way to endure them and pass through them.
- Times of trial provide opportunities to trust God by faith and bring glory to His name.

NOW LET'S TAKE A MOMENT AND PRAY TOGETHER:

DEAR FATHER, THANK YOU FOR BRINGING CLARITY AND UNDERSTANDING TO MY MIND AND HEART CONCERNING THESE MISCONCEPTIONS ABOUT FAITH. HELP ME TO FULLY ADJUST MY THINKING ABOUT ALL THESE THINGS. HELP ME TO SEE THEM AS YOU SEE THEM. LORD, I DO WANT TO LIVE BY REAL FAITH, AND I DO WANT TO GLORIFY YOU THROUGH MY LIFE. LORD, OPEN MY UNDERSTANDING TO THE TRUTHS CONTAINED IN THESE PAGES, AND HELP ME APPLY THEM TO MY LIFE. THANK YOU, LORD JESUS, FOR SAVING ME, KEEPING ME, AND FOR USING ME IN THE DAYS TO COME. I LOVE YOU, LORD JESUS. IN YOUR NAME I PRAY. AMEN

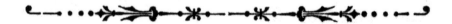

The Faith Life Is a Spirit-Filled Life
Part One:
What It Means to Be Spirit-Filled

"The opposite of sight and feeling is faith. Now it is the soulish person who gains assurance by grasping the things which can be seen and felt, but the person who follows the spirit lives by faith, not by sight."
Watchman Nee (1)

Upon looking at this chapter title you may wonder why we are including one about the Spirit-filled life in a book about faith. Should that not be in a book about the Christian life in general? Well, as we have said before, the faith-life IS the Christian life. Dr. J. Dwight Pentecost expressed it this way, "God has only one operating principle - the faith principle. A man is saved by faith, a Christian walks by faith, a child of God lives by faith, a soldier of God fights by faith. The Christian life is a faith life, step by step" (2). To understand the necessity of talking about being Spirit-filled we have only to look at our operational definition of faith (Choosing to act upon the revealed will of God using power and resources that only He has access to). The key phrase we are dealing with here is **the revealed will of God**. There are two crucial truths we will discuss fully later. The first is that the process of real faith begins with knowing the will of God, and the second is that the will of God is revealed only to the spirit of man by the Holy Spirit - not through intellect, emotion, environment, human influence, or circumstances. It therefore follows that if a person is going to receive the will of God, he must be proper spiritual condition to do so. He must be a Spirit-filled believer in order to hear the voice of God. I Kings 19:12 tells us God's voice is "still and small," detectable only to a sensitive spirit that is controlled by the Holy Spirit. I Corinthians 2:14 says, *"...the things of the Spirit of God...are spiritually discerned."* In the things of God, trust is a two-way street. In order for me to trust God, I must first be in a condition for Him to trust me.

What I mean is, I cannot believe God for anything without knowing His will first, but He will not trust me with the knowledge of His will without me being in a spiritual condition to receive it. The exercise of real God faith takes place from within the spirit. Therefore, in order to be a faith-filled Christian (II Corinthians 5:7), you must first be a Spirit-filled Christian (Galatians 5:25). In the Greek, the word "filled" means "controlled." When we are Spirit-filled, we are being controlled by the Spirit of God. When we are not Spirit-filled, we are being controlled by ourselves, our flesh. Which state we are in, at any moment, depends on our obedience.

Baptism and Filling

Before dealing specifically with the process of being filled with the Holy Spirit, we are first going to observe that there is a difference between being <u>baptized</u> with the Spirit of God and being <u>filled</u>. We read in I Corinthians 12:13, *"For by one Spirit are we all **baptized** into one body, whether we be Jews or Gentiles, whether we be bond or free; and have been all made to drink into one Spirit."* Then in Ephesians 5:18 we read, *"And be not drunk with wine, wherein is excess; but be **filled** with the Spirit."* The word "baptized" means to be immersed or placed into, and the word "filled" means to be controlled or dominated, in the sense that the thing that is doing the filling or controlling is replacing everything else. An example from the natural world would be the condition I was in before I came to Jesus. Before I was saved, I was "baptized" and "filled" but with the wrong thing. I was not only immersed in the secular music business, but it was in me, it "filled" (controlled) me and dominated every area and every minute of my life. Thank God all that has now been replaced with new life in Jesus Christ.

> The Christian life does not depend upon the strength of the Christian. Strength in the Christian life is Jesus Christ. Power in the Christian life is Jesus Christ. We may appropriate that strength and power by faith.
>
> *J. Dwight Pentecost (3)*

I Corinthians 12:13 presents a statement of fact, which says that all Believers <u>are baptized</u> (placed into) one body, the body of Christ, as a living member. That happens at the moment of salvation. It is a once and for all event that cannot be undone and cannot be done a second time. It is a past event in the life of every Believer. Ephesians 5:18, on the other hand, is not a statement of fact but a command. The Greek verb translated "be filled" is in the imperative mood and the present tense, which means two things: first, it is a command and second, it is continuous action. It does not say all Christians ARE Spirit-filled, rather it is a command to BE Spirit-filled, indicating that all Believers CAN be if they CHOOSE to be. It literally means, "Be continually getting filled."

Baptism with the Holy Spirit is once for all and never repeated, but filling is repeated daily, hourly throughout the Christian life. The verb is also in the passive voice, which means that we are not commanded to fill ourselves, but for the Holy Spirit (the One Who indwells our "temple," our life) to possess and continuously control every part of it and every minute of it. Baptism deals with our **union** with Jesus (we are joined to His <u>person</u>), but filling deals with our **communion** with Him (we are filled with His <u>power</u>). Baptism affects our **relationship** with Jesus while filling affects our **fellowship** with Him. Holy Spirit baptism provides deliverance from the **penalty** of sin once and for all, while filling provides deliverance from the **power** of sin in our daily walk. Holy Spirit baptism makes you a "new creature in Christ", while being controlled by the Holy Spirit enables you to live like the new creature you have become. Baptism gives you life **eternal** and filling gives you life **more abundant**. The result of Spirit baptism is a **changed** life and the result of Spirit filling is a supernatural, spiritually **energized** life. Baptism gives you **position** <u>in</u> Christ and filling gives you **power** to live <u>for</u> Christ. Holy Spirit baptism **provides the potential** for a holy life while filling **produces the practice** of a holy life.

Salvation is optional for the unsaved, but being filled with, or controlled by, the Holy Spirit is a command to every Christian without exception or exemption. Ruth Paxson expressed it this way, "Be filled with the Spirit is a command given to every Believer. No Christian is refused the blessing of such a precious experience and none is exempt from its responsibilities. As the refusal of life in Christ is the greatest sin of the unbeliever so the refusal of life more abundant in the Holy Spirit's fullness is the greatest sin of the Believer. To be filled with the Holy Spirit is not the privilege of a few, but it is the prerogative of all Believers. Since it is a command, it is not optional, but it is incumbent upon <u>every</u> Christian" (4).

Natural - Spiritual

In relationship to God, there are two categories of people, those who are connected to Him (the saved) and those who are separated from Him (the unsaved). A saved person is one who has received Christ as Savior and is indwelt by the Spirit of God. An unsaved person is one who has not received Christ and is void of the Spirit of God. An unsaved person is "natural"; his or her human spirit has not been brought to life through the new birth. He or she is alive physically, intellectually, emotionally, and volitionally, but that is all. The saved person, on the other hand, is "spiritual"; he or she has not only been born physically and soulishly but also spiritually. A saved person is a member of two families, earthly and heavenly.

Now, if all saved people are "spiritual" in terms of their relationship to God, then why does Paul address the Christians in Corinth the way he did when he said, "And I, brethren, could not speak unto you as unto spiritual, but as unto carnal, even as unto babes in Christ (1 Corinthians 3:1)." They were obviously saved people (brethren - babes in Christ) and yet Paul does not classify them as spiritual, but carnal. Why does he do that? The answer is found in verse three with Paul's indicting question, "are ye not carnal, and walk as men?" Paul calls them "carnal", which means fleshly or soulish, because they were still very immature. They had not grown to the reasonable level of spirituality that he expected from them. They were saved, but they were still living very much like people who are not. When Paul called them carnal, he was not speaking in the sense of salvation. He was speaking in terms of the way they were conducting their Christian life.

Sadly, there are many born-again believers in the modern church that seem to have the same problem as the Christians in Corinth. They are saved, but because of a lack of teaching or wrong teaching or some other reason, they are immature in their growth in Christ. They are spiritual, positionally, in that their human spirit has been brought to life by the Holy Spirit. But practically, they are "carnally-minded", because as a general rule of life they still rely more upon self (intellect, emotion, and will), than upon the Holy Spirit Who indwells them. In terms of his or her daily walk, a spiritual, or "spiritually-minded", Christian is one who sincerely endeavors to adjust the many aspects of life to the guidance and influence of the Holy Spirit. A carnal, or "carnally-minded" Christian is one who usually does not. In relation to daily living, every Christian has two options available to him at any given moment - to walk in obedience to, and reliance upon, the Holy Spirit or to walk by the thoughts, desires, and impulses of the flesh (his own intellect, emotions, and will). We therefore have this instruction from Galatians 5:16, *"Walk in the Spirit, and ye shall not fulfil the lust of the flesh."* It is incumbent upon every child of God to assume responsibility for his or her own personal walk with God. Failure to do so results in a carnallly-minded Christian life.

So what assessment should be made regarding a person who has supposedly received Christ and yet never takes on the likeness of a child of God? II Corinthians 5:17 says, "Therefore if any man be in Christ, he is a new creature: old things are passed away; behold, all things are become new." Scripture is very clear that a saved person will eventually become a changed person. If a person is truly spiritual positionally, he will become spiritual practically as well. If that does not happen, then he should give very serious consideration to whether or not he has genuinely been born of the Spirit of God. The likelihood is that he has not.

Earlier we talked about three types of life pictured in the Old Testament – Egypt life, Wilderness life and Canaan life. The unsaved are pictured as those who were living in slavery in Egypt prior to God's miraculous deliverance. The Spirit-filled Christian is the one who has entered into God's Promised Land of Canaan, that place of God's supernatural peace, power, provision, and protection. The third person is the one who has been delivered out from under the bondage of sin, but has not gone on into the spiritual

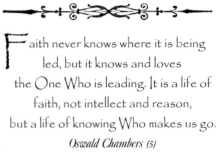

Faith never knows where it is being led, but it knows and loves the One Who is leading. It is a life of faith, not intellect and reason, but a life of knowing Who makes us go.

Oswald Chambers (5)

land of Canaan. He is living in the Wilderness and wandering in circles. He belongs to God, but is living a powerless life. It may be active and busy, but it is accomplishing nothing for God's Kingdom. That is the picture of the carnally-minded Christian. He may or may not be outwardly sinful, but he is inwardly living in the sin of unbelief. Because of that unbelief, he is continually robbed of experiencing the deeper life that God desires to draw all of His children into, the Spirit-filled life of real faith.

Carnally-Minded or Spiritually-Minded

To further our understanding of what it means to be a faith-filled spiritual Believer, we are going to compare carnally-minded with spiritually-minded. The word "carnal" is translated from the Greek word "sarkikos", which is derived from the word "sarx" meaning "flesh." It refers to everything about us that is human, that is, the body and soul (intellect, emotions and will). Again it is important to note that carnal does not necessarily mean sinful in the sense of outward practices such as immorality, anger, drunkenness, gossip, stealing, or lying. In fact, it is possible for a person to conform to Christian culture and maintain the appearance of a clean life in terms of outward behavior and still be a carnally-minded Christian. There are many Believers who attend church, give their offerings, read the Bible, pray, and serve in leadership positions yet live lives that have not been brought into subjection to the Holy Spirit. Believe it or not (and sad to say) some are even pastors, evangelists, seminary professors, and missionaries.

Carnality means to be controlled by, and dependent upon, self rather than the Holy Spirit. Romans 8:5 says, *"They that are after the flesh* [self], *do mind the things of the flesh; but they that are after the Spirit the things of the Spirit."* The Greek word for "mind" means "to regard, to show interest in, to pay attention to, to entertain, or to obey." A carnally-minded Believer lives by the impulses and stimulation of intellect, emotions, and external influences rather than by the directives of the Holy Spirit. His life is soulish. The Spirit-filled child of God, on the other hand, lives a life of obedience to the inner guidance of the Holy Spirit. The spiritually minded Believer is driven and motivated by the will of God, and the

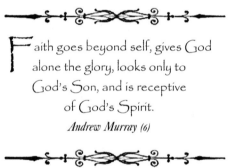

Faith goes beyond self, gives God alone the glory, looks only to God's Son, and is receptive of God's Spirit.

Andrew Murray (6)

carnally-minded Believer is driven and motivated by ideas and impulses that originate from within his own natural thoughts and feelings. A Spirit-filled person operates by God's interests, the carnal person operates by self-interests. Sometimes the differences from one side of that page to the other can be hard to see apart from the revealing light of the Holy Spirit. There are many church members and Christian workers who have been deceived into believing that they are all out for God when in reality, deep in their hearts, they are acting out of their own self aim and interests. They are often very active and involved in many good works. The problem, however, is that they are just that, "good" works, not GOD works. In order for his life and ministry to truly count for God, every Christian should lay himself bare before God and ask the Holy Spirit to reveal the deep, secret motives of his heart. To be truly effective and pleasing to God, he must be Spirit-filled, because only by being Spirit-filled can he live by real God-honoring faith.

God's Word warns us, *"...to be carnally minded is death; but to be spiritually minded is life and peace. Because the carnal mind is enmity against God: for it is not subject to the law of God, neither indeed can be. So then they that are in the flesh cannot please God"* (Romans 8:6-8). That applies to church members, ministers, and Christian workers alike. No matter how sincere, religious or hardworking we may be, it is not possible to live by the flesh and live by faith at the same time. They are contrary one to the other. Therefore in Galatians 5:16-17 Paul exhorts, *"This I say then, Walk in the Spirit, and ye shall not fulfill the lust* [strong desire] *of the flesh. For the flesh lusteth* [sets its desire] *against the Spirit, and the Spirit* [sets its desire] *against the flesh: and these are contrary the one to the other: so that ye cannot do the things that ye would."* The word "lust" means "craving" and the word "flesh" is the same as the "self." So Paul is saying that if we walk (live) by the Spirit then we will fulfill the desire of the Spirit rather than the cravings of self. He goes on to say in verses 24-25, *"And they that are Christ's have crucified the flesh* [self] *with the affections and lusts* [desires]. *If we live in the Spirit, let us also walk in the Spirit."* Again, the cravings of the flesh (self) may not be for things that are sensual, addictive, dishonest, or hurtful to others. They may be for things that are more subtle and deceptive such as worldly success, ambition, recognition, power, popularity, prestige, possessions and money. The phrase "to lust" means to "set your heart upon." It is imperative to the life of real faith that we set our hearts upon the person, plan, purpose, power, and provision of God.

Again, the carnally-minded person is not carnal simply because he has yielded to sin or satan. He is carnal because he has yielded to self, to the flesh, and to the old nature. That, however, makes him an easy target for the devil, because satan always attacks from the outside in. His strategy is always to use an enticement or a threat from the physical world to make an appeal that begins in the mind and then moves to the emotions, with the goal to capture the will. A Christian who has his heart set upon the things of the flesh is easily enticed, and one who trusts self more than God is easily threatened. Satan's strategy will not work on a Spirit-filled believer, however, because the spiritually-minded Christian is operating from within his spirit, where satan has no access or influence. Our struggle as Christians is not so much with sin itself, but with the old nature (the old man, the carnally-minded self) which yields to temptation that <u>results</u> in sin. The carnally-minded person does not necessarily want to go the wrong or sinful way and do the wrong and sinful thing; He just wants to go HIS way and do

HIS thing in HIS time. The spiritual person wants to go GOD'S way and do GOD'S thing and is willing to wait on GOD'S timing.

The carnally-minded Christian lives a powerless, conflicted, and compromised life. He is trying to maintain a supernatural life, a spiritual work, and fellowship with God out of natural, soulish energy and fleshly resources, and it will not work. His efforts are doomed to failure, spiritual fatigue, discouragement, disillusionment, and defeat. The same is true for any Christian worker (pastor, evangelist, teacher, missionary), because he cannot sustain a spiritual ministry out of the energy of the flesh. If he tries, and many do, he will find himself immersed in a dead, powerless, faithless, frustrating and fruitless situation. The difference between a ministry that is a vibrant, reproducing, living, fruit-bearing <u>organism</u> and a ministry that is a dead, self-perpetuating <u>organization</u> is the presence and power of the Holy Spirit. HE makes ALL the difference! The only way possible for any Christian to fulfill the plan and purpose of God in his life is to live by real faith, which results in the supernatural power and provision of God. That can only happen if he is in a position to receive the will of God in his spirit, and that can only happen if he is filled with the Holy Spirit.

To begin to get an idea of which side of the page our Christian life is on, lets look at the list below which compares the carnally minded Christian with the spiritually minded one. It is by no means intended to be exhaustive, but it will at least give us an idea of where we are, where we need to be and where we want to be. We are going to divide the list into several different categories beginning with the Christian life in general.

THE CARNALLY- MINDED CHRISTIAN (Baptized but *Not* Filled)	THE SPIRITUALLY- MINDED CHRISTIAN (Baptized *And* Filled)

THE CHRISTIAN LIFE IN GENERAL

Lives according to the flesh	Lives according to the Spirit
Motivated by self interests	Motivated by God's interests
Christ only has a place IN his life	Christ IS his life – reigns supreme
Has Christ in his life, but needs more	Christ alone is enough
There is divided control over his life	God is in total control of his life
Tries to serve two masters	Jesus is his only Master

Maintains multiple identities	His only identity is with Jesus
Lives partly unto self and partly unto God	Lives in total surrender to God and gives Him unhindered access
Ignorant of the deep things of God	Knows, understands, and enjoys the deeper life
Tires easily of the things of God	Tires easily of things of the flesh
Ruled by common-sense peace	Ruled by the peace of God
Lives in spiritual infancy (1 Cor. 3:1)	Becomes a mature Believer
Lives defeated life, a roller coaster ride	Continuous victory, a steady walk
Little time for prayer, private worship	Much time spent with God alone
May attend church to show others he is dedicated	Desires real fellowship of other Believers
Wants to be entertained, made to feel good	Desires to be taught the Word and to grow
Wants to be ministered to	Desires to minister to others
May view worship as only corporate and/or emotional	Views real worship as private, spiritual
Superficial understanding of the Bible	Grasps deep truths of the Word
Often mistakes Bible head knowledge as real spirituality	Knows that real spirituality is being led by the Holy Spirit
Often excuses sin	Repents, makes no room for sin
Cannot genuinely praise God (Eph 5:19)	Praise is spontaneous and real
Gratitude to God is conditional (Eph 5:20)	Gratitude is continuous
Difficulty living under authority (Eph 5:22)	Joyously submits to authority
Lives his life in reserve	He is all out for Jesus
Leans toward will of the self and ways of the world	Leans towards the will and ways of God
Tends to be protective of self	Protective only of God's interests
Lives a spiritually irresponsible life	Lives as an ambassador for Christ
Has an independent attitude	Welcomes total dependence on God
Easily swayed by opinions, advice of men	Moved only by the will of God
Will talk about Jesus, but only with Christians	Wants to talk about Jesus ALL the time
Does not want to be thought of as foolish	Willing to be a fool for Christ
Material needs are primary– spiritual needs are secondary	Spiritual needs are primary– material needs are secondary .

THE WILL OF GOD

He cannot know the will of God, is void of spiritual knowledge	Filled with the understanding of God's will received in his spirit
Makes judgments based upon reason, logic, and common sense	Makes judgments based upon the will of God
Makes decisions based on circumstances	Relies on guidance from inner man
Reacts to external influence	Acts according to inner guidance
Will yield to outward pressure	Yields only to God's voice

FAITH

As a Christian he lives a "natural" life	Lives a supernatural life
Sees with the eyes of the flesh, cannot see into the invisible	Sees with the eyes of his spirit, sees beyond the visible
Hears only with the ears of intellect, reason, logic, and common sense	Hears the voice of God with his spirit, with his inner man
Operates by his own abilities, resources	Operates by God's power, resources
Afraid to exceed limits of self, the visible	Will boldly venture all on God
Tends to live in the safe harbor	Will launch out in faith
Mostly resides in the sensible and possible	Expects miraculous and impossible
Lives a limited life – cannot please God	Limitless life – pleasing to God
Tends to view faith as impractical	Views faith as only sensible approach
Reaches for goals	Believes for faith objects
Sees the desired outcome as a future event	Sees the desired outcome as a finished work

MINISTRY AND ACTIVITY

Moves by impulse	Moves by inspiration
Often has independent attitude	Desires to cooperate with others
Tends to have "localized" view of ministry	Tends to have world view
"How will it benefit MY ministry, MY church?"	"How will it benefit God's Kingdom?"
"How much will it cost?"	"Is it God's will?"
Often serves because he "ought to"	Serves with joy for love of Jesus
Seeks to work FOR God	Seeks God to work THROUGH him
Emphasis on WORK of the Lord	Emphasis on LORD of the work
Makes plans and sets goals and asks God to bless them.	Waits to know the plan of God and joins Him in it.
Can be done without the supernatural intervention of God.	Requires supernatural intervention and resources of God.
Can be satisfied with GOOD works	Satisfied only with GOD works
Measures success by human standards	Measures by spiritual standards
Often takes pride in and credit for results	Humbled by results, gives God credit
Can be happy and satisfied with activity that does not lead to changed lives	Deeply desires to see lives changed as a result of ministry
Often results in no real spiritual fruit	Bears real spiritual fruit
Often uses money, power, and position to influence people, circumstances	Relies upon faith and prayer to move men, circumstances
Tends to have little concern for souls	Deeply burdened for souls

GIVING

Views giving as a duty, obligation	Views giving as a joy, privilege
Sees his money and possessions as his own, he is the owner of what he has	Sees his money and possessions as God's, he is in management only
"How much MUST I give?"	"How much CAN I give?"

On one side of the page, in the comparative list above, we have looked at some of the characteristics and conditions of the carnally-minded person, as well as some of the resulting attitudes and practices produced by "walking after the flesh." On the other side of the page, we see the same as related to the spiritually-minded person who is living a Spirit-controlled life. As I said, the list is by no means exhaustive, but it should be enough to at least help us determine, as a true follower of Jesus Christ, which side we want to be on. The truth of the matter is, every Believer is living with one foot on one side of the page and one foot on the other. Whether we are "in the spirit" or "in the flesh" at any given moment is strictly dependant upon which way we lean - whether we are yielding to God or self. I sincerely believe, however, that once any born-again child of God has seen a clear picture of the carnal life versus the spiritual, he will desire to live a clean, faith-filled, fruit-bearing, God-honoring, Spirit-filled life.

What It Means to Be Spirit-Filled

We have already said that to "be filled" with the Spirit in Ephesians 5:18 means the Holy Spirit, Who came to indwell us at the moment of salvation, now takes complete and continuous control of every aspect of our life. But what does it mean to be "controlled" by the Holy Spirit? It means we are not just owned by God, but we are "owned and operated" by Him. It means that as Believers, we are **transformed** into totally different beings (Romans 12: 2). A Spirit-filled Christian is not only saved but **separated** from all that does not conform to God's standard of holiness (II Corinthians 6:17). His life <u>in</u> Christ has been apprehended <u>for</u> Christ (Philippians 3:12) and is **yielded** to God entirely (Romans 6:13).

In an earlier chapter I shared with you the illustration of the construction of our home in Tennessee, "Pilgrim's Rest." I would like to refer to it again here. The analogy is not perfect by any means, but I believe it will offer, to some

Pilgrim's Rest

degree, a picture of what it means to be Spirit-filled. As I shared with you before, there came a point when we finally had the deed to the property secured and we could say with all legal assurance that we owned it. But that was not nearly as far as we intended to go. Our goal was not just to own it, but to occupy it - to live there. Before that could happen, however, construction of a house had to be completed. But before the CONstruction could begin some DEstruction had to take place. The property was completely covered with big trees, and they had to go in order to make room for the house and the people that would live in it. It all had to be done because occupation and full possession was the goal, not just legal ownership. Finally the house was completed and we moved in. And when we did, we moved in completely. When we unloaded all our "stuff", we occupied it alright - every square foot of it. But that was the way it was supposed to be. That is also the way it is when the Holy Spirit takes control of our life. His desire in the life of every Believer is not just <u>ownership</u>, but complete <u>possession</u>. His goal is not just to live <u>in</u> us but to live <u>through</u> us.

Remember, the word "filled" means to be in control or to dominate. It means to cancel out, overrule, and replace everything else. While we were building our house I jokingly said to Sheila many times, "Honey, I fully understand that this is YOUR house, and I am just grateful that you are going to let me live in it." In reality, however, there was a lot of truth in that statement. The fact is, Sheila designed the house from top to bottom with specific purposes in mind (just the way God designed each of us), and she stayed home for a year to manage the construction of it while I was overseas doing campaigns. Out of necessity, she took complete control of the project, and you can be sure that everyone on the job knew exactly who was in charge. Every decision made about the house was made by her. When it was finished it had Sheila written all over it – inside and out. You might say it had her signature on it, her "stamp." Our house took on the character, the personality, the very nature of the one who was in charge – my wife. We have even had people walk into our house and say, "This looks just like Sheila." What do they mean? They mean it is dominated by her presence. It became a projection of her personality. It is reflective of her choices. In other words, the house is "filled" with Sheila.

That is exactly what happens when the Holy Spirit "fills" or takes control of our life. When He takes charge, our life takes on His personality, His character, His nature, and His likeness. It becomes reflective of His choices and a projection of Who He is. When our life is filled with the presence of God it begins to look like God. It has His signature on it. We are "stamped" with God. Ephesians 2:22 says that we are, *"...builded together for an habitation of God through the Spirit."* Oswald Chambers wrote, "The Holy Spirit cannot be located as a guest in a house, He invades everything. When I decide that my 'old man' should be identified with the death of Jesus, then the Holy Spirit invades me. He takes charge of every-thing" (7). By means of salvation through Jesus Christ we receive a <u>changed</u> life and become new <u>creatures</u> in Christ. By means of being filled with the Holy Spirit we receive an <u>exchanged</u> life and become new <u>containers</u> for God. Being saved means that God takes ownership of our life. Being filled with (controlled by) the Holy Spirit means that He moves into every square inch of our life with all His "stuff" and takes complete and full possession. Salvation makes us His **purchased** possession (Ephesians 1:14) and Spirit-filling makes us His **possessed** possession.

When the Holy Spirit fills us, He brings life and warmth and light into the dwelling. I remember that last day when we moved out of our house in Memphis to relocate to the country. As we were about to leave for the final time, I walked back into the house that had been our home for fourteen years and took one last look around. The walls were bare, the rooms were empty, and all of a sudden it was not a home anymore; it was just an empty house - just a shell. All the life was gone. There was no more fire in the fireplace, no more smell of Sheila's cooking in the kitchen, no more sound of voices throughout the house. The life, the warmth, the light was gone because the ones who had owned it no longer filled it and possessed it.

But then I also remember that cold day in January when we moved into the new house and how quickly it became a home. The electricity was turned on allowing light and heat to pour into the house. Pictures went up, curtains were hung, furniture was placed, dishes were put in the cabinets, meals were cooked, and voices were heard throughout the house. Life and warmth and light entered the house, the owners took complete possession, and it became much more than just a house; it became a living, functioning home. Without the filling of the Holy Spirit, our life is just a house. It may look good on the outside but there is no life, no energy on the inside. But when the Holy Spirit takes complete control, when He takes full posses-sion, it becomes filled with the warmth of God, there is a fire in our heart, and the house becomes a real home for Jesus. It becomes reflective of His likeness. The difference in the Christian life between being filled with the Holy Spirit and not being is the difference between being fully alive and just existing. Dear Chrisitan friend, is your life just a house or is it a real home? Is it just God's **purchased** possession or is it His **possessed** posses-sion? How do you know? The next chapter will help you with the answer to that question.

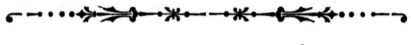

Summary of Truth

❖ In order to be a faith-filled Christian, I must first be a Spirit-filled Christian.

❖ Satan has a counterfeit for everything pertaining to God, including the Spirit-filled life.

❖ Baptism with the Holy Spirit places me in Christ and produces the potential for a holy life. Filling with the Holy Spirit places the fullness of Christ in me and produces the practice of a holy life.

❖ There are two categories of people - natural and spiritual

❖ Christians can be spiritually-minded or carnally-minded..

❖ Spiritually-minded Christians live according to the Holy Spirit and carnally-minded Christians live according to the flesh, or self. Our choices determine which side we are living on.

❖ All Christians are baptized with the Holy Spirit, but not all are filled.

❖ Being filled with the Holy Spirit means to be controlled by Him.

NOW LET'S TAKE A MOMENT AND PRAY TOGETHER:

HEAVENLY FATHER, MORE THAN ANYTHING, I DESIRE TO BE PLEASING TO YOU, TO HONOR YOU AND BRING GLORY TO YOUR NAME. I KNOW THAT TO DO THIS, I MUST BE A SPIRIT-FILLED BELIEVER. LORD, I KNOW I AM SAVED AND I HAVE BEEN BAPTIZED INTO JESUS, BUT LORD I WANT TO BE CONTROLLED BY YOU AS WELL. I DO NOT WANT TO SPEND MY LIFE DEPENDING UPON MYSELF AND WANDERING IN THE WILDERNESS. LORD, I WANT TO BE A FAITH-FILLED, FRUIT-BEARING CHRISTIAN. I WANT TO BE FILLED WITH YOUR SPIRIT AND I WANT MY LIFE TO LOOK LIKE YOU. SO LORD JESUS, I ASK YOU TO TAKE CONTROL OF MY LIFE ENTIRELY. FILL EVERY ROOM WITH YOUR PRESENCE, AND USE ME FOR YOUR PURPOSE AND GLORY. LORD, I PURPOSE RIGHT NOW IN MY HEART TO BE COMPLETELY YIELDED TO YOU, AND I ASK YOU TO HELP ME AS I CONTINUE IN THIS STUDY. THANK YOU LORD, FOR LOVING ME AND SAVING ME. IN YOUR NAME I PRAY. AMEN

Chapter 14

The Faith Life Is a Spirit-Filled Life

Part Two : How to Be Spirit-Filled

Paul's Prescription: Know – Reckon – Yield

In Romans 6:1-18 we find Paul's prescription for the Spirit-filled life. He tells us that there are three steps of faith to becoming a "servant of righteousness (v.18)", which is what a Spirit-filled Child of God is. We must KNOW, RECKON, and YIELD. First, we "<u>know</u>" *(v.3-5)* that those of us who are saved, *"baptized into Jesus Christ",* have entered into His death, His burial and His resurrection, and therefore *"should walk in newness of life."* Second, we "<u>know</u>" (v.6) that *"...our old man* [unrenewed self] *is crucified with him, that the body of sin might be destroyed, that henceforth we should not serve sin",* because (v.7) *"...he that is dead is freed from sin."* Third, we "<u>know</u>" (v.9,10) that Jesus will not die again, death has no more dominion over Him, and He now lives unto God. That means that, in Christ, we can and should live unto God also. Now, verse 11 tells us that since we know these things then we are to "<u>reckon</u>" (consider to be true) ourselves *"...to be dead indeed unto sin, but alive unto God through Jesus Christ our Lord."* Verse 12 goes on to add, *"Let not sin therefore reign in your mortal body, that ye should obey it in the lusts thereof."* Now we come to the final word, "yield". First we are to know some things, then we are to choose to consider them to be absolutely true and relevant to us personally, and finally we are to commit a definite act of surrender. Verse 13b tells us to *"...<u>yield</u> yourselves unto God, as those that are alive from the dead..."* Verse 14 tells us why, *"For sin shall not have dominion over you: for ye are not under the law, but under grace."* So in Romans 6 we clearly see the process of faith outlined (know - choose - act) in becoming a "servant of righteousness," a Spirit-filled Believer.

Receiving the Filling of the Holy Spirit

So then, how do you come to the place in your Christian life where you can say with confidence that you KNOW that the "old man" is crucified with Jesus, you RECKON you are alive unto God through Jesus, and you are YIELDED in complete surrender unto Jesus. In other words, how can you say with assurance you are filled with the Holy Spirit? Let me tell you right up front that it is not an experience to seek; it is a choice to make. It is an act of receiving from God, by faith, His free gift. Just like salvation, it is a transaction of faith between you and God whereby He offers and you accept; He gives and you receive. It is a conscious decision of your will that results in a conscious choice from your heart. It begins with a **discovery** of where you are in your relationship with God. You must face the truth about your present spiritual condition and then choose how you want to continue. A careful and prayerful examination of the comparative list in the previous chapter (between carnal and spiritual) will give you a pretty realistic idea of where you are right now, as well as where you can be. If your discovery is followed by a **dissatisfaction** with your condition, then there will be a **desire** to change, which will give way to full **disclosure** of all that hinders you from being filled with the Holy Spirit. A person cannot be saved without realizing that he isn't and that he needs to be, and the same applies to a Christian becoming Spirit-filled. Disclosure is followed by a **definite act of faith** and a **determination** to remain that way.

DISCOVERY: Come to a realization of where we are and what our condition is. Where are YOU right this minute in YOUR personal journey with God? Are you settling for less than God wants to give you? You begin the process of being filled with the Holy Spirit by discovering anything and everything in your life that would hinder Him from taking total possession of you. Ask Him to shine His light into your private life and reveal the "real you." Get alone with God, and in the light of His presence ask yourself some questions - and answer them honestly.

Do I have a hunger for the Word and a thirst for righteousness? Do I long for fellowship with God and set aside time for that purpose? Am I ever compelled in my spirit to share the message of Christ with the lost? Am I burdened for the unsaved? Are my thoughts pure and occupied with the things of God? Do my conversations include the Lord Jesus? Am I embarrassed to speak of Him in public? Is my language clean? Do I compromise Christian standards in order to fit in? Is there anything in my private life or in my thoughts that I would not want brought out in the open for all to see? Are there any habits in my life that need to go? Am I completely honest in my business? Have I ever cheated anyone? Do I do things that are "legal" but I know are not right in God's sight? Do I ever stretch the truth? Do I find it difficult to rejoice in someone else's blessings, or am I envious or jealous? What am I most interested in, things that are of God or things that are not? What do I have my heart set upon most of the time? What is important enough to me to claim my time, thoughts, energy, and money? What am I most often focused on, things that pertain to my self-interests or things that pertain to God's interests? What do I talk about most, things that pertain to God or things that pertain to everything else? These questions could go on forever but you get the idea. The objective here is for you to examine yourself and, even more, for the Holy Spirit to examine you and reveal to you exactly what your spiritual condition is. When you get that picture clear in your heart, then you will be ready to move on.

DISSATISFACTION AND DESIRE: Come to the realization of where we can go and what we can be. In order for the process of being Spirit filled to continue beyond the discovery phase there must be present in our heart a deep **desire** for change. In order for such a desire to arise, there must first be intense **dissatisfaction** with not being Spirit filled. If we are satisfied we will never desire to change, which means that we will never live by faith and we will never please God. In order to become Spirit-filled, we must not only be aware of our condition, but we must also be alarmed by it and ashamed of it as well. We must become so discontent with it that a longing for change comes into our heart. We must come to the place where we are determined to settle for no less than being filled with the Spirit of God and entering into the victorious Christian life, regardless of the cost. And there will be a cost. The flesh will not give up easily without a fight, and it is not going to go away quietly. Our choice, however, is simple. We can spend our Christian life wasting away in the wilderness, or we can move on to conquering for Christ in Canaan. Dr. Pentecost wrote, "We need to become so dissatisfied over our present state of spiritual attainment that we will come to Him and say, 'Lord, I can't do it. I cannot attain to that which is Your goal and purpose for me as Your child. But I want to turn my life over to the Holy Spirit and let Him empower me so that the righteousness of Christ might be manifested through me' " (1).

Jesus said in John 7:37-38, *"…If any man thirst, let him come unto me, and drink. He that believeth on me, as the scripture hath said, out of his belly* [innermost being] *shall flow* [continuously] *rivers of living water."* Before we can be Spirit-filled we must find enough dissatisfaction in the desert of carnality to create within us a desire that drives us to drink from the well of Jesus. His promise to us is that if we will come, we will be filled.

DISCLOSURE: Come clean with God. Now comes the step at which the flesh, the old man, the carnal nature is surely to rebel. The flesh (self) is very proud and independent and the last thing it wants to do is to admit it is wrong about anything. In order for real Spirit-filling to take place, however, that is exactly what must happen. Our dissatisfaction with where we are and our desire to enter the Spirit-filled life must be sufficient to bring about a **full disclosure** of the truth – about our life, our heart, our thoughts, our affections, our behavior, our motives, our attachments, our relationships, our secrets, our sin. Then disclosure must be followed by complete surrender to God. There must be an emptying, a giving up, a removal of and a turning from, everything in our life that does not conform to God's will, God's Word and God's way. Anything that says, "I must have it MY way" must go. We must experience true repentance (which simply means "a change of mind") about where we are. Willingness to conform to God's standard only occurs as a result of conviction brought about by the Holy Spirit, a conviction that is deep enough to produce the kind of confession of sin that results in cleansing.

Before Sheila and I moved into Pilgrim's Rest she insisted upon one thing – that it be clean! She said she knew the house would get dirty as we lived in it and would have to be cleaned continually. But it could at least be clean when we moved in and she would have it no other way - neither will the Holy Spirit. He will not fill a "dirty house" with His presence. When we moved into the house it was not quite finished. There was still some painting to be done, some trim to be put up, some fixtures to be installed, and so on. But Sheila didn't mind that. She said all along that our house would be a "work in progress" for some time to come. Her insistence was not that the house be finished when we moved in but that it be <u>clean</u>. Her demands were the same as those of the Holy Spirit. He knows that our Christian life is a "work in progress" and will not be complete until we see Jesus face to face. He does not demand <u>completion</u> before filling us, just cleansing of everything that is not of God.

God has one means of cleansing and that is through confession. The word "confession" means "agreement with" and "admission of." To confess our sins simply means that we admit our guilt of them and we agree with God about them. I John 1:9 tells us that the instant we do this, the forgiveness of the cross is applied and cleansing occurs. *"If we confess our sins, he is faithful and just to forgive us our sins, and to cleanse us from all unrighteousness."* We must ask the Holy Spirit to shine His light into all the corners of our life and *"...bring to light the hidden things of darkness..."* (1 Corinthians 4:5). I do not know what the "hidden things of darness" are in your life and you may not know all of them yourself. But God knows and He will reveal them to you if you want Him to. Furthermore, He will cleanse you of them and He will empower you to let go of them in order to make room for Himself. Are you dissatisfied with where you are now? Do you have a desire for a change? Are you willing to get on God's side against everything in your life that does not meet with His will and approval? Are you willing to let go of those things? If so, you are on your way to making that transaction of faith that results in being filled with the Holy Spirit.

When the Holy Spirit cleans house, He may shine His light on some things that we considered to be not so bad. I remember when the trees were removed to make way for the house, there were a couple of them that looked as if they might could stay because they were not right in the spot where the house would sit. They looked harmless and we really hated to cut them, but the contractor wisely told us that even though they were not right in the spot, they were still too close - on the borderline of possibly causing a lot of damage to the house later on. He put them in the "questionable" category and encouraged us to not take the risk. So down they went. Friend, there may be some things in your life that look harmless to you, but if the Contractor of Heaven says they are "too close" and calls them "questionable," then don't take the risk of letting them harm your walk with God. Just let them go. After the landscaping around our home was complete, it was so beautiful that we never even missed those trees. Likewise, I can assure you that when the Holy Spirit finishes "landscaping" your Christian life, it will be so wonderful that you will never miss the things you decided to let go.

DEFINITE ACT OF FAITH: Coming to a point of decision and decisive action. Beyond discovery, dissatisfaction, desire and disclosure, there is only one step that remains in the process of being Spirit-filled, it is a **definite act**. It is a choice, a transaction of faith. Let's go back to the moment of salvation in your life. Three things happened. First, you faced and accepted the truth about yourself – your lost condition and your separation from God because of your sin. Second, you faced and accepted the truth about Jesus – you concluded that He could and would forgive you of your sins based upon His shed blood on the cross. Third, you chose by faith to *receive* as a free gift Christ in your heart, forgiveness of sin, and eternal life. You admitted you were a sinner, you chose to believe on Jesus, and you called upon Him to come into your heart. You exchanged your sin for His righteousness. It was that transaction of that resulted in your changed life. It was a definite act, an act of receiving.

That is exactly what is required in being filled with the Holy Spirit. First, as a Believer, you face and accept the truth about the fact that you are under the control of self and not the Holy Spirit. Second, you face and accept the truth about the Holy Spirit and believe that He will cleanse you of your sin based upon the shed blood of Jesus. Third, you choose by faith to call upon Him, to receive Him in His fullness, to receive His cleansing from all unrighteousness, to receive His filling. You admit you are not Spirit-filled, you believe He will forgive you and fill you, and you call upon Him to take control of your life. It is this transaction, this definite act, this act of receiving, which results in a cleansed, Spirit-filled life. When you were saved you asked Jesus to come into your heart, you believed that He had, and based upon His promise (Romans 10:13), you thanked Him by faith for saving you. You receive the filling of the Holy Spirit the same way. You ask Him to fill you (a definite request), you choose to believe that He has, and based upon His promise (Luke 11:13, John 7:37, 38), you thank Him by faith for doing it. After you asked Jesus into your heart, you could confidently and boldly testify that you were saved. It was not because of feelings, experience, or bright lights flashing from heaven but based upon His promise. Likewise, when you call upon the Holy Spirit to fill you, you can also believe that He has because His Word says He has, *"If any man thirst, let him come."* Listen to the words of Andrew Murray, "What are the conditions of this fullness of the Spirit? God's Word has one answer – faith. It is faith alone that sees and receives the invisible, that sees and receives God Himself" (2).

I think it is worth noting here the words of Ruth Paxson in reference to faith and being filled with the Holy Spirit, "Surrender opens the door; faith believes that Christ enters, fills, abides. With no exception, everything in the Christian's life is a gift. Grace gives and faith takes. Faith is man's one activity. Faith must reach up and lay hold upon all that grace has sent down and bestowed in Christ. Grace provides; faith possesses. God has given you every spiritual blessing in Christ. But this life with all its accompanying blessings can only be actualized through faith. Your faith must make experiential what grace has made possible. Are you a child of God? Then by virtue of your sonship you may be filled with the Holy Spirit. Such fullness has been promised to you. Then why is it that you do not possess your birthright? There is one way by which you may possess the Holy Spirit's fullness. It is the gift of God. What does one usually do with a gift? He receives it and thanks the giver. This is precisely what God wants you to do with this wondrous gift of the Holy Spirit's fullness" (3).

Receive - Right Now!

Now it is time for you to act, to take a step of faith, to reach out by faith, and to receive by faith what is rightfully yours as a born-again Child of God. You do not have to earn it. You can't earn it. You do not have to beg and plead with God to give it to you. He won't respond to that. You do not have to try to make deals with God or offer promises that you can't keep. He doesn't make deals. You do not have to measure up or qualify in some way. You have already measured up in Christ. You do not have to pray more, attend more, study more, learn more, or do more. You did not have to do all that in order for Jesus to come into your heart and you do not have to do it in order for the Holy Spirit to fill you. All you had to do was believe and receive. There is no reason whatsoever why you should go any further in your life, without receiving the filling of the Holy Spirit. So - are you ready? Then let me ask you the following questions:

1. Are you a born-again Child of God?
2. Do you understand the difference between carnal and spiritual?
3. Have you discovered which side you are on?
4. Are you dissatisfied with where you are?
5. Do you sincerely desire to change, to be controlled by the Holy Spirit, to truly make Jesus Lord of your life?
6. Are you willing to do whatever it takes, to let go of whatever God demands in order to be filled with the Holy Spirit?

If you can honestly answer "yes" to all these questions, then I am going to ask you, right now, to take three simple steps – CONFESS, RECEIVE, THANK.

1. **CONFESS YOUR SIN** - Get alone with God in a private place where you will not be disturbed or rushed. Then simply ask the Holy Spirit to shed His light into your heart and reveal anything and everything to your heart and mind that you must let go of in order to be clean before Him. It may be helpful for you to write them all down. Ask Him to shine His light into your private life, into your home, into your marriage, into your relationships with your children, parents, co-workers, school mates, fellow church members and so on. Let Him bring to light everything that is displeasing to God in relation to your business, your ministry, your speech, your public conduct, your appearance, your entertainment and your thought life. If the Holy Spirit brings to mind some point of disobedience or if He convicts you that you need to make restitution in some area, then commit to Him to do it as soon as possible. If you need to be reconciled to some one, then commit to make that reconciliation as soon as possible. When the list is complete, then confess it all, simply agree with God regarding everything on the list, receive His forgiveness by faith and renounce them once and for all. This may take some time. If it does, then give it time. It may also be somewhat traumatic for you. Breaking the chains of sin and self from your heart and life often comes as a crisis point, but let it come. Once you get on the other side of it, the joy and gratitude you feel toward Jesus will far outweigh any pain you had to experience to get there. Then when you come to the place where you know in your heart you have come completely clean before God and have held nothing back, that there is nothing else to bring to the light and you now have a "clean house" to invite the Holy Spirit to possess, then move on to step two.

2. **ASK AND RECEIVE** - Now pray a prayer like this one, and as you do, envision yourself stepping down from the throne of your life and Jesus taking His proper place there, "Dear Heavenly Father, I believe in the filling of Your Holy Spirit and I want You to fill me right now. I surrender completely to You and I yield every aspect of my life to You at this moment. I ask You to take full control and possession of my life. Take the throne of my heart. I believe You are doing it even as I speak and I receive Your fullness by faith. I confess that You are not only my Savior, but You are my LORD and MASTER, and I ask You to live Your life through me from this moment forward."

3. **NOW - THANK HIM FOR HIS FULLNESS** - "Dear Father, I believe I am filled with Your Spirit and I thank You for taking control of my life. Thank You Lord Jesus for taking the throne of my heart. Now help

me Lord to continue to walk in Your fullness all the days of my life. In Jesus' Name. Amen."

Dear Christian, if you just took those three steps, then I can assure you that you are now, at this very moment, filled with the Spirit of God. Jesus has taken the throne of your heart. The "house" is clean and it is fully occupied. It is possessed by the presence of God. Write this date in your Bible, as a reminder to yourself, that on this day you entered the land of Canaan and the Holy Spirit took total possession of your life. There was a day when we closed on our house and took ownership, but there was another day when we moved all our "stuff" into it and took possession. Today the Holy Spirit has moved all His "stuff" (the fruit of the Spirit) into your heart and He has taken possession.

Now, let me say to you that you may or may not "feel" anything, but it does not matter. Being filled with the Holy Spirit is not an experience (emotional or physical). It is a transaction of faith, which, like salvation, may be accompanied by feelings of joy or excitement, or it may not. The reality of it, however, does not depend on emotion but on the fact of God's Word. Many people who pray to receive Christ do not feel anything, but they are saved nonetheless. Remember that Spirit-filling, like salvation, is not an experience to seek; it is a choice to make. If you have made the choice, then praise God, you are Spirit-filled! You are now ready and equipped to trust God by faith.

Results of Being Spirit-Filled

Before our house was anywhere near completion, Sheila had a crystal clear picture of what it would look like. She knew because she was working from a photograph of it that was published in an architectural book. Time after time she said to the builders, "Just make it look like the picture." You don't have to guess what your life will look like, what it will *be* like, when you are possessed by the Holy Spirit. There is a picture of it published in a Book, God's Word. It is found in Galatians 5:22-23. The characteristics of the new life created in us by the Holy Spirit are the characteristics of Jesus and they are called the **FRUIT** of the Spirit. The first one is **love**, the kind of love that is unconditional. It gives without demanding or expecting anything in return. It is never out to collect. Next is **joy** or rejoicing. This word carries with it the idea of a person who is calm, cheerful, happy, and filled with gladness. Third is **peace**, which also means quiet and tranquil. The next characteristic is **longsuffering** or patience. This refers to a person who is even-tempered, forgiving, and lenient. Fifth is **gentleness**, which also means kindness, graciousness, excellence of character, and usefulness. Sixth is **goodness**, which refers to a benevolent, giving person who performs good deeds and actions out of tenderness and compassion. Next is **faith** or faithfulness. This is a person who lives by faith and is faithfully obedient to God. Then there is **meekness**, which also means humility. This is the person who accepts all that comes from God as good and is not resistant toward Him. He is not meek in the sense that he has no power, but in the sense that his power is under God's control – as was Jesus on the cross. The last item is **temperance**, which is self-control or self-restraint.

In addition to Christ-like character (the fruit of the Spirit), the Spirit-filled life also produces a Christ-proclaiming **FOCUS**. A person who is controlled by the Holy Spirit <u>will</u> become a proclaimer of Christ. He WILL become evangelistic. He <u>will</u> become concerned about and burdened for lost souls. He <u>will</u> become a witness for Jesus. Acts 1:8 tells us in no uncertain terms, *"But ye shall receive power, after that the Holy Ghost is come upon you: and ye **shall** be witnesses unto Me."* In John 15:26 Jesus said that the Holy Spirit *"...shall testify of Me."* It is not possible for a person to be controlled by the Holy Spirit and not be moved by Him to proclaim the Gospel. If a Christian has no interest whatsoever in seeing others come to Christ, he is not Spirit-filled. If we are Spirit-filled we <u>will</u> participate in His agenda, the redemption of the human race. Not every Christian has the gift of evangelism and not every Christian is called to be an evangelist. There are many differing gifts given to the body of Christ. But, every Spirit-filled Believer will be open to the possibility of being used evangelistically, and regardless of what his gift is and what ministry he performs, winning the lost will be the "why" behind the "what."

Then to new fruit and new focus we add new **FAITH.** The Spirit-filled life is a supernatural life, a faith-filled life. The Holy Spirit will always move the Believer to trust God for the impossible, because that is how the Father is glorified. He reveals the will of the Father to our inner man and then empowers us to believe Him for the fulfillment of it. Does the fruit of the Spirit exist in your life? Are you joined to God's agenda? Are you living a supernatural life of faith? Do these things form a picture of what your life looks like now, or what it <u>should</u> look like? May God help us to come to a place where we can sincerely say to Him, the Master Builder, "Just make it look like the picture."

Remaining Spirit-Filled

Once again we see in Ephesians 5:18 that "be filled" is a command and it is continuous action. The command is to "be continually getting filled", which indicates that it is possible to get "unfilled." Or we could say it this way, "Continuously choose to remain under the control of the Holy Spirit." The Spirit-filled life requires maintenance. It cannot be left unattended. Like a garden it must be watered, cultivated and cared for daily. If it isn't, then weeds (sin) will spring up and choke out the fruit. So how do we keep the weeds out? The best way to deal with weeds is to pull them out as soon as they appear. You don't wait until they grow and spread and take over the entire garden. And in the light of God it is easy to spot the weeds. I John 1: 7 tells us, *"But if we walk in the Light, as he is in the light, we have fellowship one with another, and the blood of Jesus Christ, his Son, cleanseth us from all sin."*

It is imperative that we keep the garden of our spiritual life "weeded," watered and cultivated by walking in the Light. We do that by making time for God, by spending time in His Word and in prayer. By doing so we will become saturated with the things of God and we will develop a keen sensitivity to the "still, small voice" of the Holy Spirit. John 16:13 says that as we become sensitive to His voice, the Holy Spirit will *"guide you into all truth"* and He will *"show you things to come."* The surest way to remain filled by the Holy Spirit is to begin every day in God's presence, asking Him to reveal to you if there is even the tiniest thing that would stand between you and Him. If He shows you there is, if you spot even the smallest weed of sin or disobedience, then confess it immediately, claim cleansing by the blood of Jesus, and thank Him for again taking control of your life.

The Bible uses two words to express what causes Him to stop working in our life. The first word is "quench", found in I Thessalonians 5:19, *"Quench not the Spirit."* The word means "extinguish or suppress." The idea is that of snuffing out a flame. The second word is "grieve" and is found in Ephesians 4:30, *"And grieve not the Holy Spirit of God..."* This word means "to cause distress, sadness, or sorrow." It also means "to be ignored." We extinguish the fire of the Holy Spirit, we suppress His power in us, and we sadden Him by one thing - disobedience. We must be sensitive to His leading, whether He says start or stop, do or don't, go or stay. Spiritual sensitivity is cultivated through quick confession, quick obedience, time in the Word, and time in prayer.

Now, let me say this to you, dear Believer; you will never completely eliminate the pull and influence of the flesh (self, old nature) in your life altogether, but you can give it a lot less to work with. Paul exhorts in Romans 13:14, *"But put ye on the Lord Jesus Christ, and make not provision for the flesh, to fulfil the lusts thereof."* The word "provision" means "supply." If you ask God to shine His light into your heart, He will quickly identify the things that so easily cause you to sin. When He does, let them go, including things that may be in the "questionable" category. That might include certain television programs, reading material, movies, music, or maybe the internet. Let go of anything and everything the Holy Spirit makes an issue of. Perhaps you are wrongly influenced by associating with certain people or going to certain places. If so, then stop if at all possible. I realize all these things are external and there are many internal influences as well, but the point is to cut off the supply to the flesh as much as possible. In order to protect your walk with God you should avoid anything that takes your focus away from Him. II Corinthians 6:16,17 says, *"...for ye are the temple of the living God; as God hath said, I will dwell in them, and walk in them; and I will be their God, and they shall be my people. Wherefore come out from among them, and be ye separate, saith the Lord, and touch not the unclean thing; and I will receive you."* A flame deprived of air will not burn. If you think you can allow things to remain in your life that are displeasing to God and not be hurt, you are wrong. You do not have the power to "deal with them" and not be affected by them. Paul did not tell Timothy to deal with youthful lusts; he told him to flee from them.

Now you may ask, "But am I not to live in the world and be a testimony to it?" Yes, you are to live in the world, but the world is not to live in you. In John 17:15 we find these words of Jesus in reference to the disciples, *"I pray not that thou shouldest take them out of the world, but that thou shouldest keep them from the evil."* When we built our home, we had something installed in the house that would provide it with constant protection day and night – an alarm system. In order for someone to enter the house they must know the disarming code, and those who are not supposed to enter do not know it. If an intruder tries to enter, a loud alarm goes off and the police are notified by a monitoring service. Well, God has equipped you and me with an alarm system to protect us from unauthorized intruders. It is the inner voice of the Holy Spirit. Intruders come in many forms such as thoughts, feelings, threats, enticements, and fear. When they come, the Holy Spirit will set off an alarm deep within your spirit to alert you something is wrong; there has been a security breach. You may feel disturbed, troubled, guilty, or convicted. But regardless what you call it, you will know that something is wrong. When that happens, look to God immediately and ask Him to shine His light and reveal the problem. At that point it may be necessary to confess sin, resist the devil, or renounce an old encroaching worldly attachment. But whatever it is, do it, and then continue to walk in the Spirit.

You are now filled with the Spirit of God and are therefore prepared to walk by faith according to His will received in your inner man. Your garden is filled with His fruit and it is growing. Now keep it watered with His Word, cultivated through prayer, cleansed through confession, and yielding fruit through obedience. Your alarm system is on and the Holy Spirit stands ready to alert you to unauthorized intruders. Now, just walk in the light as He is in the light. As you do, you will find that the promises from God's Word listed below will apply to you. May God bless you as you continue to learn more about living the Spirit-filled life and the life of real God-faith.

Promises to the Spirit-Filled Believer

I want to close this chapter by giving you some wonderful promises from the Word of God that are yours to claim now that you are "owned and operated" by the Holy Spirit. They were written in a tract published long ago by my pastor, Brother Don Milam, who is now with Jesus. He wrote first of all that the Holy Spirit will give us a **LIFE OF PEACE**. He will emancipate our soul, freeing it from the bondage of fear and anxiety (II Corinthians 3:17). He will enrapture our heart, flooding it with His love (Romans 5:5). He will encourage us through every trial (Acts 9:31). He will entomb the old nature, fighting our battles for us and killing off the sins of the flesh through surrender (Romans 8:13). Second He will give us a **LIFE OF POWER**. He will energize us (John 6:63). He will endue us with divine power (Acts 1:8). He will enact Christ's mighty works through us (I Corinthians 12:4-11, John 14:12). He will endorse our testimony for Christ (Hebrews 2:4). Third, the Holy Spirit will give us a **LIFE OF PURPOSE**. He will enlighten our minds (I Corinthians 2:12). He will engineer our life, leading us into ALL truth (John 16:13). He will equip us for His calling (I John 2:20,21). He will enthuse us with joy in His purpose for us (Romans 14:17). Fourth, the Holy Spirit will give us a **LIFE OF PLENTITUDE**. He will enrich all our needs filling us with all the fullness of God in Christ (Ephesians 3:16 – 20, 5:18). He will <u>endow</u> our life with the vast inheritance of the saints (Ephesians 1:13, 14). He will <u>enshrine</u> the glory of Christ in our life, furnishing us with all righteousness (II Corinthians 3:18). He will <u>engage</u> God in prayer for our victory in Christ (Romans 8:26). What a glorious picture that is! What a life to aspire to! And, praise God, it now belongs to you.

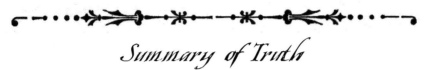

Summary of Truth

- ❖ Paul's prescription for a holy life is to know, reckon and yield.
- ❖ Receiving the filling of the Holy Spirit is not an experience to seek, but a choice to make.
- ❖ Being filled with the Holy Spirit begins with a discovery of who and where we are.
- ❖ There must be a desire for change brought on by dissatisfaction with where we are now.
- ❖ The Holy Spirit will only fully possess a clean life.
- ❖ Cleansing is brought about through confession, agreement with God regarding our sin.
- ❖ Receiving the filling of the Holy Spirit is a definite act, a transaction of faith.
- ❖ To be filled we must confess, ask and receive, and thank the Giver.
- ❖ Spirit-filling produces new fruit, new focus and new faith in the Believer's life.
- ❖ In order to remain Spirit-filled we have only to walk in the Light of God.

Now Let's Take a Moment and Pray Together:

Dear Father, I thank You for revealing to me what it means to be filled with the Holy Spirit and I thank You that I am now, at this very moment, completely possessed by You. You are in total control of every aspect of my life. I praise You that my Lord Jesus is on the throne of my heart. I am surrendered to You and by Your grace I shall continue to walk in the Light as You are in the Light. Make me super sensitive to the leading of Your Spirit and help me to be quick to obey You. Dear Father, I am open to Your instruction and I am ready to live by real God-honoring faith. Thank You Father for doing this great thing in my life. In Jesus Name I pray. Amen.

Chapter 15

Real Faith Requires Time Alone with God
The Necessity of Real Worship

"We have to pitch our tents where we shall always have quiet times with God,
however noisy our times with the world may be."
Oswald Chambers (1)

On a Hillside in Africa

In 1975 on a remote hillside in Tanzania, Africa, God spoke to me and told me to leave my staff position at Briarcrest Church in Memphis, Tennessee and go into international evangelism. We will save that story for another book, but suffice it to say, it was an unexpected shock to my system. But I knew God had spoken, and I had to obey. The question was, how? We had no money, no backing, no organization, no contacts overseas, and no idea of how to get started. The answer would be by faith alone – standing upon the will and promises of God. Upon returning home something happened that I had never experienced before. God began waking me up at exactly 4:30 every morning. I would get up, throw on some jeans and a tee shirt, grab my Bible ("Big Red") and go down to a public park near our house. There, in the quiet and seclusion of the early morning, I would walk, read the Bible, and pray. That went on for months, and during that time I got to know God in a way that I had not known Him before. I had been saved and in the ministry for eight years. I had been to Bible College and University, had preached hundreds of times, had led thousands to Christ, and was currently serving on a church staff. I <u>thought</u> I had a real working relationship with God, but those mornings in the park showed me that I didn't. I spent two or three hours out there, day after day, becoming familiar with Him Whom I was seeking to serve. Sheila and I had already "lived by faith" for years, but now God was preparing us for our life work and a new level of faith. It was a level of faith that required an intimate and personal understanding of Who God really is, what He really has, and what He can really do. God was leading us into a level of faith that not only required us to trust Him for our daily needs but also for the needs of others and the needs of a ministry. It was a new level of responsibility that required a new level of faith, and there was nowhere to learn it other than in the presence of God Himself. Out of those months of early morning fellowship with God came the ministry we have been in for the past thirty years. The experience I had back there years ago of daily meeting with God alone in the early hours set the standard for the remainder of my life. During those days in the park, I learned something that I did not learn in Bible College, or by attending church services, or from reading books; I learned to worship God and to recognize the voice of God in my spirit. Since then I have maintained the practice of meeting with God at the beginning of the day in private worship, because the necessity in my life for the intimate fellowship with God, that can only be found in the early hours of the day, has never diminished. In fact, it has increased as the years have gone by and as my responsibility has grown. Once you have experienced that fellowship, it is impossible to live a happy, faith-filled, satisfying Christian life without it. The one thing that we <u>should</u> be addicted to in our Christian life is time alone with God.

Hearing His Teacher's Voice

Some years ago I was on a campaign in Malawi, Central Africa preaching in remote villages throughout the country. My interpreter was Chief Hardwick Adam Kachaje, better known as Mfumu Thumba (Chief of Thumba Village). Many years ago "the Chief" was a schoolteacher. One afternoon he and I were out in a very remote area, preaching to a group of people under some trees using a sound system powered by a portable generator. There was nothing unusual about that, but that day something very unusual happened. About five miles away, there was a man sitting in a bar (yes they

even have them in the bush country) and, amazingly, he very faintly heard the sound of Hardwick's voice. He recognized it because long ago as a child he had been one of the Chief's students. He got up from where he was sitting and began to run toward the voice, and as he ran he listened to the message. When he arrived, he embraced his old teacher and received Jesus into his heart. Later he told, "I <u>had</u> to respond because I recognized the voice and I could not resist it." The voice of the old teacher, even though very faint, came into the man's ears with an irresistible compelling just as the voice of God comes into the spirit of the Believer with that same irresistible compelling.

Now you may ask, how could it be possible for that man to hear the voice of the Chief as far away as five miles, and how could he recognize a voice he had not heard in over twenty years? I cannot answer the first question; I frankly wonder myself. But I can answer the second. He could recognize the voice because he had spent years in the presence of the Chief, listening to his voice every day. He recognized the voice because he had spent time listening to it. My dear friend, essential to the Christian life, and to the life of faith, is knowing the voice of the Master. Jesus said in John 10:27, *"My sheep hear my voice, and I know them, and they follow me."* The only way to know His voice is to spend time listening to it. There is no short cut. We learn His voice as we spend time with Him alone in private worship and fellowship.

God wants to take you out beyond the ordinary, and He will - IF you want Him to and IF you ask Him to work in your life. Your Heavenly Father, the Creator of the universe, wants you to realize that He has a much greater plan and a much higher purpose for your life than just going along day by day. He never meant for any Christian to live in neutral or in "cruise control." God wants you to join Him in His eternal enterprises by real faith. One thing you notice quickly about the life of Jesus is that it was not defensive and passive. Rather it was offensive and active. One thing is for certain - His life was not ordinary. Why? Was it because He was God? No, it was because He was man, trusting God. Jesus was God in human flesh - ABSOLUTELY! The secret to His life, however, was His perfect unwavering faith in the Father. His ear was constantly and acutely attuned to the Father's voice, and His will was continuously set upon doing the Father's will. The secret to Jesus' earthly ministry was not that He **was** God (which He was, 100%), but that, as man (which He was, 100%), He spent time **with** God. God's desire and plan for your life, regardless of your calling or vocation, is that you live by the same faith as Jesus (Galatians 2:20). But the only way for any one of us to be involved in the plan of God is to ask Him to lead us into a life of real faith - to make space in our life for His supernatural intervention. God wants to maximize your life for Himself, for His Kingdom, and for His glory. For that purpose He endowed every Believer with the capacity of real God faith. He has supernaturally enabled each one of us to be active participants in the *"greater works"* Jesus promised in John 14:12. God wants to perform the impossible, and He want to do it through YOU.

Moving Forward into Real Faith

Having accepted all this as true, however, you must now ask yourself – how do I begin moving forward into a life of real faith? How do I begin seeing things happen in my home, my business, my church, my ministry, my family and my life, that are explainable only in terms of God's presence, power, and provision? How does a Christian reach the place where the supernatural power of God changes from mere theory to working reality? How does he come to a place where his life truly brings glory to God? How does the potential for faith become the practice of faith in a Believer's life? It begins with one thing only - knowing God Himself, learning to discern His voice, and that only happens as we spend time in His presence. There is no substitute.

The first step in moving into a God-honoring life of real faith is to become convinced that living by faith is not just for "those other folks," but it is for you, for EVERY Christian without exception or exemption. Once that is settled, the next step is to become intimately familiar with God Himself. Satan hinders many Believers at this point, however, by presenting them with two very wrong ideas about God. The first is that He is far away, "out there" somewhere. It is the old idea of separation left over from the fall. The truth, however, is that His Spirit indwells your spirit. He is "out there," of course, because He is everywhere, but He is also in you and *in* your present situation and circumstances. Another wrong idea is that we must struggle to qualify for God, to earn His approval. This leaves the Christian with the wrong belief that he must strive to serve God, and work hard for Him, and by doing so he might be able to please Him - someday - maybe. Real faith is impossible to experience if, at the very core of your being, you believe there are times when the Father doesn't approve of you. But, praise God, we have already qualified in Christ. Striving and struggling are not necessary. All God wants is to work through you, not have you struggle to work for Him. Listen to Ephesians 1:5-6, *"Having predestinated us unto the adoption of children by Jesus Christ to Himself, according to the good pleasure of his will, To the praise of the glory of his grace, wherein he hath made us **accepted** in the beloved."* What fantastic verses of Scripture! The word "accepted" is the Greek word "charitao," which means, "to grace or endue with special honor - make accepted and be highly favored." What a wonderful description of how God views those of us who have trusted Jesus as Savior and Lord. Satan would have you believe that you can know <u>about</u> God, but you cannot actually <u>know</u> God, either because He is out of reach or because you are not good enough. Both of those ideas are lies from the enemy.

Because of satan's deception, millions of Christians do not know God intimately and do not believe they can, thus making a life of real faith impossible. Faith is built upon trust (persuasion of fact), and it is impossible to trust some one you do not know. The secret to living a joyful and fruitful Christian life is not just <u>believing</u> in God, or <u>serving</u> God, or even <u>loving</u> God. The secret is **knowing** God. Once you come to know Him then all the other will follow as naturally as breathing. Once you become intimately familiar with God, and become persuaded of His faithfulness and His unwavering love for you, then the choice of faith becomes much easier to make. Every Believer has a relationship with God as His child, but in order for faith to develop, that relationship must become one of close intimate fellowship and friendship. The only way for that to happen is to spend adequate personal private time with God alone. Jesus said to the disciples in John 15:15a, *"Henceforth I call you not servants; for the servant knoweth not what his lord doeth: but I have called you friends..."* James 2:23 tells us, *"...Abraham believed God, and it was imputed unto him for righteousness: and he was called the Friend of God."* You see, what God is seeking from us is intimacy. The transition from theory to reality is made only through time spent in the Father's presence in intimate worship and fellowship. There is no other way. There is no short cut. We have often heard it said in relation to our children that you spell love T-I-M-E. The same is true in our relationship with God.

Jesus, Our Supreme Example

Lets look for a moment at the life of Jesus. His is the supreme example of a life lived by faith. The life our Lord Jesus Christ lived on earth was a life of continuous <u>prayer to</u> the Father, <u>worship of</u> the Father and <u>fellowship with</u> the Father. The result was a life of total obedience to the will of the Father by faith. Now, I know what you are going to say, "Yes, but Jesus was God in the flesh. Of course He obeyed God and trusted God. He WAS God!" Correct. But, He was also man and the faith that Jesus exercised toward His Father was the faith of a man. He was exercising the same identical capacity for faith that God placed in you and me when we were born again by His Spirit. Very often we look at the life of Jesus and view it as different from our own, but it wasn't. Hebrews 2:16-17 tells us plainly, *"For verily he* [Jesus] *took not on him the nature of angels; but he took on him the seed of Abraham* [man]. *Wherefore in all things it behoved him to be made like unto his brethren* [you and me], *that he might be a merciful and faithful high priest in things pertaining to God, to make reconciliation for the sins of the people."* Then in 4:15 we read, *"For we have not an high priest which cannot be touched with the feeling of our infirmities; but was in all points tempted like as we are, yet without sin."* Dear friends, Jesus had emotions. He experienced joy (John 15:11) as well as grief and sorrow (Isaiah 53:3). He became hungry (Matthew 4:2) and thirsty (John 19:28) and tired (John 4:6) just like we do. The Bible tells us very plainly that,

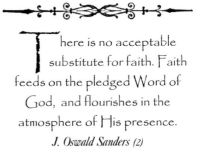

There is no acceptable substitute for faith. Faith feeds on the pledged Word of God, and flourishes in the atmosphere of His presence.

J. Oswald Sanders (2)

"Jesus wept" (John 11:35). He was one hundred percent God – YES! He was God Incarnate, God in human flesh, but He was also one hundred percent man. He Himself said in John 5:30, *"I can of mine own self do nothing: as I hear, I judge: and my judgment is just; because I seek not mine own will, but the will of the Father which hath sent me."* Jesus obeyed the will of the Father revealed to Him in His spirit - by faith. The same faith that Jesus exercised toward God is resident in you and me by His indwelling Spirit, *"...the life which I now live in the flesh, I live by the faith of the Son of God..."* (Galatians 2:20). The faith life is simply Christ-life lived through a child of God. Jesus CHOSE to trust God, not because He WAS God, but because He KNEW God.

Jesus was not born into the world with a super-human knowledge of Scripture. He studied and learned the Scriptures from childhood. The Word of God soaked into His heart and became part of Him, preparing Him for a life of trusting His Father for the impossible. In Matthew 4:4-10, what weapon do we find Jesus using so skillfully against satan? It was the Word of God. At the age of twelve, where do we find Jesus? He was in the temple. His life was a life of worship. In Mark 1:35 we read, *"And in the morning, rising up a great while before day, he went out, and departed into a solitary place, and there prayed."* His life was a life of prayer. In Mark 14:36

we see Jesus in the Garden of Gethsemane facing the greatest trial of faith a human being has ever encountered. There in the early hours we find Him on His face before the Father – praying and worshipping and yielding to His will - by faith. There was an atmosphere of total trust established in His life. It was established by spending time with God. Now let's ask ourselves, if our Lord Jesus Christ, God Almighty in human flesh, found it necessary in His humanity to spend personal private time with God alone, then how necessary is it for you and me to do the same? The answer is obvious.

Time with God Alone

So let me ask you, **do you spend time alone with God?** Now before you answer too quickly, let's look at the question again, do you spend **TIME** alone with **GOD**? I am not asking if you spend time reading a daily devotional book, or reading through the Bible in a year. For you pastors and evangelists, I am not asking if you spend time in Bible study or preparing sermons and getting ideas for messages. Your time with God may eventually lead to that, but it should not begin with it. Your sole purpose in setting aside time for God should be to meet with HIM, to worship HIM, to fellowship with HIM, to become more intimate and familiar with HIM. What we are talking about here is not spending time at church or in fellowship with other Christians, or attending Bible studies or prayer meetings. What we are talking about is spending time with God Himself. There IS a difference. The question is this; do you spend unhurried, uncluttered, regular, daily time focused upon God alone? The answer is either yes or no, not "sort of" or "sometimes." It is either "yes I do" or "no I don't." The reason I am pressing this point is because real God faith cannot exist in your life unless you spend time in worship, prayer, and fellowship with God alone. A pivotal point we will discuss later is that **faith begins with knowing the will of God,** and that is impossible to discover without spending time with Him. You see, the faith life is "God life." Faith begins and ends with God. The faith life is anchored in the **person** of God Himself. It counts upon the **presence** of God and works according to the **plan** of God. It is assured by the **promises** of God and overcomes by the **power** of God. It is supplied by the **provision** of God and conducts warfare against satan and opposing circumstances under the **protection** of God.

Now there is certainly nothing wrong with reading a devotional book or reading through the Bible or attending prayer meetings. In fact, there is everything right about doing those things. I have an old daily devotional that I bought in a used bookstore in York, England twenty years ago, "My Utmost for His Highest" by Oswald Chambers. I have carried it with me all over the world and I read it every day. In fact, all the quotes by Chambers contained in this book come from that old volume. Some days I read several selections at random. I always enjoy them and they always minister to me, but I do not consider time reading "Oswald" as time with God. I also read the Bible daily and go to church regularly and enjoy fellowship with other Believers. But, again, these things are not what I am talking about when I ask if you spend time with God. If we are not very careful, these things can actually become a substitute or competition for spending time with God alone. There have been many students in Bible colleges and seminaries who have become hard and cold and faithless toward God because they are so busy studying about Him that they have no time to spend with Him. I know, because I have been one. There have also been many preachers of the Gospel who have been so busy telling the world about Jesus that they have no time or energy left to spend with Him. I know, because I have been one of those also. There are millions of Christians who are so busy attending things and doing things that pertain to God that they have no time left for actually spending time with God. Are you one of those? How do you know? The answer is found in John 7:38, "*He that believeth on me, as the scripture hath said, out of his belly* [heart] *shall flow rivers of living water.*" The key word here is, **believe**. The flow is a result of believing God. Believing God is made possible only by knowing God, and knowing God is made possible only by spending time with God - alone. Dear friend, are the rivers flowing from you? Are you full of faith? Are you believing God for the impossible - right now? Studying, preaching, attending and doing will not fill you with faith and make you soft and pliable and red hot for Jesus - only intimate, personal, unhurried, private time in the Father's presence will do that.

Real Faith Is All About Real Worship

Now you may ask, "Okay, if I am not going to study the Bible as such during my time alone with God or read a devotional book, or go through my prayer list or get ideas for sermons or Bible lessons, what AM I going to do?" What we are talking about in spending time alone with God can be summed up in one word - worship. Now with that you may have another question, "But what is worship - exactly?" Good question. We hear the word "worship" used a lot these days - worship services, worship leaders, worship music, worship experiences, worship groups, worship conferences - but, again, what IS worship? How do you know if and when you are engaged in real worship? Well, let's go to the authority, the Word of God, and find out. The word most often translated "worship" in the New Testament is the Greek word "proskuneo", which literally means "to come forward and kiss." It means "intimate contact." It is also depicted as a dog licking his master's hand, desiring his touch. It is a picture of total abandonment and submission. It denotes total devotion and adoration. John 4:24 tells us that *"God is a Spirit: and they that worship him must worship him in spirit and in truth."* In verse 23, the Bible calls those that do *"true worshippers"* and says, *"...the Father seeketh such to worship him"*. **Real worship occurs when your spirit connects with God's Spirit in intimate fellowship**. That is what "communion" means: intimate fellowship, mutual participation, and a time of sharing. **Real worship is private and personal, just between God and His child**. It is not intellectual, and it is not an emotional "warm and fuzzy" experience. It involves thought processes, of course, and it may elicit emotion, but it is a spiritual experience. Your spirit joined to His Spirit opens up communication that is only possible in the Spirit realm, the realm that real faith operates in. It is the routine, the habit of private times of fellowship with God and worship of God that must be established in your life in order for real faith to spring forth, because real faith originates with God. Does the habit of real worship exist in your life? Again, I am not asking if you attend worship services or fellowships. Real worship in the sense we are talking about is not corporate - it is private and personal. Real worship is not what occurs in church in the company of other people; it is what takes place in "the closet" between you and God alone. My pastor, "Brother Don" Milam, always said to me, "Shad, remember that every man walks with God alone." Ultimately our walk with God is private and personal, and it begins with worship that is also private and personal.

Confusion in the church today regarding worship arises from a lack of understanding that man is a three-part being - body, soul and spirit - and of the three parts, only one is regenerated, the spirit. Therefore only the spirit of man can relate to and communicate with God. Only the spirit can hear the voice of God and only the spirit can worship God. If our "worship" does not originate from within the inner man, then it is counterfeit and mere flesh, no matter how loud it may be or how good it may feel. But doesn't worship involve the whole man? Yes it does. With our intellect we remember the works of God, with our voice we sing and praise God, with our emotion we experience love and devotion and with our body we lift our hands, bow our heads and bend our knees. Worship involves every aspect of our being, but to be real it must **originate** in our spirit.

One of the greatest examples of the real faith life in the Bible is the life of Abraham. Notice how he worshipped God. When he went up on the mountain to sacrifice Isaac, he told the men that were with him that he was going up to "worship." He left the men at the bottom of the mountain and went with Isaac - alone. Again we see that real faith-producing worship involves intimate contact with God alone and it involves doing real business with God. What was it that enabled Abraham to commit such an act of real worship, such an act of obedience, such an act of real faith as sacrificing his son? It was his life of worship that produced a life of faith. The first thing he did upon entering Canaan was to build an altar, a place of worship. Before doing anything else he made sure that a place of communion with God was established and maintained in his life. He always had two things, an altar and a tent. He was always ready to worship and always ready to move, to obey God's command at any moment. It was the place of worship that provided the anchor for his life and produced a constant enabling for faith. Even when he veered off course after receiving the promise of God, the anchor held and he returned *"Unto the place of the altar, which he had made there at the first: and there Abram called on the name of the Lord." (Genesis 13:4)* He <u>trusted</u> God because he <u>knew</u> God, and he knew God because he spent time with God alone. Again we read in James 2:23 that *"...Abraham believed God, and it was imputed unto him for righteousness: and he was called the Friend of God."* Why? Because of three things in his life; **fellowship** <u>with</u> God, **faith** <u>in</u> God and **obedience** <u>to</u> God. He spent time in constant fellowship with God and out of it grew a faith that believed God for the impossible.

Early Will I Seek Thee

Once we have accepted the fact that it is absolutely essential in our walk with God to spend unhurried time with Him in private worship and fellowship, we must then answer the question as to when that time should be. Some Christians say that setting aside a specific time to spend with God is not necessary because we should spend all our time with Him. Of course that is true in the sense that we walk before God continually, and the Bible does instruct us to "pray without ceasing." There is, however, overwhelming evidence from the Bible to suggest that every Believer should set aside a specific time every day that is dedicated to worship, prayer, and fellowship with God alone, and that time should be at the <u>beginning</u> of the day. In Psalm 63:1 we read the words of David, *"O God, thou art my God; early will I seek Thee."* Then in Proverbs 8:17 we find the words of Solomon referring to the wisdom of God, *"I love them that love me; and those that seek me early shall find me."* We see in the lives of the men of God throughout the Bible that there was one outstanding consistency; they all spent time with God in the early morning. In Genesis 19:27 we see that *"Abraham gat up early in the morning to the place where he stood before the Lord."* We are told that Job, the man that God called *"perfect and upright* (1:1)*", "...rose up early in the morning and offered burnt offerings..."* (1:5) on behalf of his ten children. We find man after man, Jacob (Genesis 28:18), Gideon (Judges 6:38), Samuel (I Samuel 15:12), David (I Samuel 17:20), and Jehoshaphat (II Chronicles 20:20), rising up early to pray, worship, and do business with God. Then as we look at the Lord Jesus Himself we see again in Mark 1:35 that, *"In the morning, rising up a great while before day, he went out, and departed into a solitary place, and there prayed."* It was the custom of His life to spend the early hours of the day in private with the Father.

> The one thing needful is to have the heart filled with faith in the living God: in that faith to abide with living contact with Him; in that faith to wait and worship before His holy presence.
>
> *Andrew Murray (3)*

The word "early", in both the Old Testament Hebrew and the New Testament Greek, means "dawning" or "first light." It also has the additional meaning of "to search," "to seek diligently," or "to be in earnest." We discover that throughout Christian history, the men and women who have been used of God the most are those who were "in earnest" with God, evidenced by the fact that they made it a practice to daily spend time with Him in the early hours of the day.

An outstanding example of such a person was the man who introduced Sheila and me to Jesus, Rev. Don J. Milam, Pastor of Park Avenue Baptist Church in Memphis, Tennessee. I believe that "Brother Don" walked in the power and presence of God more than any other man I have ever known.

I remember one Sunday after his retirement, he walked into the morning service of the church Sheila and I were then attending. He was there as a visitor. I saw him enter the room and then I, for lack of a better word, "felt" the overwhelming presence of God. People were still talking and getting settled, but when Brother Don entered all talking ceased, a silence fell over the congregation, and people all over the auditorium began weeping for no apparent reason. Some may have wondered how such an unassuming man as Brother Don Milam could have such a walk

Bro. Don Milam

with God that his entrance into a room seemed to usher in the very presence of God. The answer is really very simple - he spent time with God alone. In addition to preparing sermons and counseling people in his office, he also made many soul-winning calls every day and visited every hospital in Memphis. He was a very busy man, but he made time to spend with God alone. How? He did it early in the morning. You could drive by the church at 4:30 in the morning any day of the week and see the light on in the window of his study. If you went inside you would find him on his knees before God. He spent the first two to three hours of every day of his life on his knees in private worship and fellowship with God. After he retired he had a little room next to his garage that was used for the same purpose until the very day he died at age 86. The secret to Brother Don's life was simply that he continuously drew upon the power he received in the early hours of the day. Oh that God would enable me to be such a man as my Pastor, and oh that God would raise up such pastors as Brother Don to lead His church today.

The greatest advancements in missions were born out of the faith of individuals who did the same thing. They consistently drew strength from God in the early morning hours. Martin Luther said, "If I fail to spend two hours in prayer each morning the devil gets the victory through the day. I have so much business I cannot get on without spending two hours daily in prayer" (4). Dr. Adoniram Judson, pioneer missionary to Burma, advised, "Arrange thy affairs, if possible, so that thou canst leisurely devote two or three hours every day not merely to devotional exercises but to the very act of secret prayer and communion with God" (5). Robert Murray McCheyne wrote, "I ought to pray before seeing anyone. I feel it is better to begin with God - to see His face first, to get my soul near Him before it is near another" (6). James Hudson Taylor, the great pioneer missionary to China and founder of the China Inland Mission, made it a daily practice to rise at four in the morning and spend at least two hours prostrate before God in prayer and worship. He wrote, "The one thing we need is to know God better" (7). He advised his fellow workers, "Do not be so busy with work for Christ that you have no strength left for praying"(8). The same was true for C.T. Studd, pioneer missionary to the Congo, Africa. He got up at four every morning and spent two hours in prayer and Bible study, always using a Bible that was no more than a year old so that what he read was fresh and new. George Muller of Bristol, England, who by faith alone, fed, clothed, sheltered and educated over 2000 orphans daily, spent the early hours of every morning in worship and prayer. The list goes on and on of those who were enabled to believe God, by faith, for the miraculous because they spent time with God alone and knew Him intimately. No matter which biography you read of those who have had the greatest impact for God down through the centuries, you will see that the secret of spiritual power in their lives came from spending the early hours of the day with God alone. From E.M. Bounds we read, "The men who have done the most for God in this world have been early on their knees. He who fritters away the early morning, its opportunity and freshness, in other pursuits than seeking God will make poor headway in seeking Him the rest of the day. If God is not first in our thoughts and efforts in the morning, He will be in the last place the rest of the day"(9). There appears to be a power and productivity that only comes from meeting with God alone in the early hours. This has certainly proven to be true in my own life.

No Excuses

The most common objection offered by most Christians to spending time with God in the early morning is simply, "I don't have time." Many say, "I'm just too busy to do that" or "I have too much to do in the morning to take time out for that." Or maybe, "I cannot go without sleep." Dear friend the list of excuses for not meeting with our Heavenly Father at the beginning of the day goes on and on, but that's all they are - excuses. I am familiar with all of them and have used many of them myself. I know what it is to have to stay up late studying or working and then get up in the morning and get the kids off to school. I fully understand the word "busy." I understand the tendency to fall back on excuses, but none of them are acceptable. There is no good reason for neglecting time with God. There is also no escaping the fact that such neglect undermines the formation and growth of faith in our life. Personally, I am busier now than I have ever been in my life, but correspondingly, I am also more aware than ever before of the necessity of spending time with God alone. If you are living a busy life with a crowded schedule, I can certainly empathize, but I cannot offer you an acceptable or suitable alternative for spending time with God. There simply isn't one.

Now let me say this to you, "early" for you may not be four in the morning. Hudson Taylor, C.T. Studd, George Muller and others chose that time because if they waited until daylight their time would be occupied with the affairs of the day, which were already underway. The most important thing is not the hour on the clock itself, but that you give God the FIRST part of the day. Meet with HIM before you do anything else. Your particular schedule and lifestyle may allow you to do that at six or seven or eight in the morning. The important thing is to have quiet, uninterrupted time with God alone at the beginning of your day, regardless of what time it is. I promise you that any day of your life will go better if it begins by meeting with the "Eternal Committee," the Father, the Son and the Holy Spirit. They are always in session and are always anxious for you to join Them.

It Is Worth It!

One thing I have learned about human beings is, generally speaking, they do what they WANT to do. You might tell me that there is no way you could get up at four in the morning, or even at six or eight, and spend two hours in prayer and fellowship with God. Well let me ask you this, if someone called you and told you they wanted to give you one million dollars but to get it you would have to meet them at a restaurant at four in the morning and spend two hours talking with them, would you go? I guarantee you would. Why? Because you would WANT to. Why? Because it would be WORTH it to you to make the effort. I assure you there is far more waiting for you in the presence of God in the first hours of your day than could ever be measured in monetary terms. Consider this: someday your life on earth will come to an end and after that you will spend ALL your time with God. Why not start now and add some huge quality to the small quantity of life you have left. To his team of missionaries on the field in China, Hudson Taylor wrote these words, "The hardest part of a missionary career is to maintain regular, prayerful Bible study. Satan will always find you something to do when you ought to be occupied about that" (10). Oswald Chambers wrote, "The great enemy to the Lord Jesus Christ is the conception of practical work that has not come from the New Testament, but from the systems of the world in which endless energy and activities are insisted upon, but no private life with God. It is the innermost of the innermost that reveals the power of the life" (11).

A Solitary Place

Once you have decided that you are going to set aside a specific time in the early morning to worship God alone, the next question is - where? Looking again at Genesis 19:27 we see that when Abraham got up early in the morning to meet with God he did not go to "a" place, but he went to "...*THE place where he stood before the Lord*." And again Mark 1:35  tells us that Jesus went to a solitary place and there He prayed. In Matthew 6:6 Jesus tells us when we pray to "*enter into thy closet.*" Our place to meet with God should be specific, suitable and solitary. Brother Don went to his study and later to his little room at home. I have two places that I go to meet with God. One is my rocking chair in my study at home and the other is the swing on our back porch. Both are very private, quiet and secluded. The important thing is that you find a place where you can have quiet uninterrupted time with God, a place where you will be free from distractions.

Enemies of Private Worship

Now, let me ask you, as you approach the end of this chapter do you sense a determination rising in your heart to begin spending time alone with God, or to increase and intensify the time you are already spending with Him? I do, and I'm the guy writing the book. I already spend a lot of time with God in the first hours of the day. But, I am going to make a confession to you. There are still mornings, even after all these years, when it is a battle to get out of bed and get to my time and place with God alone. The reason is that I have two relentless opposing enemies to contend with, my own flesh and the devil. We must remember that there is only one part of us that is saved and cares anything at all about worshipping God - our spirit. Our body, our intellect and our emotions have yet to be redeemed.

They are still natural and the natural man has no interest in God. Then there is the devil who has been in competition with God from the very beginning, and is to this day, for the thing he craves the most - worship. Listen to how satan phrased the temptation when he approached Jesus in the wilderness, *"All these things will I give thee, if thou wilt fall down and worship me"* (Matthew 4:9). The very last thing satan wants is for any Christian to spend time in worship and fellowship with God. He does not want us to hear the voice of God and he does not want God to hear ours. He will do all in his limited power to cut off our communication with the Father. Why? Because, if there is no communication with God, then there will be no knowledge of His will and no obedience to carry it out, thus eliminating the opportunity for faith and the possibility of bringing glory to God. Satan knows that real worship leads to real faith.

So then, how do we break through and get to that time and place of worship? We must come to a place where we realize how much is at stake, and we must come to a place where we want God more than we want anything else. Time alone with God in private worship and communion must become more important to us and more valuable to us than anything else in life. It must become the one thing in our life we are willing to fight for and that we will not give up. Until that happens, the faith life will not develop. Listen to how David expressed his desire for God *"As the hart panteth after the water brooks, so panteth my soul after Thee, O God"* (Psalm 42:1). *"O God, thou art my God; early will I seek thee: my soul thirsteth for Thee..."* (Psalm 63:1). *"My soul longeth, yea, even fainteth for the courts of the Lord: my heart and my flesh crieth out for the living God"* (Psalm 84:2). The development of a life of faith within our Christian life begins with total consecration to God Himself. Desire for God Himself is the very air in our spiritual lungs. Desire for church, for Christian fellowship, for Bible knowledge, and so on will not suffice. Those are good and wonderful things, but it is the longing for God Himself that makes us breathe spiritually. Ask yourself, and be brutally honest, is there anything in life you want more than God? Is there anything in your life you ascribe more value to than your relationship with Him? Let's ask it this way, if God removed everything from your life that you hold dear and you were left with nothing but Him, would He be enough? That can be a frightening question if you allow satan to turn it into one. But it doesn't have to be. Let me answer it for you. Yes, God would be enough, because by His grace, He would make Himself enough for you. So right now, gain victory over satan and declare out loud, "Lord, I desire You above everything else and I place You above everything in my life." Dear friend, real worship is not only **private** and **personal**, it is also **primary** for the development of your life of faith.

Start Now

All it takes for you to change the course of your life is for you to boldly declare "NO MORE!" No more will I allow satan to deceive me or cheat me out of the powerful, productive, and extraordinary life that God wants me to have. No more will I be diverted from faith that pleases God. No more will I be distracted from worship and intimate fellowship with the Father by activity that does not originate with Him. No more will I make empty excuses for not giving God the first place in my schedule and my day. From this day forward my God gets the **first**, the **best,** and the **most**.

Now, you may ask, "But how do I get started?" Friend, you just start. Don't plan it to death, just do it. There have been many "plans" published over the years to help Christians in their attempt to spend meaningful time with God. But, right now you don't need a plan; you need a <u>decision</u>. The idea here is to focus on GOD, not a plan. Don't try to get too organized. That will come in time. The first thing you do is set a time to get out of the bed in the morning and designate a specific place where you are going to go to meet with God every day. Set your alarm clock and put it some place where you will have to get out of bed to turn it off. I suggest that in the beginning you allow yourself an hour. That will give you time to wake up, get some coffee, and settle in for a time of worship and fellowship with God. No, God doesn't mind if you drink coffee. In fact, in my case He may <u>prefer</u> that I do.

Now, how do you begin? Well, again, there is no set pattern, prescription, plan or program for spending time with God in private worship, communion and fellowship. You may want to begin by just saying to God, "Lord, here I am. I have come to spend time with You, to worship You, to have fellowship with You, but I really don't know exactly how to go about it, so guide me during this time and make it meaningful and beneficial to You and me both." Then just let it happen. As you do you will notice day by day that your time with God will include at least four recurring elements. The first is **repentance**. It is not possible to abide in the presence of God with a dirty heart, with sin in our life. Therefore, if there is anything that needs correction, the Holy Spirit will point it out so that we may confess it to God and receive cleansing by the blood of Jesus. Very often I begin my time with God by simply saying to Him, "Lord, if there is anything standing between You and me, if there is any sin, any disobedience, hindering my fellowship with You, please tell me so that I can confess it and be cleansed of it and have unhindered access to You." Faith depends upon communication with God and communication is hindered only by one thing - sin. The second recurring element is **reflection**. As you enter into your time with God you will invariably find yourself simply reflecting upon Who He is. Just thinking upon the goodness of God, His love, mercy, kindness, longsuffering, gentleness, majesty, sovereignty and eternal "almightiness" will cause praise, adoration, and faith to rise up in our hearts. Then there will be the element of **remembering**, not only Who God is, but what He has done for us in the past and how He is blessing our life right now. In Psalm 77:1-9 we find David in desperation and depression, but in verses 10-13 everything changed. Listen to what he said, *"And I said, This is my infirmity: but I will remember the years of the right hand of the Most High. I will remember the works of the Lord: surely I will remember thy wonders of old. I will meditate* [reflect upon] *also of all thy work, and talk of thy doings. Thy way O God, is in the sanctuary: who is so great a God as our God? "* All it took for David to shift out of despair into declaring the goodness of God was simply taking time to remember, to reflect, to worship. In doing so everything changed - his thinking, his language, his vision, and his faith. The fourth element that will always come from worship is **receiving**. In the presence of God we will receive new and afresh the filling of the Holy Spirit which always brings renewed joy, peace, comfort, vision and faith. You will receive instruction from the Holy Spirit in your inner man, and you will receive the knowledge of the will of God concerning various issues in your life, as well as His enabling to trust Him for specific faith objects.

Dear Christian, you do not have to struggle to cause these elements to occur in your time with God. They will come on their own. You do not have to strive for structure. It will develop as you go along. The important thing is that you start. The important thing is that you spend time with God alone and take the first step in the development of a life of faith. As you wait quietly before Him, God will begin putting things in your heart to trust Him for. He will begin to reveal His will to you and He will empower you to trust Him by faith to fulfill it. As you spend time with God alone in private worship and fellowship, a spiritual atmosphere will develop and out of it, the faith that pleases God and believes for the impossible.

I want to close this chapter by saying again that to have a real faith life you must have a real worship life. Faith begins with knowing the will of God, and you can't know it apart from spending time with Him. Very often my worship time gives way to a working time. For that reason, I always carry my Bible, my pen, and a legal pad into my times with God. As I worship God and wait before Him in the quietness of the early hours, He will very often reveal things to me and give me instructions that I will not receive any other time. I pay very careful attention to what comes to me during these times, because it is coming from Him. By His Spirit, He is speaking to my spirit. What I am hearing is not just a good idea, but it is God's instructions. I have found over the years that I can trust what comes to me in those times with God alone. Why? Because it is not from me, it is from Him.

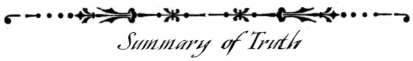

Summary of Truth

❖ For faith to develop in my life, I must spend time with God alone

❖ God wants to take me beyond the ordinary.

❖ There is never a time when God does not approve of me.

❖ The life of Jesus, Christian history, and the Word of God suggest that the best time to spend with God is the early part of the day.

❖ Jesus found it necessary to spend time with the Father in the early hours of the day.

❖ The men and women who have had the greatest impact upon the world for Christ are those who made it a practice of spending time with God alone early in the morning.

❖ In order to trust God I must first KNOW God. The only way to know Him is to spend time WITH Him.

❖ There is no substitute for spending time with God and no acceptable excuse for neglecting to do so.

❖ If I spend time with God it will be because I WANT to and because I think it is WORTH the effort.

❖ Satan is doing all within his power to prevent me from spending time alone with God.

❖ I have the power to change the course of my life by choosing to spend time with God alone in the early morning. By doing so I will begin creating an atmosphere for faith.

❖ I can trust what God says to me during my time alone with Him.

NOW LET'S TAKE A MOMENT AND PRAY TOGETHER:

DEAR FATHER, I KNOW THAT THE MOST IMPORTANT THING IN MY CHRISTIAN LIFE IS SPENDING TIME WITH YOU ALONE. IT IS ONLY IN YOUR PRESENCE THAT I FIND SPIRITUAL POWER. HELP ME TO NOT MAKE EXCUSES FOR NEGLECTING YOU. I DECLARE BY THE AUTHORITY OF THE LORD JESUS, THAT I WILL NOT ALLOW MYSELF TO BE CHEATED OUT OF THE POWERFUL, PRODUCTIVE, EXTRAORDINARY LIFE THAT YOU WANT ME TO HAVE. NO MORE WILL I BE DIVERTED FROM FAITH THAT PLEASES YOU. I WILL NOT BE DISTRACTED FROM WORSHIP AND INTIMATE FELLOWSHIP WITH YOU BY ACTIVITY THAT DOES NOT ORIGINATE WITH YOU. NO MORE WILL I MAKE EXCUSES FOR NOT GIVING YOU FIRST PLACE IN MY DAY. FROM THIS MOMENT FORWARD LORD JESUS, YOU GET THE FIRST, THE BEST AND THE MOST. THANK YOU FOR SAVING ME, LOVING ME, AND BLESSING ME AND FOR WELCOMING ME INTO YOUR PRESENCE. IN YOUR NAME I PRAY. AMEN.

Chapter 16

Real Faith Requires Knowing God's Will First

"What does God say about it? What God says is always original, always in the impossible, and great enough to be worthy of Him."
Norman Grubb (1)

One of the most enlightening and liberating truths contained in this book is found in the title of this chapter – **faith requires knowing**, in fact faith <u>begins</u> with knowing. One of the deadliest misconceptions concerning faith is that it begins with me and relates only to the future. From our natural human perspective it does, but as we will see later, from God's viewpoint it is anchored in the past and in the present and rests <u>entirely</u> upon His will. Real faith is based in the known, not the unknown. It relates to what we have, not what we hope to have. It relates to the finished work. It is not a blind leap into the dark; it is a deliberate step into the light – into the received will of God.

In the following chapters we are going to deal with <u>where</u> to find God's will and <u>how</u>, but here we are going to discover <u>why</u> real God-faith is only possible by **knowing the will of God FIRST**. We begin by observing that real prayer and faith is not just YOU deciding what you want God to do or provide and then asking Him for it and <u>hoping</u> He will do it. It is far more than that. In fact that's not even close to the real thing. Nothing about faith involves hoping or wishing. Real faith is GOD telling you in your spirit what HE is going to do or what He is going to provide in relation to your need, desire, circumstances, etc., then you asking Him and believing Him for what He shows you to be His will. Real faith is not YOU developing a plan and then calling God in to bless it and fulfill it. Real faith is having HIS plan made known to you and then you joining Him in it. Real faith begins with God, not you. It begins with knowing His will first and that requires spending private time with him in personal worship and fellowship. God <u>activates</u> our capacity of faith by various means (which we will look at later), but those means do not <u>reveal</u> His will, they cause us rather to <u>seek</u> His will. It is always God who takes the initiative in the faith process. It is not possible for anyone, regardless of how earnest or sincere they may be, to believe God for something that He is not going to do or not going to provide - something that is not His will. He will not call upon you to do that, and furthermore He will not <u>allow</u> you to do that. What He <u>will</u> do is meet with you, make His will known to you, and then enable you to trust Him by faith to fulfill it. Real faith is **knowing** and then acting upon what you know. Real faith is **receiving and possessing** and then using what you have received and now possess.

Jesus, Our Supreme Example

The Christian life, the Spirit-filled life, the abiding life, the faith life is simply walking in accordance with the will of God. It is literally living out the will of God moment by moment. That is exactly what Jesus did as He walked upon earth, and we are to do the same thing. He is the supreme example of the life of real faith. It is important for us to remember that even though Jesus was God incarnate, God in human flesh, He did not perform His earthly ministry <u>as</u> God, but as man <u>trusting</u> God. Listen to His revealing words to His disciples in John 4:34, *"...My meat* [food] *is to do the will of him that sent me, and to finish **his** work."* Then in 5:30, *"**I can of mine own self do nothing**. As I hear, I judge: and my judgment is just, because I seek **not mine own will**, but the will of the Father which hath sent me."* Again in 6:38 Jesus said, *"For I came down from heaven, **not to do mine own will but the will of him that sent me**."* Jesus had no program, no plan, and no agenda

How important it is to ascertain the will of God, before we undertake anything.

George Muller (2)

of His own. Very clearly, He never acted out of His own will or impulse. Everything He did, every decision He made, and every word He spoke was in strict compliance with the will of the Father. Even in the Garden of Gethsemane He prayed, *"...Father, if thou be willing, remove this cup from me: **nevertheless, not my will, but thine, be done**"* (Luke 22:42). His will was brought into subordination to that of the Father. Jesus was the channel through which the Father's will flowed, and so are we to be. Every act performed and every word spoken was an act of faith and a word of faith performed and spoken in accordance with the will of God.

Jesus told us in Matthew 6:10 to pray, *"...Thy will be done in earth, as it is in heaven."* How? Through us, as we speak and act in faith in compliance with the revealed will of God. When Jesus walked upon the earth HE was the channel through which the will of the Father flowed. The Father had the thought, the Son spoke the word, and the Holy Spirit used the word to create and bring the will of God to pass in the natural realm. After Jesus ascended, He sent the Holy Spirit to indwell those of us who believe on Him, thus placing us in the same position He occupied while on earth. Now the thought of God, His will, is placed in our heart, we speak the word (of faith), and the Holy Spirit brings it to pass. We will look at this more closely later on, but for now suffice it to say that God's way of transferring His will from heaven to earth, His way of executing the work of His Kingdom in the natural world, is through His children - His church. This is the process of real faith: hearing the voice of God in our spirit, speaking and acting in accordance with it, and then seeing the object or outcome brought to pass by the Holy Spirit.

Real Faith Is Based in the Fact of God's Will

We must know the will of God first because real faith is based in <u>fact</u>. As I said, a common misconception is that faith relates to what we do not have and what we do not know. That is wrong. Real faith rests in real fact – what we DO have and what we DO know. Looking again at our operational definition we see that real Bible-faith is **"Choosing to act upon the revealed will of God, using power and resources that only He has access to."** The key phrase here is "<u>the revealed will of God</u>." We have said that faith is **persuasion of fact followed by corresponding action.** Faith operates according to established fact – in the natural realm as well as the spiritual. An example we used before is that of sitting in a chair. You perceive with your natural senses that the chair is real and reliable, and based upon that perception you act; you sit in it. Spiritual faith operates the same way. There is no guesswork in real faith because it is anchored in real fact. The thing that makes real faith real is that it is attached to an object or outcome that is real – that actually exists,

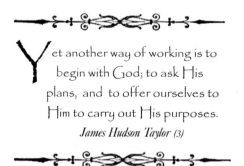

Yet another way of working is to begin with God; to ask His plans, and to offer ourselves to Him to carry out His purposes.

James Hudson Taylor (3)

whether it be in the visible, natural realm or the invisible, spiritual realm. Natural faith works because it has something in the natural world it can see, that it knows is real – like the chair. In like manner, the thing that enables spiritual faith to work is that it also has something in the spiritual realm it can "see" with the eyes of the spirit, something it knows is real – the settled will of God. You might have an urgent need in your life or a strong desire in your heart or a pressing situation in your circumstances, but that need, that desire, that situation will never turn into real faith without an actual existing object or outcome to become attached to. **Real faith must have a guarantee.** So where do we find that object, that assured outcome, that established fact or guarantee? In the natural realm it is provided by your natural senses and in the spiritual realm it is provided by your spiritual senses – that is, the knowledge of the settled will of God made known to your spirit by the Holy Spirit.

Hebrews 11:1 says, *"Now faith is the **substance** [the assurance, the* title deed] *of things hoped for, the **evidence** [the proof, the conviction} of things not seen."* Faith is a process that begins with the activation of the capacity of faith followed by certainty, concrete assurance, and a solid knowledge of God's will. Certainty is THE key factor in effective prayer, real faith, and decisive obedience. Reliable knowledge of fact produces real faith, which results in right action. Real faith will not occur in our life unless there is a "title deed" (assurance) to go with it. You will discover later on in your experience that **the very fact that faith exists in your heart is indication that the object or outcome exists also.** One cannot exist apart from the other. I know that an object or outcome is real, is God's will, because my capacity for faith (to believe for it) has been stirred up and activated by the Holy Spirit. **Real faith does not need evidence; it IS the evidence.**

Without the assurance of God's will all we can do is guess, hope, or wish. Real faith, whether in the visible or in the invisible, is not guessing or hoping or wishing; it is knowing, possessing, receiving, taking, and using. It is not hoping in what might happen or in what might be provided. Real God-faith is believing based upon assurance of God's will. It is acting and speaking in accordance with what we know (from God's viewpoint) has already happened and has already been provided.

Throughout the Bible we find God telling individuals that He was going to do this or that. Then He would tell them to go, say what He had said, and believe Him for the completion of it. In Hebrews 11, we find a long list of ordinary people who did great exploits of faith because of one thing; they had God's say-so and chose to step out on it. They believed (acted) because they "heard" the voice of God, *"...faith cometh by hearing..."* (Romans 10:17). They "saw" into the invisible. *"By faith, Noah, being warned of God of things not seen as yet, moved with fear, prepared an ark to the saving of his house..."* (Hebrews 11:7) That is the process of faith - **hearing** the voice of God, **believing** Him for what He has promised, **proclaiming** publicly that it is going to come to pass, and then **continuing to say it** and **acting** as if it is true until it *does* come to pass - **even if it means waiting until the very last minute,** and it often will.

In Acts 27 we see Paul in the storm telling his shipmates that they need not fear because God had told him they would all survive. He was just repeating what he had been told. Now you may say, "Well that's easy. Sure you can believe God for something and say it is going to happen if God tells you it is." That is the whole point. We can do the same thing. In fact God does not want or expect you to believe for something or to say it will happen unless He first confirms it to you in your spirit. It is not necessary that He speak in an audible voice, or by means of an angel, or by visions and dreams, because we are now indwelt by the Holy Spirit Who speaks clearly within our inner man. All we have to do is listen. We can hear with the "ears" of our spirit and see with the "eyes" of our spirit. Therefore God expects us to look and listen and to believe and receive.

Real Faith Is Entering the Finished Work

A concept I have already alluded to, and that may be a little difficult to grasp, is that from God's standpoint everything is already accomplished and complete. Therefore, real faith is simply entering His finished work. Hebrews 4:3 tells us, *"...the works* [of God] *were finished from the foundation of the world."* To put it another way, God has no "future." As humans living in the natural world, we view events as past, present, and future. God does not look at it that way. From His viewpoint everything in history is already accomplished. He even revealed part of it to the Apostle John who, under the inspiration of the Holy Spirit, recorded it in the book of the Revelation. Now, is there any possibility that history will not turn out the way John recorded it? No, of course not. God's will is settled in eternity and does not change. It is absolute. From God's perspective it has already happened. He is not making His will up as He goes along or as we go along in our lives. God is not trying to figure out what He is going to do next based upon the ever-changing circumstances of my life. He is never caught by surprise or caught off guard. He is not making up His plan for my life on the fly. God's will is, and always has been, a settled issue - for everything, including the very life I am living right now.

The literal meaning of the word "finished" in Hebrews 4:3 is "brought to their predestined end." The meaning of the word "foundation" is "conception." So what the Bible is telling us is that even from His very conception of the world, God's works were completed, brought to His intended conclusion. There is nothing left for God to do and nothing left for us to do other than enter into His finished work by the choice of faith. All God is looking for is

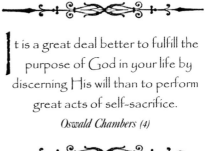

It is a great deal better to fulfill the purpose of God in your life by discerning His will than to perform great acts of self-sacrifice.

Oswald Chambers (4)

some one who will receive His will, take Him at His Word, and believe Him, by faith, to do what He says He will do. God is looking for channels (Believers who will believe) through which He can flow His will into this earth. The weakest, feeblest Christian alive can be that channel by making the choice of faith.

As I said, this is a truth that is sometimes hard to grasp because we think of the future in terms of things that are yet to happen, not as things already accomplished. But to understand the ways of God and His working in our life, we need to see things from God's viewpoint; we need to get on His side of the page. It is this understanding that makes real God-faith possible. Imagine yourself standing at the end of a long highway and looking toward the other end. That highway you are looking down is what you call your future. If you begin walking down it you will be entering into events and circumstances that you think of as yet to happen. But on the other end is God, and He is looking at it from an entirely different perspective. He views it as finished. As far as He is concerned you have lived your life in its entirety, you are already in heaven with Him, and He is already enjoying your worship and fellowship (Romans 8:29-30).

Now suppose it was possible for God to move you from your end of the highway down to His, so that you could turn around and look not at what is yet to come but at what has already happened. Would that add a different dimension to your life? Of course it would. Well, my friend, part of the operation of real faith is trusting God to do just that - show you His will concerning specific objects and outcomes that He is calling upon you to trust Him for. You see, in the issue of faith, the question is not, "What is God going to do or provide?" The real question is "What <u>did</u> he do and what <u>did</u> He provide?" Jesus said in John 16:13 *"...when he, the Spirit of truth, is come, he will guide you into all truth; for he shall not speak of himself* [out of His own will], *but whatsoever he shall hear* [from the Father], *that shall he speak: and he will <u>shew you things to come.</u> "*

Let's look at , Mark 11:24, *"Therefore I say unto you, what things soever ye desire, when ye pray, believe that ye receive them, and ye shall have them. "* This passage assumes that the thing you desire is within the will of God since the desire has come as a result of prayer. It is <u>not</u> something I desire so I keep praying until I receive it. It <u>is</u> a desire that God places in my heart and the more I pray about it, the more the desire grows because it is from Him. Also, remember that the word "believe" means "to act." Now notice the word "receive". It is in the past tense, so it literally reads, "believe that you <u>have already received</u> them." The last phrase in the verse that is translated "and ye shall have" in the KJV, means "it shall be" or "it shall come into existence to you." In other words, by means of your believing, the will of God (His acts and His provision), which exists in the invisible (God's dimension), will be transferred into the visible (our dimension). Therefore, if we act in accordance with the fact that the thing we are asking for has already been done or provided, then it will be. Let me say once again, **real faith is simply entering into the finished work.**

Let me share with you an incident that took place in my life back in 1980, one that God used to teach me a great lesson about faith and knowing the will of God. I was planning to go to Korea in September for an evangelistic campaign and I did not have the money to go. I also had no idea where it could come from. I prayed for days and weeks, but nothing happened. I knew in my spirit it was the will of God for me to go, but I could not seem to move beyond that point into faith, into believing God for the money. Satan bombarded my mind with questions, doubt and fear.

Finally one afternoon, while I was sitting outside praying and contemplating the situation, I heard a jet airplane passing over. As I looked up at that plane something happened that changed everything. All of a sudden, it was if God pulled back the veil and allowed me to see something. I saw myself on that plane three weeks into the future taking off to go to Korea. As the plane lifted off, I looked back over the city and saw my house with the rent and bills paid. I saw Sheila and the kids well supplied with groceries, gas for the car, and money for school lunches. I even saw what I was wearing on departure day, a plaid sport coat. I saw myself sitting on that plane in peace. At that moment something happened in my heart - I believed what I saw and I received it as finished. It was done - not in the physical natural world, but in the spiritual realm. God had taken me to the other end of the highway and allowed me to look backwards. It was as real to me as if I was already holding the money in my hand. I bowed my head, asked God to make it so, received it from Him, and then thanked Him for doing it. I still had three weeks to go before leaving, and I still had to wait for the money to come. But the struggle was gone because in my heart I had already received it. I had seen through to the other side. God's will, along with God's supply, had become solidified in my heart, and I was persuaded of its reality. From that moment forward I was operating according to what I knew, not according to what I was hoping for. All fear and doubt was gone. Satan's questions were silenced. The "what ifs" no longer applied. I was living out the finished work. I did not know how God was going to supply or through what channels, but it didn't matter. I knew He was going to, because in my heart He already had.

When the day of departure came it was exactly as God had shown me, even down to the plaid sport coat. I learned something there that day, a simple lesson - the lesson of waiting upon God and trusting Him to show us the other side, to show us the finished work. He will do that in every occasion of faith if we will just wait upon Him. Now, does God always help me believe when I am going somewhere by allowing me to see myself on an airplane? No, of course not. That was the only time in my life that happened. His ways are always fresh and new and original. But He will make His will known to us in such a way so that we can become persuaded of it and make the choice of faith.

Have you ever worked a jigsaw puzzle? I don't care for them myself, but Sheila loves them, the big ones with thousands of pieces. I have watched her work many of them and I have noticed that she has a method she uses

every time. She always sets the box up on edge and then begins to lay out the pieces. Do you know why she sets that box up so she can look at it? Of course you do. It has a picture on it of what the puzzle will look like when it is finished. During the entire process she is working according to the picture and when she is finished she will know it is correct because it looks just like the box. That is exactly what takes place in real faith. At the very outset God shows us the "picture on the box" in our spirit. Then as we walk in obedience to His will, He puts the pieces together in such a way that, in the end, the object or outcome looks exactly like what He showed us in our heart.

REAL faith starts with God and ends with God. It is based in and upon His finished work, and that fact equals total security. He painted the picture on the box, He made all the pieces to the puzzle and He knows how to put them all together. In any venture of faith, in any occasion for faith, if you can see the clear initiation of God in it, then you can be sure He will bring it to completion. The key is to know the will of God first. Hebrews 12:2 says that Jesus is *"...the author* [starter] *and finisher of our faith."* Looking to Him produces certainty. In order for faith to be real it must originate in the thought and will of God. If I know that God started it, I can be sure He will finish it - regardless of any opposition encountered along the way, whether it be human, satanic, or circumstantial.

Many years ago my wife and I responded to the call of God and entered, by faith, the ministry of international evangelism. We had no idea as to how we were going to meet our daily needs, let alone how we were going to travel all over the world preaching the Gospel. But we did not have to know, because what we did know was that we were doing the sure will of God. We could see with crystal clear vision the initiation of God. We could see it then, and we can see it now all these years later. There have been many trying days along the way, days in which we did not know where our next penny or our next meal would come from, but we have always been secure. Why? How? Because we have always known two things; God told us to do what we are doing, and He has not told us to do anything else. Between those two points is total security. There is nothing more secure than walking in the settled will of God, because along with it comes His unfailing supply.

God's Will Equals God's Supply

To walk in the will of God is to also walk in the constant supply of God. If a person lives in accordance with his own will, apart from the will of God, then he also lives within the limitations of his own ideas, imagination, abilities, and resources. Regardless of how limited or limitless our natural abilities and resources seem to be, they will never take us to where God wants us to go. But, the choice to live in accordance with God's will extends our reach into the invisible, into the realm of the impossible, and will take us where God wants us to go. It places at our disposal limitless resources that we could never have access to otherwise. Along with the knowledge of God's will always comes the supply to carry it out. Allow me to share a simple illustration.

When I was about ten years old we lived in the Mississippi Delta town of Yazoo City. All the rest of our family lived in Memphis. As you would expect, we made periodic trips to visit them. I remember one Friday morning Dad told us that after he closed the store on Saturday night we were going to Memphis. Then later that day my fourth grade teacher, Mrs. Byrd, asked me what I was going to do over the weekend. I answered with absolute certainty; "I am going to Memphis on Saturday night to see my Grandparents." Now, how could I, a ten-year old kid, make that bold statement? I had no car, I did not know how to drive, I had no money, and I did not even know the way to get there. I could make that statement because I was simply repeating what my father had said, and I knew he had everything necessary to make it happen. He had money, a car, the ability to drive it, and he knew the way. It would have been impossible for me to make that two hundred mile trip out of my own will and resources, but it was no problem to do it in compliance with Dad's will using his resources. The moment I entered into his will, his plan, I had everything I needed. During the day on Saturday I packed up everything I wanted to take on the trip. That was a simple act of faith. I was acting upon persuasion. I was persuaded that what my father said was true. I could act in full assurance because I knew his will first.

As I write this it is now November and we are planning to go to Kenya in January. At this point we do not have the money to go. Nothing new about that. Furthermore, we will not be appealing for funds because our ministry policy of non-solicitation (which God instructed us to live by) prohibits us from asking for money. But I am as sure that we are going to do a campaign in Kenya in January, as I was that I was going to Memphis on that Saturday night long ago. How can I be so sure? I have no money, no one has indicated they are going to send us any, I do not own an airplane, and I certainly do not know how to fly one. But, what I do have is the Father's say-so. I have the assurance in my spirit, in my inner man, that it is God's will, and I know that as we step into His will, His abundant supply becomes available to us. He has the money to cover all the campaign costs, a jet airplane to get us there, and a pilot to fly it. We can continue to prepare to go, to promote the project in Nairobi and so on, and we can do it with full assurance of completion because of one thing and one thing only - we know God's will FIRST. I have seen the picture on the box and I believe it. Hudson Taylor made a statement long ago that we still find to be true today. He said, "God is too wise to allow His own purposes to be frustrated for lack of a little money" (5).

God's Will Sets the Parameters for Faith

In an earlier chapter, "Misconceptions," we talked about the fact that no Christian has any greater amount of faith than any other Christian. What they do have, however, are different spheres or areas in which to exercise faith. Those areas or parameters are set by the fixed will of God. Real faith is not open-ended; it has limits, and those limits are set by God's will. It is therefore imperative that we know what the will of God is; otherwise it is impossible to know what to believe God for. It is tragic to believe God for less than He wants to do or give, but it is futile, foolish and frustrating to attempt to believe God for more than is encompassed by His will.

Years ago, when we were first learning about faith, we needed a refrigerator. Now, in those days, a new refrigerator was WAY out of our league. I asked Sheila what kind she would like, and she said, "I would love to have one of those side-by-side refrigerators with an ice-maker." Man, she didn't want much, did she! I could just imagine what that would cost! Then I asked what color she wanted and she said "Harvest Gold. It will look good in the kitchen." So, we started praying about it. After a few days, God

 said, "Yes, you can have that kind of refrigerator, and it's going to cost $300." I said, "But God, I don't have $300. I was thinking more like $200." Now, I didn't have $200 either, but somehow that just seemed more feasible than $300. Well, the Holy Spirit spoke right back in my heart and said, "You can think all you want, but it's going to cost $300, and that's how much you are going to have to trust me for." I finally said, "OK God, you show me the refrigerator, and I will trust you for the money." So, I told Sheila what God had said to me, and we agreed to trust God for $300. The next day I found an ad in the paper for used refrigerators and felt impressed to go look. There in the store was a beautiful, harvest gold, side-by-side refrigerator. I mean it looked brand new! I asked the man about it and he said, "Oh, I just got that in yesterday. This lady was remodeling her kitchen and the gold color just wouldn't work anymore." I opened the

door, and sure enough, there was an icemaker. With fear and trepidation I asked the price. "$300 bucks," he said. As soon as the words left his mouth, God said, "This is the one. I've been saving it for you." Instantly, the peace and assurance of God flooded my heart, and I told the man I would take it. I asked if he would hold it till I could go home and get the money and he said he would. On the way home, I thought, "OK God, now what do I do?" When I got home, I told Sheila that I had found THE refrigerator. She was so excited and then said, "What do we do about the money?" Just then I heard a knock on the door, and there was a friend of mine. He said, "Shad, God woke me up this morning and told me to bring this to you right away." He handed me an envelope, and in it was $300. Oh friend, the joy that flooded my soul! Sheila and I were overwhelmed at the provision of God for us. We couldn't praise Him enough or tell enough people of how he had met our need!

Now, you might ask, "Why was God so insistent on that amount?" I don't know. Only God knows the answer to that question. What I do know, however, is that it would have been a mistake to settle for a lesser refrigerator to save money, and it would have been a mistake to try to believe Him for a more expensive refrigerator. The key in that situation, as in all others,

God Himself, God alone, is sufficient for God's own work.

Hudson Taylor (6)

was to find God's plan, to know His will, and to believe Him for THAT. As I said, real faith has boundaries and knowing God's plan will prevent us from trying to exceed them and from stopping short of them. Dear friend, this applies to every area of life for every Christian – not just guys like me who are in the ministry. And by the way, it was a great refrigerator, and Sheila loved her gift from God right up to the day it quit working – 18 years and an "Almond" paint job later.

Extremeties of Faith

The Bible is filled with examples of ordinary people who did extraordinary exploits of faith by simply receiving the plan of God and joining Him in it. You will find a long list of them in Hebrews eleven. One of the most outstanding examples, of course, is the life of Abraham. God told him in Genesis 17:19, *"...Sarah thy wife shall bare thee a son indeed; and thou shalt call his name Isaac: and I will establish my covenant with him for an everlasting covenant, and with his seed after him.* " There it was, the will of God – unbelievable, impractical, impossible, contrary to natural law, and defiant of common sense – but the established will of Almighty God nonetheless, revealed to a human being. In chapter 21 we see the child born to a ninety-year-old woman, *"...and the Lord did unto Sarah as he had spoken. "*

Now in chapter 22 we see Abraham called upon once again to trust God for the impossible. God told him to take Isaac up on Mount Moriah and sacrifice him, and Abraham did exactly as he was instructed. He took two young men along with Isaac and when they arrived at the base of the mountain he told them, *"...Abide ye here with the ass; and I and the lad will go yonder and worship, and come again to you"* (v.5). When Isaac asked about the lamb to be sacrificed his father told him, *"...My son, God will provide himself a lamb for a burnt offering..."* (v.8). Abraham took Isaac to the top of the mountain, built an altar, laid the wood on it, and bound Isaac and placed him on the wood. As he raised the knife to slay his son, God stopped him and said, *"...now I know that thou fearest God..."* (v.12). Hebrews 11:17 tells us that he *"offered up Isaac"* because he had *"received the promises. "* Abraham knew it was God's will for the nation of Israel to come through Isaac and that could not happen if Isaac was dead. He therefore thought God was going to raise him from the dead. The bottom line is that Abraham was willing and was enabled to go to the very extremities of faith for one reason only – he knew the will of God FIRST.

Twenty-six Minutes Before Departure

There have been many times over the years when God has called upon us to go to the extremities of faith concerning our overseas campaigns. Allow me to share a brief story. We had a project in Malawi, Africa on the calendar some years ago, and we knew without a doubt it was God's will to go. He had given us deep assurance in our hearts early on in the year, and it was a settled issue. We were scheduled to depart at 10:00 in the morning on Thursday, November 7. During the afternoon on the day before, Sheila and I sat in her office discussing the fact that we needed $3,000 for expenses and we had nothing. So we prayed, confessed to God that we were confident that it was His will for us to go, and asked Him to provide the needed $3,000 before our departure the next day. We both sensed in our spirit that He was doing it right then. We received it by faith and thanked Him for it in advance. That evening we finished packing our bags (we didn't need any money for that) and went to bed. Nothing happened over night, so we left for the airport at 8:00 with no money. We boarded the plane at 9:30 and began our trip to Africa, via Boston and London, with no money. Had God failed us? Had we made a mistake about His will? It sure could appear that way except for one thing, we knew for a fact that God had initiated this project and we were in His will. God had placed His peace in our hearts, as well as His supernatural enabling to persist in faith even past the "deadline."

So as we flew to Boston I said to Sheila, "Honey, God said we are to go, and He gave us the assurance that He was going to provide that money before we left. So let's just thank Him for doing it." Did we feel a bit foolish? Yes, a little. The devil is always on hand to tell you how stupid you are for trusting God. But we bowed our heads and prayed and thanked God anyway for the $3,000 even though we couldn't see it. Then in Boston, just as we were about to board the flight to London, God very definitely prompted me to call a friend in Texas. I barely had enough time to rush to a pay phone and call him. He said, "Hey brother, when are you leaving for Malawi?" I said, "We are in Boston on the way right now. In fact we are just about to get on the plane to London." Then he said, "Oh man, I am too late. I thought you were leaving tomorrow and yesterday I sent a check to your house by FedEx. It should have arrived this morning." I said, "Brother, do you mind me asking how much it is?" He answered, "No, of course not, it is $3,000!" I called our daughter, Rachel, and asked her to rush to the house as quickly as possible to see if it was there. She called back just in time, before we had to get on the plane and said that it was. It was delivered to our home at 9:34 in the morning, twenty-six minutes before our flight departed from Memphis, just as we had asked God to do. Rachel deposited the check and we accessed it in Malawi. We were almost the last ones to board the plane, but we did so knowing that God had kept His promise. As always He was right on time. So, could God not have arranged it so that the money came the day before we left? Of course He could! But, waiting until the last minute accomplished two great things; it gave us the opportunity to build our faith, and God received glory because of His timely provision.

Now you may be saying, "There is no way I could do that." Let me assure you that you could. All it would take is for you to know beyond doubt that you are in the settled will of God. Without that, I couldn't do it either. Furthermore, I wouldn't do it. There is no way I would get on a plane and go half way around the world with no money if I did not know for a fact it was God's will. That would be utter foolishness. But, when you know the Father's will, when you have His say-so, then you can go to the extremities of faith. The key to it all is to know His will first. When the fact of God's will is settled in your heart you can believe Him for anything - regardless of how much opposition is thrown at you by the devil, the world, common sense, circumstances, appearances, and public opinion. Sheila and I did not tell one living soul what we were doing. Not one single human being knew we were going to that airport with no money. It was enough that God knew. If they had known, they might have stepped in, out of love or sympathy, and tried to "bail us out" or talk us out of going. But we didn't need bailing out, and we certainly didn't need any discouragement. What we needed was God's <u>provision</u> in God's <u>time</u>. And as always He was faithful to give it.

Depend upon it, God's work done in God's way will never lack God's supplies.

Hudson Taylor (7)

I have heard people say that there is no way they could ever have "enough faith" to do something like what I have shared in this story. But that is not true, and don't you allow the devil to convince you otherwise. I promise you that if you know for a fact the will of God, you can and you will go to the extremities of faith. The issue is not an **amount** of faith. Every child of God has the exact same capacity to believe God. Remember, He does not play favorites. The issue is the **choice** of faith, and the key to making the choice of faith is to know God's will first.

Real Faith Is for Every Believer in Every Walk of Life

I realize that the story I have just shared with you relates to ministry and reaching people for Jesus. But I do not want to leave the impression that the faith life is just for "ministers" or just for "ministry." Walking in the will of God and trusting God by faith is for every child of God, in every situation, in every walk of life. It is not just for those who are "serving the Lord." No child of God is excused or exempt from living a life that is pleasing to God and that brings honor and glory to Him. God wants all Believers, regardless of their vocation or calling, to know His will and to trust Him for specific faith objects in <u>every</u> area of their lives.

You need to realize that God is just as concerned about your business, your home, your job, and your family, as He is my ministry. If you are a born-again Christian then your business IS your ministry, your home IS your ministry, your job IS your ministry, and your family IS your ministry. So let me ask you, are you asking and trusting God to reveal His will to you, in your spirit, about the various issues of your life and then acting in accordance with what He says? You should be. What are you persuaded of right now concerning your business, your family, your church, your ministry, or your giving?

I hear many Christians say, "Oh, I'll just be happy with whatever God sends. It is all up to Him." Now that may sound good, but it is not good, because it is not faith. That kind of answer only reflects spiritual ignorance or laziness, not robust, God honoring belief. If you want to please God you must trust Him by faith in every area of your life. When you take the easy way out and say, "Oh, I'm willing to take whatever God sends," all you are doing is allowing satan to set the parameters for your life. You are settling for good when God wants to give you the best. You are settling for some when God wants to give you His "much more." You are settling for the mediocre when God wants to give you the miraculous.

Christian businessperson, what is God's will for your business this quarter, this year? Has He told you? He will, if you will take time and ask Him to reveal it to you. If you don't, then you are operating blind. What, specifically, are you believing Him for? Will it require the supernatural intervention of God? If not, then you do not yet know His will. You have a choice – you can work hard, do your best, figure it all out on your own and be satisfied with whatever happens – or – you can take time to know the will of God, trust Him by real faith to bring it to pass, and see God do the impossible. Which do you think would bring more glory to God? Christian Homemaker, what is God's will for your family, for your home? What, specifically, are you confidently expecting God to do? What has He told you in your heart, your inner man? Does it require His supernatural intervention? It should.

Brother Pastor, what has God revealed to you that He is going to do in and through your church this year? What is your faith object? What are you trusting God for? Does it take you out beyond what you have and what you can do? Does it take you into the realm of the impossible? It should, and it will, if it is of God. Brother evangelist, have you met with God and asked Him to tell you what He is going to do through your ministry this year? If you haven't, then how do you know what to believe Him for? Are you content to just "take what God sends?" Again, that sounds good, but it is not good, because it is not faith. No matter what walk of life you are in, you should be walking in the knowledge of the will of God, trusting Him by faith. You should be looking at the "picture on the box" and trusting God to bring it to pass. God wants every child of His to know His will for their life, for their situation, and to trust Him by faith for the accomplishment of it.

Ask the Right Question - Get the Right Answer

Over the years I have invited many people to go with us on projects overseas and nearly every time I get this type of question – "Well, how much does that cost?" Then when I tell them they say, "Boy, that's a lot of money." Or they may ask, "How much time does a trip like that take?" Then when I answer many will say, "Well, I just don't know if I could get that much time off", or "I don't think I could be away from my business that long." Now I know those questions seem perfectly legitimate and reasonable, and in a sense they are. The problem with them, however, is that they reflect an automatic wrong focus, which often leads to an automatic wrong conclusion. The focus is on what they have and what they can do in the natural realm rather than on what God has and what He can do in the spiritual realm, it is on the visible and the possible, rather than the invisible and the impossible.

The right question is not "how much" or "how long." The right question is not a "how", but a "what"; what is the will of God. If it is God's will for a person to go, then God's supply has already been set aside for the going and the time as well. My Dad would have never told us that we were going to Memphis on that Saturday night long ago if he did not have the ways and means to make it happen. In like manner, God will never tell you to do something that He does not have the supply for, whether that supply is in the form of time, money, or opportunity. The first question to ask about anything is, <u>what is the will of God</u>. Once you know THAT, then everything else is secondary.

If we can only wait right up to the time, God cannot lie, God cannot forget: He is pledged to supply all our need.

Hudson Taylor (8)

God's will is not mysterious and He is not keeping it a secret. He wants to get glory to Himself through every Believer. <u>His desire is that every Christian should live his life constantly reaching into the invisible and</u>

believing for the impossible. He wants every life that has been transformed by the blood of Jesus to be a continuous testimony to His faithfulness and goodness. That is made possible only by real faith, and real faith is made possible only by knowing the will of God first. In the following chapters we are going to deal with the process of coming to a knowledge of God's will. But first, let's stop to reflect and pray.

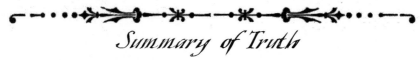

Summary of Truth

- ❖ Real faith is based upon the revealed will of God and nothing else.
- ❖ Real faith begins with God, not me.
- ❖ Jesus performed His ministry by faith, not in His position as God, but as man trusting God.
- ❖ He continues His ministry on earth today through me as I occupy the position of being a channel through which His will can flow.
- ❖ Real faith is entering the finished work of God.
- ❖ Real faith is based in the past and present, not the future.
- ❖ Real faith occurs by hearing the voice of God and seeing into the invisible. It is seeing the picture on the box and acting in accordance with it.
- ❖ The will of God is always accompanied by the supply of God.
- ❖ Real faith always has parameters, which are set by the fixed will of God.
- ❖ Any Christian can go to the extremities of faith if he knows the will of God.
- ❖ God wants every Believer to know His will and walk by real faith.

Now Let's Take a Moment and Pray Together:

Dear Father, I want more than anything to bring honor and glory to You and I know the only way I can do that is to live a life of real faith. I also know that to do that I must know Your will first. So Lord, teach me to hear Your voice, Your say-so in my heart. Teach me to look into the invisible and see Your will. Lord, help me to see the picture on the box and trust You to bring it to pass. Lord I desire to walk in the continuous flow of Your supply and endless resources. I do not want to settle for less than You want to give me. Lord, I choose right now to receive Your will in my heart and to obey You completely. Thank You for giving to me the same capacity to believe as every other child of God. Lord, help me to exercise it to Your honor and glory. Thank You again, Lord Jesus for coming into my heart and for revealing these truths to me today. Continue to enlighten me as I continue in this study. In Your matchless Name I pray. Amen.

Chapter 17

God's Will Is Revealed on the Inside

"...that ye may stand perfect and complete [fully assured]
in all the will of God."
Colossians 4:12b

*T*he most difficult and perplexing question in the lives of many Christians is "How can I know the will of God?" We have established that real faith begins with knowing the will of God. In fact, the only way to exercise real faith is to know God's will pertaining to some particular object or outcome. In Colossians 1:9, Paul tells the church that his desire for them is, *"...to be filled with the knowledge of his will in all wisdom and spiritual understanding."* Scripture certainly indicates that God wants us to know His will and that it is possible, but how do we go about it? The key that unlocks the mystery of how to know the will of God is in that verse. It is the phrase "<u>spiritual</u> understanding."

Now, before we can adequately deal with the HOW of knowing the will of God we first need to deal with the WHERE. The reason the quest for God's will seems so difficult to so many is because we begin by looking in the wrong place and in the wrong direction. We tend to approach our search for the will of God the same way we do everything else – by looking to the natural and the visible. We look <u>out</u> instead of looking <u>in</u>. You will never find the will of God by looking in the natural, because it is revealed only in the spiritual and the invisible. **God's will is revealed on the inside** and never by anything external other than the Bible. Apart from the general revelation of God through the Word, it is the Holy Spirit illuminating the Word in our inner man that helps us to know His will for us in our particular situation. Concerning those things not covered specifically in His Word, God speaks His will into our born-again human spirit by His Holy Spirit and no other way.

As already stated, God often uses various means in the external world to stimulate us to <u>seek</u> His will, but never to <u>reveal</u> His will. He may use need, desire, thoughts that arise in our mind, things that touch us emotionally, circumstances, or trials to draw us into the closet to search out His will, but only by His Spirit speaking in our inner man will we <u>know</u> it. I realize this truth may very well cut cross-grain to the way many Christians view the issue of knowing the will of God, but it is crucial that we become fully persuaded of it in our heart. Otherwise, we will never move forward in faith. God does not use anything from "without" (other than the Word) to save us, and He does not guide us from "without." The Bible tells us in Colossians 2:6, *"As ye have therefore received Christ Jesus the Lord, so walk ye in Him."* We received Jesus "within," by the renewing of our spirit. Likewise we walk in Him by the guidance of the Holy Spirit received in our spirit - from within, not from without. God may use eternal things to cause us to look to Him and listen for His voice, but ultimately, His guidance comes from the Holy Spirit to our inner man.

As we have said, God often uses our physical environment, circumstances, thoughts, and feelings to motivate us to seek His will, but He will never use them to tell us His will. It is not that these things have no say at all, or that they are not real, or that they are not relevant; they just do not have the final word. That is reserved for the Holy Spirit as He speaks in our inner man. Other than in matter dealing with salvation, moral conduct, and life in general, **God's will is made known only to the regenerated <u>spirit</u> of a <u>saved</u> person.** Apart from God's general revelation to man from His Word, a lost person (regardless of how religious or sincere he is) cannot know God's will about <u>anything</u>, because his spirit is still dead and cannot communicate with God. I Corinthians 2:14 says, *"...the natural man receiveth not the things of the Spirit of God: for they are foolishness unto him: neither can he know them, because they are **spiritually** discerned."* A Spirit-filled child of God, on the other hand, can know God's will about <u>everything</u> by discerning it in his spirit. Notice that I said "Spirit-filled." That is because a carnally-minded Christian, one who is "living after the flesh" (relying solely upon intellect and emotion) cannot know God's will either. Why? Because he is only looking to circumstances, reason, and feeling just as the natural man does, and the will of God cannot be found there. They that "walk by faith" are those who "walk by the Spirit." The Bible tells us in I Corinthians 2:16, *"...we have the mind of Christ."* But to know His mind, His thoughts, and His will, we

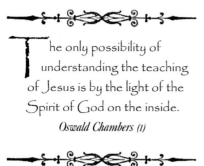

The only possibility of understanding the teaching of Jesus is by the light of the Spirit of God on the inside.

Oswald Chambers (1)

must receive it in our spirit. No person, saved or unsaved, can think or feel his way to the will of God. Many Christians make the mistake of trying to figure out God's will solely by reason, logic, and common sense or by weighing "pros and cons," but it won't work. That is the way of the world, the devil, and the flesh. The Chinese evangelist, Watchman Nee, put it this way, "Knowing the will of God in the inner man and walking in the Spirit are the same thing. Both require waiting upon God. Both require faith. This is the faith walk" (2).

Once again we observe that God created human beings with three parts, body, spirit and soul. We have already seen that from the very beginning, God's way of communicating with man was to speak to his spirit through the Holy Spirit , not to his intellect or emotion. That has not changed. The knowledge of God's will is **received** in the spirit, **interpreted** by the intellect, **expressed** by the emotions, **obeyed** by the will, and **executed** by means of our physical being. God's will begins in the spirit, moves through the soul, and culminates in the physical. God always calls upon His child to <u>act</u> in response to His guidance received in the inner man, not to <u>re-act</u> to the external pressure of circumstances (adverse or favorable) whether in my life or someone else's. We are also not to re-act to internal pressure (logic, reason, common sense) or to feelings, whether good or bad.

Quite often, Christians attempt to determine God's will based upon how things appear, and that is a mistake. For instance, just because you can make more money by moving from one job to another does not necessarily mean it is God's will. Maybe a pastor has been issued a call from a church that is much larger than the one he is currently serving – does the fact that it is a bigger church mean it is God's will? No. Does the fact that college "A" offers a scholarship and college "B" doesn't mean that it is God's will to go to college "A?" No. Perhaps, as an evangelist, I discover that I can likely win ten thousand people to Christ by holding a campaign in Brazil. Does that automatically mean I should plan to go to Brazil? No. It just may be God's will to take the other job or go to the bigger church or go to the college offering the scholarship or for me to go to Brazil. But if it is, I will never know only because of things in the external circumstances or because it makes sense. **I will only know as I wait before God and trust Him to reveal His will to me in my spirit.** At that point the outward conditions and circumstances become incidental. We could use many examples, but you get the point. The bottom line is, God's will cannot be discerned by simply weighing pros and cons or by looking merely at circumstances. A good deal doesn't automatically indicate the will of God.

Why God Speaks His Will into Our Spirit

There are at least three reasons why God speaks His will into our spirit rather than to our intellect or emotions or through circumstances. **First, it is the one place in man in which satan cannot speak or interfere, thus eliminating any possibility of confusion.** The spirit of man is reserved solely for God. When we hear the voice of God speaking in our inner man we never have to question whether we are hearing from God or satan, because the only voice you CAN hear in your spirit is the still small voice of God. Satan can talk to you in your thoughts, he can threaten you or entice you in your emotions, and he can oppose you or tempt you through circumstances and physical environment, but he cannot speak to you in your spirit. The surest way to avoid confusion about the will of God is to listen with your spirit. Do not try to figure it out according to reason or common sense. Do not make judgments based upon what feels right or wrong, comfortable or uncomfortable. Let me say it again - never try to determine God's will by means of "pros and cons" in circumstances or by how things appear. It is always a mistake to try to determine God's will by what looks good, seems best, makes sense, or feels right. It is quite possible, even probable, that what God tells you in your inner man will not make sense to your intellect or feel right to your emotions, but there will be a "knowing" in your spirit that it IS right because it is the voice of God. Remember, you are a citizen of two worlds, natural and spiritual. The will of God always <u>originates</u> from the spiritual and <u>culminates</u> in the natural.

The second reason God makes His will known to the spirit is that by so doing, He establishes a level playing field among the Body of Christ. He creates the same potential and opportunity in every Believer alike to know His will. There are obviously some people who are more intelligent than others, who think more logically or seemingly have a greater capacity for reasoning things out. If the will of God could be determined merely by means of the intellect, then the "smart" Christians would be more able to know His will than us ordinary folks. The same would be true if His will was determined by means of our emotions, the way we feel about things. The well-balanced, steady-on, "level" person would surely have a greater chance of knowing God's will than those of us who sometimes have "off days." Intellectual capacity might change from one Christian to another as might emotional stability, but the Holy Spirit and His ability to speak to the inner man is the same for every Child of God. The glorious good news is that every Christian has the exact same ability to receive the will of God in his spirit and thus the same ability to trust God by faith. God is not a respecter of persons.

The third reason why God makes His will known to our inner man is because it is the only way of producing certainty, and certainty is the key to it all. Paul did not say in Colossians 1:9 that he desired they be filled with a <u>feeling</u> of God's will or a <u>thinking</u> of God's will or an <u>appearance</u> of God's will. No, he said a <u>knowledge</u> or knowing of His will. The only way for assurance to exist in any process, especially a venture of faith, is for the initiation of it to be based upon an absolute, something that is concrete and guaranteed not to change. That "something" is the will of God made known to our spirit

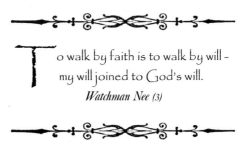

To walk by faith is to walk by will - my will joined to God's will.

Watchman Nee (3)

by the Holy Spirit. Our thoughts, feelings and circumstances are changing by the minute, but the will of God is settled forever. As we are "walking something through" by faith, we must be able at any point to look back and see clearly the **initiation of God**. Hearing and obeying the voice of God produces total security. Thoughts from my mind will not result in certainty, because there is always the possibility that there is something I do not know or something I overlooked. But hearing the voice of God, spoken by the Holy Spirit in my inner man, results in certainty, in an unshakable "knowing" that will stand the test of time and opposition. There is no possibility that God has overlooked anything.

Satan Works from the Outside In

Now let's look at how satan operates. It is always from the outside to the inside, and always in the form of a temptation to think, feel, decide, and act contrary to and irrespective of God's will. God guides, comforts, instructs, and disciplines. Satan tempts, lies, deceives, and destroys. Satan uses two kinds of temptation, <u>threat</u> or <u>enticement</u>, and often both at the same time. They always come as suggestions that bring the goodness, character, and faithfulness of God into question. Look at how he approached Jesus in the wilderness in Matthew 4:1-11. His goal is always to capture the will. *"...if thou **wilt** fall down and worship me"* (Matthew 4:9). Notice how satan communicated with Eve. He moved from the outside to the inside. He made an issue out of something from the external physical world and appealed to her intellect with the suggestion that God could not be trusted and would not meet her needs. He reasoned with her, suggesting that God was withholding something from her. He also appealed to her emotions by implying that God did not really care about her. He does the same thing with us. He says, "If God really loved you He would not allow these trials, these needs, these problems to come into your life." Then he says, "But now that you have the trials, what are you going to do about it?" He always comes to us with questions that are designed to bring doubt, fear, uncertainty, and disappointment. He did it with Eve, and he does it with us. The result was that satan captured her will, and the outcome was disastrous. It ended in separation from God. He worked from the outside to the inside, because he could do it no other way. He did not have access to the spirit of man, and he still doesn't. Therefore he is still making his appeals to human beings, lost and saved alike, the same way he did in the Garden. His desire is to keep the unsaved separated from a relationship with God by a lack of faith in Jesus and to keep the saved separated from fellowship with God the same way. His goal is to prevent our will from being joined to the will of God.

The Secret Room

The last thing the devil wants a Christian to learn is this truth: any Child of God can assuredly KNOW the will of God in his inner man and then confidently step out in faith to obey it. He will do anything to keep that truth a secret, because it is THAT secret that unlocks the door to the impossible. Satan will do everything in his power to create as much noise and confusion as possible in our intellect, emotions, and circumstances so that we will not withdraw to the quiet place and listen for the voice of God. But we must. It is essential to the faith life to learn to deliberately step aside from the roar of thoughts, feelings, and circumstances and listen for His voice. Jesus made it a practice to be alone in a quiet place with the Father. If it was essential for His life, then how much more is it for ours? Listen to the words of Oswald Chambers, "When we live in the secret place it becomes impossible for us to doubt God, we become more sure of Him than anything else. Enter the secret place and right in the center of the common round you find God there all the time. Pray to your Father in secret, and every public thing will be stamped with the presence of God" (4).

There is a secret room that satan does not want you to know about and if you do know about it, he does not want you to go there. It is called the Holy of Holies, the inner chamber of your spirit. Why does the devil not want you to go there? Because you <u>can</u> and he <u>can't</u>. The Psalmist wrote in Psalm 91:1, *"He that dwelleth in the secret place of the most High shall abide under the shadow of the Almighty."* It is in that place where we come into the very presence of God and enter into private conversations that satan cannot listen in on. You remember that the Tabernacle, the dwelling place of God (Exodus 25 and following), was constructed in three sections. There was the outer court, the inner court or holy place, and then there was the most holy place or the Holy of Holies, which contained the Ark of the Covenant. These three areas correspond with the three parts of man. The outer court represents the physical realm and was lighted by daylight. The inner court was lighted by

GOD
Speaks to Believer in the Inner Man
Works from the Inside Out

TABERNACLE

Holy of Holies
SPIRIT of MAN
(Secret Room)
God's Will and Plan Is Revealed Here

Inner Court
SOUL
(Emotions, Intellect, Will)
The Decision to Obey God's Will Is Made Here

Outer Court
BODY
(Five Senses)
Acting Upon God's Will Is Done Here

Completion of God's Will

Satan approaches from the outside with threat or enticement. Cannot gain access to the Spirit

lamplight and represents the realm of intellect and emotion. The Holy of Holies, the place reserved for the presence of God was lighted by the glory of God and represents the spirit of man. It was in the Holy of Holies that the presence of God resided, and it was there that the High Priest received instruction for the people of God. The Holy of Holies could only be entered by the High Priest once a year and only by the blood of the perfect sacrificial lamb. The Bible tells us that through the shedding of His innocent blood on the cross, Jesus, the Lamb of God, became our "Great High Priest" (Hebrews 4:14), and through Him we now have free and constant access into the very presence of God (Hebrews 4:16). Therefore, we now have continual access to His instruction, to His will. Satan can approach us in the physical realm and in the realm of thought and emotion, but he cannot enter into the realm of our spirit, into the Holy of Holies where we meet secretly with God, come into the light of His glory, and receive His will on the inside. The place of our spirit is off limits to the devil, because it is protected by the blood of Jesus. It is there we must go so that we can come into the presence of God and hear His voice.

Jesus said, *"But, thou, when thou prayest, enter into thy closet, and when thou hast shut thy door, pray to thy Father which is in secret; and thy Father which seeth in secret shall reward thee openly."* (Matthew 6:6) Interestingly, the word "closet" means a place of retirement, a secret chamber, and a storehouse from which supplies are dispensed. It is not always possible to find a physical private place to meet with God, but it is not necessary. Regardless of where you are or what is going on around you, just imagine a secret room with a door that can be closed to shut out everything except you and God. Also imagine on the door a sign that reads "Enter by the Blood." That means that you can go there and satan cannot. That is your private room where you go to meet with God, the storehouse from which His instructions and His supplies are dispensed to you. Whether I am on an airplane or in the midst of a crusade service, I can always retire to my secret room and meet God. Christian, you can and must do the same. You may be in your car, at your desk in your office, or in a crowded restaurant, but it doesn't matter. Your secret chamber, your private room is always available, the secret chamber of your inner man. You will always find God there.

Make a habit of entering into your spiritual closet the moment you wake in the morning and make a habit of returning often. Every day of your life you get up and go to your clothes closet and get yourself physically dressed for the day. You select clothes that equip you for particular activities. You must also develop the habit of entering into your spiritual closet at the beginning of the day in order to become spiritually dressed for whatever God leads you into that day. When I first go into my closet on a typical day I put on my "office clothes." Then later in the afternoon I might come home and change into my "yard-work" clothes. Then after that I might change into "going-out-to-eat" clothes. When I am out preaching in Africa

I have on my "field evangelism" clothes. The point is this; I need to be properly clothed for each activity I am involved in, and that requires return trips to the closet. We also need to be properly clothed for each activity God puts us in throughout each day, and there can be hundreds of them. Thankfully God has made it possible for us to carry our "closet" with us all the time. It is the secret room of the spirit where we go to be clothed in the will of God, in the instruction of God and in the provision of God.

The Gatekeeper

It is important for you to understand that your own human will is the determining factor in whether or not you enter into the secret room to know the will of God. If you go in there, it will be because you choose to go there. If you form the habit of going there, it will be because you continue to choose to go there repeatedly. Satan does not want you to make that choice and he will do all in his power to prevent you from developing the habit of going there. Why? Because our human will stands as the gatekeeper between the outer court, where satan has influence, and the Holy of Holies (the secret room) where he has none. For this reason, the devil's chief aim is to capture our will and he will use any means to do it. He may not understand all there is to know about the operation of faith, but he knows from observation that it works and he also knows it is activated when my will is joined to God's will. For this reason, you must constantly make the deliberate choice to know and do the will of God. It is a choice that may at times be difficult to make, and it may require some effort, but for the sake of the development of your life of faith, you must make it.

The Still Small Voice

Let me encourage you and caution you not to expect the voice of God to be loud and thunderous. His voice <u>can</u> be, but to the spirit of His child it is most often soft and gentle. That is why we must wait patiently, quietly, and attentively before the Lord in unhurried prayer and fellowship with Him so that we can hear when He speaks His word and His will into our spirit. We read in I Kings 19:11-12 that the Lord was not in the wind or the earthquake or the fire, but *"a still small voice."* Isaiah 30:21 tells us, *"And thine ears shall hear a word behind thee, saying, This is the way, walk ye in it..."* You may ask, "But how can you tell the difference between the voice of God and the voice of the devil?" That is a good question, but we have already answered it. Only GOD can speak into your spirit. But in addition to that, let's remember that the voice of God, spoken to His child, brings light, peace, assurance, and largeness in our hearts. It is redemptive, points upward, and produces faith. The voice of the devil appeals to the mind or emotions and usually begins with questions that are accusatory, point inward to self or outward to circumstances, and produce fear. In John 10:4-5 Jesus, referring to Himself as the Good Shepherd, said the sheep follow Him because they know His voice and the voice of strangers they will not follow. To those who know Him, the voice of Jesus brings peace. The voice of the "stranger" brings fear and confusion. If, while you are praying, a voice of condemnation, accusation, doubt, and fear arises in your heart, just ask yourself, does that really sound like my Lord Jesus? Although God definately does chasten and discipline His children, He does so as a loving Father. If the voice you hear does anything other than comfort, encourage, guide, instruct, and correct, it is not the voice of the Good Shepherd. You will know His voice when you hear it, and you will hear it when you spend time with Him and listen.

Thought and Guidance

There is a very definite difference between thoughts in the mind and guidance in the spirit. There are obviously thoughts that arise in my intellect as a product of my own natural capacity of reason and imagination that may not originate with God and may have nothing to do with His will. How can you tell the difference? We might distinguish between the two by saying that what takes place in the mind is "cognitive" and what takes place in the spirit is "intuitive." In other words, the intellect thinks, calculates, speculates, and draws conclusions based upon acquired knowledge, assumptions of fact, and logic. The spirit, on the other hand, "senses" and merely receives from God. You might say it "just knows" without having to go through a "process." The person operating solely by intellect arrives at conclusions and chooses a course of action based upon his own reasoning. He just does what makes sense. The person operating by the Spirit arrives at conclusions based upon guidance received in his spirit and simply follows the course of action given to him by God, whether it makes sense or not.

There are many contributing factors to the formation of thoughts in the mind, such as external circumstances, stimuli from physical senses, and memory. But the only contributing factors in receiving instruction from God are the written Word and the voice of God spoken into our spirit by the Holy Spirit. To the "ears" of the intellect there are many speakers, many voices, and they are often conflicting and confusing. But to the "hearing" of the spirit there is only one single Speaker, only one Voice - the voice of the Holy Spirit Himself. If what we are hearing is the voice of God in our spirit then it will be accompanied by a quiet persistence that will not give way to the pressure of delay, opposing opinion, or circumstances. If what we are hearing is from God, there will be no debate, no doubt, and no disturbance in our heart. There will be assurance and certainty. There will be calm and peace. *"For God is not the author of confusion, but of peace..."* (I Corinthians 14:33).

If there is a single guideword in discerning the will of God, it is the word **peace**. *"And the peace of God, which passeth all understanding, shall keep* [guard] *your hearts and minds through Christ Jesus"* (Philippians 4:7). Do not act until you are certain your action is accompanied by the peace of God. *"And let the peace of God rule* [govern or prevail] *in your hearts..."* (Colossians 3:15). God's leading may take you in a direction that defies all logic, counters opposing circumstances, and makes you look utterly foolish to the world, but it doesn't matter because there is a peace connected to it that is not explainable in terms of common-sense. The peace of God will act as a wall of protection, a shield, against the onslaught of the enemy. In John 14:27 Jesus told us, *"Peace I leave with you, my peace I give unto you: not as the world giveth, give I unto you. Let not your heart be troubled, neither let it be afraid."* The word "heart" in this verse means "mind and emotion" and the word "troubled" means "agitated or stirred up like a pool of water." Jesus is telling us to not allow our minds to be confused or stirred up, or our emotions to be fearful, by looking at the wrong thing. Rather, we are to look to God and let His peace to settle in on us by receiving His word in our inner man. The will of God brings with it a peace that cannot be explained in any natural human terms and a certainty that cannot be shaken by satanic opposition. Satan cannot produce real peace, only a counterfeit. His "peace" is based on reason and circumstances, things that change. God's peace is based upon Himself and His will, things that cannot change.

In reference to the peace of God, Oswald Chambers said, "Inner peace is impossible unless it is received from Jesus. When our Lord speaks peace He makes peace. It is a peace, which comes from looking into His face and realizing His undisturbedness. Reflected peace is the proof that you are right with God" (5). He goes on to say, "Whenever you obey God His seal is always that of peace, the witness of an unfathomable peace, which is not natural, but the peace of Jesus. Whenever peace does not come, tarry till it does, or find out the reason why it does not. If you are acting on an impulse, or from a sense of the heroic, the peace of Jesus will not witness; there is no simplicity or confidence in God, because the spirit of simplicity is born of the Holy Ghost, not of your decisions" (6).

So What about Our Thoughts

Our intellect plays two roles in knowing the will of God – collector and interpreter. First, by means of our intellect, we gather the facts as we think we know and understand them, and then place them before God. In coming to God's will over some particular issue, I often write down on paper everything I know about the situation - all the facts as I see them. I write down the possible options and scenarios, the things I can think of that might apply to my situation. The best way to clear your mind is to write it all down and get it out in front of you in a tangible form. I do not make any suggestions to God, and I do not ask Him to do what is on the paper. I just lay it before Him, and ask Him to speak to me in my inner man and give me His direction. It may ultimately turn out that what He says will have nothing to do with what I wrote down, but it was a place to start. I am confident, though, that as I wait before God (the operative word being *wait*), He will speak into my spirit and reveal to me His specific will. Then at that point, I can go back to the paper, write down what He said, put a date by it, and stand upon it until it is fulfilled.

Second, by means of our intellect, we interpret or give definition to God's will so that, through us, it may be expressed and executed. Remember, the purpose and function of the soul (intellect, emotion, and will) is to give expression, not make decisions. The Bible tells us there is a "reasoning" that is of God. When Jesus rebuked the disciples in Matthew 16:8, *"O ye of little faith, why reason ye among yourselves..."*, He used a word which means "according to logic." They were choosing to believe what they thought to be real rather than the voice of God. But when God said in Isaiah 1:18, *"Come now, and let us reason together..."*, He used a word that means "to be correct." Job used the same word in Job 13:3 when he said, *"Surely I would speak to the Almighty, and I desire to reason* [be correct] *with God."* The kind of reasoning or thinking that God wants from us is "spiritual reasoning." It is the kind that makes us "correct" with Him. In other words, it puts God and us on the same page. Our will is joined to His will. Proverbs 16:3 says, *"Commit thy works unto the Lord, and thy thoughts shall be established.*[will become agreeable to His will]." Then verse 9 says, *"A man's heart* [mind] *deviseth his way, but the Lord directeth his steps."*

Normally about mid-year I begin the process of getting on the same page with God concerning our proposed ministry activity and budget for the coming year. In our ministry we do not solicit funds, or have accounts receivable. We do not have guaranteed or predictable income based upon tithes or pledges. Therefore, it is necessary that we know God's will concerning the amount of money to trust Him for over the course of a fiscal year, and how we should spend it. I begin by reviewing the facts as I <u>think</u> I know and understand them. We have done 158 international campaigns over the past thirty years and have developed a good frame of reference concerning what it takes to do them. I have a pretty good idea of what to expect in terms of home expense, overseas team support, campaign costs and so on. But we cannot stand in faith on a "pretty good idea." "Projection planning" will not work in a faith ministry. We must <u>know</u> the will of God, and that can only be received in the inner man. But how do we get there? We begin by writing it down, prayerfully making a list of expenses based upon what we believe God wants us to do over the coming year. Then there is more prayer, discussion, and revision. The process may take a week, a month, or several months, but it takes what it takes. Eventually the mind of Christ will become very evident, and a solid "knowing" will settle in upon our hearts that this amount of ministry activity, and this amount of money to pay for it, is what we are to trust God for throughout the coming year. To logic and common sense it may look like too little, or it may appear to be more than we need, but it doesn't matter, because it is ultimately not determined by reason or calculation. It is revealed in the spirit. It can <u>begin</u> with **thinking** in the mind, but it must <u>end</u> with **knowing** in the spirit.

Once God's will is known, then we put in a request and simply ask God to do it. We receive it in our hearts and then proceed to move forward on the basis of what we believe to be God's will. One thing we can always be sure of, though, is that the completion of the will of God will require His supernatural intervention, and it will bring glory and praise to Him. But once we are on the same page with God, once we are certain of His will, then we can proceed with absolute confidence and assurance that every need will be met. We do not know how God is going to do it, but we do know that by entering His will we also enter the flow of His supply. Of course satan will oppose us as we go along, and there will be days when we are tempted to doubt and fear as a result of looking at the visible. But the thing that will prevent us from giving up will be the fact that we can look back and see the **initiation of God**, the **assurance** of His will. <u>If He started it, He will finish it.</u>

Dear friend, you can apply this same approach, this same methodology, to your business, your household, to every area of your life. In fact you must, if you are going to walk correctly before God in real faith. Get before God and ask Him to tell you His will for your business, your family, your career, and your life. Let Him speak to you in your inner man. Make room for God to raise up real faith objects in your life and create a life within you and through you that will bring honor and glory to His name. Submit every area of your life to God as a tool with which He can establish a fresh testimony to His faithfulness. Sound exciting? I assure you it is. There is nothing more stimulating and satisfying to a Child of God than watching God be God in your own personal life.

But What if I "Get It Wrong?"

Let's look at a question that may have arisen in your heart - "What if I get it wrong?" "What if I am spending time with God in prayer and Bible study, and I am sincerely seeking His will, and yet I still somehow misinterpret it and confuse my own thoughts with what God is saying?" If you are spending time with God, seeking His will, and receiving His peace to guide you, it is not likely that you will get it wrong. But let's just suppose you do. Do not be discouraged. The world will not stop spinning if you misinterpret God's will, and you will certainly be no worse off for making the effort. However, as you progress in the faith life you will begin to "get it right" more often than not. Our Heavenly Father is never displeased with a child of His who is trying to know and do His will. We only grieve the Holy Spirit when we refuse to listen to God or when we know His will and refuse to obey. If you do try and "fail," don't despair. With time and experience you will learn to distinguish between what you hear in the intellect and what you hear in your spirit. Don't give up; just keep at it. You must

not allow satan to use the fear of failure to hinder you from taking beginner steps in faith. He would have you believe that God will be disappointed with you, but that is a lie.

When a baby is first learning to walk every step is a challenge and an experiment, and the falls are frequent. But the parents are thrilled at every effort. They do not scold or punish when the baby falls; they help him up and stand out in front of him with outstretched arms of encouragement. I promise you that your Father will be thrilled at every effort you make to know and do His will, even if you do sometimes "get it wrong." A child is not born into his earthly family knowing how to recognize the voice and interpret the words of his parents, and a child of God is not born into his heavenly family knowing how to recognize the voice and interpret the words of his Heavenly Father either. But in both cases, over time, we learn, and it doesn't take very long.

Let me assure you, if you want to know the will of the Father, then you will know it. The important thing to remember is to look in the right place. God reveals His will through His Word and in your spirit, on the inside, not through external situations and circumstances. Now that we know **where** to find God's will, we are going to move on and discover how. But first let's take a moment to pray and review.

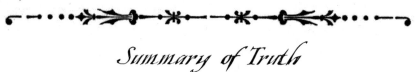

Summary of Truth

❖ God's will is received on the inside, in our spirit, and only to a person who is saved and Spirit-filled.

❖ Our thoughts, feelings, and circumstances can stimulate us to seek the will of God but can never reveal it.

❖ There are three reasons why God reveals His will only to our spirit.

  ♦ Satan cannot interfere there and there is no possibility for confusion.

  ♦ Every Christian has the same opportunity to know the will of God.

  ♦ Absolute certainty comes from hearing the voice of God.

❖ Every Child of God has a "secret room", his inner man, where he can hear from God.

❖ The voice of God is soft and gentle and heard only within our spirit.

❖ There is a difference between thought and guidance. Thought is reasoning in the mind and guidance is God's will revealed in the spirit.

❖ There is no way to "fail" in seeking to know the will of God.

NOW LET'S TAKE A MOMENT AND PRAY TOGETHER:

DEAR FATHER, THANK YOU FOR REVEALING TO ME THAT I CAN KNOW YOUR WILL BY HEARING YOUR VOICE IN MY SPIRIT. THANK YOU FOR PROTECTING ME FROM CONFUSION AND FOR GIVING ME THE ASSURANCE THAT COMES FROM HEARING YOUR STILL SMALL VOICE. LORD, I CHOOSE TO SEEK AND TO KNOW YOUR WILL AND TO OBEY YOU AS YOU GUIDE ME IN A WALK OF FAITH. THANK YOU FOR LOVING ME, SAVING ME, AND GUIDING ME. IN YOUR NAME I PRAY AND THANK YOU. AMEN.

Chapter 18

God's Will in Our Daily Routine

"For as many as are led by the Spirit of God, they are the sons of God."
Romans 8:14

F aith is for everyday living, not just for special times of need, trial or challenge. It is easy to understand the necessity for the conscious exercise of faith in relation to special times where supernatural intervention from God is obviously required, situations that necessitate a "miracle". But what about the ordinary days of life? Or to put it another way, are we to live by faith ALL the time? Absolutely. There are no "days off" in the life of faith because there are no days off in living a life that is pleasing to God. You see the faith life is just that, a faith LIFE. Every second of every minute of every hour of our Christian life is to be lived out by faith. Trusting God is not limited to just "special events."

In my own personal life I maintain what I call a "program of faith," which we will look at in chapter 25. I always have a written list of specific faith objects that are in varying degrees of fulfillment, things I believe to be the will of God that I am actively trusting God for. They may relate to needs in our ministry or to our home and family. Some relate to the vision God has given me for the expansion of our work and some to desires I have in my heart. Some are short term and some are long term. There are many faith items on my list, and I spend time every morning discussing these specific issues in detail with God, making adjustments and alterations as He directs. Now, there are some days that involve very definite activity related to my list and there are some that don't. There are some days when life seems to just sort of go along without anything happening that appears to relate to my list at all. There are some days that do not contain "earth shattering events" that call for a deliberate, conscious choice of faith. But even those days are to be lived out in an attitude of trusting God.

Three Categories of Life

I think you would agree that for most of us life seems to divide itself into three general categories. First there is the everyday living category, then there is the <u>special situations</u> or unusual circumstances category and finally the <u>change</u> category. Or we might say the "little things" and the "big things." The "everyday living" area of life involves such things as going to work, going to school, taking care of the house, family activities, grocery shopping, hobbies, and recreation. Routine daily living is filled with thousands of choices and details we normally don't give a great deal of thought to, or prayer to for that matter, because they are just that, daily routine. This area of life seems to just go along and we pretty much just "go along" with it unless interrupted by some unusual circumstance. Most Christians, even those who spend regular daily time with God, do not give much conscious consideration to the will of God or to the issue of faith concerning the ordinary activities of daily life such as those mentioned above. For instance, if you have a job you normally don't spend time in prayer each morning asking God if you should go there or not. You just assume it is His will that you do. But what about a more random "spur of the moment" choice, such as going shopping or going to play a game of golf this afternoon? Yesterday, before Sheila and I left the office, I asked her if we needed to go by the store on the way home. She said, "Yeah, I guess we could stop by there and pick up a few things." So we did. Now when I began my day yesterday I spent time with God in prayer, asked Him to direct my thoughts and steps throughout the day, and then entered into the day assuming, by faith, He would do just that. I believed that He would guide my life from within my inner man. So Sheila and I did not sit down in the office and have a prayer meeting and spend time searching through Scripture to see whether or not we should go to the store; we just went. Was that wrong? Of course not. As long as we are abiding in Jesus, (that is, we are living in a continuous attitude of worship, fellowship, and obedience with Him, trusting Him to guide us moment by moment) it is not necessary to set aside time for prayer concerning every detail of daily life. In fact, it would be impossible. Therefore, God has arranged it so that it is not necessary. By means of His indwelling Spirit, He has made it possible for us to have constant guidance for our life from our inner man.

God's word says, "...*Walk in the Spirit, and ye shall not fulfil the lust* [yield to the pull] *of the flesh"* (Galatians 5:16). That is, we will not do or say or even think outside the will of God. "Walking in the Spirit" is our sure safeguard from error. The Holy Spirit indwells the renewed spirit of every Believer and therefore directs his steps from within his spirit. When I ask God to "direct my thoughts and steps", that is what I am asking Him to do - to guide me from within my inner man. The spiritual man is the whole man governed by the inner man. The spiritual man is simply one who walks in harmony with God's will. The Bible gives us the secret to the daily walk by telling us that, as children of God, *"...we have the mind of Christ"* (I Corinthians 2:16). And in Philippians 2:5 we are instructed to *"Let this mind be in you, which was also in Christ Jesus."* But how do we "let His mind" be in us? We do it by simply choosing to recognize that we are indwelt by Him, and choosing to walk in accordance with His guidance. At the beginning of every day simply make the decision, the choice to walk in sync with the will of God, and if, as you go through the day, God puts a "check" (a hesitancy, a warning) in your spirit, then stop immediately and ask Him to redirect you. You must always make room for God to break through at any second with a change of direction. Let me suggest a simple prayer with which to start your day. You may want to write it down and put it on your nightstand, or in your Bible, or both. It will adjust your attitude, set your focus on God and send you forth into the day in an atmosphere of faith, trusting God to flow His will through you moment by moment. I call it the "ABC prayer of faith." It goes like this:

Lord today,
    I ADMIT that I cannot run my own life, my family, my business, my church, my ministry, or anything else. But Lord today,
    I BELIEVE in You.
        I believe in Your PRESENCE in my life, family, business, ministry, and circumstances.
        I believe in Your PURPOSE for every area of my life.
        I believe in Your PROVISION to meet every need.
        I believe in Your POWER to control every circumstance and guide every situation.
        I believe in Your PROTECTION from every form of harm and evil.
        I believe in Your PLAN for my life today.
        I believe in Your PEACE that surpasses all human comprehension. Therefore Lord,
    I CHOOSE Your will for every area of my life today whatever it may be. I choose to receive, by faith, all that You have for me today, and I thank You for sending it.
In Your Name I pray. Amen.

Watch for God's "Breakthroughs"

Now let me ask you, have you ever been going along through your daily life, and all of a sudden just "gotten the feeling" that God was telling you something? Sure you have. If you are a born-again child of God, I know you have had that experience. And at that moment it may or may not have made sense to you. Maybe He was telling you to do something that really didn't seem convenient at the time, but somehow you just "knew" you were hearing from God. There was an urgency, a compelling attached to it. Well, that is not a "feeling" at all. It has nothing to do with emotion. That is God's Spirit breaking through and speaking into your spirit. It is the spiritual dimension of God, the <u>invisible</u>, overriding the natural dimension, the <u>visible</u>. When that happens it is extremely important to listen and obey immediately, whether it makes sense or not.

Faith is living in a state of expectancy - leaving room for God to come in at any moment. Leave room for the element of surprise.

Oswald Chambers (1)

We tend to look at things from a "snapshot" present-moment viewpoint, but God sees the panorama, the "big picture" from beginning to end. He is always operating with much more information than we are. Part of the daily walk of faith is simply trusting moment by moment in God's view of the big picture. God may break into your daily routine and tell you to stop everything and pray for someone when you are really not in the mood to pray. He may tell you to make a phone call you don't have time to make or visit someone that you don't have time to visit. God may lead you to give money that you can't afford to give. He may prompt you to share Jesus with a perfect stranger who looks like they don't have the time or inclination to listen. The important thing is to <u>obey the voice of God and to do it quickly</u>.

Let me share something with you that happened to me just this morning. It will help illustrate what I am talking about. I was in my office, mid-morning, and all of a sudden I felt as if I should call my good friend, Art Bailey, who works with the Billy Graham Evangelistic Association. God brought him to my mind, and there seemed to be a compelling to call him. I hesitated because I knew he was in New York City organizing a crusade, and I did not want to disturb him, especially since I had no apparent specific reason to call. But the compelling would not go away. So I called him, and when he answered I said, "Hey Art, this is Shad." He responded with,

"Shad! Brother, I have just been thinking about you this morning and I am so glad you called!" Then he explained that he was in the throes of securing the venue for the crusade and needed a miracle from God. So we had a good time of prayer together on the phone and sensed that God was at work. After we finished Art told me that my call was perfectly timed and desperately needed. Now I could have easily given in to that hesitation that said it did not make sense for me to call Art, and I could have ignored that feeling that I should. But it was not a feeling at all. It was the Spirit of God breaking through and making a connection between Art and me, a connection relating to the furtherance of God's Kingdom. Friends, do not ignore the "still small voice", the prompting of the Holy Spirit. Pay attention to those "nudges," regardless of what they are in reference to, because they are God talking to you.

There were times while our kids were growing up that they would ask if they could do this or that, or go here or there, and many times I would just say yes without hesitation. But then there were those other times that I would sense that God was saying no, and so I would say no to them. Of course they wanted to know why I was saying no, and sometimes I would just have to tell them I did not have a reason. All I knew was that God was leading in a certain way and that was all we needed to know. God's voice spoken into our inner man can be a valuable safeguard for our families.

I was on an evangelistic project in Brazil a few years ago and one night as I was about to preach I was suddenly overcome with severe stomach pains. For a moment I didn't think I could go on. Then it occurred to me that satan was attacking me and I said, "Lord, touch some one to pray." As suddenly as the pain came on, it left, and I was able to preach. The next day I called Sheila back home and she shared with me that a strange thing happened to her the night before. She had gotten into bed and was about to read a book when all of a sudden God spoke to her and told her, "Pray for Shad, the devil is attacking him." So she prayed and asked God to rebuke the enemy and continued to pray until God's peace settled in on her heart. When we compared notes we discovered that God was telling her to pray at the very moment I was about to preach the night before. Coincidence? No way. That sort of thing has happened many times over the years and underscores the importance of watching for God's breakthroughs and being quick to obey.

Sheila and I go into potentially dangerous places in the world to preach the Gospel, but most of the time we don't think much about the danger. We know we are in God's will, and the center of His will is the safest place we can be. But there are times when we will start to go to some place and all of a sudden we will feel we should not go there. As we have said, it is not emotion because what we experience in those instances is not fear. Rather it is a sensing of the guidance of the Holy Spirit, a warning from God. Outward circumstances may or may not offer any reason to go or not go, or to do or not do. But we do not need guidance from circumstances, we have the guidance of the Holy Spirit in our inner man. We may not ever know why God leads us in a certain way, but we don't have to. It is enough that we know we are obeying His voice.

As We Abide in Jesus We _Are_ the Will of God

When our son, Michael, was two years old, Sheila and I were attending Union University in Jackson, Tennessee. Nearly every day after classes, I would take Michael out on nature walks around the block. I would walk on the outside next to the street providing protection and he would walk on the inside. He wanted to look at everything, so we stopped frequently to look at rocks and sticks, birds and bugs, and many other things. As we walked I held my hand just behind his back, not quite touching him, but always prepared to guide him. He was not at all conscious of it, but he was walking in my will. When we reached the end of the block I would very gently touch the back of his head and turn him around the corner. The only possibility of him becoming consciously aware of being in or out of my will was if he opposed it. As he and I walked in unison he became an extension of me, an extension of my will.

The same is true with you and me as we walk with God. As we abide in Him and walk by the gentle leading of His Spirit, we are the will of God; our thoughts, our choices, and our decisions are His. If He wants to direct us some other way, all He has to do is speak into our inner man and tell us. Concerning the will of God, Oswald Chambers said, "To be so in contact with God that you never need to ask Him to show you His will, is to be nearing the final stage of your discipline in the life of faith. When you are rightly related to God, it is a life of freedom and liberty and delight, you are God's will, and all your common-sense decisions are His will for you unless He checks. You decide things in perfect delightful friendship with

God, knowing that if your decisions are wrong, He will always check; when He checks, stop at once" (2). Again in the words of Mr. Chambers, "If we are saved and sanctified, God guides us by our ordinary choices, and if we are going to choose what He does not want, He will check and we must heed. Whenever there is doubt, stop at once. Never reason it out and say - I wonder why I shouldn't" (3).

Dear Christian, our responsibility as children of God is to keep our spirit open to God, to keep our spiritual antenna up at all times so we can "pick up the signals" from the spiritual dimension. Remember you are a citizen of two worlds. We must be attuned to His voice and be obedient when we hear it. These days, nearly everyone has a marvelous invention clipped onto his or her belt or purse - a cell phone. How did we ever get along without them? Well, of course I am not receiving messages through my cell phone every minute of the day, but it is always with me, always on and always ready to receive. I dare not leave the house without my phone fully charged and ready to receive a call. And, sure enough, sometimes as I am just going along through my daily routine, that little gadget rings and changes the course of my life, especially if it is Sheila calling. I may not have thought I was going by the grocery store on my way home, but now I know I am. Well, God has given each of us a built in spiritual cell phone. It is called the spirit, the inner man. Just as my cell phone equips me to receive a word from Sheila regardless of what I am doing or where I am, my spirit equips me to receive a word from God at any instant regardless of what I am doing or where I am.

Over the past thirty years of travel, Sheila and I have flown on hundreds of airplanes, and every time I get on one, there are two things I am grateful for: a competent pilot and a control tower for him to communicate with. There have been many times over the years when we have heard the pilot announce that because of a message received from the tower, in the interest of our safety, he was going to have to alter something about our flight. On March 11, 2005 a headline appeared in the University of Texas campus newspaper, *The Daily Texan*, which read "Airport Tower Loses Communication." The story reported that at 6:28 on Saturday morning the control tower at Austin-Bergstrom International Airport lost all power, all radio communication and all radar for eighteen minutes. One of the controllers said, "When you're blind and you can't talk or hear, that's a huge impact." God has provided us with a "control tower," the Holy Spirit, and a radio to receive messages, our inner man. Thank God He never loses power and we never drop off His radar. Our only responsibility is to listen and respond when He speaks.

We talked previously about maintaining an atmosphere of faith in our life through regular worship and fellowship with the Father. Knowing God's will in regard to routine daily living requires very little effort on the part of God's child. The frame of reference established through worship and fellowship, the principles of God's Word and the inner guidance of the Holy Spirit combine to produce within us a very reliable intuitive sense of God's will. Unless He breaks through with specific direction and instruction, unless we receive a call on our spiritual cell phone, a message from the "Control Tower," then all we have to do is just walk in the assumption that we are in His will, just like Michael walking with me around the block. This morning when God prompted me to call Art, I had settled into my office for the morning to work on some routine things. But God interrupted the routine. I felt the gentle touch of the Father's hand behind my head. I heard His soft voice in my spirit. I responded, made the call, and then returned to the routine. Why could I hear the voice? Because I have spent enough time with God to enable me to recognize it, and I have grown accustomed to listening for it. I began the day by meeting with God in worship and continued in an atmosphere of fellowship. In short, my antenna was up, my spiritual cell phone was ready to receive a call, and my radio was on and tuned to the right control tower.

Perhaps we should say just a further word about how to recognize a "breakthrough" from God. As we have said already, the Christian life, the faith life, the Spirit-filled life is not a reactionary life. It is a life of acting, not reacting, in accordance with God's will. Remember, God guides from the inside, from within our spirit. Therefore a sudden change in circumstances or environment should not automatically be interpreted as God breaking through, as guidance from Him, or indication that we should change direction. Just because circumstances change doesn't necessarily mean I should. You can safely act in accordance with guidance in the inner man without agreement from circumstances, but you must never react to circumstances, good or bad, without agreement from the inner man. For instance, when we are on evangelistic campaigns we normally preach in five or six different venues per day. Usually they have been decided before the project begins. There are times, however, throughout the course of a day, when we will be on our way from one preaching spot to another, and in route we may see a place with a large crowd, maybe an open-air market we did not know about. The temptation, the impulse, is to abruptly stop there instead of going on to our planned destination, but we have found over the years that it is usually best to just "stay with the plan." Of course if God speaks by His Spirit and says stop, then we stop. But to alter the plan just because there is a big crowd there is wrong. That is purely circumstantial. We must resist the urge to react to the "snapshot" and remember that God sees the big picture.

So then where does faith enter into the area of routine daily living? Or does ordinary daily life involve faith at all? Yes, it most assuredly does. Let's recall some things. First, the faith life is the spirit-filled life, which is simply walking continuously in God's will. Second, the faith life is the balanced life in which we are functioning in both the physical world and the spirit world at the same time. Therefore as we abide in Jesus, God's will flows through us unhindered. That is the normal Christian life. Remember also that faith is "persuasion of fact followed by corresponding action." So what "persuasion" are we acting upon in routine daily life? We are persuaded of, we trust in, the truth from God's Word that, as we abide in Jesus, our thoughts are His thoughts, we have His mind operative within us, and therefore our decisions are His. Again we always make room for God to "break through" and change our direction if He so chooses.

Only One Faith, but Different Applications

Now you may ask, is there one type of faith for routine daily living and another for unusual or special situations? On one hand, the Bible does not use one word for faith as applied to daily living and another word for special events. It does not distinguish between "everyday" faith and "special situation" faith, or "crisis" faith. On the other hand, it is obvious that there are things that occur in life that are not just part of our daily routine, which at least seem to require a greater exercise of faith. Circumstances arise and changes occur, which are not part of the "ordinary." So do these things require a different type of faith? No, faith is faith. The difference is in the application - how it is used.

There are muscles in my hands, arms, shoulders, and back that I frequently use for lifting various objects. Now it obviously requires little effort, thought, or preparation for me to reach to the ground and pick up a feather. But what about an eighty-pound sack of concrete mix? You guessed it; that is quite a different story.

Heavy lifting requires much more focused concentrated effort. I am using the same exact muscles as I used to pick up the feather - the difference is that I am using them <u>more</u>. The muscles are the same but the application is different. The act of picking up the concrete mix is much more conscious than the "take it for granted" act of picking up the feather. You might say that routine daily living operates by a more "taking for granted" faith whereas special faith events require a more "heavy lifting" faith. As we will see in Chapter 22, "The Faith Process Explained," everyday faith falls under the category of GRACE faith, but special occasion faith necessitates a special assurance of God's will, which is the GIFT of faith. The **capacity** for faith never changes, but its **application** varies from one situation to another. Now, let me caution you here to not "jump ahead" in your reading to try to "shortcut" this whole process. In the chapters to follow we are going to learn how to apply "heavy lifting faith" to various kinds of situations in life. You need to read these chapters so that you will have a complete and accurate understanding of what faith living really is and what it really involves. But for the moment let's just rejoice in the fact that the God of the universe has placed within us the capacity for faith, and has made it possible for us to trust Him for the smallest details of our routine daily lives, as well as the most trying or challenging situations imaginable.

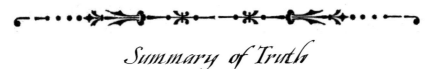

Summary of Truth

❖ Every second of every moment of my life is to be lived by faith.
❖ It is possible for every Christian to walk continuously in the will of God.
❖ We should live in expectancy of God's "breakthroughs."
❖ As we abide in Jesus we *are* the will of God.
❖ God has equipped me to receive a message from God at any second.
❖ Maintaining an atmosphere of faith in my life makes me sensitive to God's voice.
❖ Changing circumstances do not necessarily indicate a breakthrough from God.
❖ There is only one capacity for faith, but different applications.

NOW LET'S TAKE A MOMENT AND PRAY TOGETHER:

LORD JESUS, MY LIFE BELONGS TO YOU AND I DESIRE TO LIVE EVERY SECOND OF IT WALKING IN YOUR WILL AND TRUSTING YOU BY FAITH FOR EVERYTHING. HELP ME TO BE SENSITIVE TO YOUR BREAKTHROUGHS, TO ALWAYS RECOGNIZE AND QUICKLY OBEY YOUR VOICE. THANK YOU FOR EQUIPPING ME TO DO SO. LORD HELP ME TO ACT ACCORDING TO YOUR GUIDANCE AND TO NOT REACT TO CIRCUMSTANCES. HELP ME TO APPLY THE CAPACITY FOR FAITH YOU HAVE GIVEN ME TO THE HEAVY LIFTING SITUATIONS OF LIFE AS WELL AS THE DAILY ROUTINE. THANK YOU FOR THE GIFT OF FAITH AND FOR THE GIFT OF SALVATION. I LOVE YOU, LORD JESUS. IN YOUR NAME I PRAY. AMEN.

Chapter 19

Coming to the Knowledge of God's Will

"To live for the Lord means to live for His will,
for His interest, and for His Kingdom."
Watchman Nee (1)

*I*n settling upon the title for this chapter, I chose to say "Coming to the Knowledge" of God's will, rather than "How to Know." The reason is because I did not want to imply that knowing the will of God can be reduced to a formula, or stated as an equation, or explained in a series of steps. I'm sure we all wish some one would write a book called "God's Will for Dummies" that would give us a few quick and easy steps for knowing the will of God. Well that book doesn't exist and if it ever does, don't buy it. The reason that coming to the knowledge of God's will concerning things, events and situations in life cannot be reduced to a formula is because each life is different, unique, and individual, and God's ways in His dealing with each of us are just as unique and individual. In a formula the same rules apply to everyone, everywhere, every time. Not so with faith and the will of God. Therefore, like faith, getting to the will of God is better approached as a process rather than a procedure.

You Really Can Know the Will of God

Now here's the big question - is it possible to gain assurance of God's will concerning specific things and situations in our life? Absolutely! It has to be, because as we have already established, we cannot exercise real faith without first knowing the will of God. Faith is acting, and you cannot act unless you have something definite and defined to act upon. Therefore, God's Word gives us this instruction in Ephesians 5:17, *"Wherefore be ye not unwise, but understanding what the will of the Lord is."* Then in Colossians 1:9 we read, *"...that ye might be filled with the knowledge of his will in all wisdom and spiritual understanding."* Being a Child of God involves two things – beginning and continuing. First comes **salvation** (coming <u>to</u> Christ) and then **sanctification** (becoming <u>like</u> Christ). Colossians 2:6 tells us, *"As ye have therefore received Christ Jesus the Lord, so walk ye in Him."* We began our Christian life, our walk with God, by acting, by stepping into the will of God by faith. Now how did that happen? God awakened you to your need and then activated your capacity of faith to believe. The Holy Spirit used some means to draw you into the will of God – maybe the witness of a friend, a message you heard at church, or a program on television. Then at some point you became persuaded of the reality of salvation through Jesus, you acted in faith, and stepped into the will of God. You did not stumble into it; you took a thoughtful, deliberate, intelligent, rational step into it. The result was that the will of God in the eternal (in the invisible) became present reality in your life (in the visible). By faith you accessed the grace, the supply of God. The impossible (a totally degenerate human being stepping out of hell into heaven) became possible. Now, as a child of God, you are to continue in the same way - by continually stepping into the will of God by faith, thereby accessing everything that belongs to the new life God has created in you. That is the normal Christian life.

God's Will Begins with God

To get us started in understanding the process of getting to the will of God we will begin by observing that God's will begins with God. Okay, I know what you are thinking, "Well, duh! Boy this guy is really brilliant, how long did it take him to figure THAT one out?" Well, it might surprise you to know just how many Christians begin their search for God's will by looking to everything except God Himself. So many try to find God's will by means of their intellect, their emotions, by drawing conclusions from circumstances, by looking for "signs," by weighing pros and cons, or by asking for advice from other human beings. There are two things to consider here: one, as we have already settled, God's will is never revealed by thought, feeling, or anything external (other than the Word); and two, you do not "find God's will," it finds you. Those things could not bring you to Jesus and they will not enable you to walk in Jesus. The confirmation of God's will in your spirit is always initiated by Him. Your responsibility as a Believer is to maintain a continuous atmosphere of worship and fellowship with God. An attitude of receptivity to the guidance of the Holy Spirit will place you in a position to receive the knowledge of God's will when He chooses to initiate it in your heart. When sudden or unusual needs occur in your life, or desires arise in your heart, or a challenge, change, or crisis comes in your circumstances, your automatic response should not be to <u>react</u>, but to say "Speak, Lord" and then <u>wait</u> for Him to do so. We have already observed that as you go along in your daily routine life, walking in fellowship with God and abiding in Christ (the key word here is "abiding"), you <u>are</u> the will of God. Your choices <u>are</u> His choices. Your decisions <u>are</u> His decisions. Your actions <u>are</u> His actions. But there are times when things are not that simple. There are times when things arise in your life that are not routine and ordinary, things that need specific guidance and instruction from the Holy Spirit, things that will obviously require the supernatural intervention and miraculous supply of God. When that happens you must STOP, LOOK and LISTEN. First, you must stop your activity. You must refuse to react in the flesh. There will always be the temptation to try to figure or feel your way to a solution, but that will only end in results that fall short of where God is trying to take you. Second, you must look not at circumstances or outward appearances but into the invisible, and let God show you His plan. And third, you must listen not to advice or opinion but to the voice of the Holy Spirit as He speaks in your inner man.

To be content with God's will and way is rest. Mine is to obey, His is to direct.

Hudson Taylor (2)

Five Means by Which God Moves the Christian to Seek His Will

God uses five things to stimulate us to search out His will, to put up our antenna to receive His guidance, in other words to begin the faith process. They are NEED, DESIRE, HIS WORD, HOLY SPIRIT PROMPTING, and a CALLING upon our life for some special service. We will deal with these fully later, but let us observe briefly here that there are three kinds of needs. First, there are those that pertain to just living every day; the necessities of life, such as food, clothing, shelter, and so on. This is what Jesus was dealing with in Matthew 6 and what Paul referred to in Philippians 4:19. These things apply more to a "taking for granted" type faith. We know it is God's will to meet the basic needs of our life. But secondly, there are needs that arise as a result of God leading us to expand in some area of our life, such as our business, our church, our ministry, or our giving. Finally, there are needs that present themselves more in the form of crisis or trial. These last two kinds of need require a more extended knowledge of God's will and a greater exercise of the capacity of faith.

Then there are two kinds of desires, those that occur in our human nature as we interact with our natural environment and those that arise in our spirit as a result of God's direct initiation. (We are assuming here that the desire is not for something that is contrary to the written Word!) In relation to a desire, the real question is, is it within the scope of God's will; does it belong to the life God has created in me? The issue cannot be decided by my idea of "right or wrong," or "fleshly or spiritual." Whether a desire is right or wrong depends on whether or not it has God's approval, not my approval. The way to find out is to take it into the prayer closet and place it before God. If it fades in the light of God, then let it. But if it persists and intensifies, then find God's specific will pertaining to it and trust Him for it.

Regarding God's Word, there are two types here as well. First there is the written Word, the Bible, which is God's general revelation to mankind. God often speaks to us directly from the Scripture and we are reminded of some promise or admonition contained there. But sometimes through the course of your Bible study or reading, God may "energize" or "illuminate" a verse of Scripture to you. He will apply it to your heart in such a way that you know He is speaking to you, directly and personally, in relation to a specific issue in your life. You don't know exactly how you know, but you just know. That is God using His written Word to either initiate the faith process or to reinforce what He has already initiated by some other means.

Then there are times when the Holy Spirit may not use the written Word of God, but instead will prompt you in your spirit by some other means. He may use something you see or hear in your natural environment as you go through the normal course of the day. It may be something that looks and sounds very ordinary to everyone around you, but not to you, because you know God is using it to get your attention, to speak to you. He is using it to draw you into position to receive particular instruction about His will. You know because it is causing you to turn the "eyes" and "ears" of your spirit toward God.

Finally there are those special occasions that occur in the lives of some Christians in which God calls them to yield to Him for some special service. I will give examples of each of these five things later, but here I simply want to emphasize that regardless of what means God uses to get your attention, to stimulate you to be receptive to the revelation of His will and to draw you into the exercise of faith, it all begins with Him. He is the "Author and the Finisher."

Characteristics of the Will of God

Now as we turn our hearts toward God to receive His will, there are some things we should bring to remembrance and keep in mind, not necessarily as a "check list", but as a guide. Some have been mentioned already, but I am including them here again because the consideration of these truths as a whole will help us stay on track and maintain focus and clarity. I am not placing them in any particular order because they are all equally important.

1. **God's will is fixed in eternity.** You need to remember that the will of God pertaining to your particular situation is already settled. He is not scrambling around trying to figure out what He is going to do about this need or situation that has come up in your life. God is not in a panic, therefore you shouldn't be either. He already knows what He is going to do and what he is going to provide, because, from His perspective, He has already done it. Remember, faith is anchored in God's past and your present. As you step into His will you are entering the finished work and the foreordained supply. THAT is security.

2. **God's will is not a secret.** We very often treat the will of God as if it is something that is virtually impossible to know and understand, but that is not so. Quite often the reason we do not know His will is because we do not ask. In Jeremiah 33:3 God says, *"Call unto me, and I will answer thee, and shew thee great and mighty things, which thou knowest not."* The word "call" in this verse means "to encounter, to get in one's presence." The word "shew" means "to manifest or make known" and the word "mighty" means "hidden" or "fenced in." What God is saying here is "Get in My presence and I will make known to you the hidden things." If the will of God seems to be hidden or fenced in from you, it is only because you will not get in His presence and listen.

3. **God's will requires obedience.** Sometimes the problem we have concerning God's will is not that we do not know it, but that we do know it (or we at least very much suspect what it might be) and we simply do not want to <u>obey</u> it. God will not reveal Himself or His plan to an unwilling heart. To receive the knowledge of God's will, you must come to Him in an attitude of submission and obedience. You must be willing to lay aside your ideas and plans and receive His.

4. **God's will brings glory to Himself.** The ultimate end of the will of God is to bring honor and glory to Him. Our participation by faith in the fulfillment of the will of God always results in God getting glory to Himself. In every situation we should ask ourselves, what outcome would most glorify God, bring honor to His name, and prove His faithfulness? Once that question is answered, we will find ourselves at the will of God.

5. **The discovery of God's will takes place in the prayer closet.** Your search for the will of God and your desire to receive it may be stimulated by need, desire, or circumstances, but the actual discovery of it comes only as you wait before Him in private worship and fellowship. It takes time, and there is no shortcut.

6. **God's will is confirmed to us in our spirit by the Holy Spirit.** It is only as we spend time in the Word and in prayer, that God "illumines" His will in our inner man. It is therefore pointless to look anywhere else. You might as well cease looking around in your environment and circumstances for "signs" or clues that might tell you the will of God, because they are not there. God will often use circumstances to stimulate you to seek His will or to affirm and reinforce His will once it has been confirmed to you in your inner man. But the knowledge of His will begins in your Spirit. The sooner you stop figuring and feeling, straining and struggling, and seeking advice from other people about your situation, the sooner you will hear from God. Those things only make room for satan to influence you and create confusion in your life. God will not speak to you through all that noise and clutter. You must get alone with Him, put everything else aside, get quiet and still, and listen.

7. **God's will is revealed only to Spirit-filled Believers.** In order for a person to receive the will of God concerning things in his own personal life, he must be saved and Spirit-filled. Apart from the general revelation of God's Word to all mankind, it is not possible for an unsaved person to know the God's will, in terms of personal guidance, because his spirit (the part of man that God communicates with) is dead. Likewise, a carnally-minded Christian (one who is not being controlled by the Holy Spirit) cannot know the will of God because he is operating out of his flesh (his intellect, will, and emotions) rather than out of the spirit. For instance, it is easy to know God's will regarding murder, adultery,

stealing, etc. It is also easy to know God's will regarding salvation. These things are part of God's general revelation to man. But in regard to personal, individual guidance regarding God's <u>specific</u> will for <u>my</u> life, I must be saved (indwelt by His Spirit) and Spirit-filled (controlled by His Spirit). In order to hear the voice of God, there must be nothing between you and Him that would prevent it. You must come into His presence with a clean heart.

8. **God's will always agrees with His Word.** No matter how unique your situation is, the will of God concerning it will <u>always</u> line up with Scripture. Quite often there will even be specific promises from the Bible that will perfectly match what you are dealing with. Accuracy in the Christian life is maintained, not by making the Bible line up with experience, but by making experience line up  with the Bible. If some misguided person said that it was God's will for him to divorce his wife and marry another woman because God wanted him to be happy, that person would not be anywhere near knowing God's will. How do we know? Because there are four things that always work in perfect harmony – God's <u>will</u>, God's <u>Word</u>, God's <u>way</u> and God's <u>work</u>.

9. **God's will is always specific, never vague.** It is always clearly defined and easily understood by His child. If you think you know the will of God about something and the element of certainty is not present, then you don't. God's will is always accompanied by solid, unshakable assurance. If it is not there, then don't act until it is. If you do not yet have God's peace, then you do not yet have His plan.

10. **The will of God always leads to real faith.** More often than not, the will of God will stand in stark contrast to common sense, reason, and logic. Look at the cross. God's will requires His supernatural intervention and provision. It will take you out beyond your own natural abilities and resources. God may very well use what you have and what you can do in accomplishing His will, but He will not stop with that. He will always draw you into the realm of the invisible and the impossible. Real faith is reaching beyond your grasp, beyond your own abilities and resources. God's will does not ignore the natural but adds to it the spiritual, thus creating the

supernatural. Real faith stretches the visible into the invisible, the possible into the impossible, and the natural into the supernatural. Doing the will of God will always require you to do more than you can do, to go further than you can go, and to use more than you have. It always requires real faith.

11. **God's will is always original.** The Word of God, as well as Christian history, is filled with story after story of how God worked miraculously in the lives of men and women who knew His will and trusted Him by real faith to fulfill it. They are marvelous accounts of the ways and workings of God and serve to illustrate that the wisest thing a Christian can do is simply trust God with childlike faith. But that is all they are – illustrations, not models. You cannot look at another person's experience and then assume that God will do it that way for you. There has only been one Red Sea crossing and there will never be another one. You cannot look at how God worked in one church and then duplicate it in yours. You must know His plan for you. Whatever need, desire, or situation you are dealing with right now, it is unique to you. That means that God's way of dealing with it will be unique. It also means that the supply He has set aside to meet your need is specifically designated to you. He will not apply your provision to some one else's need and he will not apply theirs to yours. Not only does God not duplicate Himself from one life to another, He does not duplicate Himself in yours either. Do not look back in your life and allow yourself to believe that just because God worked in a certain way before He will do it that way this time. He won't. No two situations are alike. They don't have to be, because there is no limit to God's creativity and resources. In God's dealings with you, history does not repeat itself.

12. **God's will is always active, never passive.** Stepping into the will of God always requires you to act in faith in specific obedience to His inner command. The will of God is something you do, not something that is done to you. It requires your active participation. As we will see later, real faith is a two-sided page. God will not do for you what you can do for yourself. For instance, suppose God has told me to go to Africa and preach. I do not have the money, and the departure time is close at hand. What do I do? I do everything that does not require money. I wash and iron my clothes,

pack them in the suitcase and so on. That is on my side of the page. I do not need for God to pack my bag, or book airline tickets, and furthermore, He will not do it. What I need is for God to do the things I cannot do – supply the money, hold the doors of opportunity open in the country I am going to, hold back the rain, and so on. God will do His part, but He will not do my part. I must act in faith and do my part as if He had already done His. Why? Because He has.

13. **God's will operates according to His timing.** God's will is not affected by "deadlines." Quite often real faith involves waiting until the last minute and maybe even beyond. There are many examples in the Bible, where it appears that time has run out, all hope is gone, and the people involved are doomed. But if you are in the will of God there is no such thing as a deadline. Remember Abraham.

14. **God's will sets the parameters for faith.** Satan uses two temptations to sabotage your faith. He either tries to get you to settle for too little or to believe for too much. Either way is wrong and misses the mark. God's will has fixed limits and those limits determine the "measure" or area of faith in which a Christian can operate. The key to real faith is to know what the boundaries are and to believe up to the boundaries but not beyond them.

15. **God's will is always accompanied by God's supply.** An example of this is the feeding of the 5,000. Jesus told the disciples that it was God's will to feed 5,000 men, plus women and children - probably around 20,000 people. When asked what food supply they had available they produced the five loaves of bread and two fish. Of course they concluded it was not enough and in the natural realm they were right – it wasn't. Their mistake, however, was focusing on what they <u>did not have</u> in the visible rather than what God <u>did have</u> in the invisible. They did not take into account that from God's perspective those people were not waiting to be fed – they had already been fed. With what? With the supply that God had prepared for them from eternity past, the supply that existed in the invisible. All it took to transfer it from the spiritual realm to the material or natural realm was for someone to believe within the will of God. That someone in this case was Jesus. Those people were fed that day, not because Jesus was God in the flesh (though

He was), but because as a man He looked into heaven, saw the will of God and the supply to go with it, and acted in accordance with what He saw. As pointed out earlier, we as born-again Believers are now in a position to do the same thing. We access the provision of God by acting in accordance with the will of God. In thinking about need and supply, it is important to remember that the supply for all our needs, for all of our God-given desires, and for the fulfillment of God's will, has existed from the very beginning of creation. In God's economy, need and supply are never out of balance. It is not necessary for God to create a supply for my need because it has already been created. He has only to dispense it to me as I act in faith and believe.

16. **Coming to the will of God takes time.** It is a mistake to get in a hurry concerning God's will. Quite often you may feel pressured by man-made schedules, by deadlines, or by circumstances, but to react without knowing God's will leads to disaster. Remember, God is not in a hurry, He is not under pressure, and He is not panicked. When it is time for you to act He will tell you, and He is not going to tell you until He wants you to know. Your

> The faith that enters into the inheritance is the attitude of soul which waits for God Himself, first to speak His Word to me, and then to do the thing He has spoken.
>
> *Andrew Murray (3)*

responsibility is to wait before Him, listen for His voice, and then act when He speaks - regardless of how much time that takes.

17. **God's will is sometimes revealed in increments.** There are some situations in which God will tell you to take a step, and then after you do, He will tell you to take another one. Sometimes we make the mistake of wanting the whole picture laid out in front of us before we will act. There are times when God will do that, but there are times when He won't. It may be that you know the clear will of God concerning the first step but not the next. Don't let that immobilize you and keep you from acting on what you do know. If you will take the first step then God will give you clear guidance for the next. That is quite often the way of real faith. That is exactly what God did with Elijah in I Kings 17. First, God told him to

go to the brook Cherith, and He sent the ravens to feed him. Then He told him to go on to Zerephath and provided a widow to care for him. Finally in chapter 18, God sent him on to Mount Carmel where he challenged the prophets of Baal. The secret to getting to Mount Carmel, though, was the incremental steps of obedience to God's will on the way.

18. **God's will often includes trial and suffering.** Do not make the mistake of believing that the will of God always leads to a trouble-free life. Hebrews 11 contains a list of obedient saints who stepped into the revealed will of God by faith. God's will for some included miraculous deliverance, expansion, and blessing, but for some it included torture, trial, destitution, and death. For Jesus, the will of God included the cross. There are times when God will give you specific instructions which, when obeyed by faith, will lead to trial, hardship, and suffering. There is some teaching being spread throughout the Christian world today that says if you are truly living by faith then you never have to be sick or suffer any need. That is just not the truth according to God's Word. There were many times when the Apostle Paul suffered and had great need. Some of the people whom God has used the most are those who have suffered the most. He may call upon you to be one of them.

19. **God's will goes by way of the cross.** You will find as you walk situations through by faith, the process will move along through five stages, which could be called the garden, the court, the cross, the tomb and the resurrection. At the outset of the faith process, God will bring you to a crisis of will in which you choose not only to bring your will into subordination to His but to join your will to His. You step into the will of God knowing full well what it is going to involve. Next you go through the court where public opinion, circumstances, and common sense make a mockery of what God has told you to believe Him for. Then comes the cross, that point where you know you are acting in obedience to God, but all seems to be lost. It seems to die. You appear to be failing and everything seems to say, "You made a mistake, it is all over, it didn't work." The vision God gave you, the faith object that seemed so real in your heart in the beginning, seems to be a dead issue. In spite of everything, though, it still seems alive to you. Somehow,

you can't let go of the faith object God placed in your heart, you can't let go of His will that you <u>know</u> was confirmed to you in your spirit, and it will not let go of you. So you hang on, and as you do a miracle happens. When it seems that all is lost, God rolls away the stone, and the vision is resurrected. Why does this so often happen in the faith walk? Because God is bringing maximum glory to Himself and maximum joy to you. He is bringing His will into fulfillment in such a way that it stands forever.

20. **God's will is always opposed by the devil.** It always results in spiritual warfare. The assurance of God's will is always followed by satan's attack. He will use every means (internal and external) to discourage you, dissuade you, and divert you from hanging on and following through to the end. As we will see again later, our defense against the enemy is to <u>resist</u> his lies on the authority of the blood of Jesus, to continue to <u>act</u> in accordance with God's will, to <u>praise</u> God, and to <u>confess</u> to the outside world that God is doing it.

21. **God's will does not bend or conform to circumstances, just the opposite.** The will of God is not and cannot be determined by circumstances (good or bad) or anything else external, because they are just that – external. God's will conforms to <u>nothing</u> other than God. As we move in the direction of the will of God in obedience to Him, He will, in turn, cause all things external to conform to His will. Circumstances should be considered, but only to the extent that they help define and clarify the nature and need of the object or outcome of faith we are believing for.

22. **God's will is accompanied by peace and persistence.** Colossians 3:15 tells us to "let the peace of God rule in your hearts." The word "rule" means, "to stand guard, to act as umpire." The word translated peace means quietness, rest, and harmony. It is not possible to be in the will of God and not have an accompanying peace and harmony with God. If it does not yet exist, then you must refuse to act until it does.

Now using the above observations as a backdrop, as a frame of reference, let's look at the actual process of coming to the will of God. It is not nearly as obscure, mysterious and complicated as the devil would have you believe. Details and specifics will vary from life to life and from event to event in your own life, but the process itself will follow along these lines.

We can outline the process in five words – <u>prompting</u>, <u>preparation</u>, <u>prayer</u>, <u>picture</u> and <u>possession</u>.

Coming to the Will of God

As we have seen already, it begins with a **PROMPTING** from God by some means of His choosing. It begins with God creating a need and a desire in you to receive His will. This is done by means of some external pressure (from your circumstances and/or physical environment), from an internal pressure (from your intellect and emotions), or from within your inner man. It may be through some need that has arisen in your life that you cannot meet through your own strength, ability and resources. It may be financial or physical, or professional. Maybe it concerns the salvation of a friend or family member God has placed on your heart. Maybe a strong desire has arisen in you and you are beginning to sense it is from God simply because it will not go away. You are willing for it to, but it doesn't. In fact, as you meet with God in private prayer and worship, it intensifies.

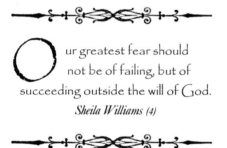

Our greatest fear should not be of failing, but of succeeding outside the will of God.

Sheila Williams (4)

Perhaps a change has occurred in your circumstances and it is causing a disturbance in your life. You may feel threatened, vulnerable, and fearful. It may involve your business, your job, your health, your ministry, your finances, your family, or your giving. Now maybe the thing that is prompting you to seek the will of God is not a crisis at all. Rather it is a "nudge" from the Holy Spirit that occurred while you were reading your Bible. A verse of Scripture seemed to just jump off the page and land in your heart, and all of a sudden you sensed God speaking to you about this or that. Maybe God is challenging you in your spirit to trust Him for expansion in some area of your life or ministry. You may sense that God is leading you in a new direction or calling you to a new place or a new work. There are thousands of possible scenarios that God could use to get your attention, but when He does, you know it. You may not be sure yet just exactly what God is up to, but you do know He is working in your life, and He is leading you to trust Him for something that only He can do and only He can provide. He has your attention, you are listening, and you are ready to know His will. In fact, you have come to a place where you know you MUST know His will. So, now what?

Now you need to take a quick inventory of your walk with God and make sure you are **PREPARED** to receive from Him what He desires to give you – the sure knowledge of His will and His plan. You can do that by asking yourself a few questions. If you come to one you cannot truly answer yes to, then make whatever adjustments are needed in your heart so that you can. When you can truthfully answer yes to all the questions, then you are prepared to meet with God. Lets look at them carefully and prayerfully. Ask yourself:

1. Do I really want to know God's will, or do I honestly just want Him to do it my way?
2. Is my heart set to obey what He tells me? Am I ready to comply with His will regardless of what it is? Do I already have a suspicion of what God's will is and just don't want to do it?
3. Am I willing for God to glorify Himself through this situation in my life regardless of what it costs me, my family, my church, or my business?
4. Am I willing to spend whatever amount of time is necessary to know His will even if it means getting up an hour or two hour earlier every day, for a while, than I normally do?
5. Am I Spirit-filled? Is my life truly under the control of the Holy Spirit? Is there anything between God and me that must be cleansed and cleared away?
6. Am I willing to take the Word of God as the final authority regarding my situation?
7. Am I willing for God to take me out beyond my abilities and resources? Am I ready to act and speak in such a way as to contradict logic, reason, and common sense? Am I willing to look like a fool to the world, to my friends, to my family if that is what the will of God requires?
8. Am I willing to completely set aside my ideas, plans, and desires and enter into His?
9. Am I willing to suffer trial and hardship if that is what God's will calls for?
10. Am I prepared to look to God alone plus nothing?

The next "square on the board," so to speak, is **PRAYER** - getting into the presence of God and conversing with Him. In order to know the will of God you must set aside time for that purpose. There is absolutely no other way and, again, there is no shortcut. It is imperative that you go directly to God Himself. Don't look at circumstances, don't read books, don't ask advice and don't try to figure it all out. None of that will help. It is GOD Who knows the will of God. Set aside time for private personal worship, fellowship, reflection, and discussion with God alone. Scripture indicates that the first hours of the day are best. In your private time with God, pour out your heart to Him and lay before Him the issue, the need, the desire, the trial, the circumstance you are dealing with. Proverbs 16:3 tells us to, *"Commit thy works unto the Lord, and thy thoughts shall be established."* Ask the Holy Spirit to guide you in His Word and speak to you from it. Listen to His "still small voice." Now you may ask, "But how many days will I have to spend meeting with God before I know what His will is?" "How long will it take?" There is no way to know, but I can tell you this from personal experience and from observing Christian history – it takes what it takes. Then you may ask, "But what am I waiting for?" You are waiting for God to give you a clear picture in your heart of what the finished work looks like concerning your need or situation. You are waiting for Him to show you His plan and His provision in the invisible so you can believe Him for it, so you can act upon it, so you can confess it and bring it into present reality. "But how will I know when I see it?" you ask. "How will I know it is real?" You'll know.

You begin by painting a **PICTURE** in words. This picture is of what the situation looks like to you now. As you wait before the Lord in private worship and prayer, write down a detailed description of your need, your situation, and your circumstances. Write down the facts, as you understand them. Then voice that to God, "Lord, this is what my situation looks like to me right now, this is what I need You to fix, to provide, to work out, to help

me with." Then paint a second word picture of what you want your situation to look like if it is possible to change it. Be honest, and be very specific. Don't hold back anything, not one detail, regardless of how small, trivial, unimportant, unspiritual, or irrelevant it may seem. In Mark 10:51, Jesus asked blind Bartimeaus, *"...What wilt thou that I should do unto thee?..."* Now Jesus already knew the answer, just like He knows what is in your heart, but He wanted Bartimeaus to express it. And express it he did. He replied without hesitation, "I want to receive my sight." That was his will, his desire. When you come to God with your need, desire, etc., the Holy Spirit is going to ask you every time, "What do you want?" There are two possible answers. You can say what you think God wants to hear, what you think is a good spiritual answer, or you can tell the hardcore truth. Coming to the will of God begins with total honesty. John 4:24 tells us that those who will worship God (have intimate contact with Him) must *"...worship him in spirit and in truth."* Notice Bartimeaus did not say, "Oh Lord, I want to be a good follower of Yours. I want to be a good man. I want to serve You well." No, he just got right to the point, made no pretense, emptied his heart, and told the truth. Then how did Jesus respond? He healed him. Bartimeaus had a crystal clear picture in his mind before he ever approached Jesus. Sometimes you may find it difficult to be completely honest with God because you are afraid you are being selfish or unspiritual. That "concern" is from the devil. It is an accusation designed to prevent you from being honest with God. But that is exactly what God wants you to be, honest. And besides, you may as well be; He knows what is in your heart anyway. Now, why does God do this? Because the moment you reach the point where you are holding nothing back from Him, then He moves into position to reveal His will to you.

After you have considered all the "facts" of your situation and have voiced to God what you would like for Him to do, then lay all of that aside and wait for Him to speak into your heart. He will. I promise you that a new picture will begin to form in your heart, in you inner man, as you meet with Him and wait before Him day by day. God told us in Isaiah 1:18, *"Come now, and let us reason together, saith the Lord..."* As we said before, the word "reason" here means to "be correct," to "be right," to "be adjusted." Real prayer and worship is meeting with God and getting correct, getting adjusted. In a sense it is you and God painting the picture together. He may do what is contained in the picture you came to Him with, but in all likelihood, He will alter it and do much more than you asked. At some point though, a final picture, a final plan, a final provision will settle in upon your heart, upon your spirit, as the will of God.

Now again you ask, "But how will I know?" You will know because the picture in your spirit will become **POSSESSION** in your heart. There will come a point where you not only see it, but you own it. That will happen long before it becomes real in your hand. Even though it has not yet happened or appeared in the natural material realm, it will be as real to you as if it had. You will become so certain of its reality that even in the face of tremendous opposing circumstances and evidence to the contrary, you will be able to say with all assurance and confidence to the world, "God has done it; God has provided." You will know when you have arrived at the will of God, because it will be accompanied by five things:

1. **PICTURE of God in my mind** – First there will be a very clear, well-defined **picture** formed in your mind, just like the picture on the puzzle box. There will be no doubt as to what the object or outcome looks like, because you have seen it already with the eyes of your heart.

2. **PEACE of God in your emotions** - There will be a **peace** that surpasses all human comprehension. There will be a certainty that cannot be shaken by opposing circumstances, logic, outward appearances, reason, common sense, or public opinion. There will be an assurance that can withstand any amount of delay and hold on past any deadline. How is that so? Because you have received the object or outcome as finished work, and God's finished work cannot be undone. The will of God is settled in eternity and once it becomes settled in your heart it is immovable, and so are you.

3. **PRESENCE of God in your spirit** - There will also be the **presence** of God abiding upon it. When something is the will of God He will find a way to put His signature on it in your heart. You don't know just how you know, but you know, and that "knowing" cannot be shaken. Once His signature has been applied, it cannot be erased. As we said in another chapter, it will take you to the furthermost extremities of faith.

4. **PERSISTENCE of God in your will** - You will also know that what you are believing for is the will of God because it is persistent, it will not go away. There is therefore a **persistence** in you that will not diminish with time or opposition. Oswald Chambers said, "I know when the proposition comes from God because of its quiet persistence" (5). You know it is from God, because you <u>cannot</u> let go of it and it <u>will not</u> let go of you.

5. **PROOFS of God in the external** - Then as you persist in faith, God will provide evidences, confirmation, **proofs** in the external world that you are in His will. As you act, speak, and continue in faith God will allow little "indicators" to pop up on your spiritual radar screen. They will likely be so small that no one could possibly see them or recognize them for what they

are except you, but they will be there just the same. Are these "proofs" necessary for you to believe? No they are not. In fact, they do not occur so that you <u>will</u> believe, they occur because you have <u>already</u> believed.

Dear friend, God wants you to know His will more than you want to know it. It is not a secret and it is not mysterious. He is anxious for you to experience the joy of real faith in your Christian life and is therefore anxious for you to know His will. That is why He is continuously bringing things into your life that necessitate faith. As I said in the beginning, coming to the knowledge of the will of God cannot be reduced to a formula or a set of steps. It is a process – an individualized process. But if you will apply the guidelines we have discussed above, you will get there. And you will know you are there, that you have arrived at the will of God because:

1. It started with God – it was confirmed to you in your spirit as you met with God in private prayer and worship.
2. It stands in agreement with the Word of God.
3. It is specific and clearly defined in your heart. You can "see" the picture complete and you have embraced it as real. You have received it in your heart.
4. It requires the supernatural intervention and supply of God; it requires real faith.
5. It is persistent – it will not go away. It is producing persistence in you.
6. It is accompanied by peace, certainty, and assurance. It has God's signature on it.
7. It has confirmation in the external world that only you can see.
8. It will bring honor and glory to God and establish a fresh testimony to His faithfulness.

Now let me ask you, is there something going on in your life right now that would indicate God is initiating certain events or things in order to get your attention? Is He drawing you into position to seek and know His will? Are there needs you cannot meet and you do not know what to do about? Do you have desires that have arisen in your heart, desires that just won't go away? Has God nudged you from His Word or prompted you by His Holy Spirit by means of something you have seen or heard? Is it possible He is calling you to serve Him in some special way? Or are you just concerned about what God wants to do with the rest of your life? If you desire for God to initiate the faith process in your life, then get alone with God and let Him speak to you. Lay your need, your situation, out before Him and listen to His voice. He <u>will</u> speak to you. Follow the guidelines above and God will reveal His will to you. Then when He does, obey Him. How? By faith. Later we will look closely at the entire faith process, but for now just let me tell you that it begins with God drawing you into position to know His will. If you are willing to start there, then you are ready to go on.

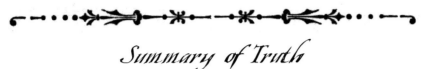

Summary of Truth

❖ Coming to know the will of God is not a procedure and not a formula; it is a process.

❖ God's will starts with Him; He takes the initiative.

❖ God uses five things to draw us into a position to receive His will: need, desire, His Word, Holy Spirit prompting, and calling.

❖ God's will:

- is fixed in eternity.
- is not a secret.
- requires obedience.
- glorifies God.
- is discovered by means of private prayer and worship.
- is confirmed in our spirit by the Holy Spirit.
- is revealed only to a Spirit-filled Believer.
- always stands in agreement with the Bible.
- is always specific.
- always leads to faith.
- is always original.
- is active.
- operates by God's timing.
- sets the parameters for faith.
- is always accompanied by God's supply.
- takes time to know.
- is sometimes revealed in increments.
- often includes trial and suffering.
- goes by way of the cross.
- is always opposed by the devil.
- does not bend or conform to circumstances.
- is accompanied by peace and persistence.

❖ Knowing God's will begins with a PROMPTING from Him.

❖ We must be PREPARED to meet with God.

❖ God will give us a PICTURE, in the invisible, of His PLAN and His PROVISION so we can believe and transfer it into present reality.

❖ It will become a POSSESSION in our heart before it does in the material realm.

❖ It will be accompanied by a PICTURE, PEACE, the PRESENCE of God, PERSISTANCE, and PROOFS.

❖ God wants us to know His will more than we want to know it.

Now Let's Take a Moment and Pray Together:

Dear Father, more than anything I want to walk in the knowledge of Your will and to please You by faith. By Your grace I am going to do the things I have just finished reading about. I am going to come into Your presence and I am going to ask You to reveal Your will to me concerning every area of my life. Lord, I am going to live by faith. I ask You now to help me by Your Holy Spirit, to understand and absorb all these truths and apply them to my own personal life and walk with You. I know You have a wonderful plan for my life and that plan is already complete. I ask You to reveal it to me as I wait before You, and help me to step into it. Lord, take me into the realm of the impossible. Glorify Yourself through me. I love You Lord and it is in Your Holy Name I pray. Amen.

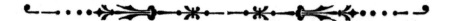

Chapter 20

Drawn to the Will of God

Part One: By Need and Desire

"It is the very time for faith to work, when sight ceases.
The greater the difficulties, the easier for faith."
George Muller (1)

s we have said already, God uses five means to draw you to the ultimate knowledge of His will. They are need, desire, His Word, prompting from the Holy Spirit, and calling. Here, we are looking at need and desire, which are like first cousins, closely related but not exactly in the same family. In differentiating between the two, we normally think of needs as necessities and desires more as wants. Though basic and simple, that is actually a fairly accurate definition of terms. According to the dictionaries I have consulted, a need is something that is required to sustain life or quality of life. It is something that is necessary for us to survive in our physical and cultural environment. It is an empty space that must be filled. A desire, on the other hand, is a longing, a wish, a craving, but not a necessity. A need is something I <u>must</u> have or do and a desire is something I would <u>like</u> to have or do. When a desire is not fulfilled it may cause you sadness, disappointment, or even distress, but it will not threaten your life. When we turn to the Word of God we find that the same definitions apply. There are 12 different words in the Bible translated need, but when you put them all together they mean the same thing, necessity. Then there are at least 35 words in Scripture translated desire, but again, taken collectively, they refer to a longing, a craving, a wish, in other words, a desire, whether good or bad, pure or evil.

Our Needs and Desires Are Equally Important to God

Now before discussing how God uses need and desire to draw us to His will, I want to first clear something up on the front end. We must understand that God is just as concerned about our desires as He is about our basic necessities. A commonly held and unfortunate misconception among many sincere Christians is that God is more apt to meet "real" needs than He is to grant desires. We tend to think of needs as those things that are important and desires as unimportant or even frivolous. Nothing could be further from the truth. Psalm 37:4 says, *"Delight thyself also in the Lord, and he shall give thee the desires of thine heart."* Then in Philippians 4:19 we read, *"But my God shall supply all your need according to his riches in glory by Christ Jesus."* Both of these verses are the inspired Word of God and they are thus equally and absolutely true. As I was checking out at the store one day, I was talking to the cashier and made a comment about the goodness of God. She replied, "Yes, He promised to meet our needs, but not our wants." I said, "You know, He really promised to do both if we walk in His will, and He sure does both for me." As I left the store I thought about how typical and tragic it is to live so far below where God wants His child to live. What a limited view of the character and Fatherhood of God, what a terrible assessment of His goodness. Listen to the words of Jesus in Matthew 7:11, *"If ye then, being evil, know how to give good gifts unto your children, how much more shall your Father which is in heaven give good things to them that ask Him?"* Dear friend, God will not only provide for every necessity you have in life, but He will also grant every desire **as long as it is within the scope of His will** . I have placed this last statement in bold type and underlined it because it is so important. I cannot simply decide I want something and "faith" my way into getting it. I can only trust God for what HE is going to do, for the desires HE places in my heart. But the things He <u>will</u> provide for us are part of a vast territory. Many times we miss out simply because we just do not believe Him, take Him at His word, and trust Him to bring it to pass.

I remember walking through my Dad's clothing store one day when I was seven years old and seeing some little blue shirts stacked up on a shelf at about my eye level. They had cowboys and horses on them, and a desire sprang up in my heart to have one. I never said a word, but my Dad saw me as I glanced longingly at those shirts. I did not need one; Dad was in the clothing business so I had lots of shirts already. But that did not matter to him, and even though I didn't say a word about it, when we left the store that day I left with a new blue shirt. My eye level glance was on the shirt, but my father's gaze from above was on me. He took great delight in giving me that shirt, in granting my desire, and so does our heavenly Father.

Let me share an incident that took place many years ago that I still remember vividly. It clearly illustrates God cares as much for our desires as He does our for our needs. Even though I was a full time staff member at a church in Memphis, I was not making much money, and therefore still had to trust God for many of the needs of my family. I am sure there are thousands of pastors and church workers around the world who can identify with that. Well, take heart my fellow coworkers; what the church cannot or does not provide for you, God will, if you will trust Him. I know from personal experience. In the fall of 1974 I found myself in an awkward position. It took every penny I made to pay for our rent and utilities, to pay for our car, and to buy food and other necessities. There was nothing left over for clothing, and therefore we had gone for a long time without buying anything. We finally reached the point where Sheila had only a couple of dresses, and I had one suit and one pair of shoes. I would not have thought so much about it except for the fact that I was required to wear a suit to the office every day, and I was required to sit on the platform in church in every service. So for over six months I wore the same suit, a mint green color (it was the 70's!), to the office and to church. I had become painfully aware it was wearing out and people were starting to notice. How could they not? Needless to say I had become burdened about the fact that I desperately needed clothes and so did Sheila. We could legitimately say we had a real need in our life that we could not meet.

But there was something else I was concerned about at that time also, life insurance. I don't know why that had become such a big issue in my heart, but it had. Now, my family could live just fine whether I had a life insurance policy or not, that is as long as I did not die. I was not planning to die of course, but the desire was still in my heart to know Sheila and the kids would be secure if I did. So my prayers were occupied with a big need and a big desire all at the same time. Then one day as I was driving back to the office I was praying and God spoke to me in my heart and said, "Shad, you have prayed about these things long enough. Just ask Me to do these things for you and believe I am going to do them." So right there in the car I prayed, "Lord I need clothes and an insurance policy and I ask You to give them to me now. Thank You. Amen."

When I walked into my office, my secretary told me that one of the church members, we will call him Mr. Smith, had called and had left word for me to call him. So I did, and he asked if I could come to his office that afternoon. I said I could and drove over there. We sat in his office making small talk for a few minutes and then he got to the point. He said, "Shad I don't want to embarrass you, but I have noticed that for the past several months you have been wearing the same suit in every service. Is that the only suit you have?" I said, "Yes sir, it is." Then he said, "Well, today God laid it on my heart to do two things for you if you will allow me to. I want to take you to my friend's clothing store, and buy you some clothes." I was stunned. Then He asked, "Do you have a life insurance policy?" I said no. He continued, "Well then, I want to buy you a $100,000 life insurance policy and I am going to pay the premiums for you." I did not know what to say. He then asked if Sheila and I could meet him the next day to take care of both items. So we went to his office the next day and signed the papers for the policy, and then drove downtown to *Julius Lewis'*, one of the finest men's clothing stores in the city.

When we walked in, Mr. Lewis himself assisted us. Mr. Smith told me to pick out a suit, so I chose a black one, good for all occasions. He said to pick out another one. I did. And another one. I did. Then he said, "You are going to need ties and shirts and shoes to match, so pick them out." I left that store with three beautiful suits and everything to match. Then on the way back to his office he turned around and handed Sheila three hundred dollars (a lot of money in 1974) and said, "Sheila, I don't know about women's clothes, so you will have to pick out what you need for yourself!" Oh glory to God, He always gives more than we ask or think! I flashed back to when I was seven years old and my dad gave me that little blue shirt. Now my Father had done it again. Oh the love and faithfulness and goodness of our Great God! Glory! Glory! Glory to His Name! When I walked into the office the next day I was wearing a new suit, and I had peace in my heart that if anything happened to me, my young family would be secure. God had not only met our needs, but He had granted our desire. And I must say, He did it in grand style, the way He does everything.

Different Types of Need

Now back to the issue of needs. In the life of every Christian there are two kinds of necessities, expected and unexpected, those you see coming and those you don't, those you are prepared for and those you are not. Expected needs, normal everyday necessities, are those things that are required to just live and get along on a daily basis. These things normally fall within the scope of daily routine faith. Included in this category are things like food, water, clothing, shelter, and money to sustain the daily operation of your home, business, ministry, church, and so on. Regardless of what your role or position is in life, it would not take long for you to make a list of your daily necessities. These are the kinds of things Jesus was referring to in Matthew 6 and that Paul referred to in Philippians 4:19. These Scriptures tell us *"...your heavenly Father knoweth that ye have need of all these things"* (good point) and that He *"...will supply all your need according to his riches in glory by Christ Jesus"* (good promise). Jesus therefore instructed us to not spend time worrying about these things, but to just assume that our heavenly Father cares more for us than He does for the birds and flowers and that He is going to meet all these daily needs. We are to *"...seek ye first the kingdom of God and his righteousness"* and then believe that *"...all these things shall be added unto you"* (good plan).

Of course there are many categories of necessity in our lives other than the physical, such as <u>emotional</u> (we all need love and affection), <u>social</u> (we all need regular interaction with other people), <u>spiritual</u> (we need time with God in His Word and fellowship with other Believers), and the list goes on. A popular term I hear a lot these days is "felt needs," which suggests something we feel we need, but may not actually be essential to survival. Well let me just say this, if you "feel" it, so does God. There are many days when I find myself asking God for things like encouragement, affirmation, and reassurance. If I don't get them, my life will not come to an end, but they are things I need nonetheless, and God will provide them. Whatever is important to me is important to Him.

Now without belaboring the point, we all know what daily necessities are and because we know about them ahead of time, we usually have at least some idea or plan in mind as to how we are going to deal with them out of our own human abilities. There is nothing wrong or unspiritual about this. In fact, God expects us to be creative, industrious, resourceful, and hard working. He expects us to use what He has given us as far as it can be used. The Word of God does not condone laziness and slothfulness. Paul wrote in Acts 20:34, *"Yea, ye yourselves know, that these hands have ministered unto my necessities, and to them that were with me."* What God does NOT want is for us to limit ourselves to living within the confines of what WE have and what WE can do and never venture out in faith. He does not want us to live independently of Him. There is nothing God honoring, conquering, overcoming, or victorious about that kind of life.

That brings us to unexpected needs, those things we do not see coming and therefore do not have a plan or provision for. There are two kinds of unexpected needs, those that are created by a change in circumstances and those that come as a result of obedience to a special leading or calling from God. Needs, or "empty spaces," that occur in life as a result of a change in circumstances, can be caused by any number of things, some as serious as natural disaster, sudden illness, political upheaval, or loss of employment, and some not so serious, such as suddenly finding out your daughter is planning to get married in three months and you don't know how you are going to pay for the wedding. Speaking from experience, I think some fathers would rather face a natural disaster.

Now what do you do when you are faced with needs that are impossible for you to meet? (And, by the way, we are all going to face them at some time or other.) No matter how capable, self-sufficient, wealthy, or in control you may be at the moment, sooner or later you are going to face a storm in life you cannot get through without God's help. So what do you do when the storm comes? First, you don't panic or become absorbed in self-pity and despair. Remember, sudden needs are not sudden to God. Maybe you did not see them coming, but He did. In fact He brought them so that He might draw you into His will and His supply. Where do you think the storm came from when Jesus was in the boat with the disciples? He brought it with Him. Through your need, crisis, or trial God is bringing about a faith event in your life that will ultimately produce joy in you and provide glory for Him.

> Faith is an attitude toward God in which you reckon God to be a faithful God Who will perform that which He has promised.
>
> *J. Dwight Pentecost (2)*

Second, you refuse to listen to satan's lies. He will tell you that you have this need, problem, or trial because you have done something wrong and you are being punished, or because God is trying to teach you some lesson. If that were the case, then Paul must have done more wrong and had more to learn than anyone else in the Bible. These lies are designed to cause you to look inward instead of upward. God does not create need in your life to teach you anything, but to give you opportunity to live out what you already know and to awaken you to His supply. God sends need into our lives so that we may be provided with opportunities to exercise real faith and receive the supernatural supply of God. He creates need in our lives so that He may enlarge us. *"Hear me when I call, O God of my righteousness: thou hast enlarged me when I was in distress..."* (Psalm 4:1). The correct response to need of any kind is to wait before God to know His will concerning the things you are facing, and then trust Him by faith to fulfill what He shows you. Ask Him to open the eyes of your heart to see into the invisible. The needs in your life you cannot meet are the things the Word of God is referring to in Hebrews 4:16 where it says, *"Let us therefore come boldly unto the throne of grace, that we may obtain mercy, and find grace to help in time of need."* The word *need* here comes from the Greek word *eukairos,* which means "special occasion of need." The answer to the question, "What do I do?", is to accept God's invitation and "come boldly unto the throne of grace," enter into the faith process, wait before God to know His will, and believe for the impossible.

Now let's look at another type of need that is created not by daily life or a change in circumstances, but by obeying a leading or calling from God. A Christian businessman could find himself with a need that he is unprepared to meet out of his own ability, not because of a decrease in business, but because God has spoken to his heart. God has told him to believe Him for expansion that is utterly contrary to common sense and totally impossible without a miracle from God. A pastor could find himself in a similar position, not because a tornado blew the church building away (as did happen to a friend of mine recently), but because God has given him a fresh vision for expansion and growth that is absolutely impossible given the current membership and income. And what about the evangelist to whom God speaks saying, "Decrease your ministry in America where you may possibly receive some income, and increase it overseas where you are guaranteed to receive none at all." Does that sound like an impossible situation to you? I assure you from personal experience, it is.

In 1975, God called Sheila and me into international evangelism, and in 1977 (at ages 29 and 31), we accepted His invitation to faith, responded to His call, and began the ministry we are in today. That act of obedience created a vast array of needs we did not see coming and that were absolutely impossible for us to meet on our own. In fact, they were more impossible than we ever imagined. The needs ranged all the way from food, clothing, and housing for our family to contacts overseas, open doors in various countries, and millions of dollars to carry out the ministry over the next thirty years. We have conducted over 158 international campaigns, and on every occasion we have had to trust God for such things as money, airline tickets, and equipment that we would have never needed had it not been for obeying God's calling upon our life. Obeying the leadership of God will always create needs that you cannot meet. It may be in relation to your business, your giving, your ministry, or something else, but whatever it is, it will lead you to a place where you must know the express will of God concerning your particular situation at this particular time in your personal history.

The Apostle Paul's life was a perfect example of one filled with constant need resulting from changing circumstances *and* calling from God. But because of his confidence in the plan, power, and provision of God, his attitude toward them was, *"But none of these things move me, neither count I my life dear unto myself..."* (Acts 20:24*)* and *"...in all of these things we are more then conquerors through him that loved us"* (Romans 8:37). The necessities created in Paul's life by circumstances and by obedience to God were unpredictable, but the faithfulness of God was not. He never viewed need as negative, but always as opportunity to glorify God.

Need Is Evidence of Supply

There is a wonderful truth that is so crucial to real faith, I am going to write it in bold capital letters and underline it - **NEED IS EVIDENCE OF SUPPLY**. In God's economy in our Christian life, there is no such thing as an empty space without God's provision to fill it. Once you embrace and internalize this fact you will have a whole new outlook toward the needs in your life, regardless of the cause, and you will be enabled to respond in faith to God's invitations to draw upon His invisible supply. Our normal reaction to sudden need is usually a feeling of fear and alarm. That's because the first thing we do is focus on the empty space in the visible, which makes us feel overwhelmed and vulnerable, rather than looking beyond it to the supply of God in the invisible, which brings comfort and security. The reason we so quickly respond to sudden need with fear and panic is because we so quickly believe the wrong thing – and we are so accustomed to doing it. That is the problem the disciples had in trying to feed the 5,000 in Matthew 14:15-21. They could not see beyond the five loaves and two fish in the visible to the inexhaustible supply of Jesus in the invisible. The reason so many of us have a faith problem is because we have a vision problem. We see in II Chronicles 20 that Jehoshaphat made the same mistake. He initially feared because he focused on the armies in the visible rather than the deliverance of God in the invisible. Earlier we talked about the fact that as born-again Believers we live in two worlds at the same time, the natural and the spiritual. Just because we cannot see the supply in the natural does not mean it does not exist. We must learn to look in the right place. We do this by spending time with God, receiving His will, and believing Him for what He shows us.

So then, should we treat the need, the lack, the emptiness that we see in the visible as unreal and just ignore it? No, of course not, that would be foolish and irresponsible. The disciples could not just pretend that those 5,000 men and their families were not there and didn't need to be fed. The need they were faced with in the physical realm was very real. But the over riding truth was that the supply of God in the spiritual realm was more real than what they were looking at in the physical. They just did not have eyes to see it. We don't need to close our eyes to the need in the visible; rather we need to open our eyes to God's supply in the invisible and believe Him to give it to us. We must discipline ourselves in our walk with God to look beyond the real to the "real" real.

Look beyond the Circle

This was brought home to me anew and fresh during the summer of 1999 while I was conducting a campaign in India. Without going into detail, let me just say that when I left for the project we were facing a huge financial obligation that was impossible for us to meet. It concerned the construction of our home in Tennessee. Night after night I lay awake in the hotel room praying and thinking and trying to figure out what to do. Day after day I went from one meeting to the next doing the same thing. I was not within a hundred miles of real faith, not even close. Then one morning as I waited to preach in a high school, God spoke to me in my heart and told me to take out my legal pad and draw a circle on the page. So I did. Then He told me to write within it everything I could think of regarding a possible solution to the problem. It did not take long to get to the end of my list. Then the Lord told me that the circumference of that circle represented the parameters of my life, the end of all I have and all I can do. I realized that within that circle there were no solutions, no supply, no answers, and no hope. Then God told me to write GOD on the page outside the circle and to look out THERE. I did it and when I did, all fear, panic and confusion suddenly disappeared. I saw the supply of God and I believed it. He led me to Isaiah 45:3, *"And I will give thee the treasures of darkness, and hidden riches of secret places, that thou mayest know that I, the Lord, which call thee by thy name, am the God of Israel."* The supply may be hidden to me and may be a secret to me, but not to God. He can see in the dark and He knows just where to look. When I looked inside the circle all I could see was limitation, emptiness, confusion and fear, but when I looked beyond the circle into the realm of God, I saw the fullness of His limitless power and provision. All of a sudden my heart was flooded

GOD TELLS US TO LOOK TO HIM
AND HIS UNLIMITED RESOURCES
"For we walk by faith, not by sight." II Corinthians 5:7

THE LIMITED CIRCUMFERENCE OF MY LIFE

ALL I HAVE
ALL I CAN DO
ALL I CAN THINK

FEAR =
LOOKING TO WHAT IS INSIDE THE CIRCLE
LIMITED RESOURCES

Reasonable
Visible

FAITH =
LOOKING TO WHAT IS OUTSIDE THE CIRCLE
LOOKING TO GOD

Circumstances — God's Will
Panic — Peace

REALM OF GOD
Unlimited Resources
Invisible
"While we look not at the things which are seen, but at the things which are not seen: for the things which are seen are temporal; but the things which are not seen are eternal." II Corinthians 4:18

SATAN TEMPTS US TO LOOK AT WHAT WE HAVE AND WHAT WE CAN DO AND TO GIVE THAT THE FINAL WORD

with peace and joy, because He had confirmed to my heart that He was meeting the need. I did not know exactly how, but it did not matter, because I had looked outside, seen the finished work, and received it as done. The unseen supply of God had become personal possession in my heart. For the rest of that trip I did not give it another thought, other than to praise God, and the need was met in full as soon as I arrived home.

In your time of need, in your trial, your crisis, your storm, do not allow satan to trap you in unbelief inside the circle. Lift up your eyes and look out to where God is. Ask Him to show you His will and His supply and receive it as yours. II Corinthians 4:18 reminds us, *"While we look not at the things which are seen, but at the things which are not seen: for the things which are seen are temporal; but the things which are not seen are eternal."* The Scripture goes on to say in II Corinthians 5:7, *"For we walk by faith, not by sight."* If we walk by what we see inside the circle we will live a defeated, limited life, but if we walk by what we see outside the circle, we will live in victory. All that is needed to transfer God's supply from His realm to ours is for someone to receive the will of God and believe. That someone is YOU. In order to become the victorious, conquering, overcoming Christians that God intends us to be, we must get it firmly planted in our hearts that for every need in our life God already has the supply, regardless of what kind of need it is or what caused it. He had it long before we came into the world. But how can we be so sure? Because it is always God's will to meet your needs, and God's will is always accompanied by His supply. The two go together and one cannot exist without the other. Your responsibility concerning a need that you absolutely cannot meet is to ask God to reveal His will to you concerning it and then believe Him for that. To step into the will of God is to step into the supply of God.

If it is food you need, He has the food. If it is money, He has the money. If it is a house, He has the house. If you have a need for education, He has the school for you to attend and a way to pay the tuition and buy the books. If it is a need for a husband or wife, He has that person for you already. God's order is always supply first, then need. No matter WHAT kind of need it is and no matter how large and impossible it is, God had the supply before you ever become aware of the need. When a need occurs in your life, your home, your business, or your ministry, God does not start looking around to try to figure out how He is going to meet it. He already knows. Think about this; which came first, redemption or man's need for redemption? Dear friend, God's plan for redemption of the human race was in place in Jesus Christ long before man was created. The fall did not catch God by surprise, and when Adam sinned, God did not panic and start searching around for a way to fix the problem. The plan was already in place and the need had already been provided in Jesus Christ. The only thing needed to make redemption complete was a place to apply it. The fall provided that place. Which came first, air or lungs to breath the air? Which came first, food or mouths to eat the food? Which came first, water or creatures to drink the water? Which came first, light or eyes to see the light? You get the idea. God has a heaven full of supply and all He needs are places to apply it. The needs in your life provide those places.

When Sheila and I began our ministry back there in 1977, where were all those hundreds of people we would work with some day? Where were all those millions of dollars we would need? Well, the people were out there in other countries being prepared by God to join hands with us in His appointed time. And those millions of dollars were in various bank accounts all over America, just waiting to be transferred into our account, also in God's appointed time which, by the way, is always perfect. We could not see the people or the money in the visible, but they were there. In fact, in the visible all we could see was emptiness, and if we had believed the apparent emptiness in the visible rather than the fullness of God's supply in the invisible, we would have never moved one foot, let alone the millions of miles He has taken us over the years.

Drawn to God's Will through Desire

Now let's say a word about desire, the first cousin to need. As I said before, they are not exactly in the same family, but they are very close. They are so close, in fact, that most of what we have said about meeting needs can also be applied to granting desires. Need and desire both represent a type of empty space in life, the difference being that if the empty space called desire is not filled, your life will not come to an end, so to speak. However, if a desire becomes intense enough it may _feel_ as urgent as a life-threatening unmet need. This is the type of desire that God uses to draw us into the knowledge of His will and ultimately into real faith. A question I often hear asked is, "How can I tell if a desire is just coming from me or if it is from the Holy Spirit? How can I tell whether or not the thing I desire is God's will or not?" In other words, how can I trust my desires? It is possible, of course, to have desires that originate purely from the flesh, but the surest safeguard against that is the Spirit-filled life. As we have said before, if a born-again Believer is walking in the Spirit, then his desires are God's desires, his decisions are God's decisions, his thoughts are God's thoughts.

Secondly, however, if you have a desire in your heart and you want to be sure it is from the Lord, then take it into the prayer closet and lay it before Him. If it is not from Him, then as you enter His presence and wait before Him, it will lose its intensity and fade and then disappear. If it does, then let it. But, if the desire is from God it will do three things. First it will clarify. A clear picture will form in your mind and heart enabling you to become very specific. Second it will intensify. It will become so strong in your heart that you cannot let go of it because it will not let go of you. You reach a point where you _must_ have it, it _must_ be granted, and you just cannot take no for an answer. It will take on the same intensity as an unmet need that is threatening your well-being. God will bring you to this point because it is there that you believe. Third it will be verified. As you walk through the faith process God will allow little indicators to appear in the external to encourage you to continue to the end. They will likely be so small that no one can see them but you. But again, if the desire fades in the light of God or in length of time, then let it. If it is from God it will endure, and in response to real faith He will move heaven and earth to fulfill it.

The Yellow House on the Corner

If I may, I would like to share another story with you as to how God grants desires. In 1977, when we resigned our church position to enter the ministry we are in today, we had to move out of the church owned home we were living in. So we moved to a townhouse where we lived for the next four years. For the first three we were very happy and content, but as the kids got older, we found ourselves desiring to live in a house. Now there was really no way we could legitimately say we needed a house. The townhouse was nice and very adequate. The kids had lots of friends in the complex, access to a pool, and it was located in a good section of the city. But all that did not change the fact that a desire for a house was settling in upon us whether we wanted it to or not. Then somehow in the spring of 1981, we became aware of four very nice, colonial style, two-story houses located on the same street that were all rental properties. I located the property manager and inquired about the houses. He told me they were all rented, but he would take my name and number. For months after that, we drove down that street and prayed about those houses and the desire to live in one became almost unbearable. Then for thirty days in a row I drove down the street slowly, looking at each house and praying. On the thirtieth day I drove past the one on the corner and as I looked at it the Holy Spirit said, "That's the one!" It was a beautiful yellow house on a big corner lot. All of a sudden, I knew in my heart it was ours. I got so excited I could hardly stand it. I went home and told Sheila that God was giving us that house. Then about three hours later the phone rang and it was the property manager. He said, "Mr. Williams, I have one of those houses available if you want it, but you have to tell me right now." I asked which one it was, and he said the yellow one on the corner." I shouted, "I'll take it!" Then he told me I would have to bring him a $350 deposit the next morning and I agreed. The problem, however, was that I did not have $350 and had no way to get it. But, that did not change the fact that we knew, without doubt, the house was ours.

The next morning about 8:30 my friend, Bill Maxwell, called me and asked how things were going. I told him about the house, and he asked if I had everything I needed to rent it. At that point I told him about the need of $350. He then asked, "Have you opened your patio door this morning?" I had not. He then said, "Go look out there." I laid the phone down and went and opened the door, and when I did I saw an envelope. On my way back to the phone I opened it and it was a check from Bill for $350! I asked him, "How did you know?" He replied, "Brother, I did not know, but apparently God did. While I was spending time with the Lord early this morning, He told me to bring that check to you. So I dropped it off on my way to work. I did not know if you needed it, but I did know that God said bring it." Of course we had a time of praise on the phone, and then I went straight to the manager's office and paid the deposit. The house was ours! The desire was fulfilled. Once again God had proven His faithfulness. I share this story with you because I want you to see that God not only goes to great lengths to meet needs, but also to grant desires. We did not <u>need</u> that house from a survival standpoint. We were surviving just fine. But God wanted us to have it, and He therefore placed the <u>desire</u> for it in our hearts. Oh, what a mighty God we serve! Oh, what a MIGHTY GOD we serve!

Ten "Ws" in the Will of God

Let me say it again, it is always God's will to meet your needs, whether they are the necessities of everyday life or the kind of needs that result from changing circumstances or obedience to God in some way. It is also God's will to grant the desires He causes to arise in your heart. Remember, your needs and your desires are not accidental; they are often caused by God for the purpose of drawing you into His will and into His supply. By means of the needs and desires in your life, God brings glory to Himself. Now you may ask, "Well if I know it is God's will to meet my needs, then why do I even need to pray? Why do I need to seek His will? Why do I have to do anything at all?" <u>Because there is more to it than that.</u> God operates in response to your faith. There are ten "Ws" involved every time God performs the impossible in meeting your needs and granting your desires, and the first one is **worship.** It always begins with worship. Jesus said in Matthew 6:6, *"But thou, when thou prayest, enter into thy closet, and when thou hast shut thy door, pray to thy Father which is in secret; and thy*

Father which seeth in secret shall reward thee openly." As I told you, the word *closet* refers to a room on the ground floor of an oriental house that was used as a private place of retirement as well as a dispensary of supplies. What a fitting word for the Holy Spirit to use in this context. We first take our need or desire to God in private and wait for Him to reveal His will concerning it. As we have said before, there is no shortcut and no substitute for getting into the presence of God. Philippians 4:19 is a wonderful promise from Scripture, but it was not written to a carnally-minded group of people. It was written to a Spiritually-minded group of folks who were enthusiastic givers. John 15:7 begins with a very large word, "if." Let's look at it, *"IF ye abide in me, and my words abide in you, ye shall ask what ye will, and it shall be done unto you."* Again this is a wonderful promise, but it is a conditional one. In coming to God concerning our needs and desires, we are not trying to find out if it is His will to meet them. No, what we need to know is the specifics concerning His will in regard to them, and the only way we can know is if we are walking in fellowship with God. So, as always in matters of faith, you must take care of first things first.

Now that brings us to the next word, **waiting**. How long will it take for God to begin to disclose the specifics of His will to you? I don't know, but it takes what it takes. There will certainly be a period of waiting before Him, but you can be sure it is not wasted time, because during this time God will begin to reveal to you the specifics of His will concerning your need or desire. One of the questions we always have is "Why is God doing this in my life?" Well, as you wait before Him He will likely give you a glimpse of the **why** behind it, and His purposes are usually much larger than just simply meeting needs and granting desires.

In meeting your needs God will always have His Own **way** of doing it, and it will not be the same as it was any time before. He will always be fresh and original. There is no point in looking at how God met your need the last time, because He is not going to do it that way now. He may reveal to you how He is going to do it, and He may not. In addition to His own way, He will usually have a certain **who** involved, some human agent that He will use as a channel through which to flow His supply. Sometimes, He even lets me know ahead of time who the person is going to be so that I can intercede for them in prayer. When God meets a need there is always a trinity; a person with a need, God with the supply, and a human agent through whom He will send it.

That brings us to **what.** God's provision is always specific and it is always exact. As we come to God in prayer concerning our needs and desires, we begin with a picture in our mind as to what we think we need, but as we wait before God, He may very well alter the picture and then show us something different. That something then becomes the specific thing that God is going to do. That specific thing then becomes the object for which we are to believe and to receive as done.

God also has His Own **when**, His Own perfect timing. Half of the equation is the will of God and the other half is the timing of God. As we will examine further in our discussion of the faith process, there will be many occasions when there will appear to be a delay according to our timetable. We must remember, however, that God has His Own time and He is never in a hurry. It may seem sometime that we have gone past the deadline, but if we have the assurance of the will of God, the deadlines will not matter. Along with the will of God comes the peace of God and the supernatural persistence to hang on until the last minute and beyond.

And while we are waiting, it is important to stay in the **Word** of God. Through His Word we will receive encouragement to hold on in faith until the need is met. Many times God will even enlighten a specific verse of Scripture to your heart, placing it into the context of your situation. This does not happen every time, but it happens sometimes. And even when it doesn't, there are still plenty of promises and examples of faith in the Bible to help you and give you strength to continue believing God. The Word of God is the most powerful weapon against attacks from satan, which will surely come. There will always be a spiritual **warfare** connected to God meeting our needs. Satan will never allow faith to go unopposed. But as we stand in faith God will supply, and His faithfulness will be proven again. It will end with what I call the **"wow** of faith." When God does the impossible, it always ends with praise and thanksgiving to Him and with a testimony to the world and the church of the awesomeness of the goodness, the power, and the faithfulness of God.

Real Faith – A Two-Sided Page

Another crucial point we need to make is that real faith is a two-sided page. It involves your doing all you can on your side of it. I am making this point in this chapter because I believe it is important for us to understand that we are not divorced from personal responsibility in having our needs met and our desires fulfilled. We always have an active part in it. Oswald

Chambers expressed it this way, "We are in danger of forgetting that we cannot do what God does and that He will not do what we can do. Take the initiative, stop hesitating, and take the first step" (3). As I have said before, real faith is not for slothful or lazy Christians. Real faith is not sitting down, doing nothing, and expecting God to provide. Real faith is always pro-active and aggressive. The Bible tells us in James 2:17-18, *"Even so faith, if it hath not works, is dead, being alone. Yea a man may say, Thou hast faith, and I have works; shew me thy faith without thy works, and I will shew thee my faith by my works."* James continues in verse 26, *"For as the body without the spirit is dead, so faith without works is dead also."* What James is saying here is that if faith is real, then corresponding works will follow.

Real faith is not mystical and ethereal or other-worldly; it is very practical, and that's where it begins, in the visible and the practical. What I am saying is that real God faith begins at the end of what you have and what you can do. So the first thing you need to do is to find out where that is and get there as fast as you can. As I have shared with you before, there have been many times when Sheila and I were going on an overseas campaign and have come right down to the last minute without the money to go. So what did we do? We acted as if we did have it. We did everything we could do on our side of the page that did not require money. We washed and ironed our "Africa clothes" and then packed the suitcases. We packed up whatever equipment we were taking plus food and other things needed for the trip. We did everything possible to get ourselves into a position where we could say, "There is nothing left for us to do, it is now all up to God." The sooner you get to that point the better, because it is there that God works. Maybe you need a car, and it is impossible for you to buy one. Well, it may not be possible for you to buy a car, but you can go look at cars. You can do enough research to at least get specific in your request. You can spend time before God and determine exactly what His will is. You may not have the money to pay for college, but you can visit campuses, apply for financial aid, and maybe investigate the possibility of some type of employment. God may use some of your efforts and He may not, but one thing is for sure, when you get to the end of you, He will do the rest. The key is to move from the possible to the impossible as quickly as you can. Again, it is <u>there</u> that God moves into action.

Pack the Boxes

One Tuesday afternoon a few years ago, I was preparing to go to Kenya to preach and I needed $32,000. I sat at my desk and prayed, "Lord, I have done all I can do." Just then the Holy Spirit said, "Oh really? Have you packed up those booklets you are taking?" I said, "No Lord." Then He said, "Why don't you go do that." So I got up, went to the garage and began packing them. About half way through the second box, the devil whispered in my ear, "You are a fool. You are out here in 95 degree heat packing booklets for a trip you are not even going on!" I kept packing and just as I finished the last one, the phone rang. It was a friend from another city. He said, "Shad, I have been meaning to call you since last Friday, because that morning I found some money in an account I did not know I had. As soon as I discovered it God told me to send it to you. I do not know why I have not called. I've been meaning to, but anyway I'm sending it right now." I said, "Brother, do you mind me asking how much it is?" He said, "No, not at all. It's $32,000." I knew exactly why he had not called. God was waiting for me to get in a position where He was no longer waiting on me and I was waiting on Him.

I know that as you read these stories, you might wonder how in the world this could have happened or how it could happen for you. Well, God is not a respecter of persons, and there is <u>certainly</u> nothing special about me or my family or ministry. You can be sure you that just as God has met our needs over all these years, God is going to meet your needs, and He is going to grant the desires that are His will for your life. But He is not going to do it independently of you. He is not going to do it without you doing everything on your side of the page.

My Own Stupid Fault

Now you may have noticed that throughout this entire chapter there is one type of need I have not mentioned. In fact you may be wondering, "But what about the needs or problems that occur as a result of my own stupid mistakes?" Well, first of all let me say that if you are walking daily in the light of God's Word and by the guidance of His Spirit, it is not likely you will make a mistake. And if you do, it certainly will not be a conscious one. But let's just say that you do make a mistake; that you do choose to disobey God in some area, and as a result, needs and problems and trials occur in your life. What do you do about those situations? Will God still meet those needs? Will He still help you through those problems, even though they are your own fault? Yes, He will. God will even meet the needs in your life that are your "own stupid fault" – IF. If you will come to Him in true repentance and confess your sin of disobedience and receive His cleansing and forgiveness by the blood of Jesus, He will forgive you, and cleanse you, and set you back on the heavenly highway. He may take you back to the place where you veered off course so you can make things right, but if He does, then so be it. The important thing is your restoration of your fellowship with God. There is not a need in your life that your Heavenly Father will not meet if you will just draw close to Him and trust Him – even the ones that are obviously caused by you. Now, He may or may not remove all the consequences of that mistake, but either way, He will take you through to the other side if you will trust Him with it.

Now let me ask you, do you have needs in your life (regardless of the cause) you cannot meet? Are you in a crisis or trial of some kind? Are you facing problems that are utterly impossible for you to solve? Are you in one of those storms of life? Are there empty spaces in your life that you cannot fill no matter how hard you try? Good. That means God is inviting you to believe and receive His supernatural abundant supply. That means that there is an opportunity in your life to see the faithfulness and glory of God. Are there desires in your life that just won't go away, longings that are pressing upon your heart? If so, then rejoice and praise God! Write them all down, take them into your prayer closet, put them before the Lord, wait to know His will, and then believe for what He shows you. The needs and desires that exist in your life at this very moment are there for the purpose of drawing you into the will of God and the supply of God. So rejoice, and again I say, rejoice!

Summary of Truth

❖ A need is a necessity, a requirement for sustaining life. A desire is a want, but not an actual necessity for life. A need is something I must have, a desire is something I would like to have.

❖ It is always God's will to meet needs and to grant desires that are from Him. He is just as concerned about one as He is the other.

❖ There are two kinds of need, expected and unexpected, those we are prepared for and those we are not prepared for.

❖ God knows about our needs before we ask and He has promised to meet them.

❖ Whatever is important to you is important to God.

❖ It is not unspiritual or faithless to do all we can with what we have to meet our own needs.

❖ It IS faithless to stop at the limits of our own best efforts and refuse to turn to God.

❖ There are two kinds of unexpected needs, those that occur from changing circumstances and those that occur from obedience to the leading of God.

❖ Every Christian will have needs he cannot meet at one time or another.

❖ Sudden needs are not sudden to God. He deliberately brings them into your life for the purpose of drawing you to His will and to faith.

❖ Need is always evidence of supply.

❖ We must learn to look beyond the emptiness in the visible to the supply of God in the invisible.

❖ God causes desires to arise in your heart so you will be drawn to His will and trust Him by faith to fulfill them.

❖ If a desire is of God it will be clarified, intensified and verified. If it fades in the light of God's presence or with length of time, then let it because it is not from God.

❖ The will of God concerning need and desire will always include 10 "Ws": worship, waiting, why, way, who, what, when, Word, warfare and wow.

❖ Real faith is a two-sided page. God will not do what is on my side, and I cannot do what is on His side.

❖ Real faith is not mystical, ethereal, or other-worldly; it is practical.

- ❖ Real faith does not mean that you sit down and do nothing and wait for God. Rather real faith is aggressive, pro-active, and hard working.
- ❖ Real faith will never exist in the life of a Christian who is lazy, slothful or carnally minded.
- ❖ If there are unmet needs and pressing, persistent desires in your life right now, that means that God is inviting you to know His will and believe by faith for the impossible.
- ❖ God will even meet needs that are "your own fault" if you will come to Him in confession of sin and true repentance.

NOW LET'S TAKE A MOMENT AND PRAY TOGETHER:

DEAR FATHER, I THANK YOU FOR THE NEEDS THAT ARE IN MY LIFE RIGHT NOW AND I THANK YOU THEY ARE BEYOND MY ABILITY TO MEET. LORD, I SEE NOW THAT THESE THINGS REPRESENT INVITATIONS FROM YOU TO COME TO THE KNOWLEDGE OF YOUR WILL. THEY ARE OPPORTUNITIES TO BELIEVE YOU BY FAITH FOR THE IMPOSSIBLE. FATHER I SUBMIT MYSELF, MY LIFE, MY NEEDS, AND MY DESIRES TO YOU RIGHT NOW. I CHOOSE TO CEASE STRUGGLING USELESSLY, AND I CHOOSE TO COME TO YOU AND RECEIVE YOUR WILL. LORD, PLEASE SHOW ME YOUR WILL CONCERNING EACH OF THESE THINGS IN MY LIFE, AND LORD, HELP ME TO TRUST YOU BY FAITH FOR WHAT YOU SHOW ME. LORD, I WANT TO KNOW YOUR WILL, AND I WANT TO TRUST YOU FOR THE IMPOSSIBLE. THANK YOU FOR LOVING ME ENOUGH AND CARING FOR ME ENOUGH TO BRING THESE THINGS INTO MY LIFE. THANK YOU FOR GIVING ME OPPORTUNITIES TO ENTER INTO YOUR FINISHED WORK AND TO RECEIVE THE SUPPLY YOU HAVE IN STORE FOR ME. THANK YOU FOR SAVING ME AND MAKING ME YOUR CHILD. I LOVE YOU, LORD JESUS. IN YOUR NAME I PRAY. AMEN.

Chapter 21

Drawn to the Will of God

Part Two:

By God's Word, Holy Spirit Prompting, or Calling to Service

*"It is faith in God that opens the heart for God
and prepares us to submit to and receive His divine working."*
Andrew Murray (1)

n the previous chapter we discussed need and desire, two means
by which God causes us to seek His will concerning a particular
issue and then act in accordance with it by faith, thus creating what
we will refer to later on as a "faith event". Now we will look at three other
means God uses to do the same thing, all of which could actually be grouped
into one category, a <u>leading</u> from the Holy Spirit. The Bible tells us in
Romans 8:14, *"For as many as are led by the Spirit of God, they are the
sons of God."* That is a very straightforward verse, and it says if you are a
child of God then you are to be led by the Holy Spirit of God Who now
indwells you as a result of the new birth. But how does He lead us? How
does He guide us into a specific direction, into the will of God? The Holy
Spirit speaks to us through our spirit, and He uses three different ways to
get our attention.

The first way is through the Word of God. God will sometimes use His
Word to open our eyes to a new direction He wants us to go in, and then
sometimes He will use His Word to reinforce His will which has already
been revealed to us by some other means. The second way is a prompting
from the Holy Spirit in which He uses something from the external. It may
be a certain thought that comes to our mind or something in outward circumstances. Regardless of what it is, it is something that the Holy Spirit
uses to draw us to the will of God. A third way God uses to cause us to seek

His will is by a calling upon our life for some particular service to Him and His Kingdom. This is often expressed as "having a burden" placed upon our heart for some specific area of service or for some area of the world.

Drawn to God's Will by His Word

Have you ever been reading the Bible while going through some situation in life or while struggling with some decision and all of a sudden a verse of Scripture seems to just jump off the page and into your heart? It happens in such a way that you know for sure God has just spoken to you concerning your particular need, issue, or circumstance. If you have been a spiritually minded, Bible reading Believer for very long, you have probably had that experience. That is one of the ways the Holy Spirit speaks to us in order to either initially reveal God's will or sometimes to clarify and confirm His will. The message you receive from the Holy Spirit by means of His energizing a verse to your heart may not be "in context" with the passage, but it will be "in context" with what is going on in your life. God deals with our lives individually. Let me say this again, however; **any leading you think you receive from the Holy Spirit, regardless of what means He uses, will never stand in contradiction to Scripture**. Every word of the Bible is inspired (God-breathed) by the Holy Spirit (II Timothy 3:16), and He will not contradict Himself. If what you think you hear God telling you does not conform to the whole of the Bible, then it is not from Him.

Another important point to remember is that when the Holy Spirit applies a verse of Scripture to some issue in your life, it is at His choosing and His initiation, not yours. You do not "find a word" from God, it finds you. In other words, you cannot force the Word of God to say something about your situation just because you want it to. The Bible is not a crystal ball and should not be treated as one. Satan attempts to pervert everything that is holy and right in the Christian life and God speaking to us legitimately through Scripture is no exception. Now, allow me to share with you some examples of the real thing.

God's Promise to Meet Our Needs

When I was saved in July 1968, I was making a living, or trying to, as the lead singer and guitar player in a rock-and-roll band. But immediately upon receiving Jesus, I knew I had to quit and I wanted to. I just did not have the heart for it anymore, and after three weeks I walked away from it, never to look back again. I also knew that God had called me to the ministry, even though I did not yet know quite what that meant. The problem now, however, was I did not know how we were going to live. I had not been to college and I had no idea how I could make a living without playing music. I also did not know that preachers got paid for preaching. That came as a real surprise!

I struggled with the issue for days, and then finally one night I did something that I would not recommend for a mature Believer or, for that matter, an immature one either. But putting that aside, I did the only thing I could think of to do at the time in order to get some guidance from God. Remember, I was a one month-old Christian who had never read the Bible or been to church much before I was saved. I laid my Bible in front of me and prayed, "Lord, this is Your Word and I know that every answer I will ever need is in this book, so Lord, please tell me what to do about this." I had no idea where anything was in the Bible so I just opened it. When I did my eyes fell upon Habakkuk 3:17-19, *"Although the fig tree shall not blossom, neither shall fruit be in the vine; the labour of the olive shall fail, and the fields shall yield no meat; the flock shall be cut off from the fold, and there shall be no herd in the stalls: Yet I will rejoice in the Lord, I will joy in the God of my salvation. The Lord God is my strength, and he will make my feet like hinds' feet, and he will make me to walk upon mine high places.* ***To the chief singer on my stringed instruments.*** *"* Now as I said, I know that may have been an immature thing to do, but immature or not, when I read that last phrase, I knew in no uncertain terms that God was talking to me (a lead singer who played a stringed instrument) and I could take what He said to the bank - literally. He was telling me that when all hope is gone, He will still meet our needs.

When I read those verses an indescribable peace and comfort flooded my heart. I became persuaded of God's provision and began, right then and there, believing Him for it. I was enabled through His Word, even as a young Believer, to exercise real faith. And now after having 40 years to become all grown up, educated, and "mature" in the Lord, I am still standing on those verses. There have been many days over the years when faced with extreme trials, especially those of a financial nature, that God has led me right back to Habakkuk 3:17-19 and once again given me the very same comfort and assurance that He gave me from those verses long ago. Praise God, His promises are timeless.

Do the Work of an Evangelist

That incident happened toward the end of July 1968 and a few weeks later in August God confirmed to me just exactly what ministry He had called me to. Through II Timothy 4:5 He told me *"...watch thou in all things, endure afflictions, **do the work of an evangelist**, make full proof of thy ministry."* Again, I was not looking for that verse when it came to me. I did not even know it was in the Bible, but God did, and He led me to it one night in the midst of a prayer time that Sheila and I were having with the young man who discipled us in the first few weeks of our Christian life. I knew God had called me into the ministry, but my question was WHAT ministry. After the Holy Spirit gave me that verse that night long ago there was no doubt, and there has never been since.

Where to Go to School

Not long after that, God began placing in my heart the need and the desire to go to school to learn the Bible. Obviously, I needed a <u>lot</u> of help in that area! Interestingly, opportunities began opening up in several different states for me to attend well-known denominational universities on a full scholarship with all expenses paid, even living expenses for my family. I don't know why they were so interested in having me come, but they were. I even had one university president from Oklahoma call me at home one day and invite me personally to come. But there was a very small, non-accredited Bible college in Memphis that had come to my attention, and the Lord seemed to be drawing me to it. The problem was that they were offering me nothing, and I had no visible way to pay the tuition or provide for my family while going to school. It made absolutely no sense for me to turn down the offer of a full ride from a big accredited university to attend a small Bible College that could not even give me an accredited degree, let alone financial aid. It became a very severe struggle until one night, while I was kneeling alone in prayer with my Bible open in front of me, God led me to Jeremiah 46:16. He lifted a phrase out of that verse and drove it right into my heart, ***"...Arise, and let us go again to our own people, and to the land of our nativity..."*** My people were in Memphis, which was also the place of my birth. God took one part of that verse, placed it in the context of my situation, and I knew the issue was settled. I went right away and enrolled. The day I arrived I discovered that I needed only $69.00 to enroll, which was the exact amount in our bank account. From that day forward I never paid another penny in tuition. Every time I went to pay, the lady who was the business manager would tell me that some one had already paid for me. I do not know to this day who it was, but I know that God led me, by His Spirit through His Word, to attend the Bible college that would lay the Biblical and theological foundation needed in my life for the work He would ultimately lead me to do. I could easily have made a wrong turn at that juncture in my life, especially as a young Christian, but God's precious Word, applied by the Holy Spirit to a specific situation in my life, prevented it. My decision did not make sense according to the world, but it made perfect sense according to the leadership of the Holy Spirit through the Word of God. Quite often common sense becomes non-sense when held up against the spiritual sense of the Holy Spirit in our inner man.

Go into All the World

Sometimes God uses His Word to draw us into faith events that last for a short while, such as attending Bible College or maybe going on a mission trip, but there are those other times that last a lifetime. One such instance took place in my life in June 1976. I was still on staff at East Park Baptist Church in Memphis, but God had been dealing with me for a year about resigning and going into international evangelism. He had very definitely spoken to my heart during a mission trip to Africa in June 1975. I knew it was God's will, but I was still struggling with it. I suppose that as you read these personal accounts, you might get the idea that the author of this book struggles a lot over many things. Yes, friend, he does. But the good news here is that the God-given capacity of faith works even for us ordinary Christians who struggle. Praise God the operation and opportunity for real faith is not reserved only for "spiritual giants" and heroes. That would certainly leave me out.

Well, one morning in June 1976 this particular struggle came to an end. I was attending a conference in Ridgecrest, North Carolina and one morning, very early, I went into a prayer garden to spend time with God. I sat for a while discussing the issue of international evangelism with the Lord, and as I did, I fanned the pages of my little New Testament. All of a sudden it seemed to just stop and when it did I looked down at the page and my eyes fell on Romans 9:17. In its context the verse was written to Pharaoh, but again, the Holy Spirit placed it in the context of my situation. It said, *"...Even for this same purpose have I raised thee up, that I might shew My power in thee, **and that my name might be declared throughout all the earth.**"* When I saw that verse I knew the issue was settled forever.

When I looked up I saw an elderly couple sitting under a pavilion just up the hill. God said, "Go tell them what I just told you." I felt very awkward, but I knew I had to do it. So I walked up the hill to the pavilion. They were praying, so I just sat down across from them and waited for them to finish, and when they did, they looked up and straight at me. I said, "Excuse me folks, but God told me to come tell you that I am going into all the world to preach the Gospel. He just gave me this verse." I read it to them and they began to weep. At that moment, the pavilion was engulfed in the presence of God in a way that words cannot explain, and I too could not hold back the tears. My heart was flooded with love, joy, peace and confirmation of the will of God. After some moments passed and we were once again able to speak, we prayed together and then parted ways. The encounter was over, but a new life had begun, and what God had spoken by His Spirit through His Word would never be unspoken. God had sealed His will and His direction for my life and ministry, and I entered a faith event that continues to this day.

Held on Course

Another instance that stands out in my memory is the time God spoke to me about our ministry in July 1983. We had just returned from Amsterdam after attending the Billy Graham Conference for Itinerant Evangelists. While there I was offered positions with no less than six internationally known organizations, and I began to wonder if God was telling me to take a turn in life. But one day soon after our return, God spoke to me clearly through His Word in Proverbs 4:25-27, *"Let thine eyes look right on, and let thine eyelids look straight before thee. Ponder the path of thy feet, and let all thy ways be established. Turn not to the right hand nor to the left: remove thy foot from evil."* When I sat down at my desk to pray that day, I was not looking for those verses. But they were looking for me, and they found me. When I read them, I knew what God was saying. He was telling me to continue on as I was going and to never be diverted. He promised me that if I would, He would bless me and take care of me, and He has. Since that day I have never been tempted in the slightest to veer off course, because I am held by the anchor of God's Word embedded in my heart.

Money for Airline Tickets

There have been many times over the years when God would use a certain verse of Scripture to help us when we were trusting Him to get us to some country to preach. I remember one time we were going to the Philippines, and as we were coming down to the last minute we still had no airline tickets and no money. Time was running out, and I did not know what we were going to do. I prayed much, but just could not seem to break through to a place of faith. Then one day God provided what I needed – a word from Him. I was at home alone during the afternoon, so taking advantage of the quietness, I went to the Lord in prayer again. This time, however, God seemed to be saying to me, "Open your Bible to Psalms." So I did. I intended to read Psalm 37, one of my favorites, but as I turned to it my eyes fell on chapter 36, verse 5, which reads, *"Thy mercy, O Lord, is in the heavens; and thy faithfulness reacheth unto the clouds."* Now I know as you read this, it may sound a little silly or at least a little childish, but childish or not, God spoke to my heart through that verse. He told me, "Shad, airplanes fly in the heavens and in the clouds, and the one going to the Philippines will have you on it." All of a sudden my faith was energized and I had the strength to believe. At that very moment, in my heart, it was a done deal, and I could see myself on that plane. I did not yet have the money and the ticket in my hand, but I had it in my heart. I had seen through to the other side, and the next day I had it in my hand. In this instance I did not need the Word to tell me the will of God; I already knew it. What I needed and what I received was reinforcement to believe.

I could go on and on with instance after instance down through the years of how God has used His Word to either reveal His will or confirm it to our hearts, but that would take another book. So let me just leave it with this, regardless of what occasion of faith you are going through in life, keep the Word close at hand. You cannot force the Bible to say something about a situation in your life just because you want it to. But you should at least be open to the possibility, because at God's choosing, it just might. Remember God reveals His will through His Word only to those who are actively continuously engaged in real worship, to those who are seeking HIM. Andrew Murray wrote, "It's only in direct and living contact with God Himself that the Word will open the heart to believe" (2). If God chooses to reveal His will regarding some issue in your life, or confirm His will to you through His Word, it will be at His choosing, not yours. But if the Holy Spirit does quicken a verse of Scripture to your heart, by all means do not ignore it. When that happens, God is reaching from the spiritual realm into the natural, and He is using His Word to do it.

Drawn to the Will of God by a Prompting of the Holy Spirit

Now I want to look at another way God causes us to turn the ears of our spirit toward Him. That is, a <u>prompting</u> from the Holy Spirit by means of our own thoughts or from something in our environment or circumstances. I am going to use just one example because I think it is sufficient. I resigned East Park Church in September 1977, and in December of that year we conducted our first campaign in Hong Kong. On our way home on Christmas Day, I was sitting there in the plane seat looking at a flight magazine. I turned to the world map in the back, and as my eyes scanned from side to side, I looked at North and South America, which were right in the middle. After a few minutes of looking at that map, I was drawn to Brazil. As I  looked at that country that I knew absolutely nothing about and had never given any thought to, the Holy Spirit spoke to me and said very clearly in no uncertain terms, "Your next trip will be to Brazil." That was it – no explanation and no details, just one simple statement. But there was no doubt that it was settled. Then, not ten seconds later, my long time friend Dr. Mel Senter, who was seated in front of me, turned around and asked, "Shad, where are you going next?" Without hesitation I replied, "I am going to Brazil." After Sheila and I returned home, I hung a world map on the wall and began to pray about Brazil every day. I knew no one in that country and I knew nothing about that country, but I knew we were going there.

Then on January 8, 1978, two weeks after our return home, I received a phone call from the man who had been instrumental in arranging the Hong Kong trip. He was Evangelism Consultant with the Southern Baptist International Mission Board . He was in Memphis and wanted to know if we could come over to his hotel and share with him about the trip. I agreed, but I did not know if we could actually get there because there was very little gas in our car, and we were so broke we could not buy gas or groceries. But we went anyway. We met with him in his hotel room and after talking for some time, "Dr. Joe" all of a sudden sat straight up and blurted out, "Shad, I know where you and Sheila need to go next!" I asked, "Where, Dr. Joe?" He said one word – "Brazil." Then He added, "We are doing a project there in March and we need for you and Sheila to go and sing and preach!" Then he explained that it would begin on March 8, exactly 60 days away, that we would have to pay our own way, and it would cost us $3,000. I replied, "Dr. Joe, we'll go. Put us down." I had no hesitation in giving my answer because the Holy Spirit had already confirmed God's will in my heart by speaking to me through the map in that flight magazine. All we needed were the details, and now we had them. We prayed with Dr. Joe and left, and as we walked across the parking lot I said to Sheila, "We are either right in the middle of God's will, or I have lost my mind. We have no gas, no food, no money, and no way to get any. And on top of all that, I have just committed us to go on a project that is going to cost us $3,000, and we have to have it in less than 60 days." But, we knew those words were just words, because God had spoken clearly two weeks before we ever saw Joe, and there was no doubt we were in the will of God. The end of the story, which will also wait for another book, is that God provided all our needs plus the money to go to Brazil. That project opened doors for us, and for others that followed us, to do ministry for many years all over that country - ministry that resulted in tens of thousands of people coming to Jesus. It all started with a prompting from the Holy Spirit using a map in a flight magazine. That prompting led us to the will of God and launched us headlong into a great faith event that brought untold joy to us, great expansion for the Kingdom of God, opportunity for others to go and minister in Brazil, and great glory to God.

I encourage you to live your life every day in the awareness that God can break through at any moment and speak to you by His Spirit through any means He chooses. In the case I cited above He used a map in a magazine. But it could be anything. If you are going along through your day, walking in harmony with God, and a thought "just comes to you" that you perceive as God speaking to you, don't ignore it. Pay attention, do what He is prompting you to do, and do it quickly. In another chapter I referred to your inner man, your spirit, as being like a cell phone – always on and ready to receive a call. Well, think of God speaking to you through His Word, or through a prompting in your thoughts or circumstances, as Him calling you on your spiritual cell phone. You cannot make your phone ring by just wishing it would, but when it does ring you can answer it. God's part is to make the call, yours is to answer and obey.

Drawn to the Will of God through Calling

Now we are going to look at how the Holy Spirit draws us into His will and into faith by placing a calling upon our life. The example I am using (again a personal one) is my and Sheila's calling to international evangelism in June 1975, which I referred to earlier. We had been on staff at East Park Church in Memphis for two years, and in that time had developed a very aggressive ministry of evangelism to the streets and public places of the city. That ministry had somehow gotten the attention of the International Mission Board, and that resulted in our church's being invited to conduct an evangelistic campaign in Kenya and Tanzania, East Africa. We would be working in conjunction with Baptist missionaries. Our pastor, Dr. Wayne Allen, accepted the invitation and began building the team. The short version of the story is that Sheila and I became part of the team and that trip was the first one we made out of the country. We had no idea that it would prove to be such a turning point in our life.

We landed in Dar es Salaam on the coast of Tanzania, and then drove five hundred miles inland to the remote mountain town of Mbeya, where  the Baptist hospital was located. We were to conduct a small crusade type event on the hospital compound as well as preach in the markets. One afternoon between meetings, I was walking around out on one of the hillsides praying, thinking, and reflecting. And then all of a sudden it happened. God spoke to me in my heart and said, "Shad, I want you to resign your church and go into international evangelism." I could hardly believe what I knew I had heard God say, and yet I knew without a doubt He had said it. I did not say anything to Sheila for a day or so, but finally I had to; I could not keep it in any longer. So I asked her, "Honey, is the Lord saying anything to you?" She replied, "You mean like go into international evangelism?" I knew then it was all over. But once again a struggle ensued. How could this make any sense at all? Our ministry at the church was phenomenal. We were seeing people saved in every service, as well as on the streets, as our young people went out sharing Christ every weekend. We had a special coffee house type ministry (called "Christian Jam") going on every Saturday night and hundreds of young people were coming from all over the city. The church was growing rapidly and we were thrilled to be a part of it. Furthermore, the church was thrilled to have us there, and at the time it seemed we could have stayed forever. But all that did not change the fact that God had spoken. He had worked a miracle for Sheila and me to be in Africa, and we thought it was for the simple purpose of having us be part of a music group for the project. We thought it would be a one-time thing and then we would go back to the church and continue our ministry there. But God had another plan. His primary purpose for taking us to the other side of the world was to get us into position for Him to speak to us. He miraculously provided for <u>both</u> of us to go because it was necessary for <u>both</u> of us to hear His call. He took us all the way to Africa because it was necessary for us to be in a context where we could <u>understand</u> the call as well as <u>respond</u> to it.

After we arrived home we did continue our ministry at the church, and it continued to grow and flourish. On the outside everything still looked the same, but in our hearts everything had changed. We had heard the voice of God and His will had been received, at least in part. There was still the issue of His perfect timing, as well as the fact that we did not know a single person outside the United States. We had no idea how we would live, let alone travel all over the world preaching the Gospel. I thought at first that maybe we could become missionaries with the International Mission Board. But, I was disqualified on two counts; I did not have a seminary degree, and I could not pass the physical due to my extremely bad eyesight. Besides, God had not called us to be missionaries to one country but international evangelists to the whole world. But the question was, how? Throughout the next year we did not tell anyone what God was doing but just kept it to ourselves. We prayed and talked and waited for God's assurance and direction. Then in June 1976, God gave that assurance in the prayer garden in North Carolina. His will was settled, and we knew for sure we were going into all the world. But the question still remained as to how.

After arriving home from North Carolina, God began waking me up every day at exactly 4:30 AM. For months I would get up and go down to a park near our house where I would walk, read the Bible and pray. Morning by morning I walked and prayed, thought and struggled, and prayed some more. Then one morning, after about three months, it happened. I was walking across the park praying out loud as I walked. I said, "Lord, I guess it just has to be by faith alone, there is just no other way; it just has to be by faith." The instant those words came out of my mouth, the heel of my shoe caught on something lying in the grass; it was something I had never seen before, even though I had walked over that piece of ground hundreds of times. It was a piece of concrete about three feet square. When I looked down my eyes fell on one word written in the concrete. It was the word **FAITH**. I could hardly believe my eyes. I knelt down and ran my hand across the letters to make sure I was seeing what I thought I was seeing. When I examined it more closely I realized it was a name, Sarah Faith Jones. The words Sarah and Jones were very faint, but the word FAITH was very clear, and God had made it very clear to me that His answer to all my questions was very simple – it is all by faith. Sheila and I continued to pray and God continued to encourage us by bringing into our lives the life stories of such men of faith as Hudson Taylor, George Muller, C.T. Studd, and others. In the summer of `75 God gave us the <u>what</u> for our life - international evangelism. In June `76 He gave us the <u>how</u> – all by faith. Then in June `77 He gave us the <u>when</u> – right now. So in September 1977 we resigned the church and entered, by faith, the ministry of international evangelism we are still in today.

Now, I want to clarify something. By "calling" I am not just talking about calling to ministry or missions or evangelism. There are different kinds of calling. I mentioned earlier my friend Dr. Mel Senter, who went with us to Hong Kong in 1977. Well, Mel was also on that trip to Africa in 1975 as part of the music group. He played the bass guitar, and at that time he was not Dr. Senter. He was just Mel. But on that same trip that God called Sheila and me into world evangelism, He also called Mel into medicine. At that time it was just as impossible for Mel to get a medical degree as it was for Sheila and me to launch a new ministry. But during that trip he answered the call of God and announced it to the whole group. Some of the group made light of what he said, because they apparently underestimated the power of God at work <u>in</u> his life, as well as the call of God <u>upon</u> his life. But Mel answered the call of God, stepped into the impossible, and is now one of the finest pediatricians in the city of Memphis.

Dear Christian, has God spoken to you through His Word, in such a way that you know in your heart He is leading you? Is that leading in some direction that is going to require more of you than you have or than you can do? Has He used some means to prompt you in your spirit to obey Him in some way that will draw you into the impossible? Is God calling you to do something or to go in a direction that will cause you to rely completely upon His supernatural intervention and provision? If He is, then you are being drawn into the will of God and into the operation of faith. Again, God's part is to issue the invitation to real faith and yours is to accept His invitation and believe. If you will, then you will receive maximum joy and God will receive maximum glory.

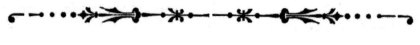

Summary of Truth

❖ God often uses His Word to reveal or confirm His will and draw us into faith.

❖ We cannot "find a word" from God. It comes only at His choosing and at His initiation.

❖ A word from God only occurs in a worshipping life.

❖ The Bible cannot be forced to say something about our situation just because we would like for it to.

❖ The Holy Spirit may speak to our inner man by means of our own thoughts or from something in our circumstances.

❖ He also reveals His will and draws us into faith by placing a call upon our life.

❖ A "call" does not necessarily mean to ministry.

❖ To be drawn into faith by the Word, or by Holy Spirit prompting, or by a call, will always draw us out beyond our own abilities and resources. It will always necessitate trusting God for the impossible by the operation of real faith.

NOW LET'S TAKE A MOMENT AND PRAY TOGETHER:

DEAR GOD, I WANT TO KNOW YOUR WILL AND I WELCOME YOUR INVITATIONS TO BELIEVE. I WANT TO GLORIFY YOU BY FAITH, AND I WANT TO KNOW THE JOY THAT COMES ONLY FROM TRUSTING YOU FOR THE IMPOSSIBLE. LORD, I ASK YOU TO HELP ME TO LIVE A LIFE OF CONTINUOUS WORSHIP SO THAT I MAY BE SENSITIVE AND ATTENTIVE TO YOUR VOICE. FATHER, SPEAK TO ME THROUGH YOUR WORD AND BY YOUR SPIRIT AS YOU SO CHOOSE. I AM READY TO ANSWER ANY CALL YOU PLACE ON MY LIFE, BECAUSE MY LIFE IS NOT MINE, BUT YOURS TO USE AS YOU SEE FIT. LORD, I AM READY TO HEAR YOU AND TO OBEY YOU. LORD, LEAD ME INTO THE IMPOSSIBLE, INTO REAL FAITH, SO THAT YOU RECEIVE MAXIMUM GLORY AND I RECEIVE MAXIMUM JOY. THANK YOU, FATHER. IN JESUS' NAME. AMEN.

Chapter 22

The Faith Process Explained
Believing God in a Faith Event

*"There are commonly three stages in work for God,
first impossible, then difficult, then done."*
James Hudson Taylor (1)

TOP! If you have skipped over any of the previous chapters and jumped to this one as a short cut to understanding the operation of faith, then <u>STOP</u>! Go back to where you jumped ahead and read to this point. The reason I am telling you this is because that is exactly what I would do if I were reading this book. Being the "type A," bottom-line, just-give-me-the-facts sort of person that I am, I would try to fast track right to the nuts and bolts of the matter and bypass all that "other stuff." Well in this case that would be a mistake. To do so would mean that you have missed far too much and you would be approaching this chapter unprepared. So go back to that place and start there. Trust me, if you don't, you will not fully grasp what you read here.

The purpose of the previous chapters has been to introduce you to the idea and concept of faith, to help you come to an accurate understanding of just what faith is, how it operates, and what it accomplishes for you and for the Kingdom of God. My aim up to this point has been to help you see that a life of faith is God's will for you, and it is possible for you. Now, in this chapter we come to what I call the "faith process," a series of progressive stages that apply to those special occasions in which we are drawn into believing God for specific objects and outcomes. In these occasions, our natural abilities and resources are clearly not enough and thus call for God's supernatural intervention and provision. These special occasions are what we will refer to as "faith events."

Before a Christian can apply the faith process to a faith event, his life must be prepared for it. He must be able to recognize it for what it is and respond to it positively as an opportunity for faith. The intent of the previous chapters is to provide you with that preparation. The <u>potential</u> for faith becomes the <u>practice</u> of faith only in a life <u>prepared</u> for faith. Our Christian life is like a mountain range containing foothills, plateaus, and great high peaks. Faith events are like the high peaks in our walk with God. They are majestic, but they are not possible without the ranges and foothills, without the prepared life underneath them. This chapter is where we are ultimately trying to get to in our climb up Faith Mountain, the place where we begin to exer- cise faith in such a way that God begins to perform the impos- sible in our life. Here we are going to discover how the will, purpose, plan, and supply of God in the invisible becomes His accomplished work through us in the visible. So, if you have read, absorbed and prayed through the previous chapters, if you have determined to put into practice what you have studied so far, then let's move on.

In this chapter I am attempting to explain the faith process by providing an overview of it, as a whole, from start to finish. Then, in the next two chapters, I will hopefully add some additional clarity to our understanding of the process by means of <u>illustration</u>. Finally, we will get to where we are trying to go, to the place of <u>application</u>. I can already hear the question you are asking, "Okay, this is all fine and good in theory, but how do I make it work for <u>me</u>?" Good question, and we *are* going to get there, but first we need to look at the situations to which the process is applied.

Faith Events – God's Invitations to Believe

Now let me ask you; is there anything in your life right now that is causing you to reach beyond your grasp? Do you feel that you are being stretched beyond your limits in some way? Is there a need you cannot meet or a desire you cannot fulfill? Are you facing adverse circumstances over which you seem to have no control? Does God seem to be pressuring you to go where you cannot go or do what you cannot do? Are you in a crisis, trial, or storm of some kind? I could keep asking this same question in various ways, but you get the point. If so, then God is drawing you into a position to enter the faith process and believe for the impossible. No, you are not doing anything wrong and God is not angry with you. Quite the contrary, you are simply receiving an invitation to faith.

If a Christian is walking in harmony with God there will be two operations of faith present in his life; faith applied to routine everyday living, and faith applied to special faith events which are brought about by God

Himself – one capacity but two operations. Daily routine faith occurs unconsciously or "automatically" as a result of just living life. As we said earlier, it is usually without thought, prayer, calculation, or seeking God's will that we sit in a chair, eat a meal, ride in a car, post a letter, or send an email – all acts of faith (persuasion of fact followed by corresponding action). Normally these routine acts of faith are met with little opposition, and if there are obstacles in the way, they are easily overcome by means of our own natural abilities and resources. For this reason they really don't feel like acts of faith at all.

Event faith, on the other hand, occurs as a result of God's drawing us into a special time of trusting Him for a specific object or outcome that is impossible to acquire or achieve without Him. It requires a <u>conscious choice</u>. A faith event, or a faith scenario, is an occurrence in life and circumstances that is out of the ordinary. If the situation is extremely severe then it may be called a crisis of faith or a trial of faith, but regardless of what label is applied, it is a time in which you are drawn into the impossible. It is a time when, above all else, <u>you need God</u>. It requires receiving the knowledge of His will in relation to some particular issue, and it requires trusting Him alone to fulfill it. It will also require some activity of faith that goes far beyond daily routine living, <u>an activity that does not solve the problem but demonstrates your belief that God is solving it</u>. Some Christians may have more faith events than others because of the particular life God has called them to. But, make no mistake about it, every Believer in Jesus Christ will have some, because it is God's will to bring glory to Himself through every Christian life. God demonstrates His "almightiness" at the end of what we have and what we can do – in the realm of the impossible.

As we walk by faith <u>in fellowship </u>with God in daily life we **are** the will of God. But as we walk through a faith event we must **ascertain** the will of God. Norman Grubb calls daily faith "elementary" and event faith "advanced." You might also call one a "ground level" faith and the other more of a "higher level" faith. Again – it is the same capacity, but different applications. Remember, if I reach down and pick up a feather, I use muscles in my hands, arms, back, and shoulders, and the whole operation requires very little thought or effort. But, if I pick up an eighty-pound sack of concrete then that changes things – a lot! I will use the same exact muscles, but this time I will also give it some careful thought and planning, and it will require quite a lot of effort. I am using the very same capacity in both instances, but in the latter I am using it much <u>more</u>. So, it is not the faith that is different, but the application. Faith events do not call for more faith, but for <u>more exercise</u> of faith. Unlike daily routine faith, event faith has three characteristics. It is **directional** in that it believes God for a clearly defined object or outcome in response to the knowledge of His will in your inner man. It is **deliberate** in that it requires you to make a definite conscious choice between believing what you see in the visible and what God shows you in the invisible. It is also **designed** in that it is initiated by God for the carrying out of His purpose in regard to a particular issue and for bringing glory to Himself.

These special times of faith in the Believer's life bring honor and glory to God as nothing else can. They establish an indisputable testimony to the world, and to the church, of His awesome power, His unfathomable goodness, and His unwavering faithfulness. That is why God sends them into your life; they are not accidental. Oh that Christians everywhere would recognize and accept such occasions in their lives as opportunities to magnify the Lord. What an impact that would have on the world. Nothing brings more joy or encouragement to the heart of a Believer than to see God work intimately, specifically, and personally in his life to accomplish those things that are explainable only in terms of His supernatural intervention. It is interesting and exciting to see the reality and power of God proven through someone else's life. But it is thrilling beyond words to see something happen in your own life that could not have taken place apart from God doing the impossible. Maybe a sudden need has occurred in your circumstances that is impossible for you to meet. Maybe a burning desire has arisen in your heart that is impossible to fulfill, but it just will not go away. Maybe you are being prompted by the Holy Spirit to do what you cannot do in your own strength, to go where you cannot go under your own power, or to give what you cannot give out of your own ability. Maybe God is pushing you in your spirit to expand your business or your ministry or your church, and you do not have a clue how to go about it. Maybe God is placing a call upon your life to some service for Him that you know you are absolutely unsuited for. In each case you might think, "This makes no sense; I must be crazy!" No you are not crazy, and in the realm of God it makes perfect sense. What is happening is that God is inviting you to a special time of fellowship with Him. He is drawing you into a faith event that will bring His provision and joy to you and glory to Him.

It Is a Process - Not a Formula

We said earlier that coming to the knowledge of the will of God is better expressed as a process than as a procedure, set of steps, or equation. The same is true for walking through a faith event and, for that matter, living the faith life. I said that you cannot "learn" the principles of faith by following a set of rules or steps. They must be <u>discovered</u> and <u>absorbed</u> through personal <u>application</u> and <u>experience</u>, as well as through trial and error. You may glean a certain amount of information about swimming by reading an instruction book or by watching a video, but you will never learn to swim until you get in the water. The same is true for faith. This book will help you get started, but you will never learn to trust God for the impossible until you launch out into the deep. You say, "But what if I try and then fail?" Well, first let me tell you that in God's school of faith it is not against the rules to "fail," but it is against the rules to never make an attempt. But, second, let me assure you that ultimately you will not fail, because God will not allow you to. When I took swimming lessons as a child, I had a coach, and there was no way he was going to let me fail. If he did, I would drown, and he was not going to let that happen. Your heavenly Faith Coach is not going to let you fail either. You may begin by "dog paddling" and barely treading water, but the important thing is that you are in the pool. That is what we are doing here: getting in the water. Granted, you may feel like you are failing at faith at times, but you are not. You may feel like you are going under, but you won't. The very act of just making an attempt to trust God, regardless of how feeble it may feel to you, makes you an A student in God's school of faith. **The only Christians that fail at faith are those who never make an attempt**.

Now, even though we cannot reduce faith to a formula, we can look at the men and women of the Bible, and in Christian history, and observe a pattern that took place in the lives of those who made the choice to believe God. By the term "faith process" we are actually referring to that pattern or sequence. We could also call it God's "way" of faith. The reason the pattern bears such close attention is because it is so consistent from one life to another, not only in the Bible, but also in the lives of those who have believed God for the impossible down through the centuries. In many cases, they were people who did not know each other, did not confer with each other, and did not read about each other. They were not copying each other; they were being led by the Holy Spirit, and His leading in each life painted a picture that looked very similar from one life to another. As we look at these lives, we will see that each time a child of God goes through a faith event, he seems to pass through a series of progressive stages. We are calling these stages the faith process, not procedure - because there are always variations from one life to another as well as from one event to another. God always finds a way to remain fresh and original.

The Faith Process Transfers God's Will from Heaven to Earth

Now, let's ask a question. What is the purpose of the operation of faith, or the faith process, in our Christian lives? We have already said that by faith we please and glorify God and bring joy into our own lives. But there is another purpose that is even more fundamental, and here it is. By the operation of faith, the will of God is transferred from heaven to earth, from the invisible to the visible. <u>What is real in the spiritual realm becomes real in the natural, physical realm by means of the operation of faith.</u>

THE FATHER - had the thought - WILL   HEAVEN (Spritual Realm)

THE SON - spoke the WORD   ME (Mediator/Channel)

THE HOLY SPIRIT - performed the WORK   EARTH

Upon examination of each event of faith in the Bible and in the lives of God's people throughout Christian history, you will see that in each case they passed through a series of stages that began with God, continued with God, and ended with God. He always takes the initiative, and He always completes what He starts. Every faith event in the life of a Christian is for the dual purpose of transferring the will, plan, and supply of God from heaven to earth, and establishing a new and fresh testimony to His name. That transfer always involves three things: a **will**, a **word** and a **work**. When Jesus was alive on the earth, it was accomplished this way: first, the Father had the thought (the will) in heaven; second, the will of the Father in heaven was revealed to the Son on earth, Who then acted and spoke in accordance with what He was told; and third, the Holy Spirit did the work. He brought the will of the Father to pass in the visible, material realm. Jesus said in John 5:30, *"I can of mine own self do nothing: as I hear, I judge* [decide]*: and my judgment is just: because I seek not mine own will, but the will of the Father which hath sent me."* After Jesus ascended into heaven, He sent the Holy Spirit to indwell His people, thus forming the church. Now you and I, as children of God, occupy the same position that Jesus occupied - a channel through which the will of the Father can flow.

God the Father in heaven has the thought (His will), which He reveals to us in our spirit. Then we act and speak in accordance with what He says. Finally the Holy Spirit, using the creative power of the spoken word, brings the will of the Father to pass in the natural realm on earth. It is by this process the post-ascension ministry of Jesus is continued on earth today.

Again, the transfer of God's will from heaven to earth, by means of a faith event in the Believer's life, involves a series of stages. I have outlined them in a diagram below that looks much like a time line. It is actually more like a <u>sequence</u> line, however, because it is not possible to attach a hard and fast time frame to a faith event. You never know how long it is going to take to come to the clear will of God concerning a particular issue, or how long you will have to persist in faith before God's will is fulfilled, even once you know His will. Remember, God is never in a hurry. He is operating on His time frame, not ours. Now, let's take a look at these stages.

The Faith Process – Seven Stages (or Sequences)

1. ATMOSPHERE for faith – Our heart and life must be **prepared** to hear from God and respond to Him properly.
2. ACCEPTING God's invitation to faith – The **process** of faith is initiated by God through need, desire, His Word, prompting from the Holy Spirit, or calling.
3. ASSURANCE of God's will – **Persuasion** of fact in the invisible.
4. ASKING and RECEIVING – The definite **prayer** of faith is offered for a specific outcome, which is then received, by faith, in the heart.
5. ACTIVITY of faith – We must **persist** in believing by:
   The WORSHIP of faith – praising God in advance for the finished work.
   The WORD of faith – Confessing publicly the outcome believed for.
   The WORK of faith - Acting in accordance with the will of God.
   The WARFARE of faith - Resisting satan through spiritual warfare.
   The WAIT of faith - Refusing to quit despite delay.
6. ACCOMPLISHMENT of God's will in God's time– His **provision** in the invisible becomes real or tangible in the visible.
7. ACKNOWLEGMENT of the power of God – His faithfulness is **proven** and a fresh testimony is established to His Name.

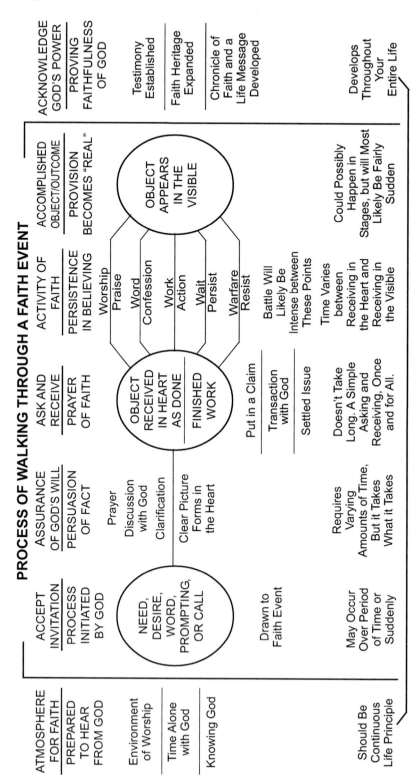

PROCESS OF WALKING THROUGH A FAITH EVENT

A Life of Worship Will Develop a Life Message and a Heritage of Faith

ATMOSPHERE for faith - PREPARED to hear from God

First, there must be an **atmosphere** for faith in your life. This is actually more of a <u>condition</u> than a stage, but I am including it because real God-faith is not possible in the life of a Believer unless his heart is right before God. Oswald Chambers wrote, "The main thing about Christianity is not the work we do, but the relationship we maintain and the atmosphere produced by that relationship" (2). I could not agree more. The older I have become in the faith, and the further I have gone in ministry, the more I believe that my personal relationship with God (my personal private walk with Him) is more important than anything else. In fact, it is the key to everything. **It is impossible for me to be truly successful in public ministry and be a failure in private worship at the same time**. As already stated, if a suitable environment of fellowship, worship, and communion with God does not exist in your life, then <u>you are not prepared to recognize and correctly respond to God's invitations to faith</u>. In fact you will most likely view those invitations as negative. Have you ever heard some one say in reference to a sudden need or crisis, "I guess God must be punishing me," or "Maybe God is testing me or trying to teach me a lesson?" Those are tragic statements because they indicate a total lack of understanding of the character and goodness of God. They also indicate a lack of the kind of relationship with God that would enable a person to recognize God's invitations to believe.

Without an atmosphere for faith, the meeting of your needs and the fulfillment of your desires will be relegated to the limitations of the natural and the visible. Without an atmosphere for faith, sensitivity to the Word of God will not exist in your life and promptings from the Holy Spirit will go unrecognized. God's calling upon your life will go unheeded, and opportunities for bringing glory to God will be lost. The purpose of all the chapters of this book, so far, is to help you develop a spiritual atmosphere that will enable you to walk by faith in your daily life and to respond correctly to God's special invitations to believe. The stage must be set before the performance can take place. An important key to living the conquering, victorious Christian life is to have the stage set, all the time, by maintaining a consistent life of intimate fellowship and worship with God.

God's invitations to faith come in all forms. Some may come in the form of a gentle nudge from the Holy Spirit, and some may come as storms. But regardless of how they come, you can and should be prepared for them ahead of time. <u>Sudden trials or crisis situations are the wrong place and</u>

time to get prepared to trust God. Of course, unexpected storms and situations are going to come in your life, but you do not have to be blown away by them. And you won't be if you have taken the time to get to know God intimately in the prayer closet.

ACCEPTING God's invitation – PROCESS of faith is initiated by God

Once an atmosphere for faith has been established, then it is possible for God to move you to the next stage – the place of **acceptance** of His invitation to exercise your capacity for faith and believe for the impossible. Here, God will draw you into position to receive His will regarding some particular thing He wants to provide for you or something He wants to accomplish in your life. As we have observed already, He uses many different ways and means to initiate occasions for faith in our lives. Regardless of what means God uses, however, you will come to the place where you know for sure that a necessity for faith has arisen. You know that in this situation, in regard to this thing, you absolutely must know the will of God, and you must trust Him for it. You become convinced intellectually, emotionally, and circumstantially that you cannot do this on your own. You are in a position where you *must* see God work on your behalf. There is no other way. So, like Jehoshaphat (II Chronicles 20:3) you "set yourself to seek the Lord." You make the wise choice of faith.

It is important to mention again that in the initiation of a real faith event, **it is always God doing the initiating**. It must be, because as you walk through a faith event, the devil is going to assault you with questions that are designed to throw you off balance and cause you to give up. The thing that will prevent you from caving in is the sure knowledge that God started the process in the first place. You are going through this occasion of trusting God because He drew you into it. If you can look back and see His hand in the beginning, then you can stand in the face of any amount of opposition, be it from the devil, from public opinion, or from outward appearances and circumstances. The sure knowledge of God's initiation will enable you to stand firm in the face of deadlines and delay. There have been many times over the years that God has told us to go to some country and preach and we have come right down to the last minute – even leaving for the airport with no money. But we could do it; we could hang on because we knew we were operating within a faith event, a faith scenario that GOD created. As I said before, if He started it then He will finish it. It may not be in the exact way or in the exact time frame that would make you feel the most comfortable, but you can be sure He will do it. He <u>will</u> do it, because He has <u>already</u> done it. Remember you are entering into the <u>finished</u> work.

ASSURANCE of God's will – PERSUASION of fact

Now we come to the third stage, the place of knowing the will of God concerning your specific situation. This involves two things: worship and waiting. You must determine to spend whatever time is necessary to come to the **assurance** of the will of God - to become persuaded of the settled facts of His finished work concerning your particular need, desire, or situation. You will know when you are there because a "knowing" will settle in upon your heart, and it will be accompanied by a peace that cannot be shaken. You will need to meet with God in private fellowship and worship, day by day, for as long as it takes. You begin by bringing to Him your assessment of the situation as you understand it - the "picture" of what it looks like to you right now. Then you present to God the picture of what you would like it to be - what you would like for Him to do or provide. You pray and discuss. You talk to God, and He talks to you, in your spirit and through His Word. Then at some point a new picture, HIS picture, will form in your heart and will become crystal clear. You will <u>see</u> the will of God, the finished work, the invisible supply. You will <u>know</u> how this is supposed to come out because you have seen the picture on the puzzle box. Again, an unexplainable certainty, peace and assurance will settle in upon your heart, and along with it will come a supernatural ability to persist in faith under pressure from opposing circumstances. It will not matter whether or not it makes sense or whether it agrees with appearances. You have <u>heard</u> the voice of God in your inner man, and you have <u>seen</u> the will of God through the eyes of your spirit. It is settled, it is a "done deal." Now you know what you are to ask for. You may not be able to explain to some one else how you know, but you just know. And, once you know the will of God, you cannot "unknow" it. Now you can confidently put in your claim because you know you are asking in accordance with the will of God. You can ask God to do what He has told you He is going to do, because you know that, from His viewpoint, He has already done it. You have reached the place of Mark 11:24, *"Therefore I say unto you, what things soever you desire, when ye pray, believe that* [act as if] *ye* [have already] *receive them, and ye shall have them."* Again quoting Andrew Murray, "Faith is the ear which has heard God say what He will do and the eye which has seen Him do it" (3).

I want to emphasize again that there is nothing vague or abstract about real faith and about knowing God's will. Faith and the will of God deals with specifics, not generalities. At the outset of the faith process, the object or outcome you need for God to provide may lack clear definition, but as you wait before God, in time, a very definite faith object or faith objective will become crystal clear in your heart. You are not ready to believe until you have something specific to believe for. I do not use the term "faith goal" because a goal is set forth by men as a thing to strive for with the realization it may or may not be reached. You do the work with no guarantee of success. A "faith object", on the other hand, is set forth by God as something to believe for with the realization it has already been reached. God does the work with absolute guarantee of success. As Believers we do not need goals in our lives which magnify our best efforts, we need faith objects and objectives that glorify God. The world is not impressed by what we do for God, but it is always impressed by what God does for us or through us.

ASK and RECEIVE– The PRAYER of faith

Coming to the will of God involves prayer, of course, and sometimes a lot of it. It is a discussion and discovery type of prayer. It is working out the details and definition of God's will. It is not the prayer of faith, but it leads to the prayer of faith, which has two aspects – definite **asking** and definite **receiving**. (Again, it must be specific.) Once you are assured of the will of God, once you have seen the picture, it is time to put in a definite request. It is time to ask God to do what He has said He will do and accept it from Him as done. It is not complicated; it is just a simple transaction between you and God. The devil will fight you at this point with questions, accusations, and fear of failure. He will try to make you hesitate by causing you to doubt your motives. He will tell you to wait until you are sure you can "do it right." He will do that, because he does not want you to perform the act that sets God in motion – the act of asking. He does not want you to ask in faith. There is nothing mystical about this at all, however, and it is not a matter of doing it the right way or even a certain way. As I said, it is just a simple transaction, just a matter of doing it – period. You know what your need or desire or situation is, and you know what God has said He is going to do about it. All you are doing is voicing back to God what He has voiced to you. So, get on your knees and ask, and when you ask, do so with an outstretched hand to receive – if not literally, at least in your mind, your heart, your imagination. Ask for the definite object, reach out with heart and take it (visualize it coming to you), and then thank God for it. Remember, you are actually asking for what you already have. From God's viewpoint it has already been done. I keep saying this over and over because it is so important to constantly look at things from God's side of the page. The late Dr. R.A. Torrey, renowned Bible professor of Moody Bible Institute wrote, "When we pray to God and pray according to His will as known by the promises of His Word, or as known by the Holy Spirit revealing His will to us, we should confidently believe that the very thing that we have asked is granted us. We should believe that we have received, and what we thus believe we have received, we shall afterwards have in actual personal experience" (4). We are going to look at the "prayer of faith" in more depth later on, but one other aspect of it that we should include here before moving on is this - one real asking is enough; it never needs to be repeated. The only prayer that is necessary and appropriate following the prayer of faith is the prayer of praise and thanksgiving. J.O. Fraser, pioneer missionary to Burma, called it "putting in a claim." He said, "When once we have the deep, calm assurance of His will in the matter, we put in our claim, just as a child before his father. A simple request and nothing more. No cringing, no beseeching, no tears, no wrestling. No second asking either. One real asking is enough for a lifetime" (5).

ACTIVITY of faith - PERSISTENCE in believing

Many times I have seen earnest sincere Christians get tripped up in faith at this point because they do not realize that asking and receiving is not the end of the faith process. You may think, "Okay, I have heard from God, I am persuaded of His will, I have seen the picture, I have asked Him for the object in faith, and have received it in my heart. I am convinced it is going to happen, and now all I have to do is wait for God to do it. Right?" Wrong! Now begins the **activity** of faith, which involves work, worship, warfare, the spoken word, and waiting. In every venture of faith Jesus will always tell us to "go and do" and "go and say." Notice, for example, the ten lepers in Luke 17:14. They came to Jesus and asked for healing, and Jesus responded with the command to *"...Go shew yourselves unto the priests..."* Jesus was telling them their request had been granted, and He was sending them to the priests for verification. Then it says, *"...as they went, they were cleansed."* When they left Jesus they were still lepers, but when they got to the priest they were healed. The asking was followed by activity, which resulted in the answer to their request. Again, Jesus will always tell us to go and do, that is, to demonstrate our faith with action. Believing is acting.

Coming to an assurance of God's will and receiving it in your heart as a "done deal" is like getting God's signature on the check. But you still have to take the check to the bank and cash it before it becomes real money. The activity of faith is like taking the check to the bank.

Now you have won the first fight (the fight against faith), which we will look at later. You resisted the flesh and accepted God's invitation to step into the arena of faith. You have also won the second fight (the fight to faith). You spent time with God resisting satan's temptation to give up and let go. Now you have come to the will of God, you have put in your claim. Now the real battle is enjoined – the fight OF faith. This will be the most difficult one of all, but it is the one that takes you to the finish line. James 2:26 tells us, *"For as the body without the spirit is dead, so faith without works is dead also."* As the man said, "It ain't over 'til it's over." And it is not "over" until the invisible becomes visible. Once you are assured in your heart of the outcome you can rest in faith, but you dare not relax. You must not allow slack in the ropes of faith until the process is complete. The prayer of faith will always be followed by the **activity** of faith, or the works of faith. I call it "walking it through." We come to a place where we assuredly know God is going to provide, to supply, to deliver, but from the moment that assurance comes in our heart until the moment it is accomplished in the natural realm, there is a period of "walking it through." This period, which is essential, involves continued worship throughout, confessing the word of faith, concentrated work (action), confronting the powers of darkness in spiritual warfare and choosing to wait until the last minute – and maybe even beyond.

One of the most powerful aids in helping you to persist in faith, beyond the transaction of asking and receiving, is simply praising God and thanking Him for the object or outcome believed for. This is the WORSHIP of faith. As you praise God for the envisioned outcome, your focus will be drawn to God, not to opposition from the visible. As we will see in the next chapter (from the story of Jehoshaphat in II Chronicles 20), satan does not know how to react when we begin praising God for the object or outcome before it appears in the visible realm. He becomes confused and his schemes against us collapse. Praise to God is an act of the will, and it is a powerful weapon against the powers of darkness.

Another powerful weapon is that of confession or public declaration. This is the WORD of faith. *"We having the same spirit of faith, according as it is written, I believed, and therefore have I spoken; we also believe, and therefore speak* (II Corinthians 4:13)." Jesus said in Mark 11:23, *"For verily I say unto you, That whosoever shall **say** unto this mountain, Be thou removed, and be thou cast into the sea; and shall not doubt* [hesitate] *in his heart, but shall believe that* [act as if] *those things which he **saith** shall come to pass; he shall have whatsoever he **saith**."* The word of faith is simply *repeating to the world what God has spoken to you in your heart.* It is verbalizing the settled will of God. The fact that you have attained to a real position of faith is evidenced by your public declaration that what you have asked is going to come to pass. Remember, Jesus only repeated what the Father told Him, and as He did, the Holy Spirit used His spoken word to bring forth the will of God in the natural realm. The same thing happens when we repeat, by faith, what God has spoken in our heart. Norman Grubb writes, "Faith must reach out and take the promises, and the public evidence of such taking is the spoken word of faith. When the decisive word of faith has been spoken, God in His grace begins to work, satan is stopped and as we persist in the stand of faith, the answer appears" (6).

Then there is the WORK of faith, that is, acting in accordance with the will of God. Manley Beasley always said, "Act like it is so, when it is not so, so it will be so, because God said it is so" (7). But how can you possibly "act like it is so" when it is obviously not so and the devil, your intellect, and everything around you is telling you it isn't? You do it by placing your focus on God's **ways**, God's **will**, and God's **word**, instead of circumstances, logic, and public opinion. You do it by moving your focus from the visible to the invisible. There have been many times when I have heard satan say, "You are really going to look stupid, and you are really going to be embarrassed when this thing doesn't happen." The truth, however, is that it is not possible for it to "not happen," because what you are believing for and confessing is the settled will of God. It has already happened. Oswald Chambers said it this way, "Take the initiative, stop hesitating, and take the first step. Be resolute when God speaks, act in faith immediately on what He says, and never revise your decisions. Take the initiative, take it yourself, take the step with your will now, make it impossible to go back. Make the thing inevitable" (8).

Later on we will look more closely at the WARFARE of faith, but for now let me just tell you that it will certainly happen. Satan will never allow a true venture of faith to go unopposed. He has too much to lose and the Kingdom of God has too much to gain. He will come against you with all sorts of accusations, questions, intimidations and enticements in an effort to get you to quit before you reach the finish line. The key is to not get into conversations with the devil and to not listen to him. Do not attempt to answer the questions he brings to your mind. Just resist him, and refer him to the home office. Refer him to the Father.

Finally there is the <u>WAIT</u> of faith. In the battle of faith, the warfare often becomes very intense and the temptation to quit can be overwhelming. But if you will just hold on, even down to the last minute, God will always come through. Real faith has no backdoor, no loopholes and no "plan B." Real God-faith can hold on even under the pressure of delay and past the deadlines. It is not necessary for the child of God to yield to pressure to "make it happen." In fact, that is always a mistake. If it looks like time has run out and the thing is going to die, then let it. Then keep holding on, and trust God for the resurrection. It will come. Abraham provides us with a perfect example of someone who tried to make it happen by forcing the issue with Hagar. The end result has been endless turmoil, and war after war unleashed upon the world for thousands of years. God does not need your help, your ideas, or your alternative fleshly schemes; He needs your trust and obedience. It is not your job to get creative; that job belongs to God. It is also not your job to protect God's Name and reputation by trying to bail out the situation through some means of your own making. God can protect His Own reputation and His Own Name. He was doing just fine before you and I came into the world, and He will be perfectly okay after we leave it. Besides, the truth of the matter is that usually we are not really all that concerned with how God is going to look. It is more often our own face we are trying to save. Your responsibility is simply to believe, to persist in the activity of faith until God brings it to pass, and just walk it through until it is finished.

Before going on I feel it is important to point out that part of walking it through, part of the wait of faith, is your doing everything that is on your side of the page. In fact, the sooner you get to the limit of what you have and what you can do the better. God <u>will not</u> do what you can do and you <u>cannot</u> do what He can do. Chambers puts it this way; "God can do nothing for me until I get to the limit of the possible" (9). There have been many times when Sheila and I have been going on a trip overseas to preach and we did not have the money to go, even down to the last minute. So what did we do? Did we wait until we had the money in our hand before we began to pack our bags and prepare equipment to take for the project? No, we did all we could do on our side of the page while trusting God to supply in His

Own time. We have found that we must, as quickly as possible, get to the place where we know we are waiting on God and He is not waiting on us. We must get to the end of the possible so that God is free to perform the impossible. There have been many times that if we had waited on the money to arrive before we packed our bags, then when it did arrive we could not have gone anyway, because we would have been totally unprepared.

ACCOMPLISHMENT of God's will – PROVISION becomes "real"

As you persist in the stand of faith, the **accomplishment** of the will of God will take place so that all can see. God's provision in the <u>invisible</u> will become yours in the <u>visible</u>. What was at first real only to the eyes of faith will become real to the eyes of men. The length of time from the initiation of faith to its fulfillment will vary, but the end result will always be the same. God will be glorified and you will be encouraged, enlarged, strengthened, and motivated to trust God again and again and again. It is important to point out, however, that it is not just the outcome of faith that glorifies God, but it

Faith does not occupy itself with itself, but with the promises of God and the God of the promises.

Henry W. Frost (10)

is the entire process from beginning to end that honors Him and proves His faithfulness. God is magnified by the very fact that you believed, that you made the choice of faith.

In Daniel 3:17-18, we find Shadrach, Meshach, and Abednego being told by King Nebuchadnezzar that if they did not worship the golden image they would be cast into a fiery furnace. Their response was, *"If it be so, our God whom we serve is able to deliver us from the burning fiery furnace, and he will deliver us out of thine hand, O king. But if not, be it known unto thee, O king, that we will not serve thy gods, nor worship the golden image which thou hast set up."* They were saying to satan, "God is going to deliver us. But whether He does or not, we are going to trust Him, and we are not going to worship you. So either way, devil, you lose." The instant we choose to believe God, satan loses, and every stage of the faith process brings honor and glory to God. Oswald Chambers said, "His end is the process - that I see Him walking on the waves, no shore in sight, no success, no goal, just the absolute certainty that it is alright because I see Him walking on the sea" (11). In Hebrews 11, we find two categories of people - those who believed God by faith and lived to see its fulfillment and those who believed God by faith and did not live to see its fulfillment. Both groups "saw" the promises of God, were persuaded of them, and embraced them as reality, which was evidenced by their public confession. Both groups went through the faith process, which for some ended in victory and for others ended in death. So which group brought glory to God? They both did. It was the process of faith, their choice to believe, that glorified God.

If you want to glorify God with your life, there is only one way to do it; you must make room for Him to initiate the faith process in your life and then choose to believe Him for the impossible. It is not easy to walk something through by faith. It would be terribly misleading if I told you that it is. In fact it can be very exhausting to the flesh. I remember a few years ago Sheila and I were going to India on a campaign, and we had walked it through down to the last minute. The battle with satan had been especially fierce and we were tired. Again it was one of those times when the money came in at the very last second, actually as we were unloading the bags at the curb at the airport. When the plane took off, Sheila and I just sat there holding hands, unable at first to speak. We had fought the fight of faith, and our hearts were filled with joy over God's provision, as well as having had another opportunity to establish a testimony to His faithfulness. But we were absolutely "wrung out" emotionally, and all we could do was just sit there and refrain from speaking for a while for fear that if we did try to talk, we would break into tears. As I said, the faith process can be hard on the flesh. It isn't always, but it <u>can</u> be. After a while though, calmness settled in upon our hearts, battle weariness faded away, and we arrived in India filled with nothing but rejoicing and thanksgiving. I tell you in all candor that faith is work, sometimes hard work, and will never be experienced by a lazy, complacent, cowardly Christian. It requires effort, boldness, and courage, but it is so well worth the effort, because it <u>always</u> results in glory to God, defeat for satan, and joy for you that cannot be realized any other way.

ACKOWLEGMENT of the power of God - PROVING His faithfulness

The final stage in the faith process is the establishment of a testimony to God's power, goodness, and faithfulness. As we have stressed all along, bringing glory to God is what faith is all about to begin with. Once the faith process has begun, and a declaration of the will of God has been made, there will be a skeptical world and an observing church eagerly waiting to see what will happen. Will God be proven faithful and trustworthy, or will the suspicions of the world and the unbelief of some Christians be justified? True faith will always establish a good testimony to the Name of God. When Jesus raised Lazarus from the dead in John 11, He prayed out loud for one reason, so that the people standing by would believe. The whole purpose for occasions for faith in our lives is to bring glory to God and cause others to believe - saved and unsaved alike.

Now, let me ask you, do you have needs that have arisen in your circumstances that you cannot meet without God's intervention? Are there burning desires in your heart that just will not go away and yet cannot be fulfilled by your best efforts? Are you faced with challenges in your life that are impossible to deal with apart from God? Maybe they are things in your business, your home and family, your church or your ministry. Are you in a financial crisis that is only going to get worse unless God performs a miracle? Is your world coming unraveled and there seems to be nothing you can do about it? Dear friend, these things are God's invitation to you to come to Him, receive His will, trust Him by faith, and see the glory of God. The question is, how are you going to respond? Let me encourage you to respond positively by accepting God's invitation to faith for what it is, an opportunity to enter the faith process and experience the reality of God for yourself. Now, I realize that even after reading this chapter, you may not fully grasp just exactly how to go about it. That is perfectly understandable. After all, this is probably new territory for you. Frankly, there are still times when I feel like it is new territory for me, and I'm the guy writing the book. But that is okay because the wonderful thing about the life of faith is that it is always new.

In the next two chapters we are going to look at illustrations of how the faith process actually works in real life situations. Observing how it works out in other lives will help you to have a better idea of how it can be implemented in your own. So keep reading; I promise you are going to get there.

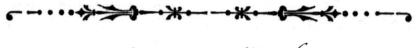

Summary of Truth

❖ The potential for faith becomes the practice of faith only in a life prepared for faith.

❖ The faith process is a series of progressive stages applied to a faith event in our life.

❖ A faith event is a special time of trusting God for a specific object or outcome that is impossible to acquire or achieve without His supernatural intervention and provision.

❖ Some Christians may have more faith events than others in their life, but all Christians will have some.

❖ There will always be two operations of faith present in a Believer's life - unconscious faith applied to daily routine living and conscious faith applied to faith events.

❖ As we walk in fellowship with God in daily life, we *are* the will of God, but as we walk through a faith event, we must *ascertain* the will of God.

❖ Event faith is directional, deliberate, and designed.

❖ Real faith is a process, not a formula.

❖ Real faith is learned through application and experience, as well as through trial and error.

❖ Ultimately, God will not allow you to fail at faith; just making an attempt at faith makes you a success at faith.

❖ The validity of the faith process is verified by the consistent pattern of faith lived out in the lives of men and women in the Bible, as well as throughout Christian history.

❖ The faith process transfers the will of God from heaven to earth, from the invisible to the visible.

❖ In order to recognize an invitation from God to believe and to respond to it correctly, there must be a suitable atmosphere for faith established in your life. It is impossible to be truly successful in public Christian living and to be a failure in private worship at the same time.

❖ The faith process is always initiated by God. Our part is to accept God's invitation and wait before Him to receive the knowledge of His will as pertains to our particular situation.

❖ You will know you have arrived at the will of God when a clear picture forms in your heart, which is accompanied by a settled "knowing" and an unshakable peace.

❖ The sure knowledge of God's will always leads to a definite prayer of faith, which includes definite asking and definite receiving.

❖ The prayer of faith is a simple one-time transaction.

❖ The prayer of faith is always followed by the activity or work of faith, which involves action and confession.

❖ The faith process often involves waiting until the very last minute and maybe even beyond.

❖ The faith process always results in glory to God, defeat for satan, and joy for the one who believes.

Now Let's Take a Moment and Pray Together:

Dear Lord Jesus, I have read this chapter and I desire for You to perform in my life what I have read. I ask You to continue to establish in my life an atmosphere for faith and help me to recognize Your invitations to believe for the impossible. Lord, help me to have the right attitude toward opportunities to enter into real faith events and see You work supernaturally on my behalf. Lord, I realize that You mean only good for me, and that all the things You bring into my life, even the storms, are intended to help me, to bless me, and to enlarge me through the exercise of faith. Thank You Father for blessing me with opportunities to enter into the faith process and see first hand the glory of God. I accept Your invitations for what they are, and I ask You to help me and enable me to walk through each new faith event to the end. Lord, I determine in my heart right now to continue my walk with You holding the shield of faith. Thank You, Lord Jesus, Almighty God Incarnate, for saving me and for continuing Your ministry through me by faith. I love You, Lord. In Your Name I pray. Amen.

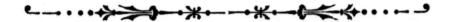

Chapter 23

The Faith Process Illustrated

Part One: From the Bible and Christian History

"The province of faith begins where probabilities cease
and sight and sense fail"

George Muller (1)

*I*n the previous chapter I attempted to explain the faith process by dealing with it as a sequence of stages throughout a faith event. These stages emerge as a pattern in the lives of those who accept God's invitations to believe Him, by faith, for specific objects or outcomes in specific situations in their lives. In this chapter we are going to look at the faith process by way of illustration, first from the Bible, and then from Christian history. Again, let me remind you that we are not talking about a precise formula, but a general pattern. It is important to remember this so that you don't find yourself trying to force your situation into a rigid mold. God's dealings with each of us are always new, personal, and original. Now let's observe the faith process at work in the lives of some people who were just as human and just as ordinary as you and me.

Jehoshaphat - A King in a Crisis

There are many instances in the Bible that clearly illustrate the faith process. But since we only have time and space for one, I have chosen to use a remarkable account from II Chronicles 20. It is a story from the life of Jehoshaphat, fourth king over the divided kingdom of Judah. First I would suggest that you get your Bible and read the entire chapter and then come back to this. As you read, you will begin to see the sequence (pattern) of faith unfold. You will see that the story begins with a young king in his mid-thirties, faced with a situation that is impossible for him to handle on his own and is sure to end in disaster if God does not do something - and quickly! Then it ends with God not only having delivered him, but having blessed him beyond his greatest expectation. Jehoshaphat would have been thrilled to just get out of the situation with his skin, but God blessed him with more "stuff" than he and his people could carry home in three days. So, how did it happen? How did he make the transition from sure disaster to supernatural deliverance?

Well it was certainly not accidental, not by any means. Faith events never are. They are deliberate, calculated invitations from God that require a deliberate correct response from us. Opportunities to trust God don't "just happen" in the life of a Christian; they are created by God for the purpose of glorifying Himself. So how was it then that the young king was enabled to make the correct response? Why didn't he just give up in despair and run away in defeat? The answer lies in the fact that there was an adequate spiritual **atmosphere** in his life. That atmosphere made it possible for him to rebound from fear and turn to God in faith rather than dissolve in panic and self-pity over what he saw in the visible. He could respond to God's invitation to believe, because he knew Him well enough to trust Him. You will never fully trust some one you do not know personally and know well. In II Chronicles 19:3 we find Jehu the seer telling Jehoshaphat, *"...thou has taken away the groves* [false gods] *out of the land, and hast prepared thine heart to seek God."* Verse 4 tells us that he went to the people and *"...brought them back unto the Lord God of their fathers."* After appointing judges, he instructed them (v.7) to *"...let the fear of the Lord be upon you..."* and in verse 9, *"...Thus shall ye do in the fear of the Lord, faithfully, and with a perfect heart."* Then in chapter 22, verse 9 Jehoshaphat was referred to as the man *"...who sought the Lord with all his heart."* In this young leader God found a man through whom He could demonstrate His faithfulness, because his heart was prepared. Jehoshaphat would not have chosen the scenario for himself, but he was adequately equipped to respond correctly when God chose it for him.

In verses 1 – 4 of chapter 20 we see Jehoshaphat's **acceptance** of God's invitation to faith. He received word that three armies had teamed up to destroy him and his kingdom, and they were on their way to do so. He was told that they were a *"great multitude"* and that they were not far away. Verse 3 tells us that he first responded naturally, *"And Jehoshaphat feared..."* But then he responded spiritually and *"...set himself to seek the Lord, and proclaimed a fast throughout all Judah."* The entire kingdom gathered together to *"...ask help of the Lord...."* His first reaction was to look at the visible, the undeniable facts in his circumstances, and in doing so he did what any sane, responsible human being would do – he feared. But he did not stay there. Because there was an atmosphere for faith in his life, because he was accustomed to worshipping God, he was able to quickly change his focus from his alarming circumstances to his almighty God. Because he was acquainted with the ways of God, he was able to move from the visible danger to the invisible Deliverer - from fear to faith. He accepted God's invitation to believe. When he compared himself to the three armies it produced fear, but when he compared the three armies to God, it produced faith. You say, "Well, he had no choice. He had to trust God; otherwise he was doomed." No, he did not have to trust God, and neither do you. He could have led his people to retreat in fear, in which case they would have been run over and killed. Or they could have fool-ishly chosen to fight in their own strength, in which case they would have still been destroyed. The thing that caused Jehoshaphat to choose to trust God was not the perplexity of the situation but the preparation of his heart.

In verses 5-17, we see how Jehoshaphat came to an **assurance** of the will of God, which enabled him to stand in faith and see the salvation of the Lord. He stood up in the midst of the people and began to pray out loud. Now keep in mind, the armies were approaching quickly, and there was little time to waste. Most leaders in similar circumstances would have been racking their brain trying to figure out what to do and would have been frantically running around trying to do it. But Jehoshaphat chose to do the only thing that really made sense, he chose to spend his precious time find-ing the will of God as well as His instructions as to how to execute it. In verse 6, he reminded God of His sovereignty and His power over heaven and earth, and in so doing he reminded himself, as well as those who heard him pray. In verse 7, he recalled the promises of God to Abraham and thus to Jehoshaphat and his people. In verses 8-10, he began to get a sense of the will of God as he recalled God's presence among them and His prom-ised protection of them. It would not make "spiritual sense," therefore, for them to be defeated. He also recalled that the land the armies were coming to claim had already been given to the people of God as a permanent pos-session. Again, defeat did not make sense in the light of God's covenant truth. With a growing sense of God's will and plan in his mind and heart, Jehoshaphat appealed to the Lord, *"O our God,* [based upon all we have discussed – Your presence and Your promise] *wilt Thou not judge them?*

for we have no might against this great company that cometh against us; neither know we what to do: but our eyes are upon thee [literally – our face is turned to You]. " He had arrived at the place we must all come to in faith, the end of himself. Through interaction with God in prayer, Jehoshaphat was rapidly becoming convinced that victory was God's will, and upon that belief he **asked** God to give it. Then it happened; the sensing of God's will became settled fact. The specific will of God was revealed for this specific situation and specific in-structions came with it. Jahaziel stood up in the midst of the people and said (v. 15), "*... Thus saith the Lord unto you, Be not afraid or dismayed by reason of* [by thinking about] *this great multitude; for the battle is not*

As God's chosen blessed sons and daughters we are expected to attempt something large enough that failure is guaranteed unless God steps in.

Bruce Wilkinson (2)

yours but God's. " Then came God's instructions, the activity of faith (the "go and do") that always occurs in a faith event. He told them (v.16, 17), *"Tomorrow go ye down against them..."* He told them exactly where to go, when to go, and what to do when they got there. He assured them (v.17) that the battle was not <u>going</u> to be won but that it had <u>already</u> been won. Jehoshaphat **accepted** it as finished and as a result was enabled to worship God in faith (v.18), praise Him in faith (v. 19), and then march out in faith (v.20).

After receiving assurance of the will of God and accepting it as fin-ished work, Jehoshaphat entered into the **activity** of faith. They (v.20), *"...rose up early in the morning and went forth into the wilderness..."* and **as they went** Jehoshaphat proclaimed victory before it actually took place, *"...Believe in the Lord your God, so shall ye be established; believe His prophets, so shall ye prosper."* God will always tell us to go, do, act, and obey. We wait to know His will, but once it is known then the <u>waiting is over</u> and the <u>work</u> begins. Now we must speak the word of faith, sing the praise of faith, and act as if it is already done. Jehoshaphat appointed sing-ers, and as they stood before the armies singing and praising God, the armies became confused and panicked and destroyed each other. The will of God was **accomplished** just as He had promised. *"And when they began to sing and to praise, the Lord set ambushments against the children of Ammon, Moab, and mount Seir, which were come against Judah; and they were smitten"* (v. 22). When the people of Judah stepped out against those armies in obedience to the will of God, all they were doing was entering into His finished work. Verse 24 tells us, *"And when Judah came toward the watch tower in the wilderness, they looked unto the multitude, and behold, they were dead bodies fallen to the earth, and none escaped."* It appeared to them that those men had just died, but from God's perspective they were dead long before Jehoshaphat even received the news that they were coming. In verses 25-27, we see the outcome of the completed faith event in the life of the Believer - abundant blessing, victory, and joy unspeakable. God always blesses in abundance, and He always gives more than we expect or ask for. Then in verses 29-30 we see the outcome from God's perspective – God is glorified and a new and fresh testimony is established to His power, goodness, and faithfulness. We read, *"And the fear of God was on all the kingdoms of those countries, when they had heard that the Lord fought against the enemies of Israel. So the realm of Jehoshaphat was quiet: for his God gave him rest round about."* The faith process always ends in supernatural rest for the child of God.

Now as wonderful as this story is, and as clearly as it illustrates the faith process, it does not end with verse 30. Rather, it continues with a warning. Jehoshaphat was truly a man of God, and he lived by faith – but he also made a mistake, a costly mistake you and I are just as capable of making. He apparently failed to see that while we can rest in faith we dare not relax. After every great victory of faith there will always be the temptation to let down, to go into neutral or "cruise control." But we must never allow slack in the ropes of faith. Coasting in the Christian life always results in compromise. We must always be careful to maintain the "tension" of trusting God in our life in order to resist the temptation of turning aside to the world. It is just as important to intensify your worship and fellowship with God after the victory as it is before, maybe even more so. Look at what happened to Elijah after Mount Carmel. Somehow, Jehoshaphat veered off course and gave up the will and ways of God for the works of his own hands, and it ended in ruin. God never intends for any of us to reach a point in our Christian life and ministry where we can do it on our own. When you start feeling self-confident and self-sufficient, you are in big trouble. So then how do we avoid getting to that dangerous place? By constantly maintaining an atmosphere for faith in our life, which continuously makes us receptive to God's invitations to receive His will and trust Him for the impossible. We must always be willing for God to get us into deep enough trouble so that only He can get us out. If we are always out beyond where we can go, then we will always be trusting the One Who keeps us there. It is imperative that we maintain a life of worship, so that we maintain a life of faith, so that we maintain a life of pleasing God. Now let's look at an example of just such a life from Christian history.

James Hudson Taylor- A Man with a Mission

If you have never read the life story of James Hudson Taylor (1832–1905), founder of the China Inland Mission and missionary evangelist to China for 51 years, I strongly encourage you to do so. Any Christian who is serious about living a life of real faith will greatly benefit from the extraordinary example of this amazing life. The story of faith I am sharing with you here involves the leading of God to expand the mission and ministry of the China Inland Mission to such an extent that was, by all human reasoning, totally impossible. You will find a brief history of Hudson Taylor and the CIM at the end of this chapter.

J. Hudson Taylor

In 1886, twenty years after Hudson and Maria Taylor landed in Shanghai under the newly formed China Inland Mission, the total number of missionaries on the field was 187. Mr. J.W. Stevenson, one of the original 24 missionaries, had just that year become Deputy Director of the mission. He and the famous Pastor Shi had spent several weeks together traveling through the northern provinces, and they were filled with enthusiasm as well as a keen awareness of the need for more workers. In a letter written to Mrs. Taylor on September 16, 1886, Mr. Stevenson said, "We are greatly encouraged out here, and we are asking and receiving definite blessings for this hungry and thirsty land. We are fully expecting at least one hundred fresh laborers to arrive in China in 1887" (3). In Mid-November a new Council was formed to help Mr. Stevenson. It was made up of the provincial superintendents of the mission. It was to this new Council that the suggestion of "The Hundred" was first made. But before it convened, Mr. Taylor, Mr. Stevenson, and others met together for an entire week for fasting, prayer, and waiting upon God. "So it was with prepared hearts that they came to the considerations of the questions before them" (4). When the suggestion of The Hundred was first mentioned to Hudson Taylor he initially offered some "practical objections," not the least of which was the additional money it would require to get a hundred new workers to the field. After all, the total number of missionaries at the time was only 187 and the mission had been in existence for 20 years. How could they possibly believe God for a hundred more in just one year? The answer was – by faith. Hudson Taylor's biography records, "So, little by little they were led on, until in the Council meetings, such was the atmosphere of faith and prayer that the thought could strike root. Begun with God, it could not fail to be taken up by hearts so truly waiting upon Him; and before leaving An-King Mr. Taylor was writing home quite naturally: We are praying for one hundred new missionaries in 1887. The Lord help in the selection and provide the means" (5).

Here we clearly see that God had created an <u>atmosphere</u> for faith among the mission leaders, not only in their private, personal lives but among them in a corporate sense as well. And in that atmosphere, He brought them to a point of <u>acceptance</u> of faith by making the needs so evident and irresistible to them that they could not say no to God's invitation. They were being prompted by the Holy Spirit to believe God for the impossible. They were being drawn out far beyond where they could go without the supernatural intervention and provision of God. They were invited to faith and they responded correctly because their hearts were prepared. Then one day when Mr. Taylor was dictating a letter he said, "We are praying for and expecting a hundred new missionaries to come out in 1887." And then he exclaimed, "If you showed me a photograph of the whole hundred, taken in China, I could not be more sure than I am now" (6)! He had moved from saying, "we are praying for" to "we are praying for and expecting." In this case, the <u>assurance</u> of God's will and the acceptance of it as done happened almost simultaneously, and right on the heels of that came the <u>activity</u> of faith. Mr. Taylor sent out a paper throughout the mission asking fellow workers to put down their name to pray for The Hundred. He sent a cable to London which read, "Praying for a hundred new missionaries in 1887." The biography continues, "Thus the step was taken and the mission committed to a program that might well have startled even its nearest friends. Yet it was in no spirit of rashness or merely human energy. Far too deeply had Mr. Taylor learned the lessons of experience to embark upon such an enterprise without the assurance that he was being led by God" (7).

At the very outset of this great venture for God, satan raised up his head through an unexpected source - a veteran missionary in Shanghai. Upon hearing the announcement of faith, he said to Mr. Taylor, "I am delighted to hear that you are praying for large reinforcements. You will not get a hundred of course within a year; but you will get many more than if you did not ask for them." Undeterred, Mr. Taylor thanked him and then replied, "We have the joy beforehand; but I feel sure that if spared, you will share it in welcoming the last of the hundred to China" (8). It happened just that way. Hudson Taylor could resist satan's temptation to doubt because he knew the settled will of God. As the year 1886 came to a close the mission gathered together for two days of prayer. On December 29 he wrote to Maria, "Tomorrow and the day after we give to waiting on God for blessing. We need two days at least this year. We have much to praise for, much to expect, but satan will be busy, and we must be prepared by living near to God, by putting on the whole armor of God" (9). The work of faith had begun and so had the inevitable warfare.

In addition to the hundred new workers, a specific request was also made for an extra ten thousand pounds ($50,000) of income for the year. In 1886 that was an enormous amount of money, especially for a mission that did not solicit funds or take up offerings. Not only was a specific amount requested, but a specific way for it to come. They asked God for it to be given in large gifts so as to not overload the home staff with additional correspondence.

On May 26 the twenty-first anniversary meeting was held, and by that time fifty-four of the Hundred had been accepted and many of those had already sailed for China. At that meeting, Mr. Taylor made these remarks, "It is not great faith you need, but faith in a great God. We need a faith that rests upon a great God, and expects Him to keep His own word and to do just as He has promised. I do want you, dear friends, to realize this principle of working with God and asking Him for everything. If the work is at the command of God, then we can go to Him in full confidence for workers; and when God gives the workers, we can go to Him for means to supply their needs. We always accept a suitable worker, whether we have funds or not. Depend upon it, God's work, done in God's way, will never lack God's supplies" (10). He later said, "The Lord wants His people to be, not rich, but in full fellowship with Him Who is rich" (11). Throughout the year over 600 candidates were interviewed and funds were miraculously received with no appeal being made. Not ten, but eleven thousand pounds were received and only in eleven large gifts! The biography of Hudson Taylor records the outcome of his faith, the <u>accomplishment</u> of the will of God. "It was about the beginning of November, when Mr. Taylor had the joy of announcing to the friends of the mission that their prayers were fully answered – all the hundred having been given and the funds supplied for their passages to China" (12).

God truly honored the faith of His servant, but that was not the end of the process in this great faith event in the life of Hudson Taylor and the China Inland Mission. The final stage was, and always is, the acknowledgement of the faithfulness of the Father, without which faith would be meaningless. Mr. Taylor wrote to Mr. Stevenson in China, "I have assured the friends that there will be a big hallelujah when they, the crowning party of The Hundred, reach Shanghai! It is not more than we expected God to do for us, but it is very blessed; and to see that God does answer, in great things as well as small, the prayers of those who put their trust in Him will strengthen the faith of multitudes" (13). In a publication entitled, "The History of the Church Missionary Society," the following statement was made in reference to The Hundred to the honor and glory of God, "Six times that number offered, but the Council, faithful to its principles, declined to lower the standard, and rejected five-sixths of the applicants; yet the exact number of one-hundred – not ninety-nine or a hundred and one, but one-hundred actually sailed within the year" (14). The last of The Hundred sailed for China on December 29, 1887. God had prompted the hearts of His servants to believe for a specific faith object and outcome and had honored their obedience to do so. They had, by faith, entered into the finished work and in doing so they saw the glory of God.

The same sequence that Jehoshaphat passed through centuries before had now been passed through by Hudson Taylor. It was not in response to a crisis, but in response to a call to expand the Kingdom of God. In the lives of both men, there was an atmosphere for faith. God had worked in their hearts so that they were willing to go through the process of believing. And in both cases the outcome was the same – the ultimate acknowledgement of the faithfulness and goodness of God, not only by those directly affected but by the onlookers as well. New and fresh testimonies were established to the honor and glory of God, one in Bible history and one in modern Christian history. Now, you may be asking, "Yes these are great examples of the faith process in action, and I can see how it works, but will it work for me?" Yes, my dear brother or sister in Christ, it certainly will. Jehoshaphat was a king and Hudson Taylor was an outstanding missionary evangelist, but they were also just plain ordinary human beings like you and me. Their capacity for faith was no greater and no different than yours. They were enabled by God to see Him do the impossible and they made the choice of faith. You and I as born-again children of God can do the same thing. Now, speaking of plain ordinary folks, I want to introduce you to a brother in Christ who was, by his own testimony, as ordinary as they come. I am referring to our old friend (now with Jesus), Dr. W. Wayne Allen, better known to those of us who knew him well as just "Brother Wayne." Brother Wayne Allen had more influence on our life and ministry of faith than anyone else. He was greatly used of God in helping initiate the ministry we are in today.

A Pastor with a Passion

In 1970, at age thirty, Brother Wayne Allen was serving as Director of Missions for the Indian Creek Baptist Association in Middle Tennessee. He was very happy in his ministry there, but he began to sense that God was leading him and his wife, Marcia, back to his hometown of Memphis. At the same time there was also a growing burden in his heart concerning the fact that high quality Christian education was available for young people attending college, but not for young people K –12. Wayne did not realize it at the time, but God was using this sensing and this burden to draw him into a faith event that would bring great glory to His Name.

In the spring of 1970, God opened the door for Wayne to become the pastor of East Park Baptist Church in Memphis. The church barely had enough people in attendance to justify the utility bill. In fact, knowing that they were about to close the doors for good, Wayne came on the condition that they would allow him to take what little money they had and do whatever he wanted to do with it. They agreed, and in June of that year he called me and asked if I would help him put on a "Jesus Festival" on the church

Dr. W. Wayne Allen

grounds. I was 23 at the time and was attending a local Bible college. Sheila and I were also heading up a citywide youth evangelism ministry and leading one of the first "Jesus bands" in the country. Ironically, the dying church was located on one of the busiest intersections of the city, and it proved to be a great location for a festival. The short version of the story, the whole of which we will tell in another book, is that the event took place and was a huge success. On the closing night over 5,000 young people gathered on the church lawn. Many were saved, and the church was re-born. Some of the deacons did not like the idea of painting the side of the church black with big psychedelic letters in fluorescent paint, but they recovered from the shock when they saw the auditorium packed inside.

Wayne was excited about the revival of the church and the rapid growth that occurred over the next couple of years, but he was still burdened about the need of Christian education in the city. God was using that burden to pressure Wayne into believing for the impossible. In 1971, he appointed a committee (they were Baptists, after all) to study the need for a school and the feasibility of building it on their existing property. The conclusion was that the school was definitely needed, but the property was too small to contain it. Wayne continued to pray and seek the will of God, and as he did, a picture began to form in his mind and the will of God began to become clear – so clear that he could take it to the church.

Now, nothing about this made any sense according to the world, or to logic, or to good business sense. Wayne was only 31 years old and had never graduated from college. He knew very little about the world of academics, and even though the church had grown, there were still fewer than 200 members and most of them were lower middle class folks. In other words, it was absolutely financially impossible for the church to buy land and build a school that had a projected cost of over six million dollars. Wayne, however, was not deterred. In fact he was challenged and energized by the magnitude of the impossibility, and he was so convinced it was the will of God to establish the school, that he began to talk about it as if it was already in existence. By the end of 1971 the church believed it too, and an effort to locate property was underway.

Wayne concluded at least ten acres of land was needed, and it should be within two miles of their present location. Weeks of search turned up nothing, however, making the project seem more impossible than ever. Then on Friday, December 29, 1971 a real estate agent called Wayne and told him that he had found a 14.2 acre piece of property that would be perfect, but it could not be bought outright. He explained that it would be sold the following Tuesday on a sealed bid basis. Wayne said he wanted to see it anyway and went with the agent to look at it. In recalling the story to me he said, "We drove out to the property, and the moment I saw it I knew that was the place. I told the agent, 'This is the property God has for us; I know it without a doubt'." All of a sudden Wayne had come to the place we will all come to eventually as we walk through a faith event, the place where you know what the specific will of God is. It is a place of settled fact and perfect peace. He now knew it was God's will to build the school, and he now knew where. He did not yet know how, but that was up to God.

Wayne went back to his office and called 34 men of the church to a special meeting to be held the following morning, Saturday, December 30. On that morning they all went out in a freezing rain to see the "promised land" and then came back to the church to pray and discuss. Wayne explained the situation, and several figures were suggested as to how much to bid for the property. Then Wayne told the men, "I want you all to bow your heads and close your eyes, and I am going to call out the possible bids we have discussed, beginning with the highest to the lowest. When I get to a number that you feel is God's will, raise your hand." He called out the highest number, which was $426,500. With every head bowed and every eye closed, every hand went up and it was settled. God had given the number – His number.

Following that meeting, every church member was called to a special business meeting on the following Sunday morning to vote on the bid. Wayne continued the story, "The vote was unanimous, and I told the people to start thanking and praising God for the land. Do not ask if I think we will get it. That is not faith. Just praise God for it in advance. We do not have to ask if we will get it because we already have it and it is ours. We have received it, and we should rejoice over it and tell everyone it is ours". Wayne had entered the activity of faith and had led the church to do the same. Now it was just a matter of walking it through to the end.

On Tuesday morning the church's sealed bid of $426,500 was submitted. The only other bid was from a very wealthy businessman, Mr. P., who was trying to buy the property for a synagogue. His sealed bid was $426,100. The church won the bid by only $400. Mr. P. was quite upset and called one of the church members (we will call him John). Mr P. knew John very well and asked him, "John, I have known you a long time, and you know I have never lost a bid unless my competitor had inside information. Now, I am asking you, did you have inside information as to how much to bid?" John then told him, "Yes we did, but I don't think you know him." Then Mr. P. demanded to know the man's name, and John told him, "His Name is Jesus Christ." With that, Mr. P. did not ask any more questions.

Within a few weeks the church held a praise celebration on the property and a faith offering was received. God miraculously provided the money to pay for the property, and by the time I joined the staff of the church in June 1973 construction of the huge new building was well underway. By mid-year, 1974 we were occupying the new facility. Across the front of the building there was a big sign that read "Nothing Is Impossible." The end result of this faith event in the life of a plain ordinary man and a very small church congregation was that a new and fresh testimony was established to the awesome power and unwavering faithfulness of God.

Now What about You?

You may not be faced with a situation like Jehoshaphat and you may not be in need of a hundred missionaries, and you may not be led of God to establish the largest private school system in America. But you are a child of God, living the life that God has called you to live. And in your life there are going to be many opportunities for you to enter into real faith events and see the glory of God. When you are faced with a need or situation in your circumstances that you cannot meet out of your own efforts and resources, do not panic and throw up your hands in despair. Rather, do what Jehoshaphat did - turn to God and trust Him for the impossible. When a desire rises up in your heart that is impossible for you to fulfill on your own, do not sink into discouragement and defeat. Look to God, and believe He loves you enough to perform the miraculous for you. If God leads you in a direction that you cannot go under your own power, then trust Him to take you there. Learn to recognize every adversity, every need, every desire, every crisis and trial, and every challenge as an opportunity to believe God. Take time to worship Him and to come to the knowledge of His will concerning your situation. Then take that step of faith. Enter the faith process and walk it through to the glorious end.

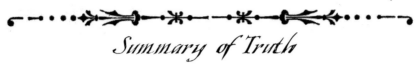

Summary of Truth

- ✤ God's dealings with each of us are always new, personal, and original.
- ✤ Opportunities in our lives to trust God (faith events) do not "just happen." They are deliberately created by God for the purpose of glorifying Himself.
- ✤ The thing that will cause you to trust God is not the perplexity of your situation but the preparation of your heart.
- ✤ After every victory of faith there will always come the temptation to let down, to relax, and to do so is always a mistake. It always results in compromise.
- ✤ God's work done in God's way will never lack God's support.
- ✤ If a faith event did not end with the acknowledgment of the faithfulness of God, it would be meaningless.
- ✤ Only one thing is required to enable us to see God do the impossible - the choice of faith in response to God's revealed will.
- ✤ God Loves YOU enough to perform the impossible through you.
- ✤ Every need, desire, crisis, and challenge is an opportunity to trust God.
- ✤ God does not demonstrate His power through the self-sufficient and the self-reliant but through the weak, the ordinary, the plain, and the simple.

NOW LET'S TAKE A MOMENT AND PRAY TOGETHER:

DEAR FATHER, I MAY NOT BE A GREAT KING, OR THE HEAD OF A WORLDWIDE MISSION AGENCY, OR THE FOUNDER OF SOME LARGE INSTITUTION, BUT LORD, I AM YOUR CHILD, AND AS SUCH I AM QUALIFIED TO EXERCISE MY CAPACITY FOR FAITH AND TRUST YOU FOR THE IMPOSSIBLE. IN ALL HONESTY LORD, IN MY FLESH, I DO NOT WANT TO BE STRETCHED BEYOND MY LIMITS AND I DO NOT WANT TO VENTURE OUTSIDE MY COMFORT ZONE. BUT LORD JESUS, IN MY HEART I DO WANT YOU TO USE ME TO GLORIFY YOURSELF AND I ASK YOU TO BRING SITUATIONS IN MY LIFE THAT WILL ENABLE ME TO DO JUST THAT. LORD, I THANK YOU FOR SHOWING ME THESE ILLUSTRATIONS OF HOW OTHERS WENT THROUGH THE FAITH PROCESS AND WALKED THROUGH FAITH EVENTS IN THEIR LIVES, BUT LORD, I WANT TO DO THE SAME THING. I WANT YOU TO DEMONSTRATE YOUR LOVE AND POWER THROUGH MY LIFE. SO, RIGHT NOW I SUBMIT MYSELF TO YOU TO USE AS YOU SEE FIT. LORD, I WELCOME OPPORTUNITIES

TO EXERCISE FAITH AND TRUST YOU FOR THE IMPOSSIBLE. I LOVE YOU, LORD JESUS AND I THANK YOU AGAIN FOR SAVING ME. IN YOUR NAME I PRAY. AMEN.

A BRIEF HISTORY OF JAMES HUDSON TAYLOR

Hudson Taylor was born to devoutly Christian parents in Barnsley, England in May 1832. From his birth his parents dedicated him to the Lord and to China. At the age of four he stated that when he was grown he intended to be a missionary to China. At age 17, however, he was still not saved. But one afternoon in June 1849 while alone in his father's library, he read a tract entitled "It Is Finished." The light of God broke through and he saw there was nothing to be done but to trust in the finished work of Jesus. He did, and he was saved right then and there. On December 2, he made a definite commitment to go to China. He found a copy of Luke's Gospel in the Mandarin dialect and began teaching himself Chinese. He did everything he could do to prepare himself for the calling God had placed upon his life. Jumping forward to September 19, 1853, we find him at age 21 departing for China under the auspices of the London based China Evangelization Society. He reached Shanghai on March 1, 1854. On Christmas Day 1856 he met his bride to be, a young English missionary named Maria. They were married on Jan 20, 1858. The following year Hudson became very ill, and they had to return to England in November 1860, seven years after his arrival in China. They referred to the next five and a half years spent in England as "the quiet years." Little did they realize at the time, however, the great purpose God had for taking them back to England rather than allowing them to remain uninterrupted in China. It was during these years that the China Inland Mission was born. It began as nothing more than a vision from God, received in Mr. Taylor's heart on the sands of Brighton Beach on June 25, 1865, and a name on a bank account which was opened on June 27 with only $50.00. But that was enough, evidenced by the fact that on May 26, 1866 Hudson and Maria, their four children and the first 24 CIM missionaries sailed for Shanghai. It was the beginning of a life and ministry that would result in 849 missionaries going to the field during Mr. Taylor's lifetime, as well as the development of a witnessing Chinese church of over 125,000 born-again Christians. Hudson Taylor died June 3, 1905 having lived by faith and having seen the glory of God.

The Faith Process Illustrated

Part Two: From Personal Experience

"God would be untrue to the very essence of His nature, which is love, and to the very heart of His work, which is grace, if He failed even once to respond to real faith."

Ruth Paxson (1)

*I*n the previous chapter, we looked at illustrations of the faith process taken from the Bible and from Christian history, but now I want to look at some that are a little closer to home. They might not be quite as dramatic as Jehoshaphat defeating three armies with the song of faith, or Hudson Taylor sending a hundred missionaries to the field in one year, or Wayne Allen building the largest Christian school in America, but they mean a lot to me because they happened in MY life. And let me say this, as you begin to enter the faith process in relation to various areas of your life, you will begin to be able to say the same thing. You see the wonderful thing about the <u>life</u> of faith is that it ultimately becomes a <u>history</u> of faith in you, and that history of faith in you becomes a <u>heritage</u> of faith for the generations that follow you. Over the years there have been many times when Sheila and I have seen the faith process play out in our lives, and I plan to share a lot of them in another book, but for now in this limited space I want to share just a few.

A Home at Last for Shad and Sheila

In the fall of 1971, Sheila and I sat out on the porch of an old house we were renting in Jackson, Tennessee. We were attending Union University at the time, and as we sat there we speculated as to whether or not we would ever own our own home. We concluded that we probably never would, considering God's call upon our life. We also concluded that we were perfectly fine with that if that's what it took to do what God had called us to do. Then after graduation in 1973, we took what we thought to be a temporary, summer staff position at East Park Baptist Church in Memphis. It turned out to last over four years, and after the first year the church moved us into a nice brick home that belonged to the church. It was located in a very quiet and desirable neighborhood. Many times Sheila and I commented to each other that, "we sure would like to own a home like this." In June of 1977 that became a real possibility, except for one thing – God had called us into the ministry we are in today, and we were about to resign our position at the church. I will tell the whole story later, but for now let me just say that in order to get the house we had to stay at the church. But that was not going to happen because God had called us to a new ministry. So for the next four years we lived in a townhouse, and then for another three years we lived in that yellow two-story house I told you about. It was very nice, but it was still rented.

That brings us to January 1984. Sheila and I had long ago given up the idea of ever having a home of our own, but as the kids grew older, the desire to have our own place settled in upon our hearts and upon the hearts of our children. We talked about it many times, but we seemed to be blocked at every turn. We had no stated verifiable income, at least not that a lender would recognize. We also had no down payment money and no way to get any. We would not allow ourselves to think much about it, and we did not discuss it with the kids, because the whole thing was just SO impossible. But, during the course of 1983 the desire seemed to grow in our hearts whether we wanted it to or not, and as ridiculous as it was, we found ourselves talking seriously about having a home of our own.

For many years I had been accustomed to getting up early in the morning to spend time with God alone. On January 2, 1984 I was up at 2:00AM and on my knees in the den of our rented house. As I knelt there with my Bible open before the Lord, I sensed God telling me to get a sheet of paper and write down some things to trust Him for during the coming year. I believe I can truthfully say there was an **atmosphere** for faith in my life at that moment. More than anything, I wanted to know the will of God. As I listened, He spoke - and as He spoke, I wrote. In the quietness of that morning God spoke and issued me a personal invitation to believe for many things, including a home for our family. There it was - an **awakening** to a new opportunity to see God do the utterly miraculous, an opportunity to accept God's option of faith. Was I dreaming? Was I imagining things? No, I was not. What I heard was not spoken to mind or emotions, but to my spirit. If it had originated in my mind, I would have listed all the reasons why it would not work and then let it go. If it had originated in my emotions, I would have succumbed to fear of failure and let it go. But because it came from God, through my inner man, I could not let it go. As I have said, one of the strongest indicators of the will of God is that you cannot let go of the thing you are trusting for, and it will not let go of you.

Now came the issue of **assurance**. God had spoken to me in my heart, and I believed what I had heard; yet there were so many questions that remained. Even though I had heard the voice of His Spirit, I still needed to come to that place where I could see the finished work and publicly proclaim it as done. During the months of January and February nothing happened. Then in the second week of March, I went on a project to Haiti and my long time friend, Art Bailey, went with me. While we were there I shared with Art what I believed God had said to me. He then said, "Brother, I have a good friend in Memphis who is a builder, and I think we should talk to him when we get home." I said, "But, Art, I have no visible income and no down payment." Art said, "Let's talk to him anyway."

So a few days after we returned home, Art set up a meeting with his friend. We went to his house and the next thing I knew he and Sheila were looking at floor plans and discussing how she would like to modify them. The whole time, in spite of what God had said, I was thinking, "This is crazy. They are talking about a house that is impossible to build!" Then the builder said, "Let's go tomorrow to look at lots." Then I thought, "Okay, this is getting out of hand." But sure enough, the next day he picked us up in his truck, and we drove around in the rain and mud looking at what would soon be subdivided lots. Sheila looked at what would be a corner lot and said, "I like that one." The builder said, "It's yours, Sheila." Then I thought, "Lord I know what You said, but I think this has gone far enough." Before we got out of his truck the builder said, "Okay, tomorrow we will talk to the banker." At that point I said out loud, "Okay, this has gone far enough. There is no way we can talk to a banker because we have nothing to talk with!" The builder said, "Let me worry about that. I'll pick you up tomorrow." So the next day we sat down with the builder in the lender's office. They talked "real estate language" for a while and then we left. When we got out to his truck the builder said, "Okay, it's all settled. I am going to build your house."

Now you would think I would have been excited, and I was, in a way. But there were still a lot of unanswered questions, and there was still something missing in my heart that the builder and the banker could not give me - total assurance of the will of God. Yes I had heard God speak in my heart, and I had heard what the builder had said, but... So I continued to meet with the Lord in the early morning hours and on April fourth God gave me what I needed – absolute assurance. And it came from His Word, very unexpectedly. I was reading from Nehemiah 6, and as I read, my eyes fell upon verse 15, which reads, *"So the wall was finished in the twenty and fifth day of the month Elul, in fifty and two days."* As I read those words, the Holy Spirit drove into my heart two phrases, "twenty and fifth day" and "fifty and two days." I was not expecting God to speak to me in that way, but He did, and right then and there it was settled. I counted forward 52 days from April 4 and it landed on May 25, the "twenty and fifth day" of the month. It was settled. I could see it. Not only would the house be built and not only would it be ours, but it would be completed on May 25. The moment I saw that, I said to the Lord, "Lord, I **ask** You to do this, and I receive it as done. Thank You for giving this to us." I can honestly say that from that moment forward there was never another doubt about whether or not it would be done, because it was <u>already</u> done. It was just a matter now of walking it through to the end.

Now came the **activity** of faith and there certainly was some. First came confession - public declaration, the word of faith. I called the builder later that day and told him, "Brother, I have some news for you. The house you are building for us will be finished on the twenty-fifth of next month in fifty-two days." He replied, "That is impossible, we have never built a house in that short a time. We just now poured the foundation and it is just not possible to finish that quickly." I said, "It is this time." Then there was acting in accordance with God's will. Long before we had the loan secured and the financing settled, long before we could legally say that the house that was going up on that corner lot was "ours," we acted just as if it was. We went out there every day to watch the construction, and Sheila had plenty of INstruction for the CONstruction. Even though we still had a lot to do to secure the financing, we did nothing but offer praise and thanksgiving to God. We never asked Him to work out the details for the loan that was impossible for us to get. We just acted as if we already had it, and then followed the steps the builder told us to take in order to get it. Of course the devil was on hand to oppose us. Without going into details, just let me say he tried everything to stop us from getting the house. He created confusion in the paperwork, tried to cast doubt about our credibility in the minds of the lender and so on, even down to the last minute. We had worked our way through the financing process and our loan was finally lying on the underwriter's desk. She said (we found out later) that she could not approve the loan, because the numbers just would not allow it. But then she looked more closely at the names on the papers and saw that it was Shad and Sheila. She then said, "Oh, I know Shad and Sheila. We went to church together. These are great Christian people and there will be no problem with this." With that she stamped it "APPROVED." God had His person, a born-again Believer, in the right place at the right time. It had already been stamped approved in heaven, and approved in our hearts, and now it was stamped approved in the visible, in the natural material realm for all to see. The will of God had been **accomplished** just as He promised.

The last painter walked out and called it finished on May 25, 1984 - 52 days from the time the foundation was poured. It was done just as God said it would be from Nehemiah 6:15. Furthermore, from the time Sheila and the builder began looking at plans to the time we moved in on May 26 we did not spend one penny – no down payment, no out of pocket costs, nothing. I do not know to this day exactly how all that happened, but I do know the first dollar we spent was on our first payment, which did not come until after we returned in July from a six-week overseas campaign. We moved into the house on May 25, and left a house full of boxes on May 26 to go to Brazil. But, that is another story. Once again the faith process had been brought to completion in the life of one of His children, a process that rightly ended in the **acknowledgement** of His faithfulness. Once again God received honor and glory because someone responded to His invitation to make the choice of faith and believe. Now, let me be clear about something. The fact that the "someone" in this case was Sheila and me is totally irrelevant. It does not matter who the someone is, just so long it is somebody - and anybody will do. Every Christian has the right, the privilege, and the responsibility to believe. All you need is a reason, and if you will ask Him to, God will provide you with that.

A Real Office for the Ministry

The next illustration I would like to share with you also comes from the year 1984 and takes place during the summer after we moved into our new home. For seven years our ministry "headquarters" had been located in our house, but with the addition of volunteer secretarial help (Wanda Bailey, Art's wife) the need for a "real" office became very apparent. As we entered 1984, it had become a concentrated matter of prayer. Our rented house was located just down the street from a beautiful office complex containing four identical buildings. Every day I would drive past them on my way to the post office, and I would dream of having our ministry head-quarters located in one of them. Then I would return to our "office" located in the living room of our house.

On January 2, 1984, the same morning God spoke to me about our new home, He also spoke to me about an office for the ministry. As I was kneel-ing before the Lord at 2:00 AM making my list, I wrote down "an office for the ministry." Then the Holy Spirit spoke in my heart and asked me a very definite question, "Where do you want to have your office?" Without hesi-tation I answered out loud, "Lord, I want to have an office in that first building in that complex, Building D, 1755 Lynnfield Road." Then I "heard" Him say in my heart, "I am going to give you that place – write it down." So, out beside "An office for the ministry" I wrote, "Building D – 1755." That same month I conducted a campaign in the Philippines and then an-other in Haiti in March. We moved into our new home in May, went to Brazil, and returned in mid July. In all that time nothing had actually been "done" about the office, but all along Sheila and I continued to believe and to confess that God was going to give us that place. When I thought about office space, there just was no alternative to what God had said.

When we returned from Brazil, we realized that something had to be done about an office, because there was no place for one in the new home. I had no idea how much office space rented for, because I had never rented any. I also had no idea how to find out. What I did know was that Sheila and I had committed the whole thing to the Lord, and we believed God would allow us to commit to $350 per month and no more. God always sets the parameters for faith. We had also concluded that to begin with we could manage with a small space if it was divided a certain way. We figured that 350 square feet would suffice. Then in looking at the schedule for the re-mainder of the year, which included another Philippines project in Octo-ber, we concluded it would be best to take on the job of setting up a new office in November. So, we were looking for:

1. An office at 1755 Lynnfield Road, building D,
2. 350 square feet of space,
3. $350 per month rent,
4. The option to move in November.

With all that in mind, I did the only thing I knew to do – I opened the yellow pages. I saw that there were hundreds of real estate people listed, and not having a clue as to which one to call, I asked God to show me. As my eyes scanned across the pages, a listing in very small print seemed to jump out at me. It was for Mr. Wyatt A. I picked up the phone, dialed the number, and he answered. I began by telling him who we were and what we did, and he responded by letting me know that he was a Christian. Then I explained what we needed. With that he responded, "Well, Shad, I think I might have just what you are looking for. Do you know where the Lynnfield Office Park is?" I could not believe he asked me that question. I said, "Yes I do, I have been looking at those buildings for years." Then He said, "Well, I have a space that will soon be available in building D, 1755 Lynnfield." My heart jumped! Then he continued, "It is fairly small, only 350 square feet, but maybe it will work for you." At that, I asked how much was the rent, and he replied, "$350 per month." I almost shouted, "Wyatt, I'll take it!" Then he said, "Okay, great. But there is just one small problem. The space has been vacated, but the current lease expires at the end of October. That means I can give you the lease now, but you cannot move in until the first of November, at which time your first month's rent will come due." I could not believe what I was hearing. God was not only providing exactly what He had promised in January, and exactly what we had asked for, but He was doing it in the exact way we had asked and in the exact time frame.

Since the space was empty, Wyatt allowed us to begin work on it in October and by the time I returned from the Philippines, Sheila had it ready to move into. What a glorious day of rejoicing we had on November 1, 1984 – the day we moved into the promised possession. The thing that had been real in our hearts for the past ten months was now real in the visible. We occupied and expanded that space over the next nine years, and there was not a day we walked through those doors that we did not recall the goodness and faithfulness of God. Through those years we were faced with many situations in which we had to see the miraculous hand of God or we would go under. But in all those times, our very surroundings provided us with a visible reminder that God is real and He can be trusted. On January 2, 1984, God stepped into the atmosphere for faith He had created in our lives and initiated a process of faith that would once again end in the acknowledgment and recognition of Who He really is.

Braces for Michael

In the last chapter we looked at a king dealing with a crisis in circumstances, a situation that threatened the national security of his country. That would certainly seem like something that God would be interested in. Then we saw a man responding to the leading of God to expand the work of a mission that would result in reaching thousands of people for Jesus. We KNOW God is interested in THAT. We can be sure also that God would be interested in helping a man establish a Christian school that would bless the lives of thousands of young people for decades to come. Then in this chapter we found a man and his wife desiring a home for themselves and their children, as well as office space from which to operate the ministry God had called them to. Of course, these things are not as "important" perhaps as national security, or the salvation of souls, or Christian education for thousands of kids, but they are still pretty important. Now, however, we come to a situation about which some may ask, "Does God really care about such small insignificant things as a kid needing braces?" Dear friend, I guarantee you He does. There is no instance, no need, no desire, and no trial in the Christian life to which the faith process should not and cannot be applied. If it is important to you, it is important to God. Remember, it is not the object of faith that brings glory to God, but the process. Let me share this last illustration with you.

It was the spring of 1983, and our son, Michael, would turn fourteen in June. Sheila and I had been noticing for some time that it appeared he needed some orthodontic work on his teeth, and if anything was going to be done about it, it needed to be done soon. Our financial condition at the time, however, would not allow us to do anything. So during my early morning times with the Lord, I began to discuss the need with Him. Sheila and I prayed together and examined our options in the natural realm. There didn't seem to be any. An atmosphere for faith in our daily walk certainly existed, and the awakening to an opportunity to believe God for the impossible had certainly occurred. The question now was what should we believe God to do? We needed assurance of His will. It was for sure we were not going to figure it out or work it out on our own. In fact I tried, and it produced nothing.

Every time I looked at Michael, I felt like the worst father and the biggest failure in the world. How could I claim to be trusting God when I could not even afford to put braces on my son's teeth? Satan, the accuser, is always on hand to level the worst kind of accusations against us. There is nothing that hurts the heart of a father more than to feel he cannot meet the basic needs of his family, especially when he is constantly telling them how they can trust God. As the days passed I became more desperate, and finally one day, feeling the pressure to do "something," I called our family dentist and asked him to recommend an orthodontist. He said, "Shad, I suggest you take Michael to see Dr. B. He is a fine Christian, and I am sure he will help you." So we called and made the appointment. When we walked into the office and looked around, I knew we were in the wrong place. I felt like I had just walked into the living room of one of the finest homes in Memphis. When I went to the window to sign in, the lady told me that before we could see the doctor I would have to pay a $100. I said, "You mean I have to pay a hundred dollars just to talk to him – before he even does anything?" She said yes, and I gave her the money – money I really needed for other things. It earned us a conversation with the doctor, during which we were informed that Michael would need extensive work, and it was going to be very expensive. He also told me that the lady at the window would tell me how to pay for it. So with that, I went back to her, and she explained that I would have to pay $500 up front and would be given a payment book as if I was buying a car. For the price, I might as well have been! So when we left I thought to myself, "Shad, you just paid $100 to find out what you already know; you can't afford to do this."

I continued to pray, and a day or so later I had an idea – not a good one as it turned out, but it was all I could think of. I wrote the doctor a letter explaining that I was an evangelist and just getting started in a new ministry. I felt embarrassed to have to tell him, but I also thought that as a Christian he might be sympathetic and consider my request. I explained our pressing financial situation and asked him if he would consider letting me pay out the initial $500 by the month. I told him I was not looking for any special treatment or a reduced price. I just needed help getting over that $500 hurdle. I was afraid to send that letter, because I was afraid that he might have the same opinion of me as a father that I did. But I felt I had to do it, so I mailed it. Then I waited – one week, two weeks - no reply. By the third week it was obvious I was not going to receive a reply, and my "great idea" was not going to work. I was out of options, completely, and that was exactly where I needed to be – in a position where the only place I could look was to God Himself.

Day by day I continued to pray and seek the will of God. Then one Wednesday afternoon I received a call from a good friend, named Chuck, with whom I regularly attended a Thursday morning prayer breakfast. He asked me if I wanted him to pick me up the next morning and us ride together. I said yes, and on Thursday morning I was up very early and ready to go about an hour ahead of time. I spent time with the Lord in prayer, as always, and again put the "braces situation" before Him, as I had done for weeks. Knowing it would be a while before Chuck would arrive, I got a cup of coffee and walked outside to sit in a swing and wait for him. Then it happened – God gave the assurance. As I rounded the corner of the house to go to the back patio, God spoke to me in my heart as clearly as if He was standing right in front of me physically. He said, "Shad, Chuck is going to pay for Michael to have braces." I was stunned. In fact I stopped dead in my tracks and just stood there holding the coffee for a minute or so. The voice was not audible, of course, but there was no doubt that God had spoken, and there was now no question about if it was going to be done; it was already finished. There was nothing left to ask for so I just said, "Lord, I accept this gift from You, and I thank You for doing this for me."

I was so excited I could hardly stand it, but then I thought, "Should I tell Chuck? Does he know about this? What should I do?" About five minutes later he pulled into the driveway, and I got in his truck. I did not say anything for a while, and he didn't either. We just made small talk on our way to the breakfast. All during the meeting I wondered what I should do, what I should say. After it was over we left, and about half way to our house Chuck said, "Shad, can I ask you a personal question?" I answered, "Sure, brother, what is it?" He asked, "Does Michael need braces?" I could hardly answer, but I finally did, "Yes, Chuck, he does." "What are you doing about it?" he asked. I said, "There is nothing I can do." Then he said, "Well, I have been praying about this, because I just suspected that at his age he might need braces. Most kids do, you know." He continued, "Well anyway, I want to pay to have him fitted for whatever he needs." I was almost speechless, but I was not surprised. Then he said, "But I need to know if you care which doctor he goes to?" I told him it did not matter to me, as long as Michael got what he needed. Then Chuck said he wanted Michael to see the man that his son went to - a wonderful Jewish orthodontist. In fact, he said he would make the appointment and go with us on the first visit.

The appointment was made and we went to see the orthodontist. He looked at Michael and then told us, "Your son doesn't need braces, all he needs is an appliance to wear in his mouth to adjust his jaw line. The worst thing you could do to this kid is put braces on him." I asked how much it would cost and he replied, "Don't worry about that right now. Let's just get Michael fixed up, and Chuck and I will take care of all that later." We thanked the doctor, and then Chuck went to the accounting lady, had a few words with her, and then we left. Michael was fitted for the appliance, Chuck paid the bill, and the faithfulness of God was proven - again.

I know this illustration of the faith process is a little different from the others, but I am including it because I want you to see that God cares about every detail of your life – even the things that, as I said before, do not threaten national security or save souls. If Michael had not gotten his jaw adjusted, it would not be the end of the world, and I am sure he would have found some girl to marry him even with his teeth sticking out. He was a nice kid after all. But that is not the issue. The issue is there was something in the life of this father, in relation to his family, that was vitally important to him – and therefore, it was important to God. It was important enough that God allowed it to be turned into a faith event, to which the faith process could be applied, with the result that the Mom and Dad received maximum joy, and God received maximum glory.

Again, What about You?

Now dear friend, let me ask you, is God drawing you into a faith event in your life? Probably. Do you have needs that can only be met by the miraculous provision of God? Are there desires in your heart that are so big that you dare not give serious consideration to them because they are so impossible? Has God nudged you from His Word over some particular issue or prompted you in your heart by some means? Has some sort of crisis arisen in your circumstances, something that has left you reeling and feeling helpless and hopeless? Have you all of a sudden found yourself in a financial firestorm? Do you think God may be calling you to some ministry you are not equipped to do by means of your natural abilities and resources? Are you being challenged by the Lord to expand your business to a level you know is impossible without His intervention? Is God telling you to increase your giving to a point that will take you out beyond your financial capabilities, maybe even to the point of appearing to threaten the security of your family? I could continue asking this same question in different ways, but you get the point of the question. Is God inviting you to make the choice of faith, to enter into the faith process and believe Him for the impossible? Is God drawing you by some means into a faith event? I have repeated the seven-stage sequence over and over. Now, you take your situation and apply the sequence to it. You may ask, "But will it work for me?" Yes, my friend, it will. Notice that Jehoshaphat, Hudson Taylor, Wayne

Allen, Shad Williams, and YOU all have something in common; we are all made of dust. We are all ordinary human beings, we all have the exact same capacity for faith, and we all have the same opportunities to trust God. The only thing that makes us different is our choices. I encourage you to choose to enter the faith process, and believe God for the impossible.

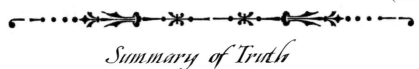

Summary of Truth

✤ Our life of faith ultimately becomes our history of faith, which eventually becomes a heritage of faith for the generations that follow us.

✤ One of the strongest indicators of the will of God is not only that you cannot let go of the thing you are trusting for but also it will not let go of you.

✤ Sometimes, even though we have heard God speak in our heart, we still need further assurance before we can take a decisive step of faith, and when we need it, God will provide it.

✤ God sets the parameters for our faith and then works according to the parameters He sets.

✤ There is no instance, no circumstance, no need, no desire, and no trial in the Christian life to which the faith process cannot be applied, regardless how large or small. If it is important to you, it is important to God.

✤ Accusations of worthlessness and threats of failure always come from the devil.

✤ God does not need our best efforts and fleshly schemes; He only needs our trust.

✤ We are all ordinary human beings made of dust. The only thing that makes us different is whether or not we choose to believe God by faith.

NOW LET'S TAKE A MOMENT AND PRAY TOGETHER:

ONCE AGAIN, LORD JESUS, I SEE FROM THESE ILLUSTRATIONS, TAKEN FROM THE LIVES OF ORDINARY PEOPLE LIKE ME, THAT THE FAITH PROCESS IS REAL AND IT WORKS FOR EVERYONE WHO WILL CHOOSE TO BELIEVE. SO, LORD, I ASK YOU TO HELP ME MAKE THE CHOICE OF FAITH. I THANK YOU THAT YOU LOVE ME ENOUGH, AND YOU CARE ABOUT ME ENOUGH, TO SEND ME OPPORTUNITIES TO TRUST YOU FOR THE IMPOSSIBLE. YOU ARE A GREAT AND MIGHTY GOD, AND I AM THRILLED YOU CHOOSE TO WORK IN AND THROUGH MY LIFE. THANK YOU AGAIN, LORD JESUS, FOR SAVING ME AND CHOOSING ME TO BE YOUR OWN. IN YOUR MATCHLESS NAME I PRAY. AMEN.

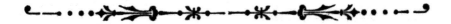

Chapter 25

The Faith Process Applied

"The faith life is the life lived by believing God under any circumstance."
Watchman Nee (1)

Thus far we have looked at the faith process by way of explanation, we have seen it illustrated from the Bible and from Christian history, and we have seen it in the life and ministry of this evangelist and his wife. But here, I want to help you to begin applying the faith process to your own life, personally and practically. Until you begin to experience it for yourself, it is all just theory.

God's Dealings with Each of Us Are Unique

Now, I know I am repeating myself, but please bear with me, and let me say to you again that the faith process is just that, a process, not a formula. I am strongly emphasizing this because I do not want you to fall into the trap of trying to copy the experience of someone else or trying to fit your situation into some kind of mold. God deals with all of us individually, personally, and uniquely. That is why I have presented the faith process as a pattern, not a rigid set of rules or steps. Everyone's experiences of faith are different, and there will be variations in the pattern from one life to another, as well as from one faith event to another in your own life. God is always original, and He is not going to do the same thing in my life that He does in yours. His creativity is not limited. So, for instance, if you are trusting God for a new home or trying to get braces for your child's teeth, don't expect God to do it the same way for you as He did for me, because He won't. He will have His Own way of doing it for you. But when it is all done, the sequence of the faith process carried out in your situation will likely be very similar to mine, even though the details are quite different.

I am pressing this point, because an often-used trick of the devil is to tempt you to try to copy someone else, rather than take the time to wait before God to know His will concerning your particular situation. It is His will for you, right now, that counts. Satan will always tempt you to take short cuts that produce only counterfeits in your life. I have seen instances when some pastor would diligently seek the will of God for his church, then believe God by faith for its fulfillment, and as a result see God produce miraculous growth. Then someone would come in and study what the pastor did, write a book about it, and begin holding seminars. The first thing you know, other pastors are reading the book, attending seminars, and trying to duplicate what they read about. Then, when it does not work in their church they are wondering, "Why did it work for that pastor and his church and not for me?" The answer is, the first pastor was following the express will of God for his particular situation, and the other pastors were following a plan and a program that was not designed for them. God will never do it the same way twice. Look again at the list in Hebrews 11. They all lived and died by faith, but there are no two lives or scenarios alike in that chapter, or for that matter, in the entire Bible. I love to read the inspiring stories of Hudson Taylor and George Muller and other "great men of faith," but while I am reading I must remember that God is not going to do in my life exactly what He did in theirs. I can glean a <u>pattern of faith</u> from their lives by watching how God led them along, but I **cannot** get from them a <u>personal plan</u> for my life. It is fine to read about someone else if you are looking for inspiration but not if you are looking for instruction. <u>That</u> must come from God. I must also remember that it was not the faith of the "great men" that produced the miracles of God, but it was the **great faithfulness of the God in Whom they believed**.

I am making a big deal out of this because the flesh, the natural part of each of us, will always seek a quick fix, a short cut, or a human scheme, rather than take time to know God's will and enter a faith scenario. But to do so is always a mistake, and it always causes you to lose. Men like Muller and Taylor succeeded with God in public, because they spent enough time with Him in private to know His will and receive His specific plan for their own personal life and circumstance. The faith life is a working life and a worshipping life. A spiritually lazy Christian will never experience a life of real faith.

Your life is unique, your circumstances are unique, God's leading in your life and His calling upon your life is unique, and He will work in your life in a way that He has never worked in anyone else's. The process or sequence of faith will always follow along the same general guidelines as we have outlined, but in the end, a new picture will emerge that has never been painted before, a picture that will create a new testimony to the faithfulness of God. You are just as capable as anyone else to receive the will of

God in your inner man and believe for the impossible. So don't waste your time and energy trying to duplicate someone else's experience. God has a plan specially designed for your life, your family, your business, your church, and your ministry.

Another Look at Faith Events

Now let me say another word about faith events, the situations in life to which the faith process is applied. Once again, by way of definition, a faith event is <u>a special time of trusting God for a specific object or outcome that is impossible to acquire or achieve without His supernatural intervention and provision</u>. They are occasions that demand more of you than you have, more than you can do, and therefore draw you into the realm of the impossible. These are situations you cannot and should not try to manufacture on your own. Real, legitimate occasions for faith are always initiated by God. They are deliberately created by God for the purpose of transferring His will and His supply into your life, and into the natural realm, by means of the operation of faith. You see, there are things God wants to give you, and things He wants to do for you, in order to expand and bless your life. There are also things He wants to give and do through you in order to bless the lives of others and expand His Kingdom. He accomplishes this by creating situations in your life, and placing burdens in your heart, that require you to reach out beyond yourself and trust Him for the impossible.

Once again, let's take a quick inventory of your life as it is right now and see if maybe God is drawing you into a faith event. We'll do this by just asking a few questions. Do you have needs in your life right now that you cannot meet out of your own abilities and best efforts no matter how hard you try? Do you need to see the miraculous provision of God in some area of your life? Are there desires in your heart that just will not go away, and yet you dare not allow yourself to believe they will come to pass because they are so impossible? Has God nudged you from His Word or prompted you by His Spirit to do something you know you cannot do; yet you know God is not going to leave you alone until you do it? Is He leading you to go where you cannot go under your own power, and yet you know that if you don't go, you will be living in disobedience? Are you deeply burdened for someone's salvation, but the more you pray for them and share with them the further away from God they seem to be? Has some sort of crisis arisen in your circumstances that has left you reeling and feeling helpless and hopeless? Have you all of a sudden found yourself in the midst of a financial firestorm that you did not see coming and you have no way out of without a miracle? Is God calling you to some ministry you are not equipped to do out of your abilities and resources, yet you know in your heart you really have no choice if you are going to stay right with God? Is God compelling you to go to some country to preach the gospel where the government does not allow anyone to preach? Do you sense in your heart God wants you to go on a mission trip and there is no way you can do it given your finances, health, or circumstances? Mr. Christian businessman, are you being led by the Lord to expand your business, when it is already a challenge to keep the doors open and pay employees? Brother pastor, has God impressed upon your heart to build a new building or begin an aggressive missions program when your current location and membership say that such a thing is crazy? My fellow evangelist, is God telling you to expand your ministry into new areas of the world when your support base hardly sustains what you are doing now? Is God telling you to increase your giving to His work to the point that if you obey, it will threaten your security and financial stability? Do you have a physical condition or illness for which there appears to be no medical solution? Dear student, are you prevented from going to college because you cannot afford the tuition, and no financial aid is available to you, yet you believe it is God's will for you to go? Mr. and Mrs. Baby Boomer, are you facing retirement with nothing on wbhich to retire?

I could go on and on asking the same question in as many different ways as there are people reading this book. But the bottom-line question is this, is there anything in your life you are not going to have or accomplish unless God gets involved in it? I am positive there is, even though you may not see it, because no Christian is excused or exempt from the privilege and responsibility of trusting God by faith. It may be that none of the examples cited above applies to you, but I promise you there are opportunities for you to trust God by faith, if you will ask Him to open your eyes to see them. Remember, without faith it is impossible to please Him. There may in fact be many opportunities in your life right this minute to enter into a faith event and see God do the impossible for you. But you may not see them, because you are blinded by the wrong attitude toward the things God brings into your life. When you look at your unmet needs, you may see only empty spaces that are never going to be filled no matter what you do. All you can see is the emptiness in the visible rather than God's supply in the invisible. When you consider your desires you automatically assume that you are not worthy enough for God to ever do something like that for you. When you look at your circumstances and your finances you just assume nothing is ever going to change, and you choose to confine yourself to the limitations of your own human abilities and resources. Now why do you do that? Because you are in the habit of doing it. Because you have spent your entire Christian life doing it. Because, until now, you may not have realized you have an alternative. Well, you do, and you can form a new habit of looking to God and trusting Him for the impossible. A negative attitude toward the things God brings into your life kills opportunities for faith. Let me give you an example.

Once, I was talking to a dedicated Christian man who had a son that would be graduating from high school in three years. Somehow we got on the subject of college and he said, "I just don't know what we are going to do. My son wants to go to college, and I want him to go. If he doesn't, he will never be able to get a good job. But I just don't make enough money to send him, and I am afraid he cannot get enough financial aid to cover it. So I guess we will just have to forget about it, because guys like me just can't send their kids to college." Now this man and his family had a wonderful opportunity for faith staring them right in the face, but they did not have eyes to see it. All they could see was doom and gloom rather than deliverance resulting in glory to God. Why? Because they were so accustomed to looking at the need, the crisis, the problem in the visible and giving it the final word, rather than looking to the reality of God's provision in the invisible and trusting Him for that. This man and his family attended church every Sunday, sang in the choir, gave their tithes faithfully, and served on every committee. But they had never developed the habit of looking into the invisible and trusting God for the impossible. Therefore, they lived in perpetual defeat. Instead of spending the next three years living in discouragement, they could have spent that time praying and seeking the will of God, looking at schools, and letting God show them which school He wanted their son to attend. You see the real issue in this situation, and in every situation, is the will of God - not difficulties, obstacles, or expense. It may

> The man who holds God's faithfulness will not be foolhardy or reckless, but he will be ready for every emergency.
>
> *James Hudson Taylor (2)*

have been God's will for this boy to go to Princeton or Harvard. Who knows? And if it was, all that mattered was the will of God, because <u>with the will of God comes the supply of God</u>. You don't get one without the other. What this family needed to focus on was God's will, not the cost of carrying it out. Their job was to trust God; it was God's job to supply. If they would do theirs, He would do His. If this family had viewed their situation as an invitation from God to believe for His supernatural provision, they could have spent the next three years rejoicing rather than dreading their son's graduation. Of course it is possibile it was not God's will for the boy to go to college at all (unlikely, since the desire was in their hearts) but the way they went about it, they would never really know for sure.

I urge you to take a long, hard, close look at your life, your home, your business, and your ministry, and let God open the eyes of your spirit to see the opportunities for faith before you right now. That thing you are calling an impossibility, a crisis, a financial setback, a business failure, an incurable illness, a circumstance out of control, or an insurmountable obstacle, may just be the greatest opportunity you have ever had in your life to see the glory of God. That unmet need, that unfulfilled desire, that burden in your heart from the Holy Spirit over some issue, that compelling from God may be just the springboard into faith you need to energize your walk with God. I urge you to change your attitude, embrace those situations, and take them before God in the prayer closet. Give Him time to make His will known to you concerning these things, then make the choice of faith and believe for the impossible. Listen to these words of Andrew Murray, "The faith that enters into the inheritance is the attitude of soul which waits for God Himself, first to speak His Word to me, and then to do the thing He has spoken" (3). There is so much that God wants to do for you and through you. There is so much inheritance He wants to give you. He has so much provision stored up for you, but you must access it by faith. And you can, if you will.

Let me suggest you do something very practical at this point; write down all your needs, desires, problems, adverse circumstances, things that are weighing in on your heart, and promptings from the Holy Spirit. In other words, write down all the things with which you obviously need God's supernatural help and guidance, whether it is financial, medical, physical, professional, emotional, spiritual, or educational. And when I say write them all I mean just that – ALL. You say, "But what if it is only something like getting money to take my family on a vacation?" Like I said, if it is important to you, it is important to God. In fact I remember one time when I desperately wanted to take my family on a vacation and it was financially impossible. I committed it to God in faith; and He miraculously supplied our family with $5,000 designated for that purpose. Remember there is nothing too small, too frivolous, too unimportant, too big, or too impossible to put on your list. After you have made your list, write on the top of the page this phrase, "GOD'S INVITATIONS TO FAITH." Now make the conscious deliberate choice to seek the will of God concerning each item and to believe Him for His miraculous provision. We are going to deal with how to do this, but first let me tell you that as you attempt to turn these things into faith events, you are going to encounter conflict – with yourself, with the devil, and with circumstances. As you go through the faith process, trusting God to work supernaturally in your life, you are going to go through three battles. Let's look at them.

Three Fights of Faith

You are going to encounter these unavoidable fights (or battles) of faith as you walk through any faith event in your life, regardless of what it pertains to. They are the fight AGAINST faith, the fight TO faith and the fight OF faith. My purpose in telling you this is not to discourage you but simply to prepare you. You don't need to be intimidated; you just need to know what's coming. As you set yourself to enter the faith process and trust God, you can do so with the absolute assurance that you will win all three battles, and it will end with the rest (or peace) of faith. How can we be so sure? Because the moment you accept God's invitation and enter a faith event that has been initiated by Him, you are entering a battle that has already been won. You are entering the finished work. All you are doing is walking it through. Remember that after God defeated the three armies for Jehoshaphat (II Chronicles 20:30) that, *"...the realm of Jehoshaphat was quiet: for his God gave him rest round about."* That is exactly what he will do for you. Now let's look at these three conflicts.

The first one is the fight *against* faith, which actually occurs before we enter the faith process in earnest. The first thing that must happen is that we get adjusted to the idea of trusting God with our situation rather than resorting to trying to work it out on our own. We must be willing to let go of it and turn it over to God. This can be very hard to do because, as we have pointed out before, we have two natures. It is as if there are two people living inside you, the old man and the new man. One loves God and wants to serve and trust Him; the other does not. There is only one part of the Christian that has any desire at all to please God and that is the spirit, that part that is born again. The flesh, on the other hand (body, intellect, emotions and will), does not want to venture out and trust God, because it is not yet fully and finally redeemed. It will be some day, thank God, but for now it still lives in prideful rebellion against God. The flesh <u>always</u> prefers and <u>always</u> chooses self-reliance and self-sufficiency over yielding to God. The operative word here, of course, is "self." That means you will always face a conflict concerning faith. Regardless of how intimate your communion is with the Father, there will always be a part of you that wants to stay in the "comfort zone" and rebels at venturing out into the "unknown."

Now, you may agree with every word you have read in this book so far; I hope so. You may also have a burning determination in your heart to live a life of faith; again, I hope so. But I can promise you there will still be a part of you that says no to faith. There will always be a fight against faith. When that sudden need or crisis arises, or that challenge to security occurs in circumstances, the automatic response of the flesh will always be to act independently of God. There will always be the temptation to "work it out on my own," to work harder, plan better, seek counsel, and do more. In other words, find some man-made solution in the natural to avoid having to cast yourself in total dependence upon the Lord by faith. The flesh will always delude itself into thinking it is easier to do "something" other than trust God, even though there is usually nothing that can be done. Satan's trick is to cause you to expend your time and energy in the natural (where you have no power or influence) rather than in the prayer closet with God where He has enormous power and influence and can accomplish the miraculous. It is a deception that we all tend to easily fall for.

There will always be a struggle in the flesh against the necessity, or even the idea, of believing God for the impossible. The old man, the natural man, just does not want to go there and will do anything to avoid it. Sadly, most Christians work so hard at insulating themselves against ever having to trust God for anything, they never see God do anything in their life that is explainable only in terms of Himself. Why do you think so many churches have millions of dollars horded away in bank accounts doing nothing? If they really believe Jesus is coming soon and the world needs to be reached for Christ, then why don't they use that money for the salvation of souls and the immediate advancing of God's Kingdom? Well, they would probably say it makes good business sense to have something to fall back on. The real truth here is that they do not want to find themselves in a position of having to venture out into the deep waters in faith and trust God. The flesh would always rather play it safe. In so doing, however, we lock ourselves into the status quo and miss seeing the glory of God. I feel very sorry for Christians and churches that are so rich, so smart, and so self-sufficient that they don't need God for anything. Oh, how poverty stricken and deprived they really are.

So what do you do? How do you break free of the strangle hold the devil, the world, and the flesh has on your life and get to the choice of faith? How do you escape from a play-it-safe, shallow water existence? You escape by saying no to the devil and by saying no to the part of you that resists faith. You say no to the flesh and you say no the world's way of looking at things. You make the choice to accept God's invitation to enter into the faith process and trust HIM. You stand up and declare, "No more! No more am I going to live my life in unbelief and fear!" You may have to actually write your need, your crisis, your situation, or your compelling from God on paper and then get up early in the morning and meet with God alone and pour out your heart before Him about it. Tell Him you are having a hard time breaking away from the hold of the flesh and ask Him to help you make the choice of faith. I promise you He will help you. Jeremiah 17:5 and 7 says, *"Thus saith the Lord; Cursed be the man that trusteth in man, and maketh flesh his arm, and whose heart departeth from the Lord...Blessed is the man that trusteth in the Lord, and whose hope the Lord is."* If you ask God to help you to trust Him, He will surely do it.

After you make your declaration of freedom you will enter the next conflict, the fight **to** faith, or to a <u>position</u> of faith. Winning the first battle (against faith) gets you to the place where you are willing to give up your human solutions and good ideas and enter into a faith event and trust God. The second battle (to faith) actually gets you in the door. Once you have accepted God's invitation to enter a faith event, it is now time to begin working your way through to the place where you are actually believing God for a definite object or outcome. That involves two things: knowing the will of God concerning your particular issue, and then coming to the place where you put in a definite request based upon the revealed will of God. It's a simple transaction of <u>asking</u> and then <u>receiving</u> the specific object or outcome from God as a "done deal." Once that happens, you have arrived at the place of faith, and the second conflict of faith has been won. Now it took me a very short space on this page to say what I just said. But let me tell you again that the time between the initiation of the faith event and the point of knowing God's will, and praying the prayer of faith, can be a long time. It may not be, but it can be. It could even take years, but again, it takes what it takes, and we must operate on God's timetable.

But when you get to that point you will know exactly what the will of God is; you will have received it as finished work, and all that will remain is to walk it through to the end. But let me caution you, it is here the battle really heats up. Even though you have received your request in your heart, and you are already rejoicing in it, the devil is still not going to just walk away and concede defeat without a fight. He is still going to challenge the outcome right down to the end.

That brings us to the third and final conflict in a faith event, the fight **of** faith, or you could say the fight <u>from</u> the position of faith, since you are now operating <u>from a position gained</u>. You are no longer trying to get to a position of believing God; <u>*you are there.*</u> You know God's will, and you have received it in your heart, but it still has not yet appeared in the physical realm. So, you must continue in faith until it does. What we are talking about here is the activity of faith, which involves the **worship** of faith (praising God in advance until the answer comes), the **word** of faith (public declaration of the answer before it comes), the **work** of faith (acting like it has already come), the **warfare** of faith (resisting satan who is trying to prevent it from coming), and the **wait** of faith (persistence to the end until it comes). Then at some point, at God's appointed time (not yours), God's provision will appear, his faithfulness will be demonstrated and you will rest – at least until the next time, which will very likely not be far away.

Applying the Process

Okay, now let's work through your situation (you may have many) and apply the faith process. To begin with, let me ask you this, and please give an honest answer. Have you spent time with God concerning your issue, or have you mostly just spent time fretting over it, worrying about it, and talking to other people about it? In reference to time with God I am talking about <u>quality</u> as well as <u>quantity</u>. I am not talking about a casual mention to God, or just a few minutes in prayer one or two mornings before rushing out the door to work. I am asking you if you are setting your clock so you can get up early, get into the prayer closet, and listen for the voice of God? If you are not, then that is where you need to start, because there are two things that must be accomplished before you can believe God for anything. First, you must be rightly adjusted to God. You must be Spirit-filled. You will never be able to truly exercise faith as long as you are living in sin or disobedience. Second, you must receive the will of God for your situation, and you cannot do that without spending time with Him.

God brings opportunities for faith into your life, but private worship is on your side of the page. It is only during this time that you will receive the will of God, and until you know the will of God you can go no further. Now, I don't need to spend paragraphs telling you how to get started in this. We have talked about it already. What you need is to just do it. Stop panicking, worrying, figuring and calculating, stop discussing it with others (they don't have the answer), stop being angry about your situation, and stop trying to figure out "why God is allowing this to happen." Just get up and meet with God. First, thank God and praise Him for this opportunity for faith in your life. Then begin your discussion with God about your need, your desire, and/or your situation. Where you are going with this is to a sure knowledge of God's will that will allow you to put in a specific request. Once you know God's will, then you will know what to ask for.

As you meet with the Lord, write down a description (that "word-picture" we talked about) of your situation as you see it. Put into words as best you can your need, your desire, and your interpretation of what you think God is leading you to believe Him for. After you have come to a clear definition of your situation that you can voice to God, then do just that; tell God in your own words how you see it. Then you must decide exactly, and specifically, what it is you want God to do or provide for you. The Holy Spirit will always ask you, just as Jesus did the blind man in Luke 18:41, *"...What wilt thou that I should do unto thee?"* The blind man did not hesitate; he answered straight away, *"...Lord, that I may receive my sight."* It did not take that man a split second to formulate his answer. That is exactly what you must do; be just that honest, just that bold and just that specific. God responds to honesty and deals in specifics, not generalities. As I said before, when the Holy Spirit presses you for a request, there are two possible answers, the one you think God wants to hear and then the truth. You don't have to worry about being "politically correct" with God, just tell it like it really is. Don't allow satan to frighten you away from a specific request by accusing you of wrong motives. If you have spent adequate time with God, you don't have to worry about that. Also, as you meet with the Lord, you should consider and ask Him what outcome in all this would honor Him and bring maximum glory to His Name. There are two purposes involved in a faith event. One is to bring joy to the Believer and the other is to bring glory to God.

Now as you spend time with God day by day (remember it takes as long as it takes) discussing your situation with Him in prayer, eventually He will break through and tell you what He is going to do. He will tell you exactly what to believe. Remember, the parameters of faith are set by the will of God, not by what you think you need or by what you desire. When the clear will of God settles in upon your heart as a done deal, it will be as if you can now see the picture on the puzzle box. An assurance, a certainty, and a peace will rise up within you that cannot be explained by common sense and cannot be attributed to circumstances. You ask, "But how will I know?" You will just know. There is no other way I can explain it to you than just that – you will just <u>know</u>. You will also have a power to persist in waiting upon God, even past deadlines, that you cannot possess apart from God putting it in you. Just the fact that the persistence is there is indication you are in the center of God's will.

You may also receive confirmation of God's will through His Word. It is important throughout the entire faith process to stay in the Bible, because more often than not, God uses Scripture to help you come to the knowledge of His will. Then after you know His will, and put in your request based upon it, He will use His Word to reinforce it and help you to continue in the stand of faith to the end. Again, I have shared examples of how He does this in a previous chapter. In addition, God may also confirm His will through "indicators" from the external circumstances, but He will only do this <u>after</u> He has spoken to you in your heart. The will of God is NEVER revealed through external circumstances. God will sometimes give you circumstantial evidences, not so you will believe, but because you have <u>already</u> believed.

The Prayer of Faith

This brings us to the **prayer of faith**. You could also call it the transaction of faith. Once you have become convinced of the will of God it is time to put in a definite request. It is time to ask God to do what He has confirmed in your heart that He is going to do. Now, you may ask, "Well, if God has said He is going to do it, then why do I need to ask?" Because asking is part of the process, and it gets us actively involved in it. Jesus knew full well what the blind man in Luke 18 wanted, and yet He still asked him. Why? Because He wanted the man to voice his request, to say it. He wanted him to ask. It is <u>asking</u> in faith that moves God into action, and it is <u>believing</u> that He has answered that moves us into action. Now remember, your request <u>must be specific</u>. God deals in specifics, not generalities. Let me break in here for a moment and share a brief story with you to illustrate.

In the summer of 1980, my son (age eleven at the time) came to me and said he wanted a new bicycle. Well, we did not have the money to buy one, so we began praying for one as a family. Our praying went on for weeks, and Michael became discouraged. So did I. Finally after about six weeks of praying together every day over the issue, I got up very early one morning and went out to a quiet place to spend time with God about this specific issue. I said, "Lord, we have prayed and prayed, and we have done all we can do about this. Lord, I just don't know what else to do." Then the Holy Spirit spoke to me very clearly in my spirit and asked a simple question, "What kind of bike do you want and what color?" I had never thought about that, and I did not know. I said, "Lord, I'll have to get back to You on that." All of a sudden I knew what was wrong. I went home and asked Michael, "Son, what kind of bike do you want?" He said, "A ten speed." I said, "What color?" He said, "Blue." Then I called Sheila and Rachel in and we prayed together, asking God for a blue, ten-speed bike. We agreed together to believe God for it – to the point of thanking Him for it right then and there. We hardly had time to continue in praising God for the outcome because He provided so quickly.

At about 3:00 PM the next day we were all at home, and a knock came at the door. I looked out and saw that it was some friends - a couple that we knew well but who had never been to our house. I opened the door and said, "Hey, what are you guys doing here?" Then the husband said, "Well Shad, today my wife and I were praying and we felt very specifially that God would have us to do something for Michael. Why don't you come out to the car and help me get this." I had no idea what was going on, but when we brought the big box into the house and opened it, it was a brand new, blue, ten-speed bicycle. All God was waiting on was for us to get specific. The bicycle has been gone now for a long time, but needless to say, to this very day, every time Michael is faced with a need or desire in his life he remembers the lesson he learned from God that day. So do I.

Once you know what the will of God is, and you can express it to Him in the form of a specific request, it is time for the prayer of faith. It is time for a simple once-and-for-all transaction of asking and receiving between you and God. When I think about the prayer of faith, I think about a time many years ago when I worked for a retail men's clothing company in Memphis. My job was to maintain a running inventory of stock and make sure we did not run out of anything. So I would watch the floor all the time, and when we were low on an item I would send a purchase order (P.O.) to the manufacturer requesting very specifically what we needed – item, style, colors, sizes, etc. Of course I had no money with which to pay for what I ordered, but I did not need any because I was operating within the authority and resources of the owner of the company. After the P.O. was sent and a confirmation was received, I would make sure there was room on the shelves in the warehouse to receive it and process it for the floor. Now, I did not know what truck line the shipper would use; that was up to them. I also did not know exactly which day the goods would arrive, but I believed they were coming, and because I believed I made room on the shelves. To this day when I get on my knees and put in my P.O. to God, my prayer order, I visualize a truck backed up to the loading dock of heaven. It is being loaded with what I need to round out the inventory of my life. I may not know what means God is going to use to send His supply to me and I may not know exactly when it will arrive, but I know it is coming because He has sent His confirmation, His assurance in my heart that it is His will. And because I believe it is coming, I make room on the shelf of my life to receive it.

Now you may be wondering exactly how you know when it is time to place your "purchase order", your prayer of faith. When is it time to make the transaction of asking and receiving from God? Once you are convinced of His will, that outcome that will satisfy your situation and bring glory to God, it is time to ask. You will come to a place where you must ask, because God is pressuring you to ask. His will has been made clear and the thing must be done, but He will only do it in response to your asking. There is no shortcut and no other way around this step. It is your asking in faith for the impossible that moves God into action. Oswald Chambers wrote, "If it is an impossibility, it is the thing we have to ask. If it is not an impossible thing, it is not a real disturbance. God will do the absolutely impossible" (4).

I suggest that you do whatever you can to make your asking as definite as possible. Pick a specific time, and go to a specific place, preferably your "altar", that place where you spend time with God daily. If possible, get some one to join you – your spouse, your pastor, or a special Christian friend and fellow prayer warrior. Jesus said in Matthew 18:18-20, *"Verily I say unto you, whatsoever ye shall bind on earth shall be bound in heaven; and whatsoever ye shall loose on earth shall be loosed in heaven. Again I say unto you that if two of you shall agree on earth as touching* [concerning] *anything that they shall ask, it shall be done for them by my Father, which is in heaven. For where two or three are gathered together in my Name, there am I in the midst of them."* With this promise from Scripture in mind, get on your knees, if possible, and voice your request out loud to God. Pray with your spiritual hand outstretched to receive, and then thank God for it. Finally, write it down and put the date beside it. Then from that time on, do not ask God for it again, just thank Him and praise Him for it until it is done. Once I filed my purchase order with the manufacturer and received my confirmation, it was not necessary to file another one. Once it was done, it was done.

Let me share with you some words written in 1914 by J.O. Fraser, C.I.M. pioneer missionary to Burma. God led him into a faith event in which he was instructed to believe God for a hundred families of the Lisu tribe. After laboring among them for three years with little results, God spoke to him and told him that he was praying much but not praying in faith. He should pray specifically for 100 families to be saved. After placing his request before God he wrote these words, "When we once have the deep, calm assurance of His will in the matter, we put in our claim, just as a child before his father. A simple request and nothing more. No cringing, no beseeching, no tears, no wrestling. No second asking either. One real asking is enough for a lifetime. I recognized the burden clearly. And it was an actual burden. I went to my room alone one afternoon and knelt in prayer. I knew that the time had come for the prayer of faith. I cast my burden upon the Lord. I rose from my knees with the deep restful conviction that I had already received the answer. The transaction was done. And since then (nearly a year ago now) I have never had anything but peace and joy (when in touch with God) in holding to the ground already claimed and taken. I have never repeated the request, and never will; there is no need. The asking, the taking and the receiving, occupy but a few moments (Mark 11:24). The past can never be undone, never need be redone. It is a solemn thing to enter into a faith-covenant with God. It is binding on both parties. You lift up your hand to God, perhaps even literally; you definitely ask for and definitely receive His proffered gift; then do not go back on your faith, even if you live to be a hundred" (5).

In reference to satan's opposition to the prayer of faith Fraser wrote, "He will first of all oppose our breaking through to the place of real, living faith, by all means in his power. He detests the prayer of faith for it is an authoritative notice to quit. He does not so much mind rambling carnal prayers, for they do not hurt him much. That is why it is so difficult to attain to a definite faith in God for a definite object. We often have to strive and wrestle in prayer (Ephesians 6:10ff) before we attain this quiet, restful faith. And until we break right through and join hands with God, we have not attained to real faith at all. Faith is a gift of God and if we stop short of it we are using mere fleshly energy or will-power, weapons of no value in this warfare. However, once we attain to a real faith, all the forces of hell are impotent to annul it. What then? They retire and muster their forces on this plot of ground, which God has pledged Himself to give us, and contest every inch of it. The real battle begins when the prayer of faith has been offered. But, praise the Lord, we are on the winning side" (6).

It is obvious that the prayer of faith is the pivotal turning point in a faith event just as it was in your conversion. There was a time when you became aware of your need of salvation, and you came to the point of wanting to be saved, but you were not yet saved. Then you made a definite decision to place your faith in Jesus, and you asked Him to come into your heart. At that moment you were saved. Jesus took your sin and gave you His righteousness. Once that transaction was complete, it was never necessary to repeat it, in fact it cannot be repeated. Once it is done, it is done. The same is true for every transaction of faith in your life following your salvation. The moment you know God's will and choose to trust Him for it, ask Him for it and receive it from Him, it is done. You are "saved" in this faith event. But now, just as you must live out your salvation until you appear in heaven, you must walk through a faith event until God's provision appears in this realm. That brings us to the activity of faith.

The Activity of Faith

Just because you have placed your request and received it in your heart as granted, that does not mean your role in the faith event is over. Far from it. You don't just sit down and passively wait for God to work independently of you. You are not only involved; you are *very* involved. I did not sit and do nothing while I was waiting on the shipment to come from the manufacturer; no, I got busy preparing for its arrival. As we have said, the activity of faith involves work, worship, speaking a word, warfare and waiting. Let's take the example of Sheila and me trusting God to provide for us to go on a trip to Africa to preach the Gospel.

We have prayed through, and we know it is the will of God for us to go. We also know that God has assured us He is going to provide the $20,000 needed for the trip. What we don't know is where the money is coming from and when it will arrive. So what do we do now? We do the five things listed above. First we begin praising God for His supply, which we have received in our hearts and believe will appear in the visible in His time. This is the **worship of faith**. It is no more necessary for us to repeatedly ask God for the money needed for this trip than it was for the blind man to ask Jesus a second time to heal him. All that is needed now is to continue to praise and thank God until the answer comes, regardless of how long it takes.

Not only do we use our voice to offer praise to God, but we also use it to make public declaration that God is supplying our need. This confession is called the **word of faith**. Remember God's sequence of transferring His will from heaven to earth. First God had the thought (His will), which He communicated to Jesus. Then Jesus spoke the word in accordance with what He was told by the Father. Finally, the Holy Spirit used the spoken word to bring to pass the will of God in the visible realm. It works the same way today, the difference being it is no longer Jesus speaking the word but you and me. When you speak a word of faith, you are simply repeating what God has told you, nothing more and nothing less. You do not have the power to "speak something into existence." What you do have is the power to agree with God, repeat what HE says, and trust the Spirit of God to bring it to pass.

Now we come to the **work of faith**, which is simply acting in accordance with the will of God. Let's go back to my trip example. Okay, we know we are going, and we are telling everyone we are. Yet there is still no money and no visible way of getting any. Furthermore, if people knew the predicament we are in, many would think we are foolish. (And we would be if we did not have the assurance of God's will.) So what do we do? We act just as if we have the money and prepare to go. We do everything we can do that does not require money. We do all the things God will not do, because it is not necessary for Him to do them. We don't need for God to wash and iron our clothes and pack our bags. We can do that, and we don't need any money for it. I don't need for God to write and print materials to take for the seminar I am going to do. I can do that. You get the point. In your situation there are many things you can do on your own, and you need to do them as fast as you can. The sooner you get to the end of you the better, because it is usually at that point God goes into action. The sooner you finish your side of the page, the sooner God will finish His. Real faith is not passive.

When we first started out, many years ago, I did not understand my role and my responsibility in Faith. I had the mistaken idea that all I was supposed to do was just pray and then sit and wait for God to act. That was wrong. Action is required of me (and you) on both sides of the faith event. When a need or desire arises, or you sense God telling you to do this or that, you must first determine what you can do to contribute to it. You might call this the work before faith. In other words, you must come to the end of your abilities and resources, the end of self. Once that is done, then you can determine what the impossible is (as per your capabilities) and then receive the will of God as to what He is going to do about it. Once you know, then you put in your definite request. Now you move into action again with the work of faith that follows the prayer of faith, which is simply acting in accordance with what you know to be the will of God. It is making preparation for the arrival of the shipment from heaven.

Then along with the work of faith comes the **warfare of faith**, which will likely become very intense. Just because you have received the outcome in your heart and see it as a done deal, that does not mean that satan is just going to give up and walk away. He is not. He is going to fight you right down to the last minute. And let me say, it is at the last minute where so many lose heart and quit. But let me assure you that if you will hold on in faith, God will come through. You might go past what you think is the deadline, but if you do, then do. Keep going on, and keep holding on, and see the salvation of the Lord. If that persistence of God is still in your heart even past the deadline, then hold on. Just because it looks too late does not mean that it is.

I remember one night before Sheila and I were leaving for Malawi, Africa. We had our tickets, but no money. We needed a minimum of $5,000 for expenses. We went to our daughter's house to say good bye, and on the way home it hit us as to what was wrong. We realized that satan was sitting on our money and had it locked up. So right there in the car we prayed and took our rightful authority over the enemy. Out loud, we commanded him in the authority of the blood of Jesus to release our money. Then we thanked God for making it real and effective and for supplying our need. It was 10:00 PM when we walked into the house, and at that moment the phone rang. It was a friend calling from out of town. He said, "Shad, I have been praying for you and Sheila and I want to know when you are leaving for Africa." I told him we were leaving the next morning. Then he said, "Well, I don't know how much money you need, but tomorrow I am wiring $5,000 into your account. I have meant to send it before now, and I don't know why I haven't, but I am sending it now." I knew why. The money reached our account as we departed for Africa, and we accessed it after we arrived there. Satan fought against the will of God down to the last minute, but he lost.

Now even though I have touched on it with this true story, I want to say another word about the **wait of faith**, because there usually is one. It has been my personal experience over the years that in most faith events, between the prayer of faith and the answer in the physical realm, there comes a point when it looks like all is lost, and it is just not going to work this time. Well take heart; just because it looks dead doesn't mean it is. Take a good look at the crucifixion and the resurrection, because your faith event will likely follow along the same line. First you will go into the garden where you come to the place of saying with Jesus, not My will Lord, but Yours. In other words, you let go of your own will and accept His. You determine to trust God no matter what it costs you and those around you. Following that, you will go through the mock court of ridicule. Satan will come to you and ridicule you, mock you, and tell you how foolish you are - just as he did with Nehemiah in rebuilding the wall of Jerusalem. But still you push on, trusting God. Then will come the crucifixion and burial, the place where all seems lost; it is all over, dead, and buried. You came to the place of knowing and accepting the will of God. You endured the devil's opposition. You won the fight against faith and the fight to faith. But now it seems it is just a dead issue. It is at this point that you must continue in the activity of faith. Regardless of time or delay, you must go on speaking the word of faith, praising God for the outcome, and acting as if it is so. Even when it is past the deadline, continue to believe. If you will, in God's appointed time, He will roll away the stone and the resurrection will take place. And when it does, you will receive maximum joy, and God will receive maximum glory.

In Romans 4:19-21 we read about Abraham, *"And being not weak in faith, he considered not his own body now dead, when he was about an hundred years old, neither yet the deadness of Sarah's womb: He staggered not at the promise of God through unbelief; but was strong in faith giving glory to God; and being fully persuaded that, what he had promised, he was able also to perform."* Abraham staggered not, because he considered not. He looked at the deadness, but he did not believe it. He chose to believe the promise of God in the invisible instead of the apparent deadness in the visible. God specializes in resurrections. So, if your situation looks dead, then let it die, and trust God to resurrect it. Hold on in faith up to and even past the deadlines. God <u>will</u> come through for you. When Lazarus died and had been dead for four days, Martha said to Jesus in John 11:22, *"...even now, whatsoever thou wilt ask of God, God will give it thee."* No matter how futile your faith event may look, dear friend, I promise you that "even now" God can and will fulfill His will and His promise in your life. He will not fail you because He cannot fail.

The key to it all, in walking through a faith event, is to keep focused on Jesus. He is the "Author and Finisher of our faith." The secret to being able to hold on is to be able to look back at the beginning and see the initiation of God. If you can do that, then you can run the race to the end. In walking through a faith event, we must learn to listen to the right voices. There is a group in Hebrews 12:1-2 that I call the "Crowd in the Cloud." Look at these verses, *"Wherefore seeing we are compassed about with so great a cloud of witnesses, let us lay aside every weight, and the sin which doth so easily beset us* [unbelief], *and let us run with patience the race that is set before us, Looking unto Jesus the author and finisher of our faith; who for the joy that was set before him, endured the cross; despising the shame, and is set down at the right hand of the throne of God."* Who is this crowd in the cloud? They are all those who have gone before us, including that long impressive list in Hebrews 11 that makes up the Hall of Faith. As you run the race of faith, there may be moments when you fall in the dust, and you may think it is over - but it isn't. Lift up your head and listen to the voices in the grandstand of heaven, that crowd in the cloud. Listen to Abraham, "Get up, you can do it, you can make it to the end. I know, because I believed God, and He gave me the promised son." Listen to Moses, "Come on brother, you can do it. I know, because I saw God part the Red Sea and take us across." Listen to Joshua, "Don't quit, keep going, God will come through for you. I know, because I saw those walls of

Jericho come down with my own two eyes." One after another come the testimonies. Listen to them; lift up your head, and look out in front of you. When you do, you are going to see a wonderful Figure motioning to you to get up and continue. That Figure is Jesus. Put your eyes on Him. The moment you do, you will be infused with enough renewed strength and energy to go to the finish line of faith. I know, because I have had my times of falling in the dust. But I have ultimately been enabled to continue by listening to the cheers of the crowd in the cloud and by focusing my sight on Jesus. Just one little glimpse of Him is all it takes.

Now you may ask, "I know that God can't fail, but what if I do? What if I miss the will of God? What if I get it wrong?" As I just shared with you, there will be times when you think you are failing, but you won't. Just making an attempt makes you an "A" student in God's school of faith. It is only those who don't even try that fail. Earlier, we used the analogy of learning to swim. Well, you may have to start out wearing floaties and dog paddling, and you might even sometimes get some water up your nose and get choked, but that is okay. The important thing is that you are in the water. Another analogy we could use is that of learning to ride a bicycle. When my little daredevil daughter, Rachel, started riding a bike at age 4, she just jumped on it and took off, but most people don't do that. Most of us ordinary folks start out with training wheels. Well, you might need training wheels for a while and even with them you might fall down and skin your knees, but in time you <u>will</u> ride with confidence. The operation of faith is learned through trial and error, and by necessity there will be some error. But that is okay; God is just thrilled you are even making an attempt. So many Christians never even try. But again, ultimately, you are not going to fail because your heavenly Father, your Faith Coach, is not going to let you. He is going to keep calling you to faith events, encouraging you to trust Him, and giving you the strength and courage to do so.

Program of Faith - Make a Faith Chart

Now I am going to ask you to do something that is simple and practical. It is something that will help you greatly in establishing an aggressive pro-active program of faith in your life. Go back to your list of invitations to faith. We are going to put them on another sheet of paper in a way that will allow you to work through them from start to finish. We are going to make a "Faith Chart." Take a blank sheet of paper and draw a line horizontally across the top. Now draw vertical lines dividing the page into seven columns. At the top of the first column write the word **"Item"**. In this column you are going to list the faith issues you are dealing with, the faith events that are being created by God's invitations to believe for

PROGRAM OF FAITH

ITEM	PICTURE	OBSTACLES	MY PART	GOD'S PART	REQUEST	COMPLETION
NEED, DESIRE, WORD, PROMPTING, OR CALLING	DEFINE IN DETAIL	WHAT IS STANDING IN THE WAY?	WHAT IS ON MY SIDE OF THE PAGE?	WHAT CAN ONLY GOD DO?	PRAYER OF FAITH	WHEN? HOW?
	WHAT DO I WANT?	WHAT MUST CHANGE?	WHAT DO I HAVE IN MY CIRCLE?	WHAT AM I ASKING FOR?	DATE OF REQUEST	CHRONICLE OF FAITH
GIVE IT A NAME	BE SPECIFIC	WHAT MUST BE PROVIDED?	WHAT IS MY PART?	WHAT AM I BELIEVING FOR?	SCRIPTURE THAT APPLIES TO MY SITUATION, A PROMISE FROM THE WORD	TESTIMONY TO GOD'S FAITHFULNESS
	WHAT DOES THE COMPLETED PICTURE LOOK LIKE?					MESSAGE TO ME AND TO FUTURE GENERATIONS
						BUILD A HERITAGE OF FAITH

the impossible. They will be in one or more of the five categories we have discussed; need, desire, Word, prompting, and call. Whatever they are, give each faith object or outcome a name. In the second column write the word **"Picture"** and underneath, give a definition in detail of each faith item. Be specific. Write down what you believe to be the will of God as received in your inner man. In the third write **"Obstacles"** and describe what stands in the way of each item, what must be provided to bring it to pass. Just because you have a clear picture of God's will, that does not mean the process is finished - far from it. You must still walk it through. In the fourth column write **"My Part"** and in five write **"God's Part."** In other words, in relation to each item, what can you do and what can only God do? Filling in these columns will tell you what your responsibility is in relation to each item and what you are believing God to do in relation to each. He will not do what YOU can do and you cannot do what only HE can do. Remember, real faith is a two-sided page. In the sixth column write **"Request."** There will come a point when you are very clear as to what God must do or provide in order to bring this faith event to completion. There will come a point when you are ready to ask Him to do it and receive it as done - not in the visible but in your heart. When that time comes, then put in your request according to what you know His will to be, receive it as done, and thank Him for it. Once that is done, then write the date of your request in the column. At this point, of course, you enter the activity of faith. If God gives you a Scripture verse, a promise from His Word, to go along with your request, then write that in the column also. He may give a promise for some items and not for others. There are times when God will energize a word from the Bible and apply it specifically to your situation, but it does not happen every time and you cannot force it to happen. If God does give you a specific promise, then praise Him for it and hold on to it. But if He does not, don't worry about it. The confirmation He gives you in your spirit is enough, and it will stand in total agreement with God's written Word. (If you ever think you have heard from God and what you heard does not conform to the Bible, then you have not really heard from God. It may sound good, but it is not from God.) As you work through this chart and through the stages of the faith process in relation to each item and event, God will, in His Own way and time, bring each one to pass. It will undoubtedly be after a season of waiting, work (including verbal confession of God's promise), worship, and warfare, but it will come to pass if you persist in faith to the end. When it does, you will fill in the last column labeled **"Completion."** Here you should tell when and how the accomplishment of God's will came about. The testimonies contained in this final column will form a chronicle of faith for future generations.

Let me also suggest something further; put all of your "Invitations to Faith" on that paper – you may need several sheets. List them one by one down the left hand side under "Items." Then deal with each of these faith issues in the same way. I keep a "running inventory" of the faith issues in my life and every day I take them into the prayer closet and meet with God about them. You can even categorize them. You may write on the top of one page "PERSONAL" and on the next "BUSINESS" or "MINISTRY" or "CHURCH." Then on another page you may write "HOME and FAMILY." You may end up with a list of faith issues under each category, and if you do – great! By doing this you are developing what I call a "program of faith" for your life. A life filled with multiple faith issues, and activity surrounding them, will prove to be a very exciting Christian life. I have been practicing this program of faith for many years, and I can tell you that, while it may be a lot of work, it is thrilling to your heart to see God do the miraculous and the impossible on a regular basis in your life.

Environment for Faith

Now, before closing this chapter, let me suggest another very practical thing for you to do, something that will greatly aid you, not only in the development of an on-going program of faith in your daily life but also in maintaining it. I suggest you do everything in your power to deliberately create an environment for faith in your life. If you, as a parent, detect an interest or talent in your child in the area of music, and you want to encourage him and support him in that direction, what do you do? You surround him with music, you expose him to musical instruments, and you provide lessons for him. Right? If you want your child to have an opportunity to develop an interest in sports, what do you do? You watch games with him on television, take him to sporting events, encourage him to get involved in athletics in school, and buy him the things he needs in order to participate. If you want your child to have any chance at all of developing an interest in literature, what do you do? You fill his environment with books and encourage him to read. Likewise, if you ever expect your children to develop spiritual leanings and a love for the things of God, what do you do? You make sure they are in church on a regular basis and are hearing the Word of God taught. So, if you want to enhance the development of your faith life, what do you do? You do the same thing; you arrange your environment in such a way that it encourages your faith. And, by the way, you will most likely have to take the initiative and do it yourself, because it is not likely that anyone is going to do it for you. Here are some suggestions.

As we have already discussed, the place to start is in the prayer closet. Spending time alone with God in regular private prayer, worship and fellowship will aid you more than anything else you can do. This is "square one" in the development of your faith life and your Christian life. If you skip this one, then nothing else counts. Moving beyond this square on the board, however, there are some other things you can do. Take your Bible (you may want to buy one especially for this purpose) and mark every "faith story" in it. Use a yellow marker and shade in all the verses in the Bible that refer to faith, trust, belief, and so on. Shade in every verse and passage that encourages you and reminds you and helps you to trust God by faith. Every verse that refers to faith in the New Testament is listed at the end of chapter 10. Go through that list day by day and when you get to the end of it, start over again. I suggest you even go so far as to pick out verses that are especially encouraging to you and print them out in big letters and put them on your walls – in your home, in your office, in your dorm room, etc. Sheila has a special verse written in large type taped to her office door, Psalm 20:7, which reads, "SOME TRUST IN CHARIOTS, AND SOME IN HORSES: BUT WE WILL REMEMBER THE NAME OF THE LORD OUR GOD." Everyone that comes in her office, including her, is reminded to trust God by faith. Hudson Taylor hung a sign over the door of the CIM headquarters which read, "THE SUN STOOD STILL AND THE IRON DID SWIM", which referred to Joshua 10:13 and 2 Kings 6:6. Every time Sheila and I pass through the gateposts at the entrance of Pilgrim's Rest, we read the words written in a marble plaque embedded in the post, "EBENEZER - JEHOVAH JIREH." Those words mean "The Lord has provided - the Lord will provide." Fill your physical environment with visual reminders to look to God by faith. You will be amazed how much it helps.

In addition, may I suggest that you always be reading one of the great biographies of one of the people of faith throughout Christian history, such as Hudson Taylor, George Muller, C.T. Studd, and J.O. Fraser. Even if you have read them all, read them again. You will always find new encouragement from them. And add to your reading a very powerful tool, the tool of conversation. You will be amazed at how much strength you receive by just talking to others about what you read in the Bible, in biographies, and what is going on in your own life. Sometimes when Sheila and I are going through a struggle of faith, we will deliberately just sit down and tell each other one of the old faith stories from the past, something that God did in our own life. It is astounding how fast your spirits can be lifted by just talking about the things God has done. Also, you may want to find a friend and share this book with them. Read it together and discuss it chapter by chapter. You may even want to form a faith study group. Read this book as a group, put it into practice together, and share with each other from week to week what God is doing in your life. You will receive tremendous encouragement from it.

I am sure you will think of many other things you can do to fill your environment with encouragements to faith, and I urge you to do all of them. Whatever it takes to bolster your decision and determination to live by faith – do it, and do it often. So, allow the program of faith to develop in your life, accept God's invitations to faith and see the glory of God!

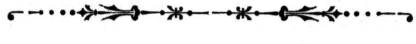

Summary of Truth

✤ The faith process is not a formula. We should never try to fit our personal situation into a mold.

✤ An often-used trick of the devil is to tempt us to copy someone else rather than trust God to do something original in our life.

✤ The flesh will always seek a short cut, some human scheme, to avoid trusting God.

✤ God deliberately creates situations in our lives to cause us to trust Him by faith.

✤ It is by the exercise of our faith that God transfers His will from heaven to earth.

✤ We must have spiritual eyes to see God's invitations to believe.

✤ We are always faced with a choice to believe what we see in the visible or what we see in the invisible.

✤ There are three conflicts involved in every faith event; the fights against faith, to faith, and of faith.

✤ There will always be a struggle between the part of us that wants to trust God and the part that does not.

✤ The process begins with spiritual atmosphere, with private worship.

✤ The prayer of faith is the pivotal point in the faith process.

✤ The prayer of faith must be specific.

✤ The prayer of faith moves God into action, and believing He has answered moves us into action.

✤ There are two periods of activity involved in a faith event, the work before faith and the work of faith.

✤ Satan will always oppose real faith.

✤ There will always be a period of waiting between the prayer of faith and the fulfillment of the will of God in the natural realm. That time of waiting will involve the activity of faith: the *worship, work, word, warfare,* and *wait* of faith

✤ There will likely be moments when you appear to be failing, but ultimately you will not.

✤ Real faith is learned through trial and error, and there will be some error.

Now Let's Take a Moment and Pray Together:

Dear Lord Jesus, I have come to the place in my life where I definitely want to believe You, by faith, for the impossible. Lord, please open the eyes of my heart to see the opportunities for faith that are in my life right now. Help me to apply the faith process to every area that it can be applied to. Lord, use my life as a channel through which to flow Your will into this world. Use my life, my needs, my desires, and my situations as instruments to magnify Yourself and bring glory to Your Name. Help me to work through the process in relation to all my needs, desires, everything. I purpose in my heart to meet with You in private, to receive Your will, and to come to the place of voicing to You the prayer of faith. Lord, help me to continue to the end and see the glory of God. Thank You again for being my Lord and Savior. I love You, Lord Jesus. In Your Name I pray. Amen.

Chapter 26

Real Faith Requires Real Warfare

"The principle of victory and triumph in the Christian life is the same principle that saved you, the faith principle."
J. Dwight Pentecost (1)

One thing that is essential to understand in regard to living by faith, as well as walking through a faith event, is that real faith will not go unopposed by the powers of darkness. Satan will not oppose attempts to serve God as long as they originate in the flesh, but when you step into the arena of real God-faith, you are in for a real fight. As we said before, there are three fights in faith; the fight against faith, the fight to faith and the fight of faith. First satan will oppose even the idea, the notion of trusting God in the first place. He will tell you to just be practical, use common sense, do what you feel is right and hope for the best. Once you get past that, and make the choice to fight through to a place of real faith, satan will use every tactic in his arsenal to prevent you from coming to the knowledge of God's will and the decision to trust God for it, rather than resorting to some human scheme. Finally, when you arrive at the place of faith, where the faith object or outcome becomes real in your heart, satan will tempt you to give up too soon and quit.

We find just such a situation as this in the first six chapters of the book of Nehemiah. Nehemiah had entered into a faith event that would surely bring glory to God, rebuilding by faith the broken wall of Jerusalem. In chapter four we read, *"But it came to pass, that when Sanbalat heard that we builded the wall, he was wroth, and took great indignation, and mocked the Jews. And he spake before his brethren and the army of Samaria, and said, What do these feeble Jews? will they fortify themselves? will they sacrifice? will they make an end in a day? will they revive the stones out of the heaps of the rubbish which are burned? Now Tobiah the Ammonite was by him, and he said, Even that which they build, if a fox go up, he shall even break down their stone wall.* " Many years ago our dear friend, Dr. Adrian Rogers (now with Jesus) preached a message at his church in Memphis (Bellevue Baptist) in which he pointed out from these verses that satan came against Nehemiah in four areas. First, satan told him the people of God were so **feeble** they would never be able to complete the task. Second, he said the task itself was so **futile** it was not worth finishing in the first place. Then he told him their faith was utterly **foolish**, and finally the work itself was so **frail** it would not stand even if it was finished.

Nehemiah's response was to pray and look to God, to resist the enemy, and to continue to build holding a tool in one hand and a sword in the other. Satan's intentions are revealed in 6:9, *"For they all made us afraid, saying, Their hands shall be weakened from the work, that it will not be done..."* But Nehemiah and the people did not yield to fear and quit and the result was that the work was completed. *"And it came to pass, that when all our enemies heard thereof, and all the heathen that were about us saw these things, they were much cast down in their own eyes: for they perceived that this work was wrought of our God"* (Nehemiah 6:15-16). That is the outcome that satan does not want and will try everything to prevent. But if we hold out to the end, we will receive the joy and God will receive the glory.

As we have already pointed out, satan is going to oppose your entering a life of faith from the start. His aim for every Christian is to live a life void of the supernatural intervention of God. He does not mind if you wander in the wilderness living a Christian life that is no more than mere religion, but he does not want you to enter into Canaan and have the real thing. There are several reasons. First, he does not want your life to please God and to bring glory to His Name. Second, he does not want the ministry of Jesus to continue on this earth. If he can prevent you from living by faith then that mission is accomplished, at least in your life. Also, he does not want the Kingdom of God to expand, which it surely will do if you are trusting God by real faith. Then if you do enter a life of faith, satan will oppose every event of faith contained in it. I have never walked through a faith event or taken a faith step that was not opposed by the devil. There has always been the temptation to avoid faith on the front end and then to quit before its completion. Real faith always results in real spiritual warfare. But looking to God, resisting the enemy, and holding out to the end always produces victory.

Satan does not have a crystal ball, and he does not know everything, but he is not stupid. He has learned that every time a child of God enters a faith event, things happen for the Kingdom and God is glorified. Thus the opposition. Every time Sheila and I have trusted God for anything, we have encountered a fight, and so will you. It didn't matter if we were believing God for a refrigerator, or for money to go to Africa and preach the Gospel. Satan knew that it would glorify God when He provided the refrigerator in response to faith, and he knew that when we went to Africa people would be saved – and he did not want either one. Satan knows Scripture better than any of us, and he has been watching Christian history for a long time. So he knows that any time a child of God enters the arena of faith, there is a lot at stake. The thing we must do, in order to stand our ground, is to realize that truth as much as he does.

Where the Battle Is Most Intense

As we have said, satan will oppose your faith at every step, but it is at one place in particular where the battle really heats up. That is at the place where you know the will of God, and you have received it as done in your heart. You have taken possession; you have taken ownership of the object or outcome believed for. You have received it. You have reached that place where you actually have it in your heart even though not yet in your hand. It is that place where you can now declare publicly with all confidence and assurance that "God is doing this for me right now." It is as real to you now as it will be when it actually appears in the natural realm. Now it is just a matter of holding on until it does. But it is at this point where the forces of the enemy will come against you with the greatest intensity. Between the time you receive the object in your heart and the time when it appears in the visible, there will be a period of waiting. During that waiting period, satan will often attempt to cloud your mind with doubt and assail your emotions with discouragement and fear. Very often an illusion of failure and defeat will settle in upon your heart, especially if there is a prolonged delay in the fulfillment of faith. There have been times while going through one of those events that I have felt utterly confused and disoriented. I have discovered that in those moments, the greatest temptation is to DO something, take things in my own hands, rather than "stand still and see the salvation of the Lord." That salvation will surely come if I will just hold on, refuse to be pressured by deadlines, and persist in faith to the end. Regardless of what circumstances say, it's not over until God says it is.

The devil's goal – always – is to get you to give up and quit just short of the finish line. When the opposition of the devil, and the pressure of circumstances, gets so intense that you feel as if your head is going to explode, take heart. That means the end is near and the fulfillment is at hand. It may seem that all is lost and it is just not going to come to pass, but that is an illusion brought on by the powers of darkness. Remember, just because your situation may look dead and buried doesn't mean it is. Just hold on. God <u>will</u> roll the stone away, and the resurrection will take place to the glory of God.

Contesting Your Inheritence

In this book I have shared with you several instances in which the fulfillment of faith (such as money needed for a campaign) has taken place at the very last second. I have also been honest enough to tell you that the battle with the devil was very intense, sometimes almost unbearable. As I mentioned before, there have been times when the fight to the finish line was so exhausting that once Sheila and I got on the plane we would have to refrain from talking for a while, regain our composure, and take some time to catch our spiritual and emotional breath. It is not like that every time, but it has been like that sometimes. When Paul told Timothy in 1 Timothy 6:12 to *"Fight the good fight of faith…,"* he chose the word "agon", which means two things, "a place of competition and contest", as well as "the contest itself." You see, what is actually happening as you walk through a faith event is your inheritance from God is being contested by the devil. You have entered an arena of competition. God has many things (possessions, opportunities, blessings, etc.) laid up for you that belong to the life He created in you through faith in Jesus. But those things are accessible <u>only by faith</u>. Satan knows that. When you enter a faith event, it is as if you just walked into a law office to receive what you inherited in a will. When someone leaves you something in a will, all you have to do to receive it is just take it. The same is true with objects of faith, those things that are part of your inheritance from God. But the taking of an inheritence can become a real battle if someone decides to contest it. That is exactly what the devil does; he contests your inheritance. He tries to produce enough pressure so that you will just give up the fight. If he can deceive you into giving up, then you will walk away and <u>forfeit</u> your interitence . He cannot take it from you, but if you forfeit it by giving up the battle, the result is the same. You can be sure that satan will always contest our receiving from God by faith, but if you will hold on to the end you will be rewarded what is rightfully yours. Your great Advocate, the Lord Jesus, will see to it.

There Is a Lot at Stake

As I said, there is always a lot at stake, usually more than we know or think. There is the gain or loss of what belongs to you, the proving of God's faithfulness, the execution of God's will in your life, the continuation of the ministry of Jesus on this earth through you, and sometimes the souls of men. Therefore, seeing a faith event through to the end is usually much more serious than we realize while we are going through it. If it were not, then the battle would not be so intense. I remember one day, several years ago, just before leaving for a campaign in the Philippines. We had come to the last minute, and we had no money. (Nothing new there!) We knew it was God's will to go, and we were fighting through, but we were nearing the final hour and nothing had happened. The situation looked hopeless, and to be honest, I must admit that discouragement had set in with a vengeance. I felt very pressured by the circumstances and the deadline and was tempted to quit. I was at home alone during the afternoon before departure day, praying and seeking God. As I knelt in our den, I prayed something like this, "Lord I am at the end, and I do not know what to do. I do not want to fail You, but I do not think I can go much further with this." It was then that God spoke to me in my heart and told me that the devil had our money locked up, that he was sitting on it and preventing it from coming. God told me to stand up, resist satan, and in the authority of Scripture and the cross of Jesus, demand verbally, out loud, that our money be released. So I stood up. Then as I started to obey the Lord, a hesitation came over me, a feeling that I was being foolish, strange, weird, and fanatical. I had to summons everything in me to do what I knew must be done, but I did it. I stood in the middle of the floor and with a loud voice commanded the devil, on the ground of the cross, to let go of our money, and release it to come to us. It went something like this, "Satan, in the Name of the risen Lord Jesus Christ, the Son of God, and on the ground of the Word of God, I command you on the authority of the cross and the blood to release our money and let it come to us right now. I resist your attempts to hinder, I order you to get off of our ground, and I call it done in the Name of Jesus." Then I knelt down and asked God to make it effectual, and a sense came over me that a breakthrough had occurred and the money had been released. About ten minutes later a knock came at our kitchen door, and the money we needed came with it.

Then a few days later an event took place that I will never forget, an event that illustrates just how important it is to fight through to the end in the fight of faith. I was preaching in a high school in the Philippines, and in the meeting about three hundred young people were saved. They prayed to receive Jesus at 11:00 in the morning. That night we had another meeting in that same location. When we arrived I learned of a terrible accident that had occurred there during the afternoon. After school that day, some of the boys were playing basketball, and during the game one of the portable goals fell and crushed one of the boys to the concrete, killing him instantly. There was a large blood stain in the concrete where he died. As I stood looking at it I was told that the boy's name was Earl Sanchez, he was fifteen years old, and he was one of the young people who had prayed to receive Jesus in the morning meeting. When he received Jesus into his heart, he was only four hours away from eternity. As I stood there, my thoughts went back to that scene in my den and to the fierce battle we had had with the devil. I thought about how tempted I was to give up, and I thanked God He had enabled me to continue to the end. Like I said, there is usually more at stake than we realize – a lot more.

Powers of Darkness

When Mrs. Howard Taylor (Hudson Taylor's daughter-in-law) shared the story of J.O. Fraser, pioneer missionary to China and Burma, in her book, "Behind the Ranges," she told the story of how he learned to deal with the powers of darkness. He was in a mountainous rainy area called Lisuland where there was not one Christian. In fact it was dominated by heathenism and was a real stronghold of satan. He labored for months and months with no results and became extremely discouraged and depressed. But the depression he experienced was not an ordinary one. Mrs. Taylor wrote, "Rain and mist in the mountains might be depressing; but as the days and weeks wore on, he realized that there were influences of another kind to be reckoned with. For strange uncertainty began to

J.O. Fraser

shadow his inward life. All he had believed and rejoiced in became unreal, and even his prayers seemed to mock him as the answers faded into nothingness. Deeply were the foundations shaken in those days and nights of conflict, until Fraser realized that behind it all were powers of darkness seeking to overwhelm him" (2).

Mrs. Taylor goes on to share how during those days God brought the much needed answer and deliverance to Fraser. It was 1913 so there was no television, email, or phone service. In fact there was hardly even any postal service, especially in those remote mountains. But somehow, God miraculously brought to him, in the limited occasional mail, a magazine called *The Overcomer*. In his own words Fraser wrote, "I read it over and over, that number [edition] of The Overcomer. What it showed me was that **deliverance from the power of the evil one comes through definite resistance on the ground of the cross**. I am an engineer and believe in things working. I want to see them work. Definite resistance on the ground of the cross is what brought me light. For I found that it worked. I felt like a man perishing of thirst to whom some beautiful, clear, cold water had begun to flow. The Lord Himself resisted the devil vocally; Get thee behind me satan. I, in humble dependence on Him, did the same. I talked to satan at that time **using the promises of Scripture as weapons of resistance**" (3).

Now you may be thinking, "Well, this does not apply to me, because I'm not on the back side of some remote mountain trying to win heathen to Christ." No, but when you are walking through a faith event in your life you may as well be. Regardless of where you are, and regardless of your situation, if you are trusting God for the impossible, you are invading the devil's territory. You are taking something he does not want you to have, because the process of doing so will bring glory to God. So, you must learn the same thing that Fraser learned; you must learn to overcome the devil by means of resistance on the authority of the cross and the authority of the Word of God. Remember, there is very likely much more at stake than there appears to be. Now let's look at a few Scripture verses to keep in your mind and heart as you resist the enemy:

Luke 10:19,20, *"Behold I give unto you power* [authority]...*over all the power of the enemy...the spirits are subject unto you..."*

Romans 8:37, *"Nay, in all these things we are more than conquerors through Him that loved us."*

II Corinthians 2:14, *"Now thanks be unto God which always causeth us to triumph in Christ..."*

II Corinthians 10:3-4, *"For though we walk in the flesh, we do not war after the flesh: (For the weapons of our warfare are not carnal* [fleshly], *but mighty through God to the pulling down of strong holds;)"*

Ephesians 6:12, *"For we wrestle not against flesh and blood, but against principalities, against powers, against the rulers of the darkness of this world, against spiritual wickedness in high places."*

Ephesians 6:16, *"Above all, taking the shield of faith, wherewith ye shall be able to quench all the fiery darts of the wicked."*

Colossians 2:15, *"And having spoiled principalities and powers, he made a shew of them openly, triumphing over them in it."*

James 4:7, *"Submit yourselves therefore to God. Resist the devil, and he will flee from you."*

I Peter 5: 8-9, *"Be sober, be vigilant; because your adversary the devil, as a roaring lion, walketh about, seeking whom he may devour: whom resist steadfast in the faith..."*

I John 4:4, *"Ye are of God, little children, and overcome them: because greater is he that is in you, than he that is in the world."*

Revelation 12:11, *"And they overcame him by the blood of the Lamb, and by the word of their testimony; and they loved not their lives unto the death."*

As we read through just these few Scripture verses, we see some things that satan would love for us to forget. Let's look at some of them. In our own strength we are very feeble, true enough, but in Jesus we have absolute authority over the power of the devil and his legions. Furthermore they are subject to us, which means they must obey what we say. We are therefore more than conquerors in Christ. We always triumph in Jesus, because our weapons are not human but spiritual and are mighty to pull down all the strongholds of the devil. We are protected by the shield of faith, which cannot be penetrated by the fiery darts of discouragement, fear, and threats. The powers of darkness have already been spoiled by Jesus, Who triumphed over them at the cross and through the resurrection – the devil's worse nightmare. Finally we are overcomers through the blood of the Lamb and the word of our testimony. In other words, we are victorious in Jesus and satan is defeated.

Now you would think that since satan has all this same information at his disposal he would just give up and quit, that he would just concede defeat and leave us alone. So why doesn't he? Well, he knows he has ultimately lost the war and his fate is sealed, but that doesn't keep him from still trying to win some battles, and that is where you and I come in. Satan cannot keep us from being saved, and he cannot prevent himself from spending eternity in the lake of fire, but he can (and does) attack us at the point of faith. His efforts are not an attempt to destroy us, but to divert us from the will and supply of God. If he can accomplish that, then he succeeds in preventing us from giving the glory to God that would occur as a result of believing Him for the impossible. Again, there is a lot at stake.

Enemies of Faith

The three fights of faith (against, to, and of) may also be thought of as the three stages in the faith process. First you make peace with the decision that you are going to trust God rather than try to work it out on your own. Then you find the will of God and reach a place of assurance where the object believed for becomes real in your heart. Finally, you hold on in the activity of faith until it appears in the visible. It all seems so simple and easy when you reduce it to a few sentences. So why does it seem so hard and complicated when you actually live it out? Because you have an enemy who stands in constant opposition to the will of God and is there to neutralize your faith at every stage, at every level. He has many weapons (fiery darts) in his arsenal to bring against us, and he uses certain ones at each stage of the faith process. Our defense, however, is to know about them before they come and to prepare for them, holding on to the promise of God in Isaiah 54:17, *"No weapon that is formed against thee shall prosper..."* Now let's look at some of these fiery darts.

Enemies in the Fight Against Faith

FALSE FAITH – One of the great enemies of real faith in general, and the real faith life, is false faith, those things that sound good and spiritual but are in fact detrimental and humanistic. Contrary to popular belief, there is no power in positive thinking, at least no spiritual power. Of course it is certainly helpful from a mental health standpoint to have a positive outlook on life, but it has nothing to do with real God-faith. Real faith is **acting upon the revealed will of God using power and resources that only He has access to.** False faith comes in many forms, which we do not have space to discuss here, but suffice it to say, if you are not looking to God alone for the fulfillment of HIS will in HIS way, then what you have is not real faith. <u>Real faith is not "going with your gut," it is going with God.</u> Also, real faith is not believing that something is going to happen or be provided just because you think it should, you want it to, and you have prayed for it. Real faith is believing (acting) upon what GOD says and upon what He reveals as His will. There is no substitute or short cut to real faith.

FATALISM – Real faith is not saying, "Oh, I will just take whatever God sends; it is all up to Him." That sounds good and spiritual, but it is not faith. There is nothing passive about real faith; it is pro-active in every sense and at every step. This attitude is one of satan's clever tricks to disengage your faith and get you into neutral, but real faith does not operate in neutral. Faith is <u>action</u>, not inaction or reaction. But what about the command to "stand still and see the salvation of the Lord?" That comes after you have "done all." Faith that is real is faith that works. James tells us clearly (1:22), *"But be ye doers of the Word, and not hearers only, deceiving your own selves."* He goes on to say in 2:17, *"Even so faith, if it hath not works* [action]*, is dead, being alone."* In reference to Abraham, James wrote in verse 22, *"Seest thou how faith wrought with his works, and by works was faith made perfect* [complete]*."* There is nothing that satan would like more for you to do than to take the lazy way out and sit passively doing nothing. Remember real faith is persuasion of fact followed by corresponding action.

FANATICISM – You could also call this <u>foolishness</u>. Millions of Christians around the world, especially in America, shy away from the principles and truth of faith, and trusting God for the impossible, because of so much fanaticism and foolishness perpetrated upon the church by false teachers who are out for their own gain. Satan uses this as an effective tool to keep Believers from ever making an attempt to trust God in the first place. A striking example is found in Matthew 4:5-7. Satan took Jesus to the highest point of the temple and told Him to jump off and let God save Him, but Jesus did not do it. Why? Because God did not tell Him to do it, and to do so would have been tempting God and utter foolishness. Of course Jesus responded the same way we should; He resisted the devil with Scripture, *"Thou shalt not tempt the Lord thy God"* (Matthew 4:7). Real faith is not crawling out on a limb just to see if God will hold you up. Real faith does not experiment, it exercises belief in obedience to God. Fatalism causes you to not act at all, and fanaticism causes you to act in the wrong way.

FLESH – Another temptation of the devil is to get you to operate out of your own abilities and resources rather than trust God - to limit yourself to what you have and what you can do. As we have said before, a person can accomplish a great deal using his own power and creativity, but all our human attributes combined will not take us into the realm of the impossible, into the arena of real faith. Again in Matthew 4:3-4, satan tempted Jesus to act out of His Own ability and turn the stones into bread, and again, Jesus responded with the Word of God, *"Man shall not live by bread alone* [the things of this world and his own resources]*, but by every word that proceeds out of the mouth of God."* In other words, we must live by the instruction of God, not our own abilities. But as you approach a faith event, the devil will always tempt you to do just that, use what *you* have, do what *you* can do, and then call it God. The problem is that it is not God, it is not faith, and it always falls short of what God wants to provide or accomplish. It is just the best that flesh can produce, and it robs you of real faith.

"FAILED" ATTEMPTS – We said at the very outset that learning to live by faith is a process and it takes time. You do not scale the heights of Faith Mountain in one great leap; it is a slow climb. Learning to apply the operation of faith requires trial and error, and along the way there are going to be some "failed attempts," which we have said are really not failures at all because any attempt to trust God is a success. But many times when God is drawing you into a faith event, satan will try to stop you by bringing to your mind some time before when you "tried" to believe God but did not succeed. Your response should be, "Sink, swim, live or die, I am going to trust God!" Remember what the men in the fiery furnace told the king? They said "The Lord is going to deliver us, but even if He doesn't, we are not going to worship your god." In other words, "Either way this turns out, satan, you lose."

Enemies in the Fight To Faith

"FACTS" – I put the word facts in quotes because what we are talking about are circumstances and appearances in the natural that present themselves as having final authority, but in reality they don't. Many times they are just appearances and nothing more. But as we fight to a position of faith (that place where we know the will of God and the object becomes real in our heart), satan will bombard our minds and hearts with certain circumstances, "facts" of reality, that stand in direct opposition to God's will. He will come against us with things that make our situation look so impossible that it seems totally absurd, and ridiculously futile, to even attempt to believe. So then, are these things not actually real? Yes they are, but they do not have the final word. When the disciples were in the boat with Jesus and the storm arose, there was no way they could look at the wind, the waves, and the water in the boat and say it wasn't real. Those things were very real, and the threat created by them was very real. But in the boat with them was a greater reality than what they were looking at, the Reality of the presence of Jesus. The water was real, but it did not have the final word in the situation. The fire in the fiery furnace was real, to the point that it destroyed the men who cast our heroes into it, but it did not have the final word. The three armies coming against Jehoshaphat were real, but they did not have the final word; God did. So what do we do about opposing circumstances, ignore them? No, we meet them head on and trust God to override them. If we will persist in faith to the end, God will bend the circumstances into conformity with His will. I have seen Him do it a thousand times.

Circumstances, good or bad, cannot be trusted, because they are always changing and they can change in a millisecond. They are totally unreliable. They are nothing but scenery. As you drive down the road and look out the window, the scenery is changing constantly. What looks real to you this second is replaced by something else the next. There are three things in the universe you can trust in; God (your Creator), man (His created being), and circumstances (God's creation in motion). Now let me ask you, which one of those three is the one that cannot and does not change and is therefore always reliable? The answer is obvious. Now let me ask you another question, which also has an obvious answer; which one should you trust? Satan also knows the answer to that question.

FIGURING – Satan often uses the weapon of our own intellect, our own thoughts, to not only neutralize our faith but to even paralyze it. Turning to human reason, logic and common sense while going through a time of faith, usually only produces a list of reasons why "it won't work" and a list of questions that either cannot be answered or don't need to be. The end result of trying to think it through is always internal conflict, torment, and confusion. Oswald Chambers makes an observation and asks a penetrating question, "Every time you venture out in the life of faith, you will find something in your circumstances that flatly contradicts your faith.

Common sense is not faith and faith is not common sense; they stand in the relation of the natural to the spiritual. Can you trust Jesus Christ where your common sense cannot trust Him? Can you venture heroically on Jesus Christ's statements when the facts of your common sense life shout 'It's a lie'?" (4) What is needed is simple obedience to the voice of God and quiet persistence in faith. Please do not fall for this trick of the devil. Do not waste time and energy, wracking your brain, trying to figure out how God is going to do it or when. Do not try to answer questions that the devil brings to your mind. You do not have the answers, and you do not need them. You can go through the mental exercise, if you just feel compelled to do so, of thinking of all the possible ways and means God may use to meet your need or bring this thing to pass, but I do not recommend it. If you wrote them all down on paper, all you would have is a list of the ways God is not going to do it.

FEELINGS – Then there are our emotions to deal with. This is an area in which satan can have a field day if we let him. But don't let him. The range of feelings possible while fighting to a position of assurance is so wide, we cannot even list them all. But you can be sure that they will come. First of all satan will tempt you to stop short of actually receiving the will of God and just do what feels right, and makes sense. You cannot, you must not allow yourself to wade into the quagmire of emotion while going through a faith event. If you do you will become bogged down and immobilized. You must remain objective and stay focused on God and His will. Otherwise you may succumb to feelings of confusion, defeat, disorientation, hopelessness, discouragement, and being overwhelmed. So how do you avoid these things? The answer is in one simple word – RESIST. Read again those Scriptures on dealing with the enemy.

FRIENDS AND FAMILY – These are the people in your life who love you the most and who, more than anyone else, have your best interest at heart. They are also the very ones satan will attempt to use to prevent you from venturing out in faith. They are not against you; they are for you, and that is what makes it so hard. When C.T. Studd answered the call of God to go to the Congo at age 51 and was in ill health, it was his family and his closest Christian friends who opposed him, not because they were against him, but because they loved him and wanted the best for him. But they could not see what he could see, and they could not hear what he could hear – the plan of God and the voice of God in his heart. They were very committed Believers who loved God, and they meant well, but they were wrong. Their efforts to dissuade him created great conflict in his life and great trial to his faith. My wife and I experienced the same thing when we entered the ministry of international evangelism. Our friends at church and our family at home eventually came around, but in the beginning, hardly anyone gave us genuine encouragement - not because they were against us or against the will of God, but because they loved us and did not want to see us go through hard times. Another aspect of this is that many times our steps of faith not only cost us, but they cost the ones closest to us, a prospect satan is quick to remind us of as we seek to obey God by faith. When you are going through a faith event, and even more when you are taking a life-changing step of faith, it is best not to confer with other human beings, especially the ones who are closest to you. It is very natural, of course, to want the support and comfort of friends, your family, your pastor, and your teachers, but it is rare to get it in a venture of real faith. It is not your fault and it is not theirs. It is just that you are wanting them to approve of, and be sympathetic with, a plan to which they are not called. God did not call them into this particular faith scenario; He called YOU. If they do not support you, do not become angry, resentful, and hurt; just understand that God has a specific plan for every person's life and ultimately we all stand before God alone. The only One who can stand with us there is Jesus.

Enemies in the Fight Of Faith

FOCUS – When you reach that place or position of faith where you have received the faith object in your heart, and now you are just waiting upon God to bring it to pass in the visible, it is as if you have come to a type of plateau. But it is not a leveling off point; it is not a place of relaxation. Quite the contrary, it is the place where you enter the activity, or work, of faith and the final stage of warfare. It is here where the fighting becomes the most intense. At this point satan will come against you with all he has in a final effort to get you to give up and quit before the finish line. One of the things he uses is a diverted focus. He will do all in his power to distract you and take your eyes off the will of God, off the provision of God, off the promise of God, and get you to look at the impossibilities and appearances in the natural. It is here that you must close your eyes and ears to everything except the voice and will of God. Satan will try to get you to look at your own weaknesses and past failures and listen to public opinion rather than to the reassuring voice of the Holy Spirit. So what do you do? You deliberately place your focus on Jesus, *"Looking unto Jesus, the Author* *and Finisher of our faith.*" II Corinthians 4:18 tells us, "*While we look not at the things which are seen, but at the things which are not seen: for the things which are seen are temporal* [earthly and temporary]*; but the things which are not seen are eternal.*" Maintaining focus can be a real struggle; that's why you need to stay before the Lord in private worship and in His Word.

FEAR – Satan's aim in trying to divert our focus is to create fear and immobilize us with it. But the Word of God says, "*For God hath not given us the spirit of fear; but of power, and of love, and of a sound mind* (II Timothy 1:7).*"* It is clear from this that if we have fear in our heart, it is not coming from God. <u>Fear is from the devil and it is always the opposite of faith</u>. Ruth Paxson points out, "Fear and faith are incompatible, doubt and faith are irreconcilable, worry and faith cannot dwell together" (5). Fear is actually faith in reverse; it is believing the wrong thing. And that is what satan will try to get us to do, to believe (act in accordance with) the wrong message. But when you think about it, what is there actually to be afraid of? Will we be physically harmed if we do not receive the object or outcome we are believing for? Probably not. So what are we so afraid of? We are afraid of failure, disappointment, and looking foolish to those who know we are trusting God, to those who may have told us we should not be attempting this step of faith in the first place. Fur-

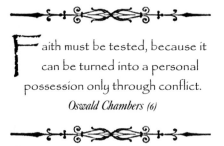

Faith must be tested, because it can be turned into a personal possession only through conflict.

Oswald Chambers (6)

thermore we are afraid that we will disappoint God and bring dishonor to His Name. But all these fears are unfounded, because if we simply persist in faith it is impossible for us to fail. Fear is an illusion from satan and a diversion from faith. So how do we deal with it? We must realize that fear is also sin. The Word of God tells us over and over again to not fear, to not worry, to not be anxious. We are told repeatedly to believe, trust and be confident. Well, no matter which side of that coin you look at, it adds up to one thing, sin. So how do you deal with sin, especially the sin of fear? You confess it to God and resist it in the authority of Jesus. Now you may ask, "But isn't fear natural?" Yes, fear IS natural and it IS often our initial response to the feeling of threat. The <u>initial</u> response of fear is not the problem, it is the <u>continued</u> response that places us in the position of disobedience and sin and paralyzes our faith.

FORGETTING – One of the chief reasons we so often and so easily succumb to fear is because we so soon and so quickly forget Who God is, what He can do, and what He has done for us. Remember in II Chronicles 20:3 we read, *"And Jehoshaphat feared..."* That was a natural initial response, but it was not sin because he did not stay there. It goes on to say that he *"set himself to seek the Lord"* and in so doing he remembered who God is (v.6), *"...art Thou not God in heaven? and rulest not Thou over all the kingdoms of the heathen?..."* He remembered what God can do, *"...and in thine hand is there not power and might, so that none is able to withstand thee?"* And he remembered what God had done for them before (v. 7), *"Art not Thou our God, who didst drive out the inhabitants of this land before Thy people Israel, and gavest it to the seed of Abraham thy friend forever?"* The cure for fear is to realize it is from the devil, recognize it as sin, and refuse to succumb to it in the authority of Jesus. Remember Who God is, what He has, what He can do, and what he has already done. Remember, while walking a faith event through to the end, you are **entering the finished work**. God has already won this battle, and the thing we are believing for has already been provided and accomplished. The will of God is settled in eternity past. We must also remember that we did not initiate this faith event, God did, and since He did, HE will finish it. God cannot fail to complete what He started. We need also to remember that this is not the first time God has performed the impossible. He is not new at this; He has a lot of experience. When the disciples were faced with the need to feed 4,000 men plus their families, and they had no food with which to do it, they came to Jesus with the problem. Then Jesus said to them, "Guys, we just did this same thing a few days ago; have you already forgotten the 5,000?" Dear child of God, take time to remember what God has already done: for those in the Bible, for those in Christian history, and for you. Read back over some of the stories in this book. They are all true.

FATIGUE – Now we come to the last item in our list, and it is one that satan uses to the fullest, fatigue: mental, physical, emotional, and spiritual. Warfare is tiring, in fact sometimes exhausting, as I have shared with you already. We have said that when you enter a faith event you are entering a contest, a fight, a race to the finish line, and there is a lot at stake. There is a lot of pressure and a lot of stress on your entire being. But don't you have peace? Yes you do – in your heart, in your spirit, but a faith event involves the whole man; body, soul, and spirit. The spirit (that part of you that is born again) loves God and wants to trust Him; it is all for exercising faith.

But the rest of you must be brought into line, and that can be, and usually is, a severe struggle. That struggle produces fatigue and it is almost unavoidable. Satan's aim is to create enough struggle, by any and all of the means listed above, so you will become tired enough to quit. What I have discovered over the years, however, is if you will lean hard on Jesus, focus on Him, persist in faith, and just refuse to quit, God will renew your strength and enable you to hold on till the end. Isaiah 40:31 assures us, *"But they that wait upon the Lord shall renew their strength; they shall mount up with wings as eagles; they shall run, and not be weary; and they shall walk, and not faint."*

Notice when satan came against Jesus in the wilderness with his temptations. It was at the end of the forty days of fasting when Jesus, in His humanity, was physically weak and tired. Now you may say, "Well yes, but Jesus could handle the stress, because He was God in the flesh." Yes, He most assuredly was, but when He resisted satan in the wilderness and in the garden, He did not do it as God, He did it as man trusting God. Therefore we can never say to Jesus, "But Lord, You don't understand how hard this is." He understands exactly how hard it is. He knows just how much grace is required to get you to the finish line, and He is on hand to provide if you will just hold on and trust Him to do it.

How to Persist to the End

The best defense against an attack from any enemy is to know ahead of time that it is coming and to be prepared for it. That includes the devil. That is what this chapter is all about – informing you and preparing you. So be duly informed, my fellow soldier in the Lord's army, you will without a doubt have a fight on your hands when you enter a time of real faith. I use the word inform rather than "warn" because "to warn" carries with it the suggestion of the possibility of impending doom, and that is not so. What we have to look forward to is certain victory. So what must we do to realize the victory that is ours? How do we hold on in faith to the very end no matter how much pressure mounts against us from circumstances, deadlines, and public opinion? We do the following:

1. Maintain private worship. Spend time with God alone in daily fellowship.
2. Remember that circumstances do not have the final word; God does.
3. Continue to praise God for His finished work. You continue to praise Him and thank Him for the object or outcome that you have

received in your heart and have yet to see in the visible. Praise will cause the forces of satan to become confused and to destroy their own schemes.

4. Speak the word of faith. Confess publicly that God has done it, and keep confessing it until it is done. The powers of darkness cannot stand in the face of praise to God and confession of the finished work. Remember Jehoshaphat in 2 Chronicles 20.

5. Act in accordance with the finished outcome. Make room for His provision on the shelf.

6. Do not allow yourself to fall into the trap of figuring and feeling. Do not attempt to answer satan's questions.

7. Keep your focus on God, His will, His ability, His supply, and His power.

8. Do not expect your friends and family to necessarily give positive advice, encouragement and support; look to God.

9. Do not yield to fear. Resist it, and refuse it.

10. Remember Who God is, what He can do, and what He has done for you already.

Now, let me finish this by just telling you again that every time you enter into the exercise of real faith, you are going to enter a warfare with the devil, with the powers of darkness. But let me tell you also that you need not be afraid. The battle has already been won and all you have to do is walk it through. So go to Ephesians 6, put on your armor, and march out in victory. Remember there is a lot at stake in your step of faith; if it were not so, then it would not take real faith to bring it to pass. But it does, and in Jesus you are up to the battle. In fact, you were born for it.

Summary of Truth

❖ Real faith will not go unopposed by the powers of darkness.

❖ Satan's aim for every Christian is to live life apart from the supernatural intervention of God.

❖ Looking to God, resisting satan, and holding on until the end always produces victory.

❖ The devil's goal is for us to give up and quit just short of the finish line.

❖ Our inheritance from God is always contested by the devil.

❖ There is always a lot more at stake in a step of faith than we realize.

❖ To trust God for the impossible is to invade the devil's territory.

❖ Our defense against the powers of darkness is to resist in the authority of the cross and the Word of God.

❖ Satan will always try to persuade us to accept a substitute for real faith.

❖ Real faith is never passive; it is pro-active at every step.

❖ Real faith is not crawling out on a limb just to see if God will hold you up.

❖ It is not possible to depend upon the flesh and operate by faith at the same time.

❖ There is no such thing as "failed attempts" in faith.

❖ Circumstances are not to be ignored, but they do not have the final word.

❖ Reasoning only produces a list of ways God is not going to act and a list of questions that cannot and need not be answered.

❖ Feelings cannot be trusted and serve only to immobilize faith.

❖ Friends and family mean well, but they cannot see what you see, and they cannot hear what you hear.

❖ If satan can divert our focus from God, he can destroy our faith.

❖ Fear is faith in reverse; it is believing the wrong thing.

❖ We so easily succumb to fear because we so easily forget Who God is, what He can do, and what He has done already.

❖ Satan's opposition is always strongest when we are weakest.

❖ The best defense for an attack from the enemy is to know it is coming and to be prepared for it ahead of time.

❖ We must remember that the battle belongs to God and it has already been won.

❖ Our Lord Jesus knows what we are going through, and in Him we are victorious.

Now Let's Take a Moment and Pray Together:

Lord Jesus, I realize I am in for a battle with the forces of evil as I take steps of faith trusting You for the impossible. I am invading the devil's territory, but You are my defense, and I am victorious in You. Lord, protect my emotions, guide my thoughts by Your Spirit, strengthen my inner man, and help me to stand in faith. Lord Jesus, I determine in my heart that I WILL cross the finish line as I look unto You, the Author and the Finisher of my faith. In Your Name I pray. Amen.

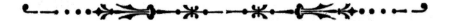

Chapter 27

Real Faith and The Timing of God

Holding On Beyond the Deadlines

"Dependence upon God makes heroes of ordinary people."
Bruce Wilkinson (1)

*I*n discussing the faith process, we observed that between the prayer of faith and the actual fulfillment of God's will in the visible realm, there will be a period of waiting, during which time the activity of faith takes place. Well part of that activity is the waiting itself, simply persisting in faith until the object or outcome believed for materializes. *"...and having done all, to stand, stand..."* (Ephesians 6:13,14). How? You must *"...take unto you the whole armour of God..."* Sometimes, however, that persistence may not be so simple, because it often takes you right up to the last minute. In fact, it sometimes even takes you beyond the last minute, beyond what men and circumstances might call the "deadline." As we said before, walking through a faith event is often like walking with Jesus from the Garden to the resurrection. The will of God is settled in the garden and surrender is made to it. It is embraced as done. Then comes the court of mocking and ridicule, which leads to the cross and the grave - that place where it looks like all is lost and hopeless. But then comes the resurrection, when the stone is rolled away and God is glorified.

There are times when it seems it is just not going to happen. You have trusted God and hung on in faith, but it appears that God is just not going to come through for you this time, as in the case of Mary and Martha and their brother, Lazarus. Well, dear friend, I have always said that in the things of God, deadlines have a way of loosening up when you don't meet them. What I mean is, God has His Own timetable and His Own deadlines. That was certainly illustrated in this instance. Jesus was never in a hurry, because He was about the higher purposes of God in everything. He was not always "on time", but He was never late. I have heard many speculations as to why Jesus delayed in getting there. The answer is simple, it was God's will to raise Lazarus from the dead, and he could not be resurrected unless he was dead. Jesus delayed in order to allow enough time for him to die. He will do the same thing in connection to faith events in your life. He will bring you to the same point He brought Martha, that point in faith where you say with her, *"But I know, that **even now** [beyond the deadline], whatsoever thou wilt ask of God, God will give it thee"* (John 11:22). In every real faith event, there is always a convergence of our need and God's supply that is perfectly timed to bring joy to us and glory to God. It is often at a time when human reason and circumstances say it is too late. Take for instance the offering of Isaac by his father Abraham in Genesis 22:1-14. It was at the very last second that God stopped Abraham from killing Isaac and showed him the ram caught in the thicket. While Abraham was going up one side of the mountain, the ram was coming up the other. God's supply converged with Abraham's need at a <u>precise</u> moment that was designed to bring ultimate glory to God and reveal Him as Jehovah-Jireh, "The Lord will provide."

Of course satan seizes upon delay to try to tempt you to become discouraged, to give up and quit. But you don't have to. If you will hold your ground and stand in faith, God will always come through for you. There are many accounts in the Bible that verify this truth, but I think they sometimes lose their impact on us because we view them as taking place so long ago, as well as involving people that seemed to have a better grip on this faith thing than we do. Well, let me assure you that the power of God is no less effective today than it was then, the people involved had no more capacity for faith than you do, and furthermore, they were just as ordinary as you are. Take Moses for instance. Yes, he was a great leader, but he was also a very ordinary human being, possessing the same weaknesses that all the rest of us have. Before putting him too high up on a pedestal, remember he did get angry and kill a man in the desert. I doubt that you have done that. And yet we find Moses in Exodus 14:13-14 saying to a whole nation of rebellious, unbelieving Israelites, *"...Fear ye not, stand still, and see the salvation of the Lord, which he will shew to you today: for the Egyptians whom ye have seen today, ye shall see them again no more forever. The Lord shall fight for you, and ye shall hold your peace."* Now, how could Moses make such a bold statement? They were hemmed in on all sides, and if they took the only possible escape route that seemed to be available to them, they would drown. He could make that statement, and he could wait until the very last second, because of one thing, he knew the express will of God. In the beginning of the chapter, *"...the Lord spake unto Moses..."* and told him exactly what He was going to do. Moses could stand still and see the salvation of the Lord, because he had the Lord's word that salvation was coming. Because he had the assurance of the will of God, the deadline did not matter.

Let's look at another leader whom we have talked about already, Jehoshaphat. Again, another very ordinary man who was just as capable of fear and panic as the rest of us. You see, what we need to understand is that these men, as well as those listed in Hebrews 11, were not spiritual super-men, they were just men being led by a supernatural God. In II Chronicles 20:20 we hear Jehoshaphat telling the people, *"...Believe in the Lord your God, so shall ye be established; believe his prophets, so shall ye prosper."* Again, another pretty bold statement for a guy who started off in a stone cold panic. In fact, he was so confident in the outcome, he appointed a praise team. So what happened? He heard the voice of God and became convinced of His will. Through Jahaziel, God told him in verses 15 and 17, *"...Thus saith the Lord unto you, Be not afraid nor dismayed by reason of this great multitude; for the battle is not yours, but God's... Ye shall not need to fight in this battle: set yourselves, stand ye still, and see the salvation of the Lord with you..."* Jehoshaphat could make that strong statement because he knew the will of God. His deadline was approaching, and from the world's viewpoint he was totally unprepared. But it did not matter, because from God's viewpoint the battle had been won already.

The wait these men were going through was not a wait of hopelessness or idleness; it was a wait of faith based upon the Word and the will of God. There comes a time when you have done all you can do and all you should do, a time when what you must do is stand still and see the salvation of the Lord. So what do you do in this time of waiting? Well, you don't just stand there with your spiritual hands folded. Again, you are not idle. You do the same thing these men did. First, you **remember**; you go back to the beginning where it all started. You recall how God drew you into the faith event you are going through. You remember how you came to the knowledge of His will. You recall how you prayed the prayer of faith and how God gave you peace and assurance in your heart that you had received what you asked for. Then, you **realize** God's will does not change. If what you are believing for was God's will a week ago, or a month ago, or a year ago, it still is. God's will is settled in eternity past, and no amount of delay or opposing circumstances in the natural realm can change the fact of God's will. Third, you **refuse** the devil's lies by the authority of the blood of Jesus. Just simply refuse to listen to him. Fourth you **rehearse** the promise and the goodness of God verbally to someone else. Confess the outcome, out loud, in spite of the apparent delay. Finally **resume** praise and thanksgiving

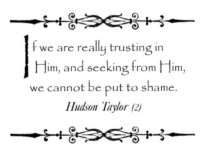

If we are really trusting in Him, and seeking from Him, we cannot be put to shame.

Hudson Taylor (2)

to God, and stand your ground, until you see in the natural what you see in your heart. God WILL do it, He WILL supply – in HIS time. And when He does, you will receive maximum joy, and He will receive maximum glory.

In Romans 4:18-22 we read of Abraham, *"Who against hope believed in hope, that he might become the father of many nations, according to that which was spoken, So shall thy seed be. And being not weak in faith, he considered not his own body now dead, when he was about an hundred years old, neither yet the deadness of Sarah's womb. He staggered not at the promise of God through unbelief; but was strong in faith, giving glory to God. And being fully persuaded that, what he had promised, he was able also to perform. And therefore it was imputed to him for righteousness."* Abraham staggered not during a long time of delay that took him well within the realm of the impossible, because he considered not the circumstances. He came to the place where the situation was "now dead", but he could continue on in faith, because he had very clear knowledge of the settled will of God. It is that knowledge that will enable you and me to continue on in faith also, even beyond the deadlines. Like Abraham of old, you can stand empowered by faith. And you can rejoice and praise God when your situation dies if you will remember that God specializes in resurrections.

Now let me give you a word of caution here. If and when you reach a point in your faith event where it appears it is going to die, then let it. Do not try to keep it alive on your own by means of some fleshly life support that not only will not work but, in the end, will cause more harm than good. If you have done all the Holy Spirit has led you to do, then don't do anything else. Just leave it alone, and let God work. Do not try, under any circumstance or any amount of pressure from within or without, to fix it or resurrect it on your own. God does not need your help; He wants your trust, your belief, and your faith. This is a place for patience and persistence, not panic. When you have done all to stand, then just stand and see the salvation of the Lord. God will roll the stone away at His appointed time. Satan will always come in at this point and tempt you to do <u>something</u>, but do not yield to it. You will only make a mistake and ruin what God is doing. This is a "faith" event, not a "you work it out at the last minute on your own" event.

Praise God – Only Six-Hundred Dollars!

Over the past forty years there have been many times when we have seen God provide for us at the last minute or beyond, so many in fact that I cannot remember them all. But there are a few that stand out in my memory. One was back in April of 1979. An evangelist friend and I, along with a pastor from Memphis, were going to Brazil, and as has happened many times, we did not have the money to go. But, believing it to be God's will, we were heading by faith in that direction anyway. We did not advertise for funds and, in fact, said very little to anyone at all about the financial aspects of the project. But as we moved along in the process, God began to provide as He always does. One morning, a few weeks before departure day, we were sitting in a restaurant talking over the trip, and in walked a businessman whom we had met only once casually at a local church. We will call him Mr. Jones. As we talked, we discussed our trip to Brazil and he said, "Well, when you guys leave, call me and let me know, because I would like to come to the airport and have prayer with you." We agreed to do that, he gave us his number, and then we parted ways.

Well, on the morning of departure day before heading to the airport, we remembered Mr. Jones' request and called him. At that moment we were still $600 short of having what we needed. That does not sound like much, and by comparison it isn't, but in the context of that present situation, it was critical. But, of course, we said nothing to anyone about it. We just went to the airport. As we were standing at the check-in counter, Mr. Jones was driving to the airport and was having a conversation with God. As he drove, God spoke to him and told him, "If those guys have a need, you meet it". He agreed. But then he began to think about what he had just agreed to and he asked the Lord, "But Lord what if they need $1,000?" God said, "You meet it." "But Lord, what if it is $5,000?" "You meet it." "But Lord, what if it is $10,000?" "You meet it." Later he said that the further he drove, the worse it became, and by the time he got to the airport he was terrified to even ask the question! When he arrived, we were still at the ticket counter and still desperately needing the $600, which no one knew about but us. As I stood there, I saw Mr. Jones coming up the escalator, and he actually had his checkbook open and a pen in his hand ready to write a check. As soon as he saw us he almost shouted, "Do you guys need any money?" We replied, "Yes, we do." He asked, almost frantically "How much?" I replied, "Brother, we need $600." With that he shouted, "PRAISE GOD!" I have never seen a man so happy and excited about writing a $600 check. Once again, God had provided 100% of all we needed, even at the last minute. Our need and God's supply converged at that ticket counter, the perfect place to bring glory to God and joy to everyone involved, including Mr. Jones. Maybe I should say, especially Mr. Jones.

Deadline for School Fees

The incident I am sharing with you here had nothing to do with reaching souls for Christ, but it had everything to do with this father trying to take care of his family. The year was 1982, and the incident involved the payment of school fees. Sheila and I had believed, from the time that our kids were in kindergarten, that it was God's will for them to attend the school that was founded by our church in 1974, and for eight years they had. Now it was August 1982 and time to register again for the fall semester and pay part of the fees, $1,200. The deadline was approaching, and if we did not pay the money on time Michael and Rachel would lose their places. There was no grace period. Now, going to public school would not have been the end of the world for them, but that was not the issue. The issue was the will of God, which we believed to be otherwise. So as the day approached we prayed and held on to the belief that they were supposed to go to that school. Finally the night came before the final day to pay the fees. We not only did not have the $1,200, we were completely broke. The mail had come that day, and there was nothing in it. It was now 6:00PM, and the fee had to be paid by 8:00 the next morning, or it was all over. I did not know what to do. I went out into a field behind our house and stood up on a little hill and prayed, "Dear God, we are at the last minute, and I have nowhere to turn, but I am believing You are going to help us."

With that I went back inside and occupied myself until bedtime. At about 10:00, I went upstairs to get ready for bed, and while I was doing so,

Sheila shouted up the stairs, "Shad, you need to come down here, brother (we'll call him John) is here to see you". So I went down, and John was sitting on the couch in the den. I said, "Brother, what are you doing here at this time of night?" Then he explained, "There is a small company out west that I have a part in, and each quarter I get a return on it. Well, just this afternoon I received my quarterly check, and as soon as I did, God spoke to me and told me to bring part of it to you. I don't know why He told me this amount, but He told me to bring you $1,200. I started to wait until tomorrow, but God impressed me that I must bring it tonight. So, here I am." With that he handed me a check for $1,200, the exact amount I needed to pay the fees and just in time to get it there by the deadline the next day. Needless to say, when I shared with him what was going on, we had a wonderful time of praise. The Lord is not only concerned about those things that relate to reaching the world for Jesus, but He is just as concerned about meeting the needs of your family, and He will move heaven and earth to do it.

Amsterdam '83

In July 1983, one of the most significant events of our life took place and, from a human viewpoint, we almost missed it because I almost gave up too soon. If it had not been for the wise counsel of my wife, I would have. The event was the International Conference for Itinerant Evangelists sponsored by the Billy Graham Evangelistic Association and held in Amsterdam. I had received an invitation to the conference in the fall of 1982, but because of certain circumstances beyond my control, I did not respond to it. Months went by and I continued to hear about the conference, but did nothing about it. Then one day in early June of '83, Sheila asked me, "Do you really think you should not go to that conference?" Just that question, coming from her, got my attention. I said, "Well, even if I wanted to go, it is probably too late now; it starts on July 12." She said, "Well, you won't know if you don't call." So, I decided to call the Billy Graham office the next morning and inquire about it. The lady on the phone was very nice, but told me, "Mr. Williams, if you have not responded to your invitation by now there is no way you can go. There are over 3,000 people from all over the world who are trying to get in, but there is just not room for them. I'm sure if you had returned your invitation you could have gone, but now it is absolutely too late." I thanked her and hung up the phone. I had asked the question and had received the answer I expected, but somehow in my spirit I could not let go of it. I continued to think about it and pray about it throughout the rest of the day, and at 3:00 in the afternoon I went upstairs to be alone and pray. I knelt down and prayed, "Lord, I have been told that it is too late and that it is impossible for me to attend that conference, but Lord, I have come to believe that I should go. God, I ask You to make a way." Just as I finished speaking those words out loud to the Lord the phone rang. I was still kneeling in prayer and when I got up and answered the phone a man on the other end said, "May I speak to Shad Williams please?" I said, "This is Shad." Then I heard, "Shad, this is Bob Williams with the Billy Graham conference in Amsterdam. I was just going through some invitations here in my office tonight, and I came across yours and wondered why you never returned it. Do you not want to attend the conference?" I said, "You mean you are calling me from Amsterdam? What time is it there?" He said, "It is 10:00PM and I was just about to go home, but I was looking at your invitation and decided to call you. So do you want to come to the conference?" I could not believe what I was hearing. I answered, "YES, Brother Williams, I DO want to attend, but they told me it is too late, the deadline has already passed." He then said, "Yes, that is true, but I am impressed of the Lord that you should come, Shad, and if you want to come we will make a place for you." I said, "Brother Bob, I will come and I don't know how to thank you for this!" Then he asked, "Do you want to bring your wife?" "Yes, if it is possible." He said it was possible, but she could not come as a full-fledged participant, only as an observer. I told him that would be okay, and then he suggested some hotels and asked in which one we would like to stay. I picked one, but then told him that we had no money. He said, "Shad, that is okay, you just bring the money with you, and I will trust God with you to provide it." I could not believe that such a huge mountain had been moved in such a short time and so far beyond the deadline.

But now we had another mountain and another deadline facing us, the money. It was going to cost $3,000 for airfare, hotel, and conference fees, and we had nothing. That phone call had come on a Tuesday. Then on Thursday afternoon while I was praying God spoke to me and said, "Shad you need $3,000, so I want you to send $300 for someone else to go." I did not tell Sheila about that, but as we discussed it later in the evening she said to me, "Shad, we need $3,000, so I think we should send $300 for someone else to go." Needless to say, the following morning there was a check in the mail to BGEA for $300. On Monday, we received enough money in the mail to pay for the air tickets and send the conference fees, $1,500. Also in the mail, we received another miracle, an invitation for Sheila to attend as a full-fledged participant. We have no idea, to this day, how that happened. Now all we needed was the remaining $1,500. Well again, God proved Himself more than faithful. Just prior to that trip to Amsterdam, we visited some friends in Johnson City, Tennessee and on our last day there a man asked us to drop by his office. So, on our way out of town we did, and as we sat in his office he asked about the upcoming trip to Amsterdam. He asked if we had the remaining money to go. I confessed we did not. Then he took out his checkbook, and wrote a check for $1,500! One more time, God had provided everything we needed, right on time – His time. Once again the circumstances said it is too late, it is impossible, just give up and quit, but once again God proved that circumstances do not have the final word.

When we left for Amsterdam we had only $300 to eat on for the entire 12 days we were gone, but God stretched that money and made it last. And during those conference days, God worked in our lives in a way that was foundational to the ministry we are in today. I am grateful to my wife for her counsel and to Bob Williams (now with Jesus) for his sensitivity to the Holy Spirit. I am grateful to the Lord for proving over and over again that, in His will, it is never too late, and it is never foolish to abandon all and cast ourselves upon God entirely.

Thanking God at Midnight

On the morning of April 4, 1984 I woke up very early thinking about the fact that after seven years of being in this ministry we were about as broke as we had ever been, and we needed $4,000 to meet our current needs. At that moment, it may as well have been four million. As I sat down in the den before daylight and began to pray, I sensed God was telling me to read Daniel chapter 10. I did not remember what was in that chapter, but as I read God began to speak to me. The Holy Spirit drew my attention to verse four and the words, *"four and twentieth day of the first month"* jumped off the page and into my heart. When I looked in the study notes of my Bible I saw that the first month in the Israelite religious calendar is April. God told me right there that He was going to send me $4,000, but it would come on April 24. All of a sudden it was settled, and I knew my prayer had been answered. But God was going to do with me just what He did with Daniel; He was going to supply in 21 days. Later in the morning I shared with Sheila what God had confirmed, and we began walking it through together.

For the next three weeks very little money came in, but we managed to survive day by day. And during the first of those three weeks a man came to visit us from the Philippines. He was the man I had worked with during a project there in January. One day God laid it upon my heart to try to help him raise some support for his ministry, so I called a dear friend (who is now with Jesus) and asked him if he would host a meeting. He said he would, and the date was set for Tuesday night, April 24. As we approached that day, our financial condition became worse. In fact, when we got up on the morning of April 24, there was no food in the house. I felt depressed and discouraged, and when the mail came I felt even worse because there was nothing in it. I had believed with everything in me that God had spoken to me on the morning of April 4, but now I was beginning to doubt. I did not know what

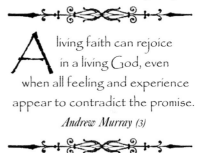

A living faith can rejoice in a living God, even when all feeling and experience appear to contradict the promise.

Andrew Murray (3)

to do, because the meeting for my Filipino friend was in a town 100 miles away, and I had no money for gas. During the afternoon I said to Sheila, "Well I guess I just missed it. I was certain that God told me He was sending that $4,000 today, but it has not come." Then she replied, "But remember, Shad, you don't have to see it in your hand for it to be real." I agreed, and felt encouraged by her words - but I still had no gas for the car.

Well, as always, God provided. My friend, Art Bailey, called and asked what was going on and I told him. Then he said he wanted to go and suggested, "Brother your car is small and so is mine; why don't I borrow my friend's Cadillac and we will go in that?" I agreed, but I still did not know what to do about gas. Praise God, when Art arrived it had a full tank. I was happy to have that issue solved, but all the way there I was thinking, "Shad you must be the biggest fool ever. Here you are completely broke, cannot buy food for your family, and you are taking this guy to a meeting to try to raise money for his ministry. And furthermore, that $4,000 you thought God was sending by today has not come and time has run out." I felt like the biggest failure that ever lived, and by the time we got to the meeting, I just wanted to get it over with and go home.

When we arrived I felt even worse, because there were only seven people there. I opened the meeting with prayer and introduced my friend.

He spent an hour talking about his work in the Philippines, I thanked everyone for coming, closed in prayer, and the meeting was over. I could hardly wait to get back in the car and go home. As I was walking out a man, whom I did not know (we will call him Don) stepped in front of me and asked if I had a card. I gave it to him, he thanked me, and then we left. All the way home, all I could think about was how could I have been so wrong about what I thought I heard God say.

I got home late, and at mid-night I sat on the side of my bed thinking through the past three weeks. Then all of a sudden, just at 12:00 mid-night, something happened. It was as if some one flipped a switch inside of my heart. I remembered what Sheila had said earlier in the day, "You don't have to see it for it to be real." All of a sudden my eyes were opened to that truth, and in my heart I had that $4,000. April 24 had now officially come and gone, the deadline was passed, and I could not see that money in my hand - but I could see it in my heart. It was as real as if it was laying on the nightstand in front of me. As I sat there on the bed I prayed, "Lord, You said You were sending that money on the 24th and I believe You sent it. I can't see it with my eyes, but I believe You sent it and I thank You and praise You for it." When I went to sleep that night my circumstances had not changed, except that they had actually gotten worse. All appearances in the visible said that the deadline was passed, I had missed the will of God, and I was broke and defeated, but my heart said that God had provided.

I woke up the next morning with joy in my heart, still no money, but joy and peace. When the mail came there was nothing in it, but it did not matter; I still believed God had provided. Then at 3:00 in the afternoon the phone rang, and to my surprise it was Don (the man I had given the card to), but it took me a couple of minutes before I realized who I was talking to. He said, "Shad, this is Don, and I just called to tell you that last night God did not tell me to help your friend." There was a long awkward pause, and I did not know how to respond so I just said, "Well thank you for calling and letting me know." Then he said, "Well, but wait a minute. What I called to tell you is that God did tell me to help your ministry and I would like for you to tell me about your financial condition right now." Since I hadn't said anything about my ministry the night before, I was really surprised! But I answered his questions and told him about the Daniel ten passage and how God had promised to send $4,000. He then asked if the money had come in, and I told him, "Not exactly."

Then he asked, "Well, what did you do last night when it had not come in?" Then I said, "Well brother Don, you see, it did not come in a way that I can see it, but it did come, because God promised it was coming, so therefore it had to come. So, at midnight, I just thanked God for sending it." I figured Don was going to think I was crazy! Instead, he said, "Shad, you are exactly right, God did provide that money yesterday. At 9:00 last night He spoke to my heart and told me to send you $4,000, and I have put it in the mail today." I could hardly believe what I was hearing, and my heart was so full of praise to God I could hardly contain it! Then Don went on to say, "And furthermore, Shad, I am going to send you another $8,000 for your next campaign. Just let me know where it is and when you need the money." Not only had God met our current need "on time," but He had supplied the money for our next project in Brazil ahead of time. When I hung up the phone, I was amazed at how God had used a man I had never met before and with whom I had never talked about our ministry. And I was also grateful and excited about the need being met, even when it appeared the deadline was passed and all hope was gone. But I cannot say I was surprised, because God had assured me the night before that it was accomplished. Once again our Great God proved it is far better to "walk by faith and not by sight!"

A Knock at the Door

In September 1985, an incident took place that involved our friend Jim McDonough (now with Jesus) of Adamsville, TN. Sheila and I were preparing to go to England for ten days and then on to Malawi, Africa for a five-week campaign. We did not need much money for England because we were staying with friends, but to cover the cost of the Malawi project we needed $10,000. In keeping with our non-solicitation policy that God gave us from the beginning, we did not say anything to anyone about it. We just made preparations to go, asked our friends to pray for the project and looked to God for His supply. As we neared departure day nothing had come in, and on the afternoon before leaving we found ourselves, once again, facing a dead- 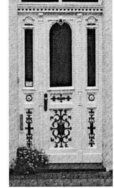 line with no hope in sight. We did have our plane tickets, and all the arrangements were in place in England and Malawi. But we had not one penny for expenses. Before going to bed that night we packed all our bags and did everything we could do that did not require money. There was nothing left to do but wait upon the Lord, which in all honesty, was becoming increasingly difficult to do with each passing hour. Finally, at midnight, I called my old beloved friend, Larry Baskin, and told him, "Larry, I am having a tough time here. I believe with all my heart it is God's will for us to go, but I am down to the last minute and I need for someone to pray and believe and stand with me and Sheila about this." With that, Larry said, "Shad, this is God's will, brother, and He is going to provide for you. He always has, and He will this time." That was all I needed. Just that little word was enough to help us hang on in faith.

But before going to bed, Sheila and I made a decision. Yes we believed God was going to provide, but we decided that one way or the other, with or without the money, we were getting on that plane. If we had to trust God to provide as we went, then so be it. We got up the next morning and prepared to go to the airport. Still no money, not a penny. The morning passed, and at 11:00 we were about to walk out the door to leave. Our flight left at 1:00PM. Sheila went to the car, and as I was reaching for the door handle to open it and follow her out I heard a knock at the front door. I thought, "Who in the world could that be?" Then I saw it was Jim. I ran to the door, opened it and asked, "Jim, what are you doing here?" Then he asked me, "When are you leaving for Africa?" I said, "Brother, right now! I was just going to the car. Our flight leaves in less than two hours." Then Jim said, "Well, I knew you were leaving soon, but I did not know exactly when. But anyway, this morning the Lord woke me up very early and told me to go around town and collect up as much money for you as I could and to bring it to you this morning. So I went around town, took up a collection, and drove over here as fast as I could. Anyway, here it is." With that, Jim handed me an envelope bulging with cash - $5,000! I could not believe it. I said, "Brother Jim, praise God and thank you so much. This is a miracle!" I stuffed the cash in my pockets, hurried to the car, rushed to the airport, and arrived just in time to make the flight. When we left, I thought we were going with half of what we needed, but I soon discovered I was wrong. God does not do things in halves. I had figured the budget according to the exchange rate that was in place during the last campaign in Malawi, but when we arrived I discovered the dollar had exactly doubled in value and God turned that $5,000 into $10,000 by means of the new rate! God had provided not half, but 100% of what we needed, and He beat the deadline by two whole hours!

He Will Do It for You

The point of these stories, which are all true, is to say to you that God will provide for you if you are just willing to wait until the last minute and even beyond if that is what it takes. In all the personal stories I share with you in this book, I try to be very honest and transparent. I certainly do not want to pass myself off as some kind of super faith guy who has a real handle on the faith life. Sheila and I are just plain, ordinary folks who have been privileged to see God do some wonderful things over the years. We have walked through many faith events, and there have been many times when we have felt like we were barely hanging on by the skin of our teeth. There have been times when we thought we could not go another step and almost gave in to the pressure of appearances and circumstances in the visible. But after all these years, I can tell you authoritatively that if you will just hold on to the will of God and believe for the impossible down to the last second and even beyond, God will <u>always</u> come through for you. I have never had an instance when He didn't. I have said before that walking through a faith event can be very hard on the flesh and often is, but that is okay. If it is hard, then so be it. The important thing is that you continue to the end. Satan will say to you, "Oh, if you really had faith, you wouldn't have fear and doubts." Dear Christian, the thing that proves you are exercising real faith is not that you don't have fears and doubts, but that even when you do have fear and doubts arise within you, you continue to hold on and believe God anyway. There may be times when you have to say with David in Psalm 56:3, *"What time I am afraid, I will trust in thee."* Faith is an act of the will, not a feeling in the emotions. Sometimes you get to walk through a faith event without being afraid, and sometimes you don't. The important thing is that either way, you keep walking until it is finished, even if it takes you beyond the deadline.

If you are going through a faith event right now in your home, your business, your finances, your church, or your ministry and have come down to the last minute without yet seeing God's deliverance, don't despair. If you have heard from God, and He has revealed His will to you, then just hang on and believe. Remember, believe means act, not feel. If you get fearful, then just be fearful, but don't quit. If you get discouraged, then do what I did and call a friend whom you can trust. Confess your fear to them, and have them pray with you. Look into the Word of God and receive strength from it. Remember that just because you can't see the ram coming up the other side of the mountain, that does not mean it isn't there. The convergence of your need and God's supply will take place at His exact appointed time. But, you can be sure there IS an appointed time. It may or may not fit your timetable and conform to your deadline, but it WILL happen.

Before we move on let me refer you again to Psalm 77. Read the whole Psalm and then look at verses 9 and 14. In verse 9 David asked, *"Hath God forgotten to be gracious? hath he in anger shut up His tender mercies?"* Then look at verse 14, *"Thou art the God that doest wonders..."* Wow, what a contrast! How did he get from "forgotten to be gracious" to "God that doest wonders"? Well in verses 10 – 13 he took four steps. First in v. 10,11 he said, *"...I will remember the years of the right hand of the most high. I will remember the works of the Lord: surely I will remember thy wonders of old."* Second in v. 12 he said, *I will meditate also of all thy work..."* Then also in v. 12 David said, *"...and talk of thy doings."* And finally in v. 13 he says, *"Thy way, O God, is in the sanctuary: who is so great a God as our God?"* When David was on the brink of giving in and giving up, he did four things. He **remembered** the years, the works and the wonders of God. He let his mind become saturated with memories of the miracles of God. Then he not only remembered, but he **meditated** upon these things. He replaced thoughts of fear and dread with thoughts of God's power and provision. Third, he **talked** about them to someone else. He confessed with his mouth the new thoughts of his mind and heart. And when he did, the **ways** of God became clear and reliable in his heart. All of a sudden, what he saw in the invisible became more persuasive to him than what he saw in the visible. So if you are in one of those last minute Red Sea situations, remember the works of God, think on those things, find some one to tell them to, and then see the ways of God and believe. Let me say it again, God will come through for you in His appointed time. If He will do it for me, I KNOW He will do it for you.

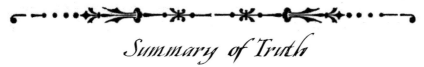

Summary of Truth

- ❖ There is always a period of waiting between the prayer of faith and the fulfillment of God's will in the visible.
- ❖ The wait of faith often takes you to the last minute and sometimes even beyond the deadlines.
- ❖ God has His Own timetable and His Own deadlines.
- ❖ In every faith event there is a perfectly timed convergence of our need and God's supply.
- ❖ Satan will always try to use delay to cause discouragement.
- ❖ Knowing the will of God enables us to wait until the last minute and beyond.
- ❖ The wait of faith is not an idle wait.
- ❖ God's will is settled, and it cannot be changed by delay or circumstances.
- ❖ Feeling fearful during a faith event does not mean that you are failing and it does not disqualify you from trusting God.
- ❖ The thing that proves you are trusting God is not that you have no fear, but that you continue on in faith in spite of fear and doubts.

Now Let's Take a Moment and Pray Together:

Dear God, Thank You Lord for showing me that I do not have to be a super saint in order to trust You. Lord, I thank You that it is okay for me to just be an ordinary human being who places his trust in You. Thank You for showing me You will always come through for me, even if I go past the deadline. Thank You for showing me that manmade, circumstantial deadlines do not matter to You, and they do not have to matter to me either. Lord, I give myself to You right now to lead me into whatever faith event You want me to walk through. And I yield myself for You to take me beyond the deadlines if You so choose. Lord, I say with David, "What time I am afraid, I will trust in Thee." Thank You Lord for revealing these truths to me today. Thank You for saving me and for loving me. In Your Name I pray, Lord Jesus. Amen.

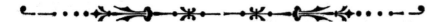

Chapter 28

God Uses the Unexpected

"We are uncertain of the next step, but we are certain of God.
He packs our life with surprises all the time.
Spiritual life is the life of a child."
Oswald Chambers (1)

One thing I learned early on, concerning faith and faith events, is that God very often uses the unexpected, in fact more often than not. Even if He tells you ahead of time that He is going to use this person or that situation to help meet your need, solve your problem, or expand your ministry, there will still be an element of the unexpected in it. You may have prayed the prayer of faith, placing your "prayer order" before the Great Supplier of heaven, and you may have an unshakable confidence in your heart that God's deliverance is on the way, but you will likely not know by what means the deliverance will come. That is up to God. The faith life is full of wonderful surprises. That night that I sat on the side of my bed at midnight thanking God for His supply of the $4,000, I knew beyond doubt it was coming. In fact, I knew in my heart I already had it, but I did not have a clue God was going to use that man to whom I gave my card after that meeting. That part of it was a total surprise. The thought never entered my mind of that man's having anything to do with me, or our ministry, beyond that meeting. I have found that if I make a list of all the ways I think God might do it, all I end up with is a list of ways He is *not* going to do it. In Isaiah 55:8,9 God plainly tells us, *For my thoughts are not your thoughts, neither are your ways my ways, saith the Lord. For as the heavens are higher than the earth, so are my ways higher than your ways, and my thoughts than your thoughts.* " God always has His Own way of conducting His Own business and how He does it is none of our business. Our business is to trust Him.

You may be walking through a faith event in your life right now, and you may be wondering how in the world God is going to do what He has confirmed in your heart that He is going to do. You have an assurance, a peace, a confidence He is going to supply, but you just can't imagine how.

Well, again, that part of it is not your concern. He may give you some idea ahead of time or He may not, but either way it does not matter. You don't need to know how, or even when or where; all you need is to know Who. If it makes you feel better to go through the mental exercise of trying to figure out how God is going to do it, then go ahead. In all probability, though, it won't help because, as I said, when you are finished all you will have is a list of options that God is not going to use. It is far better to just take Him at His Word and trust. When I was a boy I never found it necessary to ask my earthly father how he was going to do such and such; I just took him at his word and believed he was capable of doing what he said. How much more should it be with our heavenly Father. Over the past forty years God has demonstrated this truth in our life hundreds of times, but again there are some that really stand out in my memory. In this chapter I want to share a few of them with you to illustrate what I am talking about. The first one involves our second project in Hong Kong in November 1978.

Money for Hong Kong

Sheila and I, and an evangelist friend from Memphis, were going on this project with a larger group, and the travel arrangements were made by Bryan Tours in Jackson, MS. The departure date was October 28, and the deadline to pay for the air tickets was Monday, October 2. We needed a total of $4,500. Throughout the months of August and September we prayed and waited upon the Lord, but the money did not come. After receiving and accepting the invitation in early August, we published a newsletter telling everyone we could think of that we were going. We mailed it to 1241 people and thought that even though we did not ask for money, God might still use the letter to touch the hearts of some folks to help. It did not happen. We did not receive one single response from all those letters, not even an inquiry. We might have, if it had been sent in obedience to the Holy Spirit, but I am afraid it was, at best, just one of our "good ideas." All we accomplished was spending money we did not have. So when Monday morning arrived and the money did not, I called the agency and told them that we did not have the money and would therefore have to cancel our trip. I did not want to do that, because I believed it was God's will to go. It seemed, however, that we had no choice. But when I told the agent to cancel she said, "Shad, we set the deadline for today so we could finalize all this, but we can actually wait another week if you would like." So I accepted her offer and set a new deadline date for the following Monday, October 9.

Over the next week we continued to pray about the $4,500, but nothing happened. So on the next Monday I called the agent again. This time the owner of the agency, Dr. Bryan himself, came on the phone and told me, "Shad, we really want you guys to go, but time has run out; there is just nothing we can do. These tickets absolutely must be paid for today." I was just about to tell him again to cancel our trip when he said, "Shad, hold on for a second, someone is telling me something." So I waited. Then he continued, "You are not going to believe this, I just this second received word from the airline that they have extended the deadline until next Monday. I don't know why they have done it, but you have another week!" I thanked him and hung up the phone and then thought, "Lord I don't even want another week; I just want to get this over with." But I knew we had to continue to walk it through. Now we were facing the same deadline for the third time, but I knew in my heart it could not go any longer than one more week. We had to see the hand of God by Monday, October 16, or this time it was over for real.

On Thursday morning of the next week my evangelist friend and I were sitting in a restaurant discussing our situation. As we were talking, a friend (we will call him Bill) came in and joined us. He was a great guy and a wonderful Christian, but at that moment we really did not want to talk to him. All we wanted to do was just drink coffee (all we could afford), discuss how bad our situation was, and feel sorry for ourselves. But Bill wanted to know all about what was going on and about the upcoming Hong Kong trip. He asked if we had all our money and we said no. Then he wanted to know how much we needed, so we told him. We did not think there was any harm in telling him, because we knew Bill was just as broke as we were. Finally he left, and we were glad to see him go so we could resume our discussion, as fruitless and faithless as it was.

Then on Friday morning something happened that I did not expect and something that is also difficult to explain. I was talking to Sheila about the trip, and all of a sudden a peace and an assurance came into my heart that we were going - and along with it came a directive from the Lord. It was assurance followed by the activity of faith. He told me to write two letters, one to our friend Walter Wan in Hong Kong and another to missionary John Hyrons in neighboring Macau. He told me to tell both of them that we were coming for sure and to go ahead with arrangements for meetings if they had not done so already. Sheila typed the letters as I dictated, and they went in the mail that day. I knew beyond a doubt we were going to Hong

Kong and Macau, but I had no idea how. We were facing that third dead-line on Monday and there was no hope in sight.

The next day, Saturday, my evangelist friend and I drove to Houston, Texas to speak in a small church and to visit with old friends Tim and Rene Lawrence. At 3:00 Sunday afternoon, we were sitting around the dining table in their home having a late lunch, and the conversation turned to the Hong Kong trip. They asked if we had the money and I said, "No, we do not have it in our hand but it is coming. God is going to supply." Of course the final deadline was the next day. Just as that statement came out of my mouth the phone rang. Rene answered it, and to my surprise it was for me. It was Sheila calling from Memphis. I barely said hello when she shouted, "Honey, we got the money to go to Hong Kong, every penny of it!" And then she explained what had happened.

Our friend Bill, the guy we did not want to talk to and wished would just go away, had gone to his place of work earlier that afternoon to do something and when he arrived, his boss was there. As they talked, the subject of our trip somehow came up in the conversation. Then his boss, who was not a Christian and was not on our mailing list, asked if we needed any money for the trip. Bill told him we needed

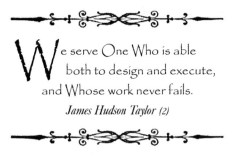

We serve One Who is able both to design and execute, and Whose work never fails.

James Hudson Taylor (2)

$4,500. With that, the man took out his checkbook and wrote a check for the entire amount, gave it to Bill, and told him to take it to us. So Bill left his workplace, drove to our house, and gave the check to Sheila. While I was confessing that the money was coming, Sheila was taking the check out of Bill's hand. She called me immediately in Houston to tell me about it. After I hung up the phone, I was able to tell our friends that God had indeed supplied, and we now had the money in hand – in time to pay for the tickets the next day.

There came a point during this faith event that I knew God was going to supply, but I would have never dreamed He would use Bill and his un-saved boss as the channel. Talk about unexpected! If I had made a list of all the possibilities I could think of, their names would not have been on it. But they were on God's list. Once again God demonstrated that He does not need our schemes and our good ideas. All He needs is our obedience and our faith. Just expect Him to use the unexpected and hold on in faith until He does. God uses the unexpected because <u>it rightly places the emphasis on His faithfulness, not our faith.</u>

Write This Name

I had an incident happen in my life in July 1991 that not only illustrates the fact that God uses the unexpected but was also a lesson in obedience, a very important element in walking through a faith event. I was leaving for a campaign in South India on July 4, and on the day of departure we had just enough money for my associate, Rick, and me to take for project expenses, but there was nothing left for home. Sheila and I had discussed it at length and had prayed much. She advised me to just go on to India, and we would trust God together to take care of the home front. Needless to say, that was hard to do, but we did it. I arrived in India three days later, and when I called home Sheila told me that there was still no money, and she needed at least $5,000. In 1991 we did not have cell phones and it was very hard and very expensive to make a call to the USA from India. So we could not be in touch every day, and that made the situation even more difficult.

For the next ten days Rick and I traveled from town to town preaching in 66 schools and villages, and we saw over 20,000 people come to Jesus. I was happy about that, of course, but every moment I was not preaching, all I could think and pray about was Sheila and the situation at home. On Wednesday, July 17, Rick and I had been gone fourteen days and still no money had come in at home. I had received word from Sheila that the situation had become extremely critical, and she had to have no less than $5,000 by Monday the 22nd. I did not know what to do. In reality, there was nothing in the natural realm I could do. She was on one side of the world, and I was on the other. But there was something in the spiritual realm I could do, and God brought that to my attention at mid-day that day.

We had conducted two meetings in one town that morning and had seven more to go in another town in the afternoon and evening. While traveling from one town to the other we stopped in a place at noon called Nazareth. There was a church compound there, and the pastor offered us a room to rest in for a short while. I intended to stretch out on a little cot for a few minutes to rest before going on to the other meetings. But just as I laid my head down, God spoke to me and said, "Shad, take out your legal pad and write down the names that I tell you to write down." I wanted to rest, but I knew I had to do it. So I began to write. After I had written four or five names, God said, "Put Pastor Dave on the list." I suspected that God was giving me a list of people to pray for who might possibly help with our financial crisis, and knowing for a fact that Pastor Dave did not have $5,000, I wrote the name of his church down instead.

Then as I looked over the list of names, the only one I was led to pray for was that church. It was as if God was telling me He was going to use that channel to meet our need. I don't really know why the other names were even on the list because all my attention was focused on that one. Then for the next five days I continued to pray, and finally late Monday night I was able to call home and talk to Sheila. When I got through to her it was about noon Monday Memphis time, and she had just come from the post office. She was so excited she could hardly wait to tell me what happened. She said that she had just received a check in the mail from Pastor Dave D's church for $5,000! Then she said there was a letter with it explaining what happened. Pastor Dave wrote, "Dear Sheila, This morning (Wednesday 17 – the day I was praying in India) a lady came in my office and gave me a check for $5,000 made out to the church. She said she wanted it to go for missions, but did not know where to send it, so she wanted me to decide. I told her that the people who came to my mind immediately were Shad and Sheila Williams. She said that would be fine. So I am sending this money to you to use any way you need to use it." He mailed it on Wednesday and it arrived in Sheila's hands on Monday, just in time to meet her deadline.

When I was sitting in India, I could not imagine how Pastor Dave could ever have $5,000, but it never occurred to me that some one might give him the money to pass on. It did occur to God, however, and after I hung up talking to Sheila, God spoke in my heart and said, "Next time I tell you to write a name, don't get creative, just obey, and do what I tell you." I said, "Yes Lord, I apologize." I know you may think, what difference does it make what name I wrote down? It makes a difference because God deals in specifics and demands absolute obedience. He allowed me some grace in this situation and proved, once again, that He always comes through, and He always uses the unexpected. He certainly did this time, because I would have never thought in a million years that the supply for our need would come through a pastor who was no more capable of giving $5,000 than I was. As He said, *"My ways are higher than your ways."* God uses the unexpected, because by doing so, He gets all the credit, all the honor, and all the glory.

From a Man I Did Not Even Know

Over the years we have had some strange and unusual things happen in relation to God meeting our needs, but this one really got my attention. I have said before that God is not likely to use someone to help us who does not even know who we are, but this incident came close to proving me wrong. It took place in November 1986. But to explain it, I must go back to the spring of 1985.

Once again our friends, Tim and Rene Lawrence of Houston, were involved. We went to visit them during the last weekend of March for the purpose of sharing the ministry with some of their friends, whom they invited to their home on Saturday night. At that meeting we met a man and his wife (we will call them Bob and Jane) who had only been saved about a month. After the meeting was over they told us that the next time we were in Houston they would like to have a meeting for us in their home. So when we went back in May, we did just that. They had over sixty people attend, and among them were his business partner and his wife (we will call them Charles and Mary Wilson). During the meeting we showed slides, shared about the work, and met a lot of people, but Charles and Mary were not among them. During the course of the evening we never met them. We had literature available, but they did not take any. So, even though they attended the meeting and listened to all we shared, we never knew they existed.

Now, fast forward to November 1986, 18 months later. Our friend, Evangelist Philip Eyster, had just come to work with us at the time, and one morning we were having a discussion about faith. As it happened, we desperately needed $2,000 that day to cover some expenses in the ministry, and we had nothing. I broke off our discussion and went to the post office, and when I opened the box I found an envelope from a Mr. Charles Wilson of Houston, Texas. I had absolutely no idea who he was. I opened the envelope and found a check for $2,000! I could not believe it, a check for the exact amount we needed from a man I did not know. I went back to the office, looked at our mailing list, and his name was not there. I asked the team if anyone knew a Mr. Wilson in Texas, and no one did. I could not figure out for the life of me who this man was. So, as awkward as I felt in doing it, there was nothing for me to do but call the number on the check and find out.

So, I called the number, and he answered the phone. I said, "Mr. Wilson, this is Shad Williams in Memphis and I just received a check from you for $2,000 – and – I am sorry I have to ask, but could you tell me who you are and how it is that you sent us that check?" Then he explained, "Well, my wife and I were at Bob and Jane's house in May of last year, and we heard about your ministry. A few days ago we were in a prayer meeting, and while we were praying, God brought you back to my mind and laid it on my heart to send you $1,000. I told my wife about it, and she said it should be $2,000. But I did not remember your name or where you live, so I called Bob a few days ago, and he gave me the information and I mailed the check." Again, if I had a made a list of all the ways God might meet that $2,000 need, Mr. Wilson's name would not have been on it, because I had no idea he even existed. Not only can God use the unexpected, He can even use the unknown. He delights in doing so because it proves His "Al-mightiness."

Three Loads of Corn for Africa

I have said repeatedly that God is always original, and He was cer-tainly no less so in this case. As we approached the month of April 1997, we were preparing to go to Malawi, Africa for a campaign, and of course we had no idea as how we would pay for it. On Monday morning, March 24, I got up at 4:00 to pray. The upcoming trip was heavy on my mind and heart, and once again I found myself cast upon the Lord for His supply. I knew for a fact it was God's will to go, but how? I prayed for two solid hours about nothing else but the Malawi project and the needs connected to it. I figured we needed about $9,000 for the tickets and project expenses.

Then at 6:00 the phone rang. I could not imagine who would be calling me at that early hour unless it was one of our team members overseas. But it was not from overseas; it was my a friend of mine, a farmer from Indi-ana. He said, "Shad, I am sorry to call so early, but I need to talk to you right now." I said, "No problem, brother; I have been up for two hours." Then he said, "Well, anyway, the reason I am calling is to tell you that you are now in the corn business." I said, "Oh really, how's that?" Then he explained, "I have some surplus corn that I am sending to be sold today, and I am going to have the broker send the check to you. I don't know exactly how much it will bring, but it is three tractor-trailer loads. What I need for you to do is call them and give them the information on where to send the check and how to make it out." He estimated it would be around $9,000! I said, "Brother, I have been up this morning praying about the money needed for Malawi, but I must tell you that in my wildest dreams, I never expected God to provide for it by selling corn. This is unbelievable." Later that day I was contacted by the broker and gave them the information. They sent me a check for $9,157. Praise God for using a harvest of corn in Indiana to pay for a harvest of souls in Africa. Who would have thought that God would supply in that way? No one! I have read about the "cattle on a thousand hills" and have even said jokingly, from time to time, that we need for God to sell some cows. But, I never thought about selling corn. It is always so much fun watching God be God by using the totally unexpected.

I Had to Bring It Now!

I realize many of the accounts I share with you have to do with going on campaigns and reaching souls and all of that, but I want to say again that God is just as concerned about your personal needs and the needs of your family or your home or your business as He is about reaching souls. Remember it is not the object of faith that is the most important element in the faith process; it is the process itself, the act of believing. I like this commentary by Oswald Chambers, "What we call the process, God calls the end. His end is the process, that I see Him walking on the waves, no shore in sight, no success, no goal; just the absolute certainty that it is alright because I see Him walking on the sea. It is the process, not the end that is glorifying to God" (3). This applies to every situation in life that draws you out beyond what you have and what you can do into a time of trusting God for the impossible, regardless of what the impossible thing is.

This story relates to a personal need that Sheila and I had in our life in September 2004. It was a need that demanded just as much attention from God as those times we are going overseas to preach the Gospel. If you cannot identify with going overseas to preach, maybe you can identify with this. It was the fifteenth of the month, our house payment was due the next day, and we did not have one penny. We had some other things to pay as well making the total amount we needed $2,000. We had been praying and asking God to meet the needs, but as of that morning nothing had happened. On the way to the office, we prayed again in the car and asked God to intervene. We went to the post office and there was nothing in the post office box. Then after we had been at the office for just a few minutes, a friend from our church came in. We will call him Mr. Jones. I said, "Hey brother, what brings you over here?" He said, "Shad I need to talk with you." We went into my office and he closed the door. I could not imagine what was going on. I thought there must be some serious problem. Then he said, "Shad, I had the strangest thing happen to me this morning that I have ever had happen." I asked him what it was and he said, "Well, about two hours ago, I was having my devotion time and all of a sudden God spoke to me and told me to give you some money. I mean it came on me all of a sudden and felt extremely urgent. So, I told the Lord I would mail you a check. Then He told me that that would not do, I had to bring it to you right now. So brother, here I am, and here is the check" He handed it to me folded up and when I unfolded it, it was $2,000! Once again God had supplied just in time and in a way I would never, I mean NEVER have expected.

Expect the Unexpected in Your Life

I am sharing all this with you, not only to illustrate the point of this chapter but also to let you know that every need you have is important to God, and He will go to any length necessary to meet it. But, again, as you wait for Him, don't wrack your brain trying to figure out how God is going to meet the need or solve the problem. You are not going to figure it out, because He is going to use an option, a channel, a way that you do not know about. Your job is not to figure; your job is to trust and obey. God is going to use the unexpected, and He is going to do it in His Own time. And when He does, you will receive maximum joy, and He will receive maximum glory. So, just let God be God, and hold on in faith until God fulfills His will in His Own way and time.

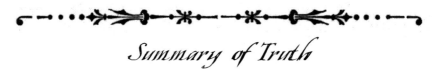

Summary of Truth

- ✧ God will nearly always use the unexpected in meeting our needs.
- ✧ It is useless to try to figure out how God is going to do what He is going to do.
- ✧ God deals in specifics and demands strict obedience.
- ✧ He needs our faith, not our help.
- ✧ God cares as much about our personal needs as He does about reaching souls.
- ✧ The issue in faith is not the object, but the process of believing.

NOW LET'S TAKE A MOMENT AND PRAY TOGETHER:

DEAR FATHER, THANK YOU FOR SHOWING ME THIS TRUTH. THANK YOU FOR FILLING MY LIFE WITH SURPRISES AS I WALK WITH YOU BY FAITH. LORD, HELP ME TO TRUST YOU AS A CHILD, FREE OF THE BURDEN OF FIGURING OUT HOW YOU ARE GOING TO DO WHAT YOU DO. HELP ME TO JUST LIVE IN EXPECTANCY OF THE UNEXPECTED. THANK YOU, LORD, FOR SAVING ME AND LOVING ME. IN YOUR NAME I PRAY. AMEN.

Chapter 29

Real Faith Requires Real Obedience

"At the risk of being thought fanatical you must obey what God tells you."
Oswald Chambers (1)

*I*n the Christian life there are two types of obedience. The first is obedience in a general sense, that is, compliance with the will and Word of God in our daily walk (John 15:1-11). Living in obedience to God on a daily basis, in the broad sense, provides the underpinning required for a life of faith that will not and cannot exist without it. A Christian who is living in even the slightest disobedience to God should not expect to be able to believe God for anything. The first order of business, therefore, in attempting to believe God by faith, is to make sure you are rightly adjusted to Him. The real faith life is a life lived in continuous fellowship with God, and fellowship with God is maintained through continuous obedience to the Spirit and the Word. All it takes to maintain a consistent harmonious relationship with God is to simply, moment-by-moment, obey the leading of the Holy Spirit and do what He says. A consistent life of obedience to God is essential to a life of real faith. Every occasion for the kind of faith that connects you to the impossible will necessitate an activity of faith that requires an act of radical obedience. The choice of radical obedience to God in relation to a faith event is much easier to make when the habit of regular, routine obedience has been formed in the daily life already.

As a side note, let me say this to you parents. The most valuable lesson you can teach your children is the habit of obedience. If a child learns from early age to unquestioningly and instantly obey his parents in the natural realm, then when he comes to Christ he will much more easily transfer that habit and pattern of life to God. The greatest contribution you can make to the life of your child, aside from leading them to Jesus, is to teach them instant and total obedience before they are saved. If they come into the Christian life prepared from day one to obey God instantly and completely, they will be miles ahead in their growth in Christ, and they will mature spiritually at a much faster rate. I have seen many young sincere Christians stumble and fall simply because they never learned to get under authority. Parents, your children can't learn if you don't teach them. Start preparing them for the Christian life from the day they are born by simply teaching them to obey, first you, then God.

Now let's look at the second type of obedience, which is what we will deal with primarily here. This is specific obedience to a specific command of God in connection with a specific faith event in your life. I referred to it above as radical obedience, and sometimes it is. In fact sometimes it is very radical. But one thing you can be sure of is that to every faith event God will attach a "go and do." The activity of faith, which follows the prayer of faith, will always include an action of faith on your part that may not make any sense whatsoever according to human reason and circumstances. What matters, however, is not how much sense it makes, but Who told you to do it. I want to share a couple of examples with you from my own life, but first let's look at some in the Bible.

From Genesis to Revelation the one issue that weaves its way through the entire Bible is that of faith and obedience. God is constantly saying to all of mankind, "Trust Me and obey Me." There is no greater example of radical obedience than the Lord Jesus Himself. In Him we find the greatest picture of obedience ever put on display for the human race. *"For as by one man's disobedience many were made sinners, so by the obedience of one shall many be made righteous"* (Romans 5:19). *"And being found in fashion as a man, he humbled Himself, and became obedient unto death, even the death of the cross. Wherefore God also hath highly exalted him, and given him a name which is above every name"* (Philippians 2:8,9). In John 5:30 Jesus said of Himself, *"I can of mine own self do nothing: as I hear, I judge: and my judgment is just; because I seek not mine own will, but the will of the Father which hath sent Me."* The greatest testimony to this statement, as well as the greatest act of obedience ever recorded, is found in the submission of Jesus to the will of the Father in the Garden of Gethsemane where He prayed, *"Abba, Father, all things are possible unto thee: take away this cup from me: nevertheless not what I will, but what thou wilt"* (Mark 14:36). Jesus understood, better than anyone, that God could perform the impossible. And He knew the resurrection was coming, but He also knew there was no shortcut. The only way to get there was through the gates of deliberate, radical obedience of faith.

When God calls upon you to enter into a faith event and trust Him for the impossible, your situation will not involve going to a cross and it will not end in a literal resurrection. But it will follow along the same route, and it will take you through the same gates Jesus walked through - the gates of radical obedience. I have heard it expressed that faith and obedience are like two oars in the water working together to propel the boat in the right direction. That is exactly right. In our walk with God, faith and obedience always work in tandem to propel us in the direction of His will. Again stating our most basic definition - faith is persuasion of fact followed by corresponding action. James expressed it this way in James 2:17 and 26, *"Even so faith, if it hath not works* [actions of obedience], *is dead, being alone* [without corresponding action]*... For as the body without the spirit is dead, so faith without works* [actions of obedience] *is dead also."*

Every time you walk through a faith event, you can be sure that, at some point, you are going to encounter a directive from God that requires you to confess publicly what He has confirmed to you as His will (the **declaration** of faith) and to act in radical obedience (the **demonstration** of faith). He is going to tell you to do this, go there, or say such and such, and you can be sure that the going, doing, and saying will contradict human reason, common sense, and circumstances. But all that doesn't matter. All that matters is what God says do. As we have said before, there may very well come a point when it seems your situation is dead. But if you will hold on in faith, and obey God to the end, He will raise up your situation and fulfill the promise He made to you, in your heart, through His Spirit and through His Word.

A Big Boat and No Water

Look again at the names in the Hall of Faith in Hebrews. The third name in the list is Noah. If there was ever an instance of radical obedience in the Old Testament, it is certainly found in Genesis six. Looking back on this event with all the information we now have 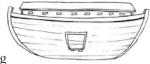 it makes perfect sense. But from Noah's viewpoint, it made no sense at all. God told this man to make a huge boat because a flood was coming upon the whole earth, and everyone was going to die. He even gave Noah specific, detailed instructions as to how to build it and how big to make it. In verse 22 the Bible simply records, *"Thus did Noah; according to all that*

God commanded him, so did he." Noah simply took God at His word and obeyed, which was a radical thing to do considering the fact that it had never even rained. Can you imagine how foolish Noah looked to all those folks that did not believe God? Can you imagine how much ridicule he received? Clearly Noah was not fazed because Hebrews 11:7 gives this testimony, *"By faith Noah, being warned of God of things not seen as yet, moved with fear, prepared an ark to the saving of his house; by the which he condemned the world, and became heir of the righteousness which is by faith."* Now how was it that Noah could just do what God said? The simple explanation is found in Genesis 6:9, *"...Noah was a just man, and perfect in his generations, and Noah walked with God."*

Going Out with No Direction

Another outstanding example, of course, is Abraham, who could obey God in relation to sacrificing Isaac because a pattern of obedience had already been formed in his life. Hebrews 11:8 says, *"By faith Abraham, when he was called to go out into a place which he should after receive for an inheritance, obeyed; and he went out, not knowing whither he went."* In verses 17 and 19 we see that *"By faith Abraham, when he was tried, offered up Isaac...accounting that God was able to raise him up even from the dead."* Abraham accounted that God was able, in this particular instance of extreme trial of faith, because in his life he already had a history of accounting God able. In connection with this wonderful display of faith Oswald Chambers makes this important observation, "The wonderful simplicity of Abraham! When God spoke, he did not confer with flesh and blood, i.e. your own sympathies, your own insight, anything that is not based on your personal relationship to God. These are the things that compete with and hinder obedience to God" (2). I agree. In times of extreme faith, which call for acts of radical obedience, all that matters is what God says, not what you think or feel, not circumstances, and certainly not what any other human being has to say. In this case Abraham was accounting God able to raise up Isaac, but in your particular situation you can just fill in the blank.

Stretch out Your Hand

In Exodus 14:1, God revealed His will and His plan to Moses and told him exactly what He was going to do. Then in verse 13, Moses spoke a word of faith, repeating to the people what God had told him. Then in verse 16, God gave Moses a sure promise accompanied by specific instructions, *"But lift up thy rod, and stretch out thine hand over the sea, and divide it: and the children of Israel shall go on dry ground through the midst of the sea."* There it was, the "go and do" mentioned above, the obedience of faith. Then verse 21 tells us, *"And Moses stretched out his hand over the sea; and the Lord caused the sea to go back by a strong east wind all that night, and made the sea dry land, and the waters were divided."* Now here is a question, was it necessary for Moses to lift up that rod and stretch out his hand over the sea in order for it to part? Could God not have side-stepped Moses and done it without him? Yes, God could have, but He was not going to. And to answer the first part of that question, yes, it was absolutely necessary for Moses to go through a radical act of obedience and it will be necessary for you to do the same thing. If Moses had not lifted up that rod and stretched out his hand, the waters would never have parted and neither will yours. Again quoting Oswald Chambers, "All the promises of God in Him are yea, and in Him Amen. The 'yea' must be born of obedience; when by the obedience of our lives we say 'Amen' to a promise, then that promise is ours" (3).

Blow Your Horns

In Joshua 6, we find God giving another promise with very specific instructions to go with it. God told Joshua in verse 2 that he was going to deliver the walled city of Jericho into his hands, but before that happened, Joshua had to "go and do." God told Joshua his entire army was to march around the city, one time each day for six days, and each time they were to be followed by seven priests walking ahead of the ark, each one carrying a trumpet made of a ram's horn. Then on the seventh day they were to march around the city seven times with the priests blowing their trumpets. Then when they gave one long loud blast, the people were to shout and the walls would come down. Now the Bible doesn't say this, but I can just imagine what was going through the minds of some of those soldiers when they heard this plan. I'm sure some must have thought, "You have to be kidding! What possible good can it do to just march around that wall and then come back to camp and sit down and do nothing?" I am sure some thought it made no sense whatsoever. But it did not matter what they thought. What mattered is what they did. What they did was obey the Lord's command to the letter, and as a result God fulfilled His promise and the walls collapsed.

Now what if they had stopped on the sixth day. Or what if they had not shouted as the Lord commanded? The answer is simple; the walls might still be standing. But they did continue, they did shout, the walls did come down, and they did enjoy the victory of God just as He promised. And so will you as you obey Him specifically. This was a radical thing to do, and in the natural realm it did not make sense or seem reasonable. But all that did not matter. All that mattered was that God said to do it, and they did. They had the sure promise of God, but without absolute obedience it would have been of no effect.

Digging Ditches

In II Kings chapter 3, we see this same truth born out again. The three armies of Israel, Judah and Edom teamed up to fight against the army of Mesha, King of Moab, and for seven days they marched through the wilderness becoming desperate because there was no water. Jehoshaphat, King of Judah, asked if there was not a prophet of the Lord that could tell them what to do. When Elisha was identified, the three kings consulted him. He told them God said to dig ditches throughout the land to contain the water He would send. He told them they would not see wind or rain, but they would see the water come just the same. He told them also that they would not only have plenty of water, but they would also have victory over their enemy. In verses 20-26, we see that as they obeyed the Lord, God not only blessed with abundant water, but gave victory as well. But, again, you can be sure that if those ditches had not been dug, the water and victory would not have come. The promise of God was contingent upon the obedience of those to whom He gave it.

Gather Some Pots

In II Kings chapter 4, we find a similar situation. A woman came to Elisha and told him her husband had died and left a debt, and the creditor was threatening to take her two sons as slaves to repay the debt. Elisha asked her what she had in the house, and she told him she only had one jar of olive oil. He told her to go and borrow all the empty jars she could find from friends and neighbors, then go into her house (she and her sons) and fill all the jars from the one she had. Now, how is it possible to fill many jars from one single jar?

It is not possible, but she obeyed God and HE did it. He made the oil last as long as there was another jar to put it in. He multiplied that oil in response to her obedience. As a result, from the sale of the oil, she paid off the debt and had money for her and her sons to live on. Once again God honored and blessed simple obedience to His specific "go and do."

Lots of Cash but No Cure

Now let's look at one more interesting event in the fifth chapter of II Kings, which also involves the prophet Elisha. This time God spoke through him to Naaman, the captain of the army of the king of Aram. Verse one tells us Naaman was a "great man", a "highly respected" man and a "valiant warrior." But he was also a leper. Now Naaman's wife had a young maid, an Israelite girl, who knew about the prophet Elisha in Samaria, and she told Naaman's wife that she wished Naaman could go see him, because she thought Elisha could cure him. When Naaman told the king what the girl said, he told Naaman to go and sent with him a letter of authorization and a large sum of money.

In verse 9, we find Naaman standing at the door of Elisha's house in all his honor, his valor, and his dignity - and in all his need. There he was, a man of great reputation, authority, and wealth. Yet he could not solve his own problem. He did not need all those things he came with; all he needed was to obey a simple command from God, which was about to come through Elisha. The prophet sent a messenger out to Naaman saying (v.10), "...*Go and wash in Jordon seven times, and thy flesh shall come again to thee, and thou shalt be clean.*" There it was, a simple specific command requiring simple obedience. But that simple obedience was something that Naaman, like so many of us, had a hard time producing. In fact he became angry. He said in verse 11, "...*I thought, he will surely come out to me, and stand, and call on the name of the Lord his God, and strike his hand over the place, and recover the leper.*" What Naaman was saying was, "I thought he would come out and recognize who I am and respect me and heal me in a dignified way. I didn't know he was just going to tell me to dip myself in some dirty river. And besides aren't there better and cleaner rivers than Jordon? Why can't I wash in them?" The problem Naaman had was the same one we often have when facing a situation that requires simple, yet radical obedience to the command of God. He wanted to rely on human reason and human resources rather than simply obey. His problem was that he was thinking instead of obeying. He needed to realize, just as we do, that <u>there is no substitute for obedience</u>.

In verse 13 we see the servants of Naaman were thinking more clearly and sensibly than he was. They asked him, "If the prophet had told you to do some great thing, wouldn't you do that? Of course you would. Then why don't you just do this simple thing and be healed?" So at their bidding, Naaman went and washed and was healed immediately. Dear friend, you may, like Naaman, have a lot of money, a lot of respect, a lot of dignity, a lot of common sense, and a lot of pride. But there is going to come a day when you are going to have a lot of need that only God can provide for. I know, because the storms, trials, and challenges of life come to every person sooner or later. But, praise God, if you are a child of His, you have the option of accepting His invitation to simply trust and obey and believe for the impossible.

Now notice again that the command of God was very specific; it always is. God did not say for Naaman to dip in just any river; it had to be Jordon. Why? Because God said so. He did not tell him to dip six times or eight times, it had to be seven. Why? Because God said so. Joshua had to march around the wall of Jericho exactly seven times. Why? Because God said so. God does not need for us to be inventive or creative; He just wants us to be obedient. In connection to your faith scenario, whatever it is, God is going to tell you to do something very specific and very literal. When He does, just simply follow the advice of Mary in John 2:5, *"Whatsoever he saith unto you, do it."*

Fishing at the Wrong Time of Day

There are so many instances of radical obedience in the Bible, but we are going to turn now to one in the New Testament. In Luke 5:1-11, we find Peter in a very discouraged state. He and his fellow fishermen had been fishing all night and had caught absolutely nothing. They had given up and were washing their nets. As they were doing this, Jesus came along, got into Peter's boat, and told him to push away from the shore a little. Jesus taught for a while and then told Peter to do something that made no sense whatsoever. He said in verse 4, *"...Launch out into the deep, and let down your nets for a draught."* Now it is easy to tell from the next verse what Peter was thinking. It probably went something like this, "But Lord (not a good way to start a conversation with Jesus), we have been fishing all night, which is the right time to fish, by the way, and we have caught nothing. Now You come along, up in the day when the sun is on the water and the fish are on the bottom, and tell us to fish where the nets won't even reach. And besides, You want us to go out there in the deep where it is the most dangerous. Lord, I have been doing this all my life, and I'm telling You it does not make sense." But then all of a sudden something happened in Peter, something clicked in his heart, and he said in verse 5, *"Nevertheless at thy word, I will let down the net."* The whole scenario turned on that one short phrase, *"AT THY WORD, I WILL."* That is exactly the place we must get to in our faith event, the place of radical obedience where we say, "Lord, this may not make any sense, but *at Thy word, I will."* Jesus told Peter to do two things. First, "Launch out into the deep," get into the place of utter impossibility. And second, "Let down your nets for a catch;" act in faith expecting results. Then verse 6 tells us, *"And when they had THIS done* [specific obedience to a specific command], *they inclosed a great multitude of fishes: and their net brake."* If you want to see the abundance of God in your life, then radically obey Him by faith and believe for the absurdly impossible.

As They Went

Let's look at one more example from Luke 17:11-19, which is the story of the ten lepers who came to Jesus to be healed. In verse 14 Jesus told them, *"...Go shew yourselves unto the priests."* Now the problem with this command was that they were not yet healed. So it appeared Jesus was telling them to do something that made no sense. Why should they go to the priests to be declared clean when they were obviously still lepers? Why? Because Jesus said so. Why? Because if they did not obey, they would not be healed. The rest of the verse says, *"...as they went, they were cleansed."* When they left Jesus they were still lepers, but by the time they reached the priests they were cleansed. Radical obedience of faith produced radical results - and God will do the same thing in your life and mine. I know, because I have seen Him do it. I have shared with you already in other chapters how God told us to get on a plane, go to another country, and preach the Gospel - even without the money to go. And as we went in obedience to Him, He supplied all we needed in order to do what He had called us to do.

Personal Experiences

There have been many times over the years when God has told us to do some seemingly irrational things in connection to various faith events in our life. I have shared some of them with you already, such as the Sunday morning we were leaving for Africa and had not one penny of the $3,000 needed for the trip. God told us to put our bags in the car, tell no one about the need, and leave for the airport after church. We did exactly as God said, and just as we were walking into church, a man stopped us and gave us the $3,000 we needed. There was another time that God told us to go with no money, which we did, and when we arrived in Boston, we found out the money had come to our house as we were getting on the plane.

In another chapter I shared with you how God told me to write letters to our friends in Hong Kong and Macau telling them we were coming. That would have been no problem except for the fact that we had already passed two deadlines in paying for our tickets, the third and final one was coming in three days, and we had no money whatsoever. But, in obedience to God, we sent the letters and on the third day God miraculously provided. I shared with you also that as we were trusting God for $3,000 to go to Amsterdam, God told us to give $300 for someone else to go. No problem, except we didn't have $300 to give. How could it make any sense at all to give money away (that we did not have) when we were looking to God for ten times that much, which we also did not have? It did not make sense, but it was God's will and God's way. Then there was that night God told me to take my Filipino friend to another city to help him raise money. I have already told you when that night came I felt like the biggest fool who ever lived, because we had no food in our house and no gas to get to the meeting. But God said go, and that was that. So I went, and you know the rest of the story – except for the part I left out. What I did not tell you before is that out of that meeting, God not only provided the $4,000 we needed that day but also, over the next several years, over one and a half million dollars of support for the ministry. And that money resulted in two and a half million people coming to Jesus. We never know how much is at stake in one simple act of obedience, especially an act of radical obedience connected to a real faith event. What do you think would have happened if I had not written those letters, or given that $300, or made that trip that night? The answer is obvious. Dear Christian, don't delude yourself into thinking God will work around your disobedience or in spite of it. He won't.

Get a Job - Or Not?

Sheila and I began early on in our Christian life encountering situations that called for radical obedience to the leadership of God. One of our first was the decision to turn down offers to go to school for free from four large, accredited universities in order to attend a small school in Memphis that offered nothing, including an accredited degree. But, as foolish as that looked, it was the will of God. Then the summer of 1971 brought us to another point of obedience to God. We were to transfer to Union University in Jackson, Tennessee in the fall. The question was, what to do during the summer? I had only one speaking engagement on the calendar and it was in July, right in the middle of summer break. We had no money and no income, and we did not know what to do. Our son was almost two and our daughter had just been born, so needless to say, we needed to make some money doing something. My thought was that as a responsible husband and father, I should find a job for the summer and work until time to move to Jackson. I would just have to cancel that one engagement. But as Sheila and I prayed it through, we sensed that God was telling us to keep that engagement and trust Him by faith to take care of us. I remember thinking that it just did not make sense to sit around for 5 weeks waiting for one little engagement, and then sit around for another 5 weeks after the engagement, when I could be out working at a job for the whole time and making money. But there came a point where I knew that to do anything else would be disobedience. So we kept the engagement on the calendar.

A day or so after making that decision, we received a call from some friends in Johnson City, Tennessee asking us to come visit for a few days. So, having nothing else to do, we accepted the invitation and went. We barely had enough money to get there in our little Volkswagen, but we made it, and after we arrived God began to do something very strange and unexpected. People we had never met, friends of our friends, started asking us to come to this meeting and that meeting in homes and churches, and as we went God began to touch the hearts of people to give us money. We had no ministry organization back in those days, and we had nothing to promote. We were just a young couple going to school and doing ministry as God opened doors. The first such occasion happened at a Wednesday night supper at a church. A man came up to me and handed me a folded bill and said, "Shad, God told me to give you this." I put it in my pocket thinking it was a dollar bill. Later I took it out and discovered it was a hundred dollar bill. As we were leaving the supper, his wife told us to come by their house the next day, and there would be something for us in the mailbox. We went, and it was a check for two hundred dollars. I know that does not sound like much now, but that was 1971 and minimum wage (which is all

I could have earned at the time) was about $1.40 per hour. Over the next few days, person after person came to us and gave us money. After about a week, we drove home with over $1,500 in our pocket. Then we received calls to do other meetings over the next few weeks, and by the time we were to move to Jackson, God had supplied over $3,000. That was *three times* what I would have made working 60 hours a week at a minimum wage job. I was more than willing to work at a regular job, but it was not the will of God. Isaiah 1:19 says, *"If ye be willing and obedient, ye shall eat the good of the land."* It certainly proved to be so with us in the summer of 1971. And, I might add, it has proven to be so ever since.

Mail the Checks

In the years that followed, God called upon us to take steps of faith that required radical acts of obedience, not the least of which was our resignation from our church staff position in 1977 to enter the ministry we are in today. But there is a particular instance that stands out in my memory that occurred about a year later in June 1978. Looking back on it now, it seems like a small thing, but at the time it was huge. On June 1, we needed $345 to pay the rent and we also needed about $250 or so to cover some other bills as well. So in all we needed about $600. Again, looking back on it today, that does not seem like much of a problem, but at that moment it may as well have been $600,000. Need is relative to where you are at any given moment.

As I sat at my desk that afternoon, looking at the bills and looking at my empty checkbook, I heard the Lord whisper a question in my heart, "Shad what would you do if you had the money?" I said, "Lord, I would write the checks." Just then the Holy Spirit said to me, "Then write them." Then I thought, "Yeah, right. Lord, You know that's irresponsible." He said, "Write the checks." As I sat there holding the checkbook in one hand and the bills in the other, a real struggle ensued between my intellect, my emotions, and my spirit. My inner man was telling me to obey the voice of God, but my logical calculating mind was telling me I would be crazy to write checks that I did not have money to cover. And when it came to choosing sides, my

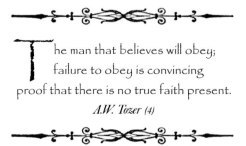

The man that believes will obey; failure to obey is convincing proof that there is no true faith present.

A.W. Tozer (4)

emotions quickly sided with my sense of logic and common sense. So I hesitated. But as I sat there the Spirit of God pressed me to obey. So I picked up my pen and began to write the checks. That pen felt like it weighed a hundred pounds. I wrote the rent check first and then the others. Then when I finished, the Lord told me to put them in the envelopes and seal them up. So I did it. Then God said, "Now Shad, you must mail them."

Again came the struggle, and at that point, I hesitated and tried to get creative. I mean, how in the world could I mail $600 worth of checks when I did not have one penny with which to cover them? So I thought (bad mistake), "I will lay these envelopes out, and as the money comes in to cover them, I will put them in the mail." My idea was very sensible, very responsible, and very disobedient. But that is what I did, and for six days I waited and nothing happened – nothing! I had no peace in my heart, the pressure from the Holy Spirit continued, and I knew it was not going to go away until I obeyed Him. So finally, on the sixth day, Sheila and I took the envelopes to the post office and dropped them in the box. All of a sudden the pressure was relieved, and peace came. Quoting from my journal entry that night, "So we took the bills to the post office and sent them on their way. We are at peace about it now. We are not free from satan's taunts, but we do have the victory in Jesus. In fact, I have more peace tonight than I have had in a long time. We are totally cast upon the Lord, and I feel very secure. Of course I have to pray constantly and remind myself that the supply is on the way." Yes, finally the pressure was off and peace had come, not because we had the money, but because we had radically obeyed the Lord and could now wait in faith on Him. We had finally reached that crucial point where we were waiting on Him and He was no longer waiting on us.

Days went by and small amounts of money came in here and there, and each time it did I put it in the bank. I knew, however, it was not coming in fast enough to keep us out of trouble, because that $345 rent check was always deposited the very day it was received. As we went through the month, I could not figure out for the life of me why we were not bouncing checks. But when we arrived at the end of the month, and received our bank statement, I found out why. This was the only month out of the forty-eight we lived there, that the management company held our check for 30 days before depositing it. By the time they did there was just enough to cover it. Coincidence? Absolutely not! The hand of God? No doubt about it!

Now, as I said, I know that in retrospect this looks like a small incident in faith, but at the time it was a huge lesson for a young couple just starting out in a new ministry and just learning to trust God. Along the way God would lead us to trust Him for much bigger things that would involve many people and lots of money, but first we needed to learn the importance of complete radical obedience. Now what about the next month? We did not have the money we needed on the first of July either. So, did we mail the bills again with no money in the bank? Absolutely not! Why not? It worked last time, why not this time? Because last time God said do it, and this time He didn't. In June it was real faith because it was done in obedience to the command of God. In July it would have been utter foolishness because it would have been no more than a "good idea" - except it would have been a terrible idea because God was not in it. The key in every situation is simple obedience. Now, let me take a moment here to caution you. DO NOT try to "work your own salvation" by "trying out" one of these events that happened in my life. If you do, you will most assuredly fail. Why? Because these were faith events for my life that were orchestrated by God and entered into by His command. I didn't think them up, and I didn't work them out on my own. Whatever need you have, and whatever faith event you enter, will be created just for you by God's own design. It will be unique to you, and will contain its own set of circumstances and instructions. Remember, there are no shortcuts!

Make the Calls

Now let me share one more incident with you. It concerns a campaign in Brazil that came about as a result of radical obedience to God on the part of several of His children, including me. In the last chapter I told you about a couple in Houston, Texas (we called them Bob and Jane) who had a meeting for us in their home on a Saturday night May 25, 1985. Well, the next morning as we were about to leave for their church, Bob showed me a verse and said God had spoken to him through it that morning. It was II Chronicles 17:11, *"And some of the Philistines brought Jehoshaphat presents and tribute silver; and the Arabians brought him flocks, seven thousand and seven hundred rams and seven thousand and seven hundred he goats."* Bob did not tell me what God had said to him, but when I looked at that verse the Holy Spirit spoke to my heart and said, "This man is going to give you $7,700." Needless to say I was excited because we were in the throes of preparing to do a six-week project in Brazil and we needed $21,500 for the project. We went to church with Bob and Jane and then to lunch afterward, and while we were waiting for the food to come Bob handed me a check folded up. He said, "Shad, God told me through that verse this morning to give you this." I opened the check and it was $700, not $7,700. At that moment my heart sank, because I knew he had made a mistake, but there was nothing I could say. So I thanked him and put the check in my pocket. I did tell Sheila later, however, that he had made a mistake and we needed to pray for him, because I was very afraid he had missed the will of God. So we did pray for him asking God to help him obey.

On the following Friday night, God said, "Shad, tomorrow I want you to get up early and begin calling people, and call until I tell you to stop. Call the names I bring to your mind and tell them you have a need, but do not tell them how much it is." I did not know what to think about that because we have a policy of non-solicitation in our ministry. I reminded God of that, and He responded , "Okay, don't call them, but you are not going to get the money you need if you don't." For me, this was a point of radical obedience, because I felt I was violating a principle we had worked hard to keep. But I knew I had no choice. With the final call at 10:00 PM, God said,

We are saved through faith alone, but the faith that saves is never alone.

John Calvin (5)

"That's enough." I told every person, "God told me to call you and tell you we have a need, but to not tell you how much it is." Every one was receptive and thanked me for calling and for giving them the opportunity to pray. I was exhausted and glad to have it over with. But I knew I had obeyed the Lord. Through that situation, God taught me a great lesson. A principle is just that – a principle. It is not Scripture. Principles are subject to change by God. I realized I must be willing to change the way I did things in response to God's instructions. He is the Author of the principles in my life. The principles in my life do not dictate the way God works in my life – God works in my life and the principles conform to His Way!

Four days later, I received a letter in the mail from Bob in Houston and with it was a check. The letter was short and read simply, "Shad, when God says $7,700, He means $7,700, not $700. Here is the rest." Of course the check was for $7,000. Bob was only a few months old in the Lord, and this was a radical step of obedience for him, but I was so glad for his sake that he was enabled to do it. And, by the way, Bob was NOT one of the people

I had called. By the next day, Thursday, we had received another $3,000 from the phone calls, making our total in hand $10,000 toward the $21,500 needed. At noon the next day, Friday, Sheila and I knelt by my desk to pray for the remaining $11,500 needed by Monday, our departure day. At 3:00 in the afternoon the phone rang. It was the man I had met a year before (we called him Don), the one who called to give $4000. He said, "Shad this is Don. I need to ask you a question, and I need a point blank answer." "Okay, brother, what is it?" "Do you need any money?" I answered, "Yes, brother, I do." "How much?" Now at that point I was thinking (there I go again) that if I had $10,000 I would somehow be able to get the other $1,500. I don't know why I thought that, but I did. So I answered, "Don, I need $10,000." At that he said, "Praise God! I have been praying for you every morning this week. For the last five days I have sensed God telling me to send you $10,000, so I decided to call you and ask you what you need. If you said, $10,000 then I would know I am right." Then he said, "Well Shad, I am out of town so I will have to make arrangements to get it to you." I said, "I know you are out of town, you live 100 miles away." He said, "No I am on my new boat down here in the Caribbean off the coast of Florida." "You mean you are calling me from a boat?" "Yes I am, on a satellite phone. So do you want me to have it brought to you or do you want to go pick it up?" I said, "Brother, I will go get it." With that I thanked him and then made plans to go pick up that check, which I did.

After I hung up that phone the realization and the amazement of the power of God flooded into my heart. Here I was sitting in my office in Memphis with a need, and there was Don sitting on a boat in the ocean with the supply. All God had to do was put the two together. I realized, all of a sudden, that Don and I both had been talking on a much bigger satellite phone than the one he used to call me on. I was talking to God about the need and all the while God was talking to Don about the supply. The wonderful thing is that even if I had thought to call Don, which I did not, I would have had no idea where he was or how to reach him. But God knew exactly where he was, exactly how to reach him, and He didn't mind calling him. *"O the depth of the riches both of the wisdom and knowledge of God! how unsearchable are his judgments, and his ways past finding out"* (Romans 11:33).

Now all we needed was the remaining $1,500 and the next day God provided that. One of our friends, Don Hemker (now with Jesus) came by my house on Saturday and gave us a check for $1000 and another friend came by and gave $500. That, of course, made the total amount needed, $21,500. On Monday we departed for Brazil, and we were able to go because some of God's children had radically obeyed the voice of the Father.

That incident took place twenty-four years ago and we have seen many days since then when we were in almost the exact same situation, but God has never told me again to call a list of people like he did on that Saturday. Also, I have never had anyone since call me from a boat, or send the balance of a check as Bob did. Every radical act of obedience is specially designed for a specific event. Never make the mistake of thinking God will repeat Himself, because He will not. There has never been another Red Sea crossing, and there never will be. It's not that God cannot do it again; He could, but He won't. He is always original. You cannot repeat those moments in your life, but what you can do is learn from them and allow them to create a history of obedience in your life and a collective testimony of God's faithfulness. You can look back on them and remember, as David did in Psalm 77, that you radically obeyed God and the outcome was miraculous. When you do, the realization will settle in upon you that the most sensible, the most rational, the most responsible thing you can do in any situation in life is to find the will of God, obey Him totally, and believe for the impossible. Are you in a faith event right now? Is God telling you to do something that looks crazy to the flesh, to the world, and maybe even to you? Well, again, just follow Mary's advice in John 2:5, *"Whatever he saith unto you, do it."*

The Christian life is not only a changed life (II Corinthians 5:17), but it is a changing life. It is not just a one-time salvation experience resulting from a one-time act of obedience in faith to Christ. It is a life of continual salvation resulting from continual obedience in faith to the commands of Christ. Yes, we have been saved, once and for all, from hell by grace through faith in Jesus (Ephesians 2:8), but the Christian life is more than that. It is a life of continually being saved through obedience to the Word and Spirit of God as we face the storms and challenges of life.

When we walk with the Lord in the light of His Word,
What a glory He sheds on our way.
While we do His good will, He abides with us still,
And with all who will trust and obey.

Trust and obey, for there's no other way, To be happy in Jesus,
but to trust and obey. (6)

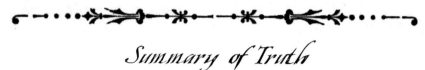

Summary of Truth

❖ There are two types of obedience in the Christian life; compliance with the will of God in our daily walk, and radical obedience connected to a faith event.

❖ The greatest lesson that parents can teach their children is simply to obey.

❖ There is no greater example than the Lord Jesus of a life of faith and radical obedience.

❖ God will not work apart from our obedience to His commands.

❖ In every faith event there will be a "go and do" from God.

❖ If you want to see the abundance of God in your life, you must learn to radically obey Him by faith and believe for the absurdly impossible.

❖ The absurd becomes the sensible when it is a directive of God.

❖ The Christian life is not just a changed life; it is a changing life. It is a life of continual salvation as a result of continuous obedience.

NOW LET'S TAKE A MOMENT AND PRAY TOGETHER:

DEAR FATHER, IT IS THE DESIRE OF MY HEART TO LIVE A LIFE OF TRUST IN YOU AND OBEDIENCE TO YOU. I DO WANT THIS HABIT OF OBEDIENCE TO BE FORMED IN MY LIFE. I REALIZE THAT THERE IS A PART OF ME THAT DOES NOT WANT TO OBEY YOU. BUT LORD, IN MY HEART AND IN MY SPIRIT I DO, AND I DETERMINE RIGHT NOW, AT THIS VERY MOMENT, TO CAST MYSELF UPON YOU AND TO TRUST YOU COMPLETELY WITH EVERYTHING. LORD, I WELCOME THE OPPORTUNITIES YOU SEND INTO MY LIFE TO BELIEVE FOR THE IMPOSSIBLE, AND I CHOOSE RIGHT NOW THAT WHEN THEY COME, I WILL OBEY YOU RADICALLY, NO MATTER WHAT YOU TELL ME TO DO. I KNOW THIS IS A BIG CLAIM, BUT LORD I AM MAKING THE COMMITMENT TRUSTING THAT WHEN THE TIME COMES, YOU WILL POUR OUT YOUR GRACE AND HELP ME. THANK YOU, LORD JESUS, FOR YOUR SUPREME EXAMPLE OF RADICAL OBEDIENCE, AND THANK YOU FOR SAVING ME AND DRAWING ME INTO THIS WONDERFUL LIFE OF WALKING WITH YOU. IN YOUR NAME I PRAY. AMEN.

Chapter 30

Real Faith Results in Real Giving

"For God so loved the world that He gave..."
John 3:16

M y intention in this chapter is not to give an exhaustive treament to the subject of giving - that would require another book. Rather, what I want to do here is simply make the important point that a life of real faith is a balanced life of giving as well as receiving. The very essence of the Christian life is giving. *"For God so loved the world that He gave..."* The very nature of the life of Jesus lived through us is giving. *"I am crucified with Christ: nevertheless I live; yet not I, but Christ liveth in me: and the life which I now live in the flesh I live by the faith of the Son of God, who loved me, and gave himself for me (Galatians 2:20)."* Notice that the operation of real love, which we have said is the driving force of real faith, is expressed through the activity of giving. Because the life of faith is powered by love, it will always be a life of flow and not containment. One of the chief characteristics of love, which you discovered the moment you were born again, is that it wants to give. As I have mentioned before, when I first met my wife, I fell head over heels in love with her. The result was I wanted to give her everything - I still do. All of a sudden I found myself spending money I did not have and buying things I could not afford to give to a girl I did not yet really know all that well. Now, why did I do that? Because I was in love and love wants to give. I might add that after forty-two years I still feel the same way. The same thing happened when I met Jesus. The moment He came into my heart, I fell in love with Him and wanted to give Him everything. I gave away money, clothes, possessions, and anything else I thought God could use for His Kingdom. I am sure you had the same experience. When you are truly in love, you just can't give enough. Amy Carmichael (1867-1951), missionary to India, said, "You can give without loving, but you cannot love without giving." In Acts 2:41-47 and 4:31-37, we see three outstanding characteristics of the early Church that resulted from being filled with the Holy Spirit - boldness, unity, and giving. These early Christians were almost intoxicated with giving, and as a result, there was no lack among them. They sold lands, houses, and possessions and gave the proceeds to the apostles to distribute to those who had need. What was it that produced this radical giving? They had been filled with the Holy Spirit, and they had fallen in love with Jesus.

The real faith life, the Christian life, is fluid like a river, not still and stagnant like a pond. *"He that believeth on me, as the Scripture hath said, out of his belly* [innermost being, heart] *shall flow rivers of living water"* (John 7:38). Just like Jesus, we as children of God are to be channels through which the blessings and provision of God flow to others, not just reservoirs in which to store them for ourselves. Sadly, many people incorrectly believe, and many falsely teach, that faith is only about acquisition; God blessing ME, providing for ME, meeting MY needs, solving MY problems, and calming MY storms. Yes that is part of it, but it is only PART of it. There is another side of the page that reaches far beyond you and your needs out into the world. If you come away from this book thinking it is only about YOU, then I have done a poor job of trying to teach you something about the life of faith. The faith life is a balanced life of receiving, yes, but also of giving, and if the giving side is not there, then the receiving side will be greatly diminished. The only way to live a full-orbed life of faith is to maintain the balance between receiving and giving.

The Law of Circulation

Norman Grubb (son-in-law of C.T. Studd and author of "The Law of Faith") refers to this balance as the "law of circulation." He writes, "Life ultimately consists in circulation. When once this principle becomes clear to us, we shall see that our attention should be directed to giving rather than to receiving. We must look upon ourselves, not as miser's chests to be kept locked for our own benefit, but as centers of distribution. If we choke the outlet, the current must slacken, and a full and free flow can be obtained only by keeping it open. We are not called upon to give what we have not yet got, and to run into debt; but we are to give liberally of what we have, with the knowledge that by so doing we are setting the law of circulation to work" (1).

In writing to the church at Corinth concerning an offering to be taken for the saints in Jerusalem, Paul expressed this truth in II Corinthians 9: 6-8, *"But this I say, He which soweth sparingly shall reap also sparingly; and he which soweth bountifully shall reap also bountifully. Every man according as he purposeth in his heart, so let him give; not grudgingly, or of necessity* [because he feels he has to]*: for God loveth a cheerful* [joyous] *giver.* " Then in Like 6:38 we read, "*Give, and it shall be given unto you; good measure, pressed down, and shaken together, and running over, shall men give into your bosom* [the pouch of your robe that is used as a bag]. *For with the same measure that ye mete withal* [the measure you use to give] *it shall be measured to you again.* " Turning back to the Old Testament we find this same truth stated in Proverbs 11:24-25, "*There is that scattereth* [gives generously], *and yet increaseth; and there is that withholdeth* [keeps for one's self] *more than is meet* [fitting or suitable], *but it tendeth to poverty. The liberal soul shall be made fat: and he that watereth shall be watered also himself.* " So we see from Scripture that as a general principle in life, especially the Christian life, there is a definite correlation between giving and receiving.

I recently read a story about a woman who is not even a Christian and yet learned a remarkable lesson. She was struggling to become a financial planner and was failing miserably. Even if she had some success one month, she was still discouraged and anxious over how she would perform the next. She was a very talented and capable person and yet lived in constant fear and defeat. One day, in an effort to briefly escape her situation, she took a day off from work intending to just spend it watching television. While doing so, she saw an advertisement by a charitable organization asking for

A simple rule is: if in need, give.

Norman Grubb (2)

donations. She said that all of a sudden she felt as if she should give, so she called and made a pledge. She said that at that moment everything began to change. She went back to work the next day energized, and new clients began to call her. From that time on, every time she began to feel discouraged, she would give, the discouragement would go away, and her business would improve. She later said that she realized she had stumbled upon something – the way to make oneself open to receive is by giving. What she "stumbled" into was a spiritual law, a spiritual principle set into motion by God. Of course she does not recognize it as such since she does not know the Lord. Like so many unsaved people, she is enjoying a principle and blessing from God without having a clue where it is coming from. So, why does the principle work in the life of this woman who is now a very successful world-famous figure in the world of finance? Why does it work in the life of someone who makes no claim to being a Christian and attaches no spiritual significance to what she discovered about giving and receiving? It works for the same reason gravity works for the saved and unsaved alike, it is a law. The question though is this, if the principle of giving and receiving works in the life of an unsaved person, how much more will it work in the life of a Christian who is indwelt by and guided by the great Giver of the universe, God Himself? The answer is obvious.

One day, some years ago, during one of our campaigns in Africa, there was a young man saved in an open-air meeting and afterwards I asked about his situation. It turned out he was trying to sustain himself by selling vegetables in the market but was not doing very well. He said if he had a little money to rent a pushcart he could do more business and better take care of himself. I asked how much he needed, and he said the carts rented for fifty cents per day. I gave him enough for his first month. With that help, he began to carry and sell more produce, and he began to make more money. He also began to give faithfully to the Lord out of what he made. The more he made, the more he gave, and the more he made. Today he is one of the most faithful members of his church, and he is also one of the best and most consistent givers.

Saving and Hoarding

Now let me be clear, I am not saying giving can be used as a "magic bullet" for having needs met, financial or otherwise. What I am saying, though, is there is an obvious correlation between giving and receiving. A selfish, self-centered, hoarding Christian (or church) should not expect to receive anything from God by faith. We all love to quote Philippians 4:19, *"But my God shall supply all your need according to his riches in glory by Christ Jesus."* What we need to consider, however, is Paul wrote those words to Christians who were very generous and had given sacrificially to meet his needs. He said to them in verse 15, *"...no church communicated with me as concerning giving and receiving, but ye only."* George Muller wrote, "Let no one profess to trust in God, and yet lay up for future wants, otherwise the Lord will first send him to the hoard he has amassed, before he can answer the prayer for more" (3). So is it wrong or faithless to have a savings account or to have money set aside that is not currently being used? No, not at all. But it is wrong, it is faithless, and it is sin to look to that for security rather than looking to God by faith. The difference between saving and hoarding lies in whether or not you are willing to let go of it at the Lord's bidding. The key question is <u>who is in control of the account</u>, you or God? Saving means you are holding, with a loose grip, money (or whatever) in reserve until God tells you what to do with it. He may tell you to hold on to it and apply it to future needs, or He may tell you to give it away. Regardless of what He says, however, you are willing to obey. Saving does not diminish faith; it simply holds supply in reserve in anticipation of God's instructions. Hoarding, on the other hand, does diminish faith because it operates out of fear. Hoarding means you are holding on  tightly to money or supplies in anticipation of future needs and you are trusting that money or supply to meet your need. If you are holding on to money or supplies in an effort to prevent yourself from having to trust God by faith, then you are hoarding, and you are in sin. You are also inevitably setting yourself up for trouble. By hoarding you are preventing yourself from giving and thus stopping the flow, which will surely result in a deficit in your situation at some point. It may take a while for it to occur, but you can be sure it will.

There is a tragic mistake I see many churches and individual Christians make when they experience a reduction in their income, for whatever reason. They start cutting back on their giving to missions, missionaries, evangelism, and anything else that does not contribute to their own building maintenance, staff salaries, and programs. Many churches also cut back on giving when they enter into a building program. Again, this is a very bad mistake for two reasons: first, cutting back, period, is not faith, and second, it is not a solution. Real faith does not cut back; it pushes forward. It does not retreat; it advances. Cutting back is always a mistake in the things of God, especially in the area of giving, and even more especially in the area of giving to missions, the one thing that is dearest to the heart of God. Cutting back in giving only stops the flow, and cutting back on giving to missions and evangelism disconnects the church from God's agenda, the redemption of the human race.

Giving with the Right Motive

One very important issue we need to mention in connection with giving is the one that Jesus addressed in Matthew 6:1-4, the issue of motive. The Pharisees were giving publicly in order to be seen and praised, not out of love for God. He told them that when they give they should do it in secret and let their reward come from God. The verses we quoted above testify to the fact that in God's economy, the more we give the more we receive. That is absolutely true – BUT – yes there is a "but" and here it is – <u>God cannot be manipulated. He cannot be forced to do anything that is not his will.</u> While Luke 6:38, *"Give and it shall be given unto you..."* is absolutely true, you cannot wave it in God's face at your own whim and choosing and manipulate Him into giving you more money or possessions or anything else. I have heard many preachers on television tell their listeners that if they will plant a "seed" (always money and always into the preacher's own ministry) then God will give them back more than they gave. They make promises like this, "You plant $100 in our ministry and God will give you back $1,000." Who wouldn't take a deal like that? Well, here is the problem with that – you can't treat God like the stock market. He will not be manipulated, and anyone who falls for the T.V. preacher's line is going to end up disillusioned and disappointed. The thing that makes the difference in giving is motive. If our motive in giving is to obey the voice of God, then we will be rewarded and blessed, but if our motives are selfish and originate from the flesh we will be disappointed. God does not author or endorse get-rich-quick schemes. You cannot manipulate God with giving or with anything else. In Matthew 4:1-11, satan tried to manipulate Jesus with Scripture, but that didn't work either.

Now, you will remember I shared with you an incident that happened to Sheila and me when we were trusting God for the money to go to the Billy Graham Conference in Amsterdam in 1983. We needed $3,000 for tickets and expenses. As I was praying about the need one afternoon God spoke to me in my heart and said, "Shad, you need $3,000 and I am going to provide it for you, but before I do I want you to give $300 for someone else to go." I knew for a fact I had heard from the Holy Spirit in my inner man, but I did not say anything about it to Sheila for two days. Then two days later she came to me and said, "Shad, I believe the Lord has told me that since we need $3,000 we should give $300 for someone else to go." Of course, there was no doubt about what we had heard God say, and we obeyed and sent the $300. The end of the story is that God miraculously provided the $3,000 in full and we went. Now you may ask, what is the difference in what we did and what someone might do in response to the T.V. preacher? The difference is that no man told us to do anything. That directive came from God alone; it was HIS idea, not ours. He was moving us, we were not moving Him. We were obeying the voice of the Holy Spirit spoken in our inner man. THAT is the difference.

One day, many years ago, a brother in Christ called me and said he was coming through Memphis and wanted to know if I would like to meet him for lunch. I agreed, and as I was leaving my office, the Lord spoke to me very clearly and said, "Shad, you need to give brother John $100." I said, "Okay, Lord, I will do that." Then God said to me very clearly, "I am going to have John return that money to you ten fold. He is going to send you back $1,000." I said, "Okay, Lord, but whether he does or not, I am going to give the $100 to him." So I wrote the check and took it with me. When I met him I gave it to him, and then he told me he was completely broke and had asked God for $100. We praised the Lord, had lunch, and he went on his way to New Orleans. Several weeks passed, and I had forgotten about the whole thing. Then one day I received an envelope in the mail from John containing a note and a check. The note said, "Shad, God has blessed me, and He told me to send you this check." It was for $1,000! At that moment I remembered what God had said and, needless to say, I praised His Name. Now again, what is the difference? The difference is that it was GOD who initiated my giving John the $100, and it was GOD who told John to give me the $1,000. My only motive in giving John $100 was to simply obey God, and John's was the same. Again, God was moving John and me; we were not moving Him. I was not trying to make some kind of deal with God or work out some scheme to get some money from Him; I was simply obeying His voice. I might add that was the only time in my entire Christian life that ever happened.

The key to giving with the right motive is the same as it is with everything else in the Christian life; wait for the voice of God to speak in your spirit and obey Him completely. Giving, or not giving (and there are times when God will tell you not to), should always be in response to the leadership of the Holy Spirit and nothing else. It should be an action, not a reaction. It should never be based upon logic, intellect, human reasoning, pros and cons, or public opinion. Giving should never be based upon circumstances (good or bad) or the state of your bank account. When God told Sheila and me to send $300 to help someone go to Amsterdam, we had no money in our account. But we wrote the check and mailed it anyway. Foolish? Yes, in the realm of logic and common sense, but not in the realm of God, Who provided the money to cover the check by the time it was needed. In the life of faith we do not give according to our human calculations, but according to what God says. We also must never give according to the dictates of our emotions. Giving should always be a spiritual response and a spiritual action, never an emotional one. We are emotional creatures, of course, and all fundraisers know that and try to capitalize upon it with words and pictures that pull at your heartstrings. So what should you do when you are "moved" to give? Wait, refuse to act immediately, take the issue into the prayer closet, and put it before God. Then do exactly what He tells you to do. But make sure it is ultimately a spiritual action, not just an emotional reaction. Why is this so important? Because satan will cleverly use emotional appeals to <u>divert</u> your giving to areas into which God is not leading you.

The Key Is Obedience

Again the key to it all, the faith life, the Christian life, and giving , is simply obedience to the Holy Spirit at any given moment. I began learning this early in my walk of faith. Just after I left my church position to enter the ministry we are in today, I received an invitation from an old college preacher pal to come to his church in South Carolina to conduct a youth meeting. He said I would be there with several other guys from different parts of the country. I accepted and went. When I arrived he told us he could only give us our hotel room, food, and $50 each for the three days we would be there. I did not mind, because I had nothing else on the calendar anyway, and it was good to see my old friends again. Besides, at that time, $50 seemed like a lot of money. At the opening dinner we each received an envelope containing our $50 check. When I received mine, God told me immediately to give it to my friend Chuck. I hesitated and let the moment pass without doing it. As I used to tell my kids, <u>delayed</u> obedience is <u>disobedience</u>. Then the evening passed and finally the whole weekend, and I still had not obeyed the Lord. Then on Monday I flew back to Memphis with one of the brothers who was there, a guy named Jim. Chuck had gone on another flight. As we were flying, God spoke one of the strangest messages into my heart I have ever heard. He said, "Shad, I told you to give your $50 to Chuck, and you did not obey Me. Now I am telling you again, and if you will obey Me I will tell Jim to give his $50 to you." Now I have to be honest here, out of all the things I have ever heard God say, I thought that was the strangest. I said in my heart, "God, why didn't You just tell Jim to give his $50 to Chuck and leave me out of it?" The Holy Spirit said, "No, you must do this My way or you are going to lose." I struggled with it and looked across the aisle at Jim. He was just sitting there. Then I prayed silently, "Okay Lord, as soon as I get to my house I will mail the check to Chuck." The instant that prayer left my heart, Jim leaned across the aisle and said, "Shad, can I borrow your pen?" I handed it to him, and he took out his check and endorsed it. Then he handed it to me with these words, "Brother, I don't know why, but God just now told me to give this to you." I knew why, and I finally had peace in my heart. Needless to say, I followed through on my promise. But that is not the end of the story. I did send the $50 to Chuck that very day. Then over the next three days, God brought at least five different people to my house with a $50 check for Sheila and me – five people that had never been to my house before. So what was this all about? It was about learning to obey God in one of the most important areas of faith – the area of giving. God was providing me with a demonstration of the law of circulation. He was showing me that He gives back more than He demands. He was showing me the value of instant obedience, an essential element in the life of real faith. Over the years to come, in our life and in our ministry, God would call upon Sheila and me to be a channel through which He would flow millions of dollars into the evangelization of the world. But it had to begin somewhere, and It began with a small $50 check. Of course "small" is relative to your current condition, and at the time fifty dollars was pretty big. But, when you demonstrate to God that He can trust you with small things, then He entrusts you with bigger ones. Again, it is all about obedience.

Sometimes, all you get in return for obeying the Lord in giving is the simple peace and satisfaction in your heart that comes from knowing that you did what God said do. But that is enough. One night Sheila and I were attending a revival service and our friend, Manley Beasley, was preaching. During the service God spoke to me and said, "Shad, give $1,000 in the offering for Manley." I could not believe what I had heard. We had the $1,000 in our account, but we needed it very badly. But I could not get out from under it and I whispered to Sheila, "Is God telling you anything?" She replied, "Yes, but you are not going to like it." I already knew what it was, but I asked anyway. Then she said, "God is telling me to give $1,000 in the offering for Manley." I said, "Get out the checkbook and let's do this before we talk ourselves out of it." So we gave the money in the offering. Now it would be a great story if I told you that in a day or so we received $10,000 or something like that, but that did not happen. As far as we could tell, nothing occurred in our financial circumstances over the next few weeks that had anything to do with our giving to Manley. But that did not matter, because we did not give for any other motive than to simply obey God, and as a result we had the great peace and satisfaction of knowing we were living in obedience to God. That was enough.

The same thing happened a few years later. One morning God spoke to my heart and told me to give $5,000 to one evangelist friend and $1,000 to another. We'll call them Bob and Jim. I told the Lord I did not have $6,000, and even if I did, I had a lot of places to use it myself. Then God spoke to me, "Shad, if I give you $6,000 will you give it away?" I told God I would. Later in the day I told Sheila what I had told the Lord and she agreed. I asked her if the money came in the mail that day would she be willing to give it? She was, and when we went to the post office that afternoon we found two checks in our box – one for $5,000 and one for $1,000. I couldn't believe it, but there it was, $6,000. We deposited the money immediately and then sent the checks, $5,000 to Bob and $1,000 to Jim. I called both of them and when I told them the money was coming Bob told me he had been praying that day for $5,000 and Jim told me he was praying for $1,000. Praise God Who knows how to match the supply with the need! Again, over the weeks that followed we did not see any obvious correlation between our giving and our financial circumstances. But what we did see was a correlation between our obedience to God and the financial circumstances of our friends.

In the Christian life, every giving/receiving scenario represents a triangle; the giver on one side, the receiver on the other side, and God at the top. In every Spirit-led incident of giving and receiving, God is matching His supply with someone's need, and He is using a giver to do it. When God calls upon you to give, He is making you part of the faith process in someone's life. For that reason we must be very sensitive to the Holy Spirit, and we must obey the voice of God implicitly and immediately. You can be sure there is more involved and much more at stake in your giving than you realize, and there are always more lives affected than just yours. A perfect illustration of that fact is found in the next paragraph.

No Such Thing as a "Small" Gift

Sheila and I would not be in the worldwide ministry we are in today had it not been for obedience in the area of giving in the life of Mrs. A. B. Clark on a Wednesday night in June 1975. Our church was going on a mission trip to Kenya and Tanzania, and the team was being finalized that night. We knew for sure the church was going to pay my way to go since I was on staff and I was heading up the music team. There was some question, however, as to whether Sheila's way would be paid, and if it was not, she would not be able to go. Our pastor, Dr. Wayne Allen, was to make the decision and tell us after the Wednesday night service. Before the service started, as we found out later, he was praying about who should go, and he said, "God, if You want the church to pay for Sheila to go, let someone give something, any amount, toward her trip." He said nothing to anyone about what he had decided. When the service was over that night, Mrs. Clark, an elderly retired missionary widow, came to Wayne and said to him, "Brother Wayne, I know this is not much, but it is all I can do and God told me to give it towards Sheila's trip." It was five dollars. Brother Wayne took it, and thanked her. In his office a few minutes later, he told Sheila that God had answered prayer and she was going. After we had been in Africa for a few days, God spoke to both of us and confirmed in our hearts we were to leave the church and launch out into international evangelism. Now, here is the significance of Mrs. Clark's gift. If she had not given it, Sheila would not have gone. If Sheila had not gone, she would not have been in position to hear from God. If she had not heard from God as I did, we would not be in this ministry today. But she did hear, because she was there, because Mrs. Clark did give that gift. Sometimes what God is telling us to do may seem small, but in God's economy it may be huge. It was certainly so in this case, and I praise God that Mrs. Clark obeyed and gave as the Lord told her. Since that night back in 1975, over seven million people have come into the Kingdom of God through the ministry that God started with Sheila and me as a result of that trip to Africa. Mrs. Clark had no idea that her "small" gift would mean so much, but it did.

One day many years later I went to the post office to get the mail and there were two checks in the box, one for $15 and one for $15,000. When I got back to the car I laid both of them on the seat of the car and prayed. I thought back on Mrs. Clark's gift and said to the Lord, "Lord, there is no one in this car but You and me, but right here and now I want to give you equal praise for both of these checks because they both come from You and they are both the same in Your sight. So Lord I praise You equally for both of them." The truth of the matter is that the $15 check may have been even more in God's sight because it came from a widow lady who had little to give, and the check for $15,000 came from a man who had the ability to give much. It reminded me of the story in Luke 21:1-4 where Jesus said of the widow who gave two mites, *"..Of a truth I say unto you, that this poor widow hath cast in more than they all; For all these have of their abundance cast in unto the offerings of God: but she of her penury hath cast in all the living that she had."* Again, the "size" of our giving is relative to our condition. Of course the $15,000 gift was "larger" than the $15 gift in that we could obviously do much more with it, but in God's economy the $15 gift was just as large, maybe even larger. We always get a clearer perspective when we look at things from God's side of the page.

From the Ends of the Earth

One thing I learned a long time ago is that God will go to any length to meet our needs if we will only be faithful to obey Him and to do it quickly. One weekend some years ago, Sheila and I were, as we say in the south, flat broke. I don't know where that expression comes from, but it means you need a miracle to get up to zero. We had no food in the house and not a penny to buy any. But on Saturday afternoon we were to sing at a wedding and we thought maybe something might come from that, and sure enough it did. We were given $100, which we planned to deposit on Monday. That meant we could now go to the grocery store. We went home first to change clothes and as we walked into the house God spoke to my heart, "Shad, you need give that $100 to your evangelist friend down the street and you need to take it to him right now!" I felt like I had been kicked in the chest by a gorilla. I crumpled into my chair in the den and tried to rationalize my way out of it, but it was useless. God had spoken and I knew it. I told Sheila about it and she said she had the very same impression. So I got up, went straight to his house, and gave him the money. Was my heart now flooded with peace? No, not this time. It was flooded with questions about how we were going to eat. But God had a surprise waiting for me. Just after I walked back in the door to my house, the mailman came, and as I was going through the mail I saw an envelope from Macau, South China. It was from a young missionary we had met there four years earlier. I opened the envelope and inside there was a note, which read, "Dear Shad and Sheila, I have been sitting here in my apartment in Macau tonight thinking about you guys and praying for you, and as I have prayed I have sensed that I need to send you this money. It is not much, but I hope it helps." The check was for $100! At that moment God spoke to me and said, "Shad, if you will just obey Me, I will meet your needs, even if I have to go all the way to China to do it." We would have been glad to go to the grocery store that day with the first hundred dollars, but with the second we were beside ourselves with joy unspeakable. God's rules, including those for giving, are simple – just trust Me, and do what I tell you.

Out of Ownership into Management

Now I know what you are going to say. You are going to tell me it is hard to give under certain conditions, when everything in you and around you tells you that you are crazy. No kidding! You are not telling me anything I don't already know and agree with. But you must obey God and this is how you can do it; get out of ownership into management. The only way to maintain the right outlook in our hearts toward giving is to stop being owners and become managers or stewards. This applies not only to individual Believers, but also to churches, ministries, and businesses. Once you relinquish all you are and all you have to God in its entirety, then it is no longer yours to keep or to give; it is His. You simply become a manager of what God has entrusted you with. At that point, giving (or not) is no longer a decision for you to make, but an instruction for you to obey. And the more we obey, the more God gives us opportunity to obey. Regarding management or stewardship, George Muller wrote, "It is the Lord's order, that, in whatever way He is pleased to make us His stewards, whether as to temporal or spiritual things, if we are indeed acting as stewards and not as owners, He will make us stewards over more" (4). In Matthew 25:14-30, Jesus illustrates this truth with the story of the master who went on a trip and gave responsibility for different amounts of money to three different servants. Upon his return he found two of them had invested theirs and the third had hidden his. He condemned the third, but to the first two He said, *"Well done, thou good and faithful servant: thou hast been faithful over a few things, I will make thee ruler over many things: enter thou into the joy of thy lord."* A huge part of the life of faith is simply taking what God has entrusted us with and doing with it what He tells us to do. The faith life calls for management, not ownership.

We Always Receive More than We Give

I have heard it said many times "You cannot out-give God." I believe that is absolutely true; Scripture supports it, and I have experienced it in my own life. I have also observed it in the lives of others. I said above that sometimes all you receive when you give is the peace and satisfaction in your heart that you have obeyed the will of God. Yes, that is true in an immediate sense, but ultimately God will pour more back into your life than you poured out. C.T. Studd, founder of the Heart of Africa Mission (later the World Evangelization Crusade), gave away an enormous fortune left to him by his father (who was saved under the ministry of D.L. Moody in 1877 and died two years later). He concluded that God would have him give it all away and cast himself completely upon Him by faith. So, he let go of his inherited fortune, in its entirety, and cast himself upon the resources of God. Part of the money was sent to D.L. Moody, who used it to start the Moody Bible Institute in Chicago. The rest of the story is, over the course of his lifetime, God poured back into his life more than five times what he gave away. He never owned a business, was never employed, and never solicited a penny. He simply trusted in the living God to Whom he had given everything. George Muller, of Bristol, England, fed, clothed, and housed 4,000 orphans every day and did it without asking anyone for anything. How did he do it? By trusting God for everything and by giving liberally to various works of God that did not involve his own ministry. He gave large sums of money to the missionaries of the China Inland Mission as well as to others. During the course of his life he gave away literally millions of dollars, and when he died his entire personal estate was worth only $300.

Now I would certainly not elevate myself to the status of a C.T. Studd or a George Muller, but I can still testify that over the course of our life, God has poured more back into us than we have given. I shared with you earlier how God called upon us to move out of a very nice home and give up the idea of ever owning one in order to enter this ministry. Well, today we own a home that is far more than we ever imagined in our wildest dreams. We did not earn it or manipulate it; we received it as a gift from God. In those first early days we began by trusting God for just our personal livelihood, but soon we were looking to Him for more to put into ministry. In a short time we were receiving three times what we needed to live on, and we were giving two-thirds into the ministry. Sheila and I have never needed or wanted millions of dollars for ourselves, but God has poured millions through us, over the years, to be used in His work. We have found that the more we send out, the more He sends in. Now, do we ever have days when we are broke and don't know where the next dollar is coming from? Yes, I have shared some of those times with you. C.T. Studd, George Muller, and Hudson Taylor had many days like that, but panoramically, in the end, God always gave back more than was given out.

Are You Giving?

Now let me ask you straight up, are you giving, or are you making excuses that do not hold up in the light of God's word? Are you applying the law of circulation to your life? Are you living in obedience to God and being used as a channel by Him, or are you stopping the flow? Is your life like a flowing river or is it a stagnant pond? Is your focus on receiving only, or are you living a balanced life of receiving AND giving? If not, then you will never be able to truly live a life of real faith. Now there are three possible answers to the question, "Are you giving?" Answer number 1 is, **"No I do not give, because I just cannot afford it in my current financial condition."** To you, my friend, I would say this – if your condition is so bad that you cannot find even a few cents to give to the Lord, then you cannot afford to NOT give, and you need to start giving <u>as soon as possible</u>. The truth of the matter is that the statement, "I cannot afford to give" is a lie from the devil, and it is his clever way of keeping you trapped in a "poor me," poverty condition and mind set. But here is the good news; you can set yourself free by starting to give in obedience to God. It may very well be that your first act of real faith will be the simple act of giving what your logical calculations say you cannot give. This may be your first step into the impossible. Get alone with God, and ask Him what to give and how to give. Ask Him to give you the ability and the courage to begin. God has some very creative ways of getting you started. If you do not have money to give, then God may lead you to sell something, or He may lead you to just give some item to His work. I have no idea what God will lead you to do, but I can guarantee He will help you begin if you are willing. I will also tell you that for your sake, for the sake of your family, and for the sake of God's Kingdom, the sooner you start the better. You may begin in a very small way the way Sheila and I did many years ago, but the important thing is that you begin and set God's law of circulation in motion in your life.

Answer number 2 is, **"Yes I give; I pay my tithes every week."** To you I would say that if you use the word "pay" in relation to your tithes, then you may very likely be doing just that – paying, not giving. The difference has to do with the attitude of our heart. Billy Graham said, "Give me five minutes with a person's check book and I will tell you where their heart is." There are two ways to tithe to God, either cheerfully out of love for God or begrudgingly out of fear and superstition. The Bible says God loves a "cheerful" giver, not just a "compliant" one. I have heard many pastors threaten their people with statements like this, "You better give that ten percent, because if you don't, God will get it out of you some other way." Now does that really sound like the voice of the Holy Spirit to you? Of course not. God does not extract money from His children or beat it out of them; He receives it as an expression of love. If you tithe to the penny out of fear of God's judgment, or out of superstition related to your finances and not out of real love for Christ, then you are not giving; you are just paying another bill. You should give to God and His work because you love Him, not because you believe your finances will fall apart if you don't. I have met many Christians who tithe, yes, but they resent having to do it, and they would not give another penny no matter what. Of course only you and God really know the truth about what is going on in your heart. But if you give resentfully or grudgingly, you may as well keep it, because in reality you are not really giving at all. I would suggest, though, if you cannot find a cheerful attitude in your heart regarding your tithe, then you need to get before the Lord and find out why.

Answer number 3 is, **"Yes I am giving, and I am so excited about it. The more I give, the more blessed I am."** The truth is, when you fall in love with Jesus you cannot give enough. There is a lot of discussion these days over the issue of tithing. But when you fall in love with Jesus it ceases to be an issue for you, because you are not satisfied with just giving ten percent anyway. When you fall head over heels in love with Christ you stop asking silly questions like, "Should I tithe on the net or the gross?" Questions like that no longer apply, because in your heart you want to give it all. You stop asking, "How much can I keep," and you start asking, "How much can I give?"

> **All to Jesus I surrender, all to Him I freely give;**
> **I will ever love and trust Him, in His presence daily live.**
> **I surrender all, I surrender all;**
> **All to Thee my blessed Savior, I surrender all.** (5)

Now let me finish this up by mentioning that there are two types of giving. I recommend both and practice both. One is regular or <u>regulated</u>

giving and the other is <u>revelation</u> giving. Regulated giving is simply setting aside a certain amount or percentage of income to give on a regular basis. Revelation giving is when God speaks to you about giving above your regular amount to some particular area of His work. This is the kind of giving God calls upon you to do when He is involving you in the faith process in someone else's life. Regulated giving is systematic and revelation giving is sporadic. Both, however, should be done in obedience to the voice of God received in the inner man. So, dear child of God, get in the prayer closet and ask God to tell you what to do in relation to your giving. Then trust Him by faith to enable you to do it. Energize your life of faith by becoming a channel through which God can flow His love and provision into a hungry and thirsty world.

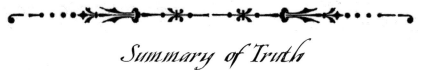

Summary of Truth

❖ The life of real faith is a balanced life of giving and receiving.
❖ Real love is expressed through giving.
❖ The faith life is fluid and flowing like a river.
❖ Liberal giving sets in motion the law of circulation.
❖ A selfish, hoarding Christian should not expect to receive from God by faith.
❖ Hoarding means you are looking to existing supply for security rather than to God.
❖ Hoarding stops the flow and ultimately creates deficit.
❖ Giving cannot be used as a means of manipulating God.
❖ The key to giving with the right motive is obedience to the Holy Spirit.
❖ When God finds out He can trust you with small things, He will then entrust you with bigger things.
❖ Sometimes all you receive immediately from giving is the satisfaction of knowing you have obeyed God, but ultimately God will pour into your life more than you gave out.
❖ Every giving/receiving scenario involves a triangle; the giver, the receiver, and God.
❖ There is no such thing as a "small" gift to God.
❖ God will go to the ends of the earth to meet your needs if you are faithful to obey him in giving.
❖ The best way to maintain faithfulness in giving is to get out of ownership into management.

NOW LET'S TAKE A MOMENT AND PRAY TOGETHER:

DEAR FATHER, MORE THAN ANYTHING I WANT TO PLEASE YOU BY BECOMING A TRUE GIVER AND BY LIVING BY REAL FAITH. LORD, I ASK YOU TO DO WHATEVER IS NECESSARY IN MY HEART TO BRING ME TO THAT PLACE IN MY LIFE. I PURPOSE IN MY HEART RIGHT NOW TO BECOME A CHANNEL THROUGH WHICH YOU CAN FLOW YOUR BLESSINGS AND YOUR SUPPLY INTO THE LIVES OF OTHERS AND INTO THE WORLD FOR THE BUILDING OF YOUR KINGDOM. THANK YOU FOR GIVING YOURSELF FOR ME, LORD JESUS, AND NOW HELP ME TO GIVE MY ALL FOR YOU. IN YOUR NAME I PRAY. AMEN.

Chapter 31

Real Faith Requires Letting Go

*"By faith Abraham, when he was called to go out into a place
which he should after receive for an inheritance, obeyed;
and he went out, not knowing whither he went."*
Hebrews 11:8

When you begin to live a life of faith, and you must in order to please God, you will soon discover it is a life of continuously letting go – of something. It is a life of stepping out from the familiar and the comfortable into the unknown and the unpredictable. It is a life in which you exchange the false illusion of the security of the world for the rock-solid real security of God. It is a life that often takes you out of step with the world in order to put you in step with God. In a life of real faith you are repeatedly required to let go of the limitations of the visible and the possible so you may reach into the limitless realm of the power and resources of God. In the faith life you are required to let go of self-dependence and walk in total God-dependence, trusting Him alone. But when you finally make that critical life-changing choice to cast yourself upon God entirely and walk by faith and not by sight, you will find letting go is much easier than you thought it would be. It is also much more liberating than you ever imagined.

Jump or Stay Put

Some years ago, on the way to a campaign in India, I was flying from Boston to Frankfurt, Germany and I sat by a lady with whom I had a very interesting conversation. I spent the first three hours trying to lead her to Christ. After graciously but firmly refusing to be saved, she said, "May I share with you something I have been doing?" I agreed, and she began telling me she had been learning to sky dive and had even done it once already. My first reaction, which I kept to myself, was, "Lady, you don't want to get saved and yet you are jumping out of airplanes. You know you really might want to rethink your decision!" Anyway, she explained she first attended classes to learn all about how to jump out of the plane, how to activate the parachute, how to land, and so on. She had even practiced landing by jumping off of a table. Then she said the day finally came when she actually went up in the plane and was going to jump. There were three people jumping that day. The first jumped, then the second, and then it was her turn. She said, "I got to the door and froze. I was so afraid. The instructor told me that I had done well in practice and I knew everything I needed to know. Now all I needed to do was just let go and trust my parachute." Then she continued, "I realized all of a sudden that it was just a matter of believing. The door was open, the wind was blowing, and I could barely hang on. All at once, I let go and jumped. I pulled the rope, the chute opened, and then it hit me; it was much easier to just let go than it was to struggle to hang on." Her confession made the hair stand up on the back of my neck. I said, "Lady, that is exactly what you need to do with Jesus. Just let go and trust Him. He wants to be your parachute."

Of course I was thinking in terms of her salvation, but what she said also applies to living the Christian life. We hang on so tightly to what we can see and touch, to what makes us feel safe, comfortable, and secure, because we are afraid to let go and simply trust God. We have received our instructions from the Word and from the Spirit, and yet we hang on. But, dear child of God, I promise you, if you will just let go and make the transaction to move from dependence upon self and dependence upon what you have and what you can do, to total dependence upon God, you will find it is "easier to let go than it is to hang on." The operative word here is "total." It is not possible to "sort of" live by faith, to partially depend upon God. It is all or nothing. You either jump or you don't. My traveling companion on that flight to Frankfurt could not sort of hang on and sort of let go at the same time. She had to make a clear choice. She could give in to fear, play it safe, and stay where she was, or she could let go and take the plunge into freedom. You and I have that same choice to make. We can hang on to the old, status quo Christian life or we can cast ourselves upon God and believe for the impossible.

The First Letting Go

When you came to Christ initially, you had to let go of everything else and trust Him alone for salvation. You had to let go of religion, "churchianity," self-effort, and preconceived ideas and cast yourself, by faith, totally and completely upon Jesus alone. You had to abandon everything that was NOT faith in Christ. You had to turn away from everything and anything that might present itself as a substitute for the real thing (Eph.2:8,9). The same is true for living a life of faith, which is the normal Christian life. Again quoting Colossians 2:6, *"As ye have, therefore, received Christ Jesus the Lord, so walk ye in him."* How did we receive Him? By faith. How must we continue in Him? By faith. Salvation from hell could not be obtained by the schemes of your intellect, the passion of your emotions, the force of your will, or the power of your physical being. And salvation from the challenges of life cannot be obtained that way either. It took pure faith in Christ to get you into the Christian life and it takes pure faith in Christ to get you through it. In order to live a life of real faith you must be willing in your heart to let go of what the world and the flesh label as safe and secure and sensible. You must let go of your attachments to the visible, the "practical," and the possible. You must let go of your own best efforts as well as your old natural ways of looking at things. You must let go of making decisions based solely upon logic, feeling, common sense, and circumstances. You must let go of reliance upon people, possessions, plans, and position, and look to God alone for security. You must let go of personal ambition and submit completely to the will of God, regardless of what it may be and what it may cost you and those connected to you. In other words, you must give up your right to yourself and surrender all to God. In the faith life you do not need self-sufficiency, self-reliance, and self-confidence. You need to look to God alone and find your sufficiency in Him. You need confidence in Who He is, what He has, and what He can do. He alone must become your Source, your Security, and your Supply.

Looking to God Plus Nothing

Now, in case I did not make that clear enough, let me say it again; real faith is **LOOKING TO GOD ALONE PLUS NOTHING**. Faith is not manipulation of circumstances. It is not "trying my best and trusting God to do the rest." God does not need or want your help. He wants your trust. In relation to the needs in our ministry, real faith is not looking to God plus our mailing list or email list. It is looking to God alone and voicing our needs to Him alone. While looking to God for our needs, He may tell us to share them with our supporters, and He may not; that is up to Him. If He says to not tell anyone, then we don't tell anyone. If He says to share the needs, then we share them. But in either case the instructions must come from God, and they must be complied with to the letter. Otherwise, what we are calling faith is not faith at all.

Now, you may want to know just what kind of "letting go" we are talking about. Well, it is hard to explain "letting go" to a Christian who has never let go, who is still hanging on and hanging back. A business-person or a Christian employee may ask, "Does entering the faith life mean I have to quit my job or give up my business and have no visible income? Do I have to empty my bank account, deplete my portfolio, and give away everything I have?" A pastor may ask, "In order to live by faith should I refuse the salary the church wants to pay me?" Well, God does call upon some individuals to do just that, and when he does, He gives them the grace to do it. Obviously, however, that is an extreme step to take, and it only applies to those individuals upon whose lives God has placed a special calling. Questions like "Do I have to quit my job?" indicate a narrow view of the faith life. The kind of "letting go" we are talking about here involves a lot more than materialism and may or may not take place in actual circumstances. You can be absolutely sure, however, that it will take place in your heart, and it applies to every area in life, not just employment, income, bank accounts and things that represent security in daily life.

Unfortunately, when people talk about living by faith, they usually limit it to the areas of finances, the necessities of life, trials, crises, and adverse circumstances; in other words, the physical. But to reduce the necessity for faith to just the issue of survival is a huge mistake. Real faith has more to do with <u>expanding</u> your life than just sustaining it. There is much more to trusting God than just acquiring things or money or getting out of trouble. If we only needed God when we were in need of something or when we were in trouble, then there would be times when we did not need God at all, and that is <u>certainly</u> not true. Contrary to what satan would have us believe, we need to believe God by faith in every detail and in every second of our lives.

Living by faith, in total dependence upon God, applies to every area of life and to every moment of life. When you cross over the line into the life of faith, you may very likely still have those things that represent security; your job, your profession, your position, your business, your home, the support of your family, and your bank account. The difference, however, is that you will no longer look to those things as the source of your supply or your security in life. And if you are called upon to let those things go, you will not panic and crumble in self-pity and despair, because you have already let them go in your heart. You have surrendered them to God, which means that satan cannot take them from you. No one can take from you what you have already given up. Also they no longer represent your base of security, because your trust has been transferred to God. You will know when you have made the transition into real faith because you will begin to see those things that formerly represented security as mere channels through which God, your Source, flows His supply. You will no longer feel threatened by the possibility of losing those things, because channels may change, but the Source never does. "Letting go" simply means casting yourself upon God and trusting Him <u>above</u> everything and <u>for</u> everything.

When our son, Michael, was almost three years old, I gave him one of those wooden jigsaw puzzles with the large pieces. I remember one night watching him try his hardest to work it. I was sitting in a chair, and he was on the floor in front of me. He struggled for a long time, and then all of a sudden he just piled the pieces up on the board, stood up, laid the whole thing in my lap, and said, "Here Daddy, YOU do it!" At that moment, God used that picture to show me something. Whatever the puzzle is, an isolated event or life as a whole, just pile the pieces on the board, lay it in the Father's lap, and let HIM do it. The key to it all, however, was that Michael let go of it *entirely*. If he had hung on to just one piece then I could not have worked that puzzle, and he couldn't either. The solution was in completely letting go. He gave it to his father in pieces, and his father returned it to him whole.

In some instances the act of letting go may very well mean a literal separation, a walking away from home, country, family, job, profession, desires, plans, and dreams. In others, it may take place only in the heart. But in either case, a definite act of the will is required. We must be willing to cross over the "Great Divide" in the Christian life, that place where we make the conscious choice to stake our all on Jesus alone. It is at that place and at that moment that real freedom, liberty, joy, and peace are obtained. Once we cast ourselves upon the Lord, and embrace HIM as our only Source and security, then all of satan's strings upon our life are cut. Victory over fear and temptation is ours, because no longer does he have anything to threaten or entice us with. Of course, the devil will forever make attempts to bring new "attachments" into our life, things that make us "feel" secure, things that appear to be a reliable source. But as long as we maintain our fellowship with Jesus, the Holy Spirit will always be faithful to warn us of the devil's schemes and keep us from falling for them, and to protect us from replacing dependence upon God with something else. Our greatest protection is to simply walk in the will of God.

The Greatest Example of Letting Go

The greatest example in time and eternity of letting go is found in the relationship of God the Father, Who let go and *"gave his only begotten Son"* for the redemption of the human race, and God the Son, Who let go and prayed in the garden, *"Nevertheless, not my will but Thine be done."* When Jesus called His disciples, He required of them that they let go of everything and follow Him, not at a distance, but closely, completely, and continuously. They let go of careers, family, friends, possessions, and any plans of their own for the future. Jesus required of them total abandonment of everything. His instructions to them were simple, clear, and unmistakable - "Follow Me." He called upon those men to leave everything; their fishing boats, their tax collector booth, their old ideas of religion, every vestige of security, and everything they were familiar with. He expected them to follow Him into the unknown, trusting Him alone for everything. He gave them no explanation as to where they were going, what they were going to do, or where they would end up. He just said, "Follow Me." Nothing has changed. Jesus calls upon us to do the same thing - to let go of the familiar and the visible and live by faith.

Over and over, throughout the Bible, we find individuals who were brought to the point of having to let go in order to obey God in acts of real faith. In Genesis 12 we see Abraham letting go of his homeland in obedience to God, to seek *"a city whose builder and maker is God."* Then in chapter 22, we find him letting go of his beloved son Isaac. Moses' parents let him go in order to preserve his life, and later, Moses would let go of the pleasures of Egypt to preserve the life of Israel. Gideon (Judges 7) had an army of 32,000 and God told him to let go of all but 300 so that when the battle was won God alone would get the glory. In Matthew 14:29, Peter let go and stepped out of the ship to go to Jesus, thus becoming the only man in history to walk on water other than Jesus Himself. Paul let go of his great intellect and oratory skill (I Corinthians 2:1-5) in order to preach the simple gospel of *"Jesus Christ and him crucified."* He abandoned his rights as a Roman citizen and a *"Pharisee of the Pharisees"* to become *a "bond-slave of Christ."* In Hebrews 11, we find a list of heroic people who made the ultimate sacrifice in letting go of life itself to obey God by real faith.

Examples from Christian History

Then there are the testimonies scattered across Christian history of those who let go in order to obey the will of God. On September 19, 1853, there was a small sailing ship, The Dumfries, moored at the dock of Liverpool, England. It would carry its crew, a load of freight, and one lone passenger on a six-month voyage to China. That passenger was twenty-one year old Hudson Taylor. Before departing, his mother came on board and had prayer with him in his little cabin. Then she went ashore to watch him sail away for what she thought might be forever. He later wrote, "I stood alone on deck, and she followed the ship as we moved toward the dock-gates. As we passed through the gates and the separation really commenced, never shall I forget the cry of anguish wrung from that mother's heart. It went through me like a knife. I never knew so fully, until then, what 'God so loved the world' meant" (1). That day, in answer to the call of God, Hudson Taylor let go of his family, his friends, and his home. He had no idea if he would ever see any of them again on this earth, but as a result of his letting go by faith, nearly 900 missionaries were planted in China by the time of his death and hundreds of thousands of Chinese were brought into the Kingdom of God.

Another life that bears testimony to the wisdom and merit of saying yes to the will of God, and no to everything that opposes it, is the life of C.T. "Charlie" Studd. For the full amazing story I suggest you read "C.T. Studd, Cricketer and Pioneer" by Norman Grubb. C.T. Studd was the greatest cricketer in England in his day and was also one of the original "Cambridge Seven," who sailed for China in 1885 to serve with the China Inland Mission. It was at this time

Tedworth, C.T. Studd's ancestral home. He gave his entire fortune to Christian work. He finished the final years of his life in the little hut pictured in the upper corner.

that God called upon C.T. to let go of home, country, family, and fortune.

C.T. served in China for ten years, returning to England in 1894. Then he preached on the campuses of America and England until 1900, at which time he went to India where he served until 1906. Then in 1908, while at home in England, God spoke to him again – about a new venture that no one believed in but him.

He attended a meeting one night, where he learned that in the middle of the continent of Africa there were numbers of tribes who had never heard the story of Jesus. C.T. asked the question, "Why have no Christians gone there?" Then God said to him, "Why don't you go?" He was fifty years old and had been in poor health for fifteen years. And besides, he had no money. He began, however, to make it known that he was willing to go, and a committee was formed among some businessmen to back him – under one condition, that the doctor approved it. The doctor said he would approve it if C.T. would promise to go no farther south than Khartoum. But he could not make that promise, because God had told him to go a thousand miles farther south.

C.T. Studd

Norman Grubb writes, "Penniless, turned down by the doctor, dropped by the committee, yet told by God to go, what was he to do? The only honest thing. Once more he staked all on obedience to God. As a young man he staked his career, in China he staked his fortune, now he staked his life. He joined the ranks of the great gamblers of faith. His answer to the committee was this, 'Gentlemen, God has called me to go and I will go. I will blaze the trail, though my grave may only become a stepping stone that younger men may follow.' He carried out his Master's word to the letter, 'He that shall lose his life for My sake and the Gospel's shall find it.' The next twenty years were to prove the last paragraph, 'shall find it'" (2).

During the last twelve years of their life, C.T. and his wife saw each other for only two weeks. She remained in England due to ill health and took care of the home affairs of the mission. That two-week visit took place in 1928. She died the next year while C.T. was still in the Congo. He died there in July 1931. Norman Grubb wrote about their last moments together on earth, "The parting was terribly hard, and Mrs. Studd did not want to go, but the hot season was starting and the home end of the work urgently needed her. They said farewell to each other in his bamboo house, knowing that it was the last time they would meet on earth. They came out together from the house and down the path to the waiting motor car. Not another word was said. She seemed completely oblivious of the group of missionaries standing around the car to say good-bye, but got in with set face and eyes looking straight in front of her, and was driven off" (3).

After C.T. died there in the Congo a gathering of men and women who had come to Jesus under his ministry came together – to sing, to worship, to glorify God, and to celebrate "Bwana's" life. There were thousands of people there. C.T. and Mrs. Studd had let go of everything on this earth, including each other, in order to obey God by faith. Was it worth it? For the answer to that question we would need to ask some of those folks who gathered that day to worship their newly found Savior.

As you read these accounts of a son letting go of his mother and a mother letting go of her son, and a devoted husband and wife saying good-bye to each other knowing they would never meet again this side of heaven, your reaction may be, "I could never do that, and if that is what it takes to serve God and live by faith, then I cannot do it." That is not true; you can do whatever God calls you to do, whatever He requires you to do. You can do it because He gives you the supernatural grace to do it. Jesus said, "...My grace is sufficient for thee: for my strength is made perfect in weakness" (II Corinthians 12:9). After a lifetime of letting go Paul testified in Philippians 4:13, "I can do all things through Christ which strengtheneth me."

In my own personal life, I don't think I have experienced a letting go that would equal what Hudson Taylor and C.T. Studd went through. But I can tell you this, it has been a life of letting go just the same, and your life will be also if you choose to live by faith. As I said before, the faith life is a continual letting go of something, and it is always relative to where you are in your walk with God and to what He calls you to do. I have learned after forty years of living by faith that the letting go is always just that – letting go, and it is always voluntary. God does not tear things out of our hands, and He does not tear you away from where you are or from what, or whom, you are holding on to. Rather, He asks us to give them up freely and trust Him. I have found therefore, that the best approach to the Christian life, and to the faith life, is to just let go on the front end; don't even wait to be asked. If we lay our lives, and all that they contains, on the altar for God, then there is really nothing left to let go of when we are called upon by God to trust Him, by faith, in some particular issue of life. The best preparation for times of letting go is to let go before the time ever comes.

Get in the habit and the practice of daily surrendering all you are, and all you have, to God.

Throughout our Christian life, Sheila and I have encountered many times of letting go. It began initially in 1968 with our walking away from the music business, which, at the time, was our only possible source of income. But in order to live for God and fulfill His purpose for our life, we had to do it. Not long after that I found myself letting go of opportunities to attend large universities so that I might do the will of God, which was to go to a small non-accredited Bible College. In 1976, I was faced with the reality of having to let go of a secure church-staff position, and a great local ministry, in order to enter the ministry we are in today. I also had to let go of my perceived ability to provide for my family, which was difficult but necessary, in order to do the will of God. Sheila and I had to let go of any hope of ever having our own home. And on and on it has continued over the years. I could keep giving example after example, but it is not necessary to outline our entire Christian life to make the point that the life of faith is a life of continually letting go. I want to be quick to say, however, that it is also a life of "much more." It has been our experience, in nearly every case, that God ultimately replaces what you walk away from with something much better and with much more.

Some years ago I was conducting a crusade in the northwest coastal city of Port de Paix, Haiti, and while I was there God showed me an illustration that has remained with me ever since. Our "hotel" was right on the beach and thus provided me with a good place to walk and pray in the early morning. While doing so, I noticed that every single day there were three guys in a little boat fishing. And every day, they went through the same routine. They would begin in the shallow water where they knew they would catch nothing, but it was safe. One man bailed water (because the boat had holes in it), another man rowed, and the third man cast the net. They would toil uselessly in the shallow water for a while, and then they would finally give in to reality and launch out into the deep where they were sure to catch fish. They repeated this process every day, without fail, and as I watched them God showed me something.

Let the attitude of the life be a continual 'going out' in dependence upon God, and your life will have an ineffable charm about it, which is a satisfaction to Jesus.

Oswald Chambers (4)

They began in the shallow water because it was safe and secure; after all, the boat did have holes in it. But eventually, in order to catch fish, they would have to let go of the security of the shallow water and go into the deep. As I watched them, God said to me, "Shad, you can spend your life playing it safe in the shallow water of worldly security and do nothing for Me, or you can let go, launch out, and count for the Kingdom of God." In my mind and heart there was no contest. The interesting thing was that because of the rough tide against the shore, the men had to work a lot harder near the beach than they did out in the deep water where it was calm. I have found it is ultimately much easier to just trust God in the deep, than to work myself to death in the shallow water accomplishing nothing. As the lady said, "It is much easier to let go than it is to hang on."

In my early Christian life, I met a pastor who meant a great deal to me and was very encouraging to me in the beginning stages of my walk with God, but his life ultimately represented a sad story to me. As a young man he attended a Bible college that was founded by a man of faith, and the faith life was taught and encouraged there. He read books on faith and the biographies of men who lived by faith. He even loaned his books to me and encouraged me to trust God and believe for the impossible. But the sad thing was, he never experienced personally what he encouraged me to do, to really let go and trust God. He would come so close, but every time God gave him an opportunity to enter a faith event and believe for the miraculous, he would revert back to some scheme of his own. He talked faith, read faith, and wanted faith, but he could never bring himself to actually embrace faith. Instead of launching out into the deep, calm waters of faith in God, he clung to the security of the little, insufficient salary provided by his small church. I watched him even resort to a secular job rather than cast himself upon God in real faith. Part of the problem was his wife; she just did not believe that God would meet their needs. Another part of the problem was his fear of what his fellow pastors would think of him if he tried to trust God and failed. He had been to the "sky diving class" and had watched others take the plunge, but he just could not let go and jump into freedom himself. He spent his whole Christian life struggling to hang on, when it would have been so much better to just let go and believe.

God Did Not Promise It Would Be Easy

My dear friend, where are you right now in your walk with God and in your climb up faith mountain? Are you still struggling in the shallow waters? Are you still hanging on to the plane for dear life? Are you being cheated out of what God wants to do in your life by the lies of the devil? Is God drawing you into a faith event by means of some need, burning desire, trial, or calling upon your life? Are you tempted to resort to some plan, some scheme, some "good idea", some source of your own rather than looking to God alone? You may at this moment be like the guy that fell off a cliff, and on the way down, his shirt caught on a branch sticking out and it broke his fall. As he hung there he looked up and called out, "I need help, is there anybody up there?" Then the voice of God called back, "Yes, this is God. Just let go, and I will save you." With that, the guy looked up and called out again, "Is there anybody else up there?" You don't need anybody else or anything else. All you need is God. Just let go, take the plunge, and jump into the freedom of faith.

The truth is, you may have been paddling around in the shallow water for so long that you don't even recognize it anymore. You may have been just hanging on for so long that you have gotten used to it. If you even suspect that may be the case, then get alone with God and ask Him to open your eyes to see where you really are. Then ask Him to help you break free into faith. He will do it if you will ask Him. One other thing I saw on the beach in Haiti those mornings was an old boat lying on the beach. It was obviously useful at one time, but now it was just lying there in a state of decay. When I looked at it, God spoke to my heart and said, "Shad, that is what happens when you hang close to the beach for too long; eventually you quit paddling in the water, you get washed up on the beach, and you become useless." I determined in my heart right then and there, that would not happen to me. I urge you to make that same decision. If God is calling you to take a step of faith in your life, then take it. Draw a line in the sand and step over it. Declare your freedom and don't look back. Burn the bridge back to the old world of living by the limitations of the natural and the visible, and plant your flag in the new world of living by faith.

I do not want to mislead you by suggesting in any way that letting go is easy. It is, once you make the decision, but like the woman in the plane, coming to the decision is the hard part. The devil will do all in his power to make it hard. As you step up to that line in the sand, that "great divide" in the Christian life, you will probably do so with mixed feelings; anticipation and excitement on one hand and fear and trembling on the other. You will experience excitement in your heart over entering a new adventure with God, but at the same time you can be sure that satan will be on hand to try to persuade you to remain in the wilderness. He does not want you to take that step because once you do he has lost all control. He knows that once you enter Canaan, the land of faith, you will never be back. But I can tell you authoritatively that once you take the step, fear will disappear and will be replaced with peace, joy, confidence, and assurance like you have never known before.

When God called Sheila and me into the ministry we are in today, it took us over two years to finally let go. It was not a snap decision, and it did not happen without a struggle. The devil saw to that. Everything about the decision to leave our fruitful, secure, church position to enter this ministry said we were crazy. We were going into international evangelism, and we had no money, no backers, no organization, no contacts overseas, no cross-cultural knowledge or experience, and no clue whatsoever as to how to begin. We also had very little encouragement from well meaning friends and deeply concerned family. What we did have, though, was the sure calling and promise of God. I remember very well that first day, September 5, 1977. All of a sudden I had no office to go to, no secretary, no position, no meetings to attend, no well defined ministry activity, no agenda for the day, no routine, no income, no health insurance, no way to meet the needs of my family and worst of all, from the world's view point – no identity. For many years I had been living a well-ordered and well-defined life and now, all of a sudden, all of that was gone. In other words, I had let go of everything – literally. Did satan tell me I was crazy? Of course. Was I tempted to believe him? Yes, there were moments when I was, but in the midst of it all there was something satan could not take from Sheila and me, something that completely balanced the scales. That something was the unshakable sure knowledge that we were right in the center of God's will for our life. We had let go of everything, but in doing so, we had caught hold of all the power and resources of God, and we had gained our freedom. And, after all these years, I can tell you honestly that we have never been tempted to go back, and there is nothing we left behind that has not been replaced with something much better. As I have said before, God always gives you back more than you walk away from.

Now as we come to the close of this book, let me ask you, is God drawing you into a life of faith? Of course He is. Is He leading you into a particular faith event by means of some need or desire or prompting from the Holy Spirit? Probably. Is God pressuring you to stretch out and expand in some area of your life by faith – in your business, you ministry, your giving, or your service to Him? I would be surprised if He wasn't. Is God calling you to leave the position, the job, the career, the church, the ministry you are in right now and follow Him into a new place of service? In other words, is God bringing you up to that place where you are required to make a definite conscious decision to either hang on or let go? You cannot do both. Are you at that point where you must either step over the line in the sand, the "great divide," and believe God or shrink back into the status quo of unbelief? As I said in the beginning, the faith life is a life of continuously letting go – of something.

No, God did not promise that coming to the decision to let go would be easy. But after forty years of doing so, I can tell you that there is one thing that makes it possible, and that is, *"Looking unto Jesus, the author and finisher of our faith."* Peter could let go, step out of the boat, and walk on the water for one reason; his eyes were on Jesus. Hudson Taylor and C. T. Studd could leave their family behind and serve God in a foreign land for one reason; their eyes were on Jesus. Sheila and I could leave the security of the life we had on staff at that church, and step out into the unknown, for one reason; our eyes were on Jesus. If you are sensing the call of God in your heart today to step out and trust Him by faith, then you <u>can</u> do it if you place <u>your</u> eyes on Jesus. For some of you, it might be to give $100 that you really cannot afford to give. For another person it might be to trust God for a particular person's salvation. For yet another, it might be to move to another city or take a different job, even though it makes no logical sense. And it might be that God is calling someone to leave all they have known and enter a particular ministry. I urge you and invite you to do whatever God is laying on your hearts. Let go, and begin your walk of faith today. Let go of being enslaved by the natural, the visible, the ordinary, and the possible. Draw your line in the sand and step over it to embrace the life of real faith. Look outside the circle, step into the will and supply of the Father, and see the glory of God. Join the ranks of those who enter heaven, having pleased God on the way, and hear Him say, *"...Well done, thou good and faithful servant: thou hast been faithful over a few things, I will make thee ruler over many things: enter thou into the joy of thy lord."*

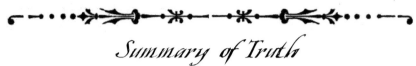

Summary of Truth

❖ The faith life is a life of continuously letting go – of something.

❖ Letting go may or may not take place in actual circumstances, but it will for sure in the heart.

❖ Faith should not be reduced to survival and acquisition; it is for expansion as well.

❖ When we choose to let go, the devil's strings are removed from our life.

❖ The greatest example of letting go was God the Father and God the Son.

❖ God's requirement to let go is always accompanied by His grace to do it.

❖ God always gives back more than we let go of.

❖ God did not promise it would be easy, but He did promise it would be a life that would please Him.

❖ "Looking unto Jesus" makes the faith-life possible.

NOW LET'S TAKE A MOMENT AND PRAY TOGETHER:

DEAR LORD JESUS, THANK YOU FOR BRINGING THESE TRUTHS INTO MY LIFE AND FOR GIVING ME THE OPPORTUNITY TO LEARN TO WALK BY FAITH. LORD, I KNOW IN MY HEART THAT YOU ARE BRINGING ME TO THAT POINT WHERE I MUST CHOOSE TO LIVE BY FAITH OR NOT. I DO NOT WANT TO LIVE THE REMAINDER OF MY LIFE IN THE SHALLOW WATER OF UNBELIEF. I DO NOT WANT TO LIVE IN THE DULL EXISTENCE OF THE STATUS QUO. LORD, YOU SAVED ME FOR MORE THAN THAT. SO LORD, RIGHT NOW, WITH ALL THAT I AM AND WITH ALL I HAVE, I HEREBY DRAW THAT LINE IN THE SAND AND I STEP OVER THE GREAT DIVIDE INTO THE LIFE OF FAITH AND FREEDOM. LORD, I WILL NOT LOOK BACK, AND I WILL NOT GO BACK. FROM THIS MOMENT FORWARD I CAST MY ALL UPON YOU BY FAITH. THIS IS A NEW DAY IN MY LIFE, AND I AM A NEW PERSON. NOW I AM NOT ONLY SAVED, BUT I AM LIBERATED. LORD, I REFUSE TO HANG ON ANY LONGER, I DETERMINE TO LET GO OF FALSE SECURITY, AND I CLING TO YOU BY FAITH. I CHOOSE TO PLACE MY EYES ON YOU. THANK YOU, LORD, FOR DOING THIS IN MY LIFE. I LOVE YOU LORD JESUS. IN YOUR NAME I PRAY. AMEN AND AMEN.

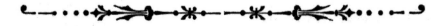

Source Notes

Chapter 1

1. Watchman Nee, *The Spiritual Man*, 2 vols. (New York: Christian Fellowship Publishers, 1977), 2:241
2. Oswald Chambers, *My Utmost For His Highest* (London: Simpkin Marshall, 1941), 242
3. Dr. and Mrs. Howard Taylor, *James Hudson Taylor and the China Inland Mission, The Growth of a Work of God* (China Inland Mission and Religious Tract Society, 1931), 279
4. Bruce Wilkinson, *The Prayer of Jabez* (Sisters, OR: Multnomah Publishers, 2000), 42

Chapter 2

1. Chambers, *My Utmost for His Highest*, 129
2. Chambers, *My Utmost for His Highest*, 126

Chapter 3

1. Taylor, *The Growth of a Work of God*, 384
2. Wilkinson, *The Prayer of Jabez*, 7
3. Chambers, *My Utmost for His Highest*, 251
4. Manley Beasley, *The Faith Workbook* (Gospel Harvesters), 2
5. Beasley, *The Faith Workbook*, 2
6. Nee, *The Spiritual Man*, 2:252

Chapter 4

1. Manley Beasley, *Alive By His Life* (Kalamazoo, MI: Masters Press, 1976), 80
2. Beasley, *The Faith Workbook*, 12

Chapter 5

1. Chambers, *My Utmost for His Highest*, 265

Chapter 6

1. Chambers, *My Utmost for His Highest*, 194

Chapter 7

1. Taylor, *The Growth of a Work of God*, 179
2. Beasley, *The Faith Workbook*, 1

470)

3. Beasley, *The Faith Workbook*, 1
4. Beasley, *The Faith Workbook*, 2
5. Beasley, *The Faith Workbook*, 26
6. Beasley, *The Faith Workbook*, 26
7. Beasley, *The Faith Workbook*, 26
8. Chambers, *My Utmost for His Highest*, 242
9. Chambers, *My Utmost for His Highest*, 22
10. Chambers, *My Utmost for His Highest*, 53
11. Chambers, *My Utmost for His Highest*, 129
12. Chambers, *My Utmost for His Highest*, 131
13. Chambers, *My Utmost for His Highest*, 225
14. Taylor, *The Growth of a Work of God*, 142
15. Taylor, *The Growth of a Work of God*, 143
16. Andrew Murray, *With Christ in the School of Prayer* (Springdale, PA: Whitaker House, 1981), 81
17. Miles J. Stanford, *The Green Letters*, Study Ed. (Hong Kong: Living Spring Press, 1968), 2
18. Ruth Paxson, *Life on the Highest Plane* (Grand Rapids, MI: Kregel Publications, 1996), 349
19. Chambers, *My Utmost for His Highest*, 88
20. Mish, Frederick C. and Morse, John M.eds. *Merrriam-Webster's Collegiate Dictionary*, 10th edition (Springfield, MA: Merriam Webster, Inc.,1993), 26
21. Beasley, *The Faith Workbook*, 24

Chapter 8

1. Taylor, *The Growth of a Work of God*, 429
2. Norman Grubb, *The Law of Faith* (Fort Washington, PA: Christian Literature Crusade, 1947), 17

Chapter 9

1. Chambers, *My Utmost for His Highest*, 58
2. Paxson, *Life on the Highest Plane*, 348

Chapter 10

1. Chambers, *My Utmost for His Highest*, 305
2. Andrew Murray, *The Spirit of Christ* (Minneapolis: Bethany Fellow ship, 1979), 183

Chapter 11

1. Norman Grubb, *The Law of Faith*, 16
2. Chambers, *My Utmost for His Highest*, 129
3. Chambers, *My Utmost for His Highest*, 132

Chapter 12

1. Nee, *The Spiritual Man*, 240
2. Chambers, *My Utmost for His Highest*, 254
3. W.E. Vine, *Vine's Expository Dictionary of New Testament Words* (McLean, VA: MacDonald Publishing Co.), 276
4. Vine, *Vine's Expository Dictionary*, 734

Chapter 13

1. Nee, *The Spiritual Man*, 30
2. J. Dwight Pentecost, *Pattern for Maturity* (Chicago: Moody Press, 1968), 247
3. Pentecost, *Pattern for Maturity*, 247
4. Paxson, *Life on the Highest Plane*, 315
5. Chambers, *My Utmost for His Highest*, 79
6. Murray, *The Spirit of Christ*, 183
7. Chambers, *My Utmost for His Highest*, 102

Chapter 14

1. Pentecost, *Pattern for Maturity*, 145
2. Murray, *The Spirit of Christ*, 206
3. Paxson, *Life on the Highest Plane*, 342, 343, 354, 358

Chapter 15

1. Chambers, *My Utmost for His Highest*, 6
2. J. Oswald Sanders, *Prayer Power Unlimited* (Chicago: Moody Press, 1977), 63
3. Murray, *The Spirit of Christ*, 181
4. E.M. Bounds, *Power Through Prayer* (Grand Rapids, MI: Zondervan, 1962), 37
5. Bounds, *Power Through Prayer*, 40
6. Bounds, *Power Through Prayer*, 42
7. Taylor, *The Growth of a Work of God*, 236
8. Taylor, *The Growth of a Work of God*, 444
9. Bounds, *Power Through Prayer*, 42
10. Taylor, *The Growth of a Work of God*, 596
11. Chambers, *My Utmost for His Highest*, 293

Chapter 16

1. Norman, Grubb, *After C.T. Studd* (London: Lutterworth, 1939), 12
2. Arthur T. Pierson, *George Muller of Bristol* (London: James Nisbett and Company, 1899), 449
3. Taylor, *The Growth of a Work of God*, 355

4. Chambers, *My Utmost for His Highest*, 160
5. Taylor, *The Growth of a Work of God*, 54
6. Taylor, *The Growth of a Work of God*, 52
7. Taylor, *The Growth of a Work of God*, 42
8. Taylor, *The Growth of a Work of God*, 55

Chapter 17

1. Chambers, *My Utmost for His Highest*, 3
2. Nee, *The Spiritual Man*, 30
3. Nee, *The Spiritual Man*, 247
4. Chambers, *My Utmost for His Highest*, 236
5. Chambers, *My Utmost for His Highest*, 239
6. Chambers, *My Utmost for His Highest*, 349

Chapter 18

1. Chambers, *My Utmost for His Highest*, 25
2. Chambers, *My Utmost for His Highest*, 80
3. Chambers, *My Utmost for His Highest*, 155

Chapter 19

1. Nee, *The Spiritual Man*, 244
2. Taylor, *The Growth of a Work of God*, 180
3. Murray, *The Spirit of Christ*, 180
4. Sheila Williams
5. Chambers, *My Utmost for His Highest*, 88

Chapter 20

1. Pierson, *George Muller of Bristol*, 437
2. Pentecost, *Pattern for Maturity*, 246
3. Chambers, *My Utmost for His Highest*, 131

Chapter 21

1. Murray, *The Spirit of Christ*, 182
2. Murray, *The Spirit of Christ*, 179

Chapter 22

1. Taylor, *The Growth of a Work of God*, 276
2. Chambers, *My Utmost for His Highest*, 217
3. Murray, *With Christ in the School of Prayer*, 81
4. R.A. Torrey, *The Power of Prayer* (Grand Rapids, MI: Zondervan, 1955), 122

5. Eileen Crossman, *Mountain Rain, A New Biography of James O. Fraser* (Singapore: Overseas Missionary Fellowship, 1982), 90-91
6. Grubb, *The Law of Faith*, 116
7. Beasley, *The Faith Workbook*, 5
8. Chambers, *My Utmost for His Highest*, 131
9. Chambers, *My Utmost for His Highest*, 145
10. Dr. and Mrs. Howard Taylor, *By Faith, Henry W. Frost and the China Inland Mission* (Singapore: Overseas Missionary Fellowship, 1988), 142
11. Chambers, *My Utmost for His Highest*, 210

Chapter 23

1. Stanford, *The Green Letters*, 2
2. Wilkinson, *The Prayer of Jabez*, 47
3. Taylor, *The Growth of a Work of God*, 422
4. Taylor, *The Growth of a Work of God*, 420
5. Taylor, *The Growth of a Work of God*, 422
6. Taylor, *The Growth of a Work of God*, 423
7. Taylor, *The Growth of a Work of God*, 423
8. Taylor, *The Growth of a Work of God*, 433
9. Taylor, *The Growth of a Work of God*, 424
10. Taylor, *The Growth of a Work of God*, 428
11. Taylor, *The Growth of a Work of God*, 430
12. Taylor, *The Growth of a Work of God*, 431
13. Taylor, *The Growth of a Work of God*, 433
14. Taylor, *The Growth of a Work of God*, 432

Chapter 24

1. Paxson, *Life on the Highest Plane*, 348

Chapter 25

1. Nee, *The Spiritual Man*, 245
2. Taylor, *The Growth of a Work of God*, 278
3. Murray, *The Spirit of Christ*, 180
4. Chambers, *My Utmost for His Highest*, 60
5. Mrs. Howard Taylor, *Behind the Ranges, Fraser of Lisuland, SW China* (London: Lutterworth Press), 112, 113
6. Taylor, *Behind the Ranges*, 114

Chapter 26

1. Pentecost, *Pattern for Maturity*, 247
2. Taylor, *Behind the Ranges*, 90
3. Taylor, *Behind the Ranges*, 91

4. Chambers, *My Utmost for His Highest*, 242
5. Paxson, *Life on the Highest Plane*, 347
6. Chambers, *My Utmost for His Highest*, 242

Chapter 27

1. Wilkinson, *The Prayer of Jabez*, 49
2. Taylor, *The Growth of a Work of God*, 211
3. Murray, *The Spirit of Christ*, 183

Chapter 28

1. Chambers, *My Utmost for His Highest*, 120
2. Taylor, *The Growth of a Work of God*, 356
3. Chambers, *My Utmost for His Highest*, 210

Chapter 29

1. Chambers, *My Utmost for His Highest*, 209
2. Chambers, *My Utmost for His Highest*, 316
3. Chambers, *My Utmost for His Highest*, 322
4. A.W. Tozier, Man the Dwelling Place of God, *World Invisible*, *www.worldinvisible.com*
5. John Calvin
6. John Stammis

Chapter 30

1. Grubb, *The Law of Faith*, 150-151
2. Grubb, *The Law of Faith*, 150
3. Pierson, *George Muller of Bristol*, 442
4. Pierson, *George Muller of Bristol*, 443
5. Judson Wheeler Van DeVenter

Chapter 31

1. Dr. and Mrs. Howard Taylor, *Hudson Taylor in the Early Years, The Growth of a Soul* (China Inland Mission and Religious Tract Society, 1931), 187
2. Norman Grubb, *C.T. Studd, Cricketer and Pioneer* (London" Religious Tract Society, 1933), 127-128
3. Grubb, *C.T. Studd, Cricketer and Pioneer*, 235-236
4. Chambers, *My Utmost for His Highest*, 2

$\mathcal{A}ppendix$

HOW TO HAVE A CLEAN HEART
(How to Be Sure You Are Saved)

In order to truly understand the meaning of faith, you must first know for sure you are in the family of God. Jesus told Nicodemus in John 3:7, *"Ye must be born again."* In response to that, Nicodemus asked a question you may be asking, "But how can a person be born a second time?" Jesus was talking about a spiritual birth, a birth every person can have by taking three simple steps. You can take them right now and by so doing you can and will receive an assurance in your heart that you are a child of God and on your way to heaven.

Step One: Face the Truth about Yourself. Every one of us is born with a problem called sin. We are sinners by birth and by choice. God created Adam and Eve with a clean heart, free from sin, and instructed them to fill the earth with people who would love and worship Him. But before the first child was born, satan tempted them and they rebelled against God and followed the devil. Their heart became dirty (sinful) and they became separated from God by sin. They lost everything - their home, their relationship with God, and even their life. Because of sin they began to die. With the entrance of sin into the human race came death (Romans 5:12). Their children were born with a dirty (sinful) heart and sin passed from generation to generation - down to you and me. When you and I were born we were born with a dirty heart, separated from God (Romans 3:23). We are all born with the same problem and we must all face the same question. How can we go to a perfect sinless heaven with a dirty sinful heart? The answer is, we cannot – unless there is a way for us to get a clean heart. The good news is, there is - through Jesus Christ.

Step Two: Face the Truth about Jesus. God provided a solution for our problem through His Son Jesus Christ. But why must the answer for the problem of sin be Jesus? God said that sin must be paid for by death. Someone who is innocent, perfect, sinless, must die for the sins of all mankind. But who could that someone be? Where could he come from? His name is Jesus and He came from heaven. God sent His Own Son from heaven to earth to become a human being so that He might die to pay for our sin. *"For God so loved the world* [you and me] *that he gave his only begotten Son, that whosoever believeth in him should not perish, but have* *everlasting life* (John 3:16)." Jesus was born through the virgin Mary. His mother was Mary, but His Father was God. Therefore, He was born with a clean heart and lived a perfect sinless life. Then, at age 33, God the Father allowed Jesus the Son to die on a cross to pay for the sin of the world. Jesus Who had no sin died for you and me. He bore our sin on the cross and paid the penalty for it with His shed blood. The moment He died, the way was opened for every one of us to become a child of the Living God and enter heaven when we die. Why? Because the problem of sin was solved. How? Through Jesus' death on the cross. He was buried in a tomb and three days later He rose from the dead victorious over sin and death. He walked upon the Earth for forty days and then ascended into heaven. He is there now preparing a home for you and me. But, in order to go there you must have a clean heart. So what must we do?

Step Three: Face the Truth about Eternity. There are two places people go when they die - heaven or hell. Now, why do people go to hell? Is it because God does not love them? No, it is because they choose to die with a dirty sinful heart. All sin goes to hell and if a person dies holding on to a dirty heart, then He goes where sin goes. But, that is not necessary because God has provided a way for every human being to have a clean heart. Jesus said in John 14:6, *"I am the way, the truth, and the life: no man cometh unto the Father, but by Me."* But why only through Jesus? Because only Jesus was qualified to die on the cross and pay for our sin. *"But God commendeth his love toward us, in that, while we were yet sinners, Christ died for us"* Romans 5:8).

So what must we do to receive Christ in our heart and be saved? There are three things: ADMIT, BELIEVE, and CALL. You must <u>admit</u> to God you are a sinner; that you have a dirty heart. Second, you must choose to believe upon Jesus. You must choose to <u>believe</u> He is the Son of God Who came from heaven, died for you, was buried and rose again, and is alive in heaven right now. Third, you must <u>call</u> upon (ask) Him to come into your heart. The Bible says, *"For whosoever shall call upon the name of the Lord shall be saved"* (Romans 10:13). Whosoever means YOU. But, how do you call upon Him? You do it through prayer, and if you want to receive Jesus into your heart right now, you may do so by praying the simple prayer like the one below. Now what is going to happen when you do? You are going to be cleansed and forgiven of all sin and Jesus Christ is going to become the Lord and Master of your life. You are going to become a child of God, a citizen of heaven, and everything about your life is going to change. You are going to become a brand new person. Now, are you ready for that? If so, then right now, bow your head and pray a prayer like this one:

Lord Jesus, I admit to You I am a sinner; I have a dirty heart. But, Lord I want to have a clean heart, I do want to be Your child, I do want to go to heaven. Lord Jesus, You died for me on the cross and I thank You for paying for my sin. Right now, Lord I ask You to come into my heart and be my Lord and Savior. I receive You right now and I thank You for receiving me as your child. Now I know I belong to You, Lord Jesus. Thank You for coming into my heart today. I will live for You from this moment forward. In Your Name I pray. Amen.

Dear friend, if you just prayed that prayer, Jesus is in your heart and you are now a child of God. *"For whosoever"* - that's YOU. *"Shall call"* - that's what you just did. *"Shall be saved"* - when? Right now and forever.

Now then, if you have not read the Bible before, then begin in the Gospel of John and read it every day. Also begin reading this book every day and stay with it to the end. In it you will discover how to live the Christian life to the fullest.

One final thing - please do me a personal favor. If you just prayed that prayer and received Jesus in your heart, please write me or call me and let me know. My contact information (address, phone number, E-mail) is on the back cover of this book. Thank you, my new brother or sister in Christ, and God bless you. I look forward to hearing from you.

Shad Williams

To view the "Clean Heart" presentation in diagram form, please visit our website: www.wegotothem.com

Author Biographical Note

Shad was born in 1946 in Memphis, Tennessee and grew up in the Mississippi town of Yazoo City. He was raised in a good home with loving attentive parents, but in those days God was not part of the picture. His family moved to Memphis in 1963 where he graduated from high school and continued to pursue his dream of becoming an entertainer in the music business. Sheila was born in Memphis in 1948. Her father was in the construction business so she moved from city to city, attending thirteen different schools before finally settling in Palmetto, Florida in the seventh grade. After graduation from high school, Sheila's family moved to Memphis where she attended Rhodes University. Unlike Shad, Sheila grew up attending church but she did not truly receive Christ until after they were married.

Shad and Sheila met in 1966 at an event at which his band was playing. It was, as they say, "love at first sight." They were married in 1967. Since Sheila had never been saved it was easy for her to adapt to the lifestyle of the music business. She quit school and joined Shad in his pursuit of success in the entertainment world. It proved to be a pursuit that would lead to despair and disappointment. It was disappointment, however, that God used to help draw the young couple to Christ. God had a plan for them that they could not imagine at the time.

Through the influence and persistence of Sheila's mother, Dr. Alta Lane, Shad was persuaded in the spring of 1968 to attend a Sunday morning service at Park Avenue Baptist Church in Memphis. There he encountered Pastor Don Milam for the first time. On the following Tuesday "Brother Don" visited Shad and Sheila in their home and shared with them the love of Jesus. Shad refused the invitation to be saved, but Brother Don did not give up. He came again and again, and each time he came he shared how to be born again. Shad testifies, "I thought Brother Don was going to condemn me and tell me how bad I was. But he didn't do that. Every time he came he just told us about Jesus, and I couldn't find anything wrong with Jesus." Finally on Sunday afternoon July 7, 1968, while at home alone, Shad reflected on Brother Don's message as well as the condition of his life and prayed to receive Christ in his heart. He says, "At that moment everything changed. My desire for the music business disappeared and all I wanted to do from that moment forward was serve God." He shared with Sheila what had happened and asked her to "Call that pastor at that church and make an appointment. I need to find out what this is that has happened to me." After meeting with the pastor, they joined the church, Shad was baptized, and they began to be discipled. A month later Sheila realized she had never been saved and prayed to receive Christ. Shad quit the music business and he and Sheila began a new life of serving God together.

In January 1969 Shad enrolled in Mid South Bible College in Memphis. While there he and Sheila and some of the students began a citywide youth evangelism ministry of music and preaching. Over the next two years it was used of God to lead thousands to Christ. In 1971 they transferred to Union University in Jackson, TN where Shad graduated cum laude in 1973. During those years Shad and Sheila sang and preached in hundreds of evangelistic events in churches, colleges and high schools. From 1968-1973 they saw over 25,000 people come to Christ.

After graduation they were prepared to move to Fort Worth, Texas to attend seminary, but God redirected them to join the staff of East Park Baptist Church in Memphis. Shad served there under Dr. Wayne Allen until September 1977. While there he and Sheila developed a youth evangelism ministry that was greatly used of God to grow the church and lead hundreds to Christ.

In June 1975 Shad and Sheila participated in a church mission trip to East Africa. It was during that trip God spoke to them and told them to begin a ministry of international evangelism. It was a long slow decision, but in September 1977 they resigned and entered the ministry they are in today. They began with nothing but the knowledge of God's will and the assurance of His promises. Over the past 33 years God has developed and grown the ministry of Shad Williams Evangelistic Association/Global Field Evangelism into a worldwide organization. Shad and Sheila have traveled over 3.5 million miles and their ministry has presented the Gospel to 13 million people. They have lived in Adamsville, Tennessee since 1998. They have two children, Michael (born 1969) and Rachel (born 1971), and six grandchildren. After 42 years of marriage and 40 years of ministry, Shad and Sheila say they have only just begun.

Ministry Profile

Shad Williams Evangelistic Association and Global Field Evangelism is an international ministry of frontline "field" evangelism which uses the "we go to them" philosophy and approach to take the Gospel to where the people are. Rather than conducting events which require people to come to us to hear the Gospel, SWEA/GFE takes the message out to where people are already gathered in groups or they easily can be. The Gospel is taken <u>out</u> to public places such as open-air markets, villages, busy streets, crowded slums, refugee camps, or bus and train stations,. It is also taken <u>in</u> to high schools, colleges, prisons, and military camps. The goal is to reach people with the message of Christ where they already are - in their own territory.

Following their conversion in 1968, Shad and Sheila began taking the Gospel to the streets of their hometown (Memphis, TN), as well as to high schools, colleges, and prisons. Then, as now, the goal was to reach unsaved people who would not or could not attend an organized Christian event, such as a church service, Christian concert, or crusade. Early on they realized that most unsaved people are not going to come to hear the Gospel, thus the necessity of taking the Gospel to them. What began on the streets and campuses of America has now spread out across the world.

Shad and Sheila's ministry of international evangelism began in 1977 when they resigned their church position to obey the call of God to take the Gospel to the world. They began as Shad Williams Evangelistic Association and in 1984 the name Global Field Evangelism was given to the network of national ministry teams beginning to develop in various countries.

As of June 2009, SWEA/GFE has conducted 158 international evangelistic campaigns in Africa, Asia, the Caribbean, Central America, and South America. Over 13 million people have heard the Gospel in tens of thousands of evangelistic events and 7.7 million have prayed to receive Christ. Hundreds of churches have been planted and millions of pieces of Christian literature have been distributed. The ministry currently has national teams operating in the Democratic Republic of Congo, India, Kenya, Malawi, Nigeria, Tanzania, and Uganda.

Our <u>mandate</u> is to take the Gospel to the whole world. Our <u>method</u> is "we go to them." Our <u>message</u> is Jesus Christ crucified, buried, and risen again for the salvation of all men. Our <u>means</u> of operation is by faith in God alone, looking to Him for His plan, His power, and His provision.

Please visit our website <u>www.wegotothem.com</u> in order to learn more.